BUSINESS INFORMATION PROCESSING SYSTEMS
An Introduction to Data Processing

The Irwin Series in Information and Decision Sciences

EDITORS   ROBERT B. FETTER, *Yale University*
           CLAUDE MCMILLAN, *University of Colorado*

Business Information Processing Systems

An Introduction to Data Processing

C. ORVILLE ELLIOTT, Ph.D., C.P.A., C.D.P.
Professor of Accounting
Department of Accountancy and Information Science
Western Illinois University

ROBERT S. WASLEY, Ph.D.
Professor of Accounting
College of Business and Administration,
and Graduate School of Business
University of Colorado

Fourth Edition   1975

RICHARD D. IRWIN, INC. Homewood, Illinois 60430
Irwin-Dorsey International, London, England WC2H 9NJ
Irwin-Dorsey Limited, Georgetown, Ontario L7G 4B3

Fourth Edition

First Printing, January 1975

ISBN 0-256-01579-1
Library of Congress Catalog Card No. 74–12924
Printed in the United States of America

Learning Systems Comany—
a division of Richard D. Irwin, Inc.—has developed a
PROGRAMMED LEARNING AID
to accompany texts in this subject area.
Copies can be purchased through your bookstore
or by writing PLAIDS,
1818 Ridge Road, Homewood, Illinois 60430.

To our patient wives
Helene and Helen

Preface

THIS BOOK is an introduction to the study of computers, the design and development of information systems, and the implementation of such systems, with particular emphasis on how they can be used in a business environment. The coverage is at an introductory level that is broad in scope but of sufficient depth so that it may be used both as a learning device and a reference source. To get the most out of the text an understanding of business terminology and the ability to envision why certain techniques are important to the business environment would be helpful. Therefore, it would be preferable if the student could have some business exposure or some basic accounting or other business courses as a background to this study.

Changes in equipment and methods of accumulating and processing data, changes in the economic environment in which this work is being done—in the attitudes of people and in costs over time—all have an extremely important bearing on the student who is interested in learning about working with data processing today. This book is designed so that the attention of the student is called to the latest and best information available.

This potential depth of coverage is relevant—and may well be essential—to students interested in data processing as a career and in all areas of accountancy (public, private, or governmental) as well as to those who have aspirations to become members of the top management team.

Major Changes

For its Fourth Edition, this book has been thoroughly revised. It incorporates several major changes:

1. More illustrations have been added throughout the chapters of the book to show what is being done in the "real world." Supplemental information is also provided by references to current periodicals and case illustrations following discussions of major subject areas.
2. All of the material has been reorganized, condensed, and brought as nearly up-to-the-moment as is humanly possible. Much of the material on the punched card and, in particular, its associated equipment, has been greatly condensed.
3. Comparative tables of all major computer systems and associated equipment are provided in each of the equipment chapters as part of the basic information on these items. These tables serve as reference to capacities, speeds, techniques used, and—for overall systems—prices. Again, these provide a means of bringing the "real world" closer to the student.
4. The chapter on Computer Systems Controls has had a completely new section added to it on the subject of Computer Security. Chapters 15 and 16 show the current state-of-the-art in what has, on the average, been accomplished thus far (20 years) in terms of the application of the computer to the solution of some of man's problems. Timesharing is discussed as a part of this.
5. The questions at the end of each chapter have been completely reoriented and rewritten.

This revision has been a major one in attempting to bring the real world to the student of data processing. It is also felt computer associated terminology and know-how is vital to all business students as even those who will not be closely associated with the operation of the computer will have to be able to communicate their needs to professional data processing personnel.

Business students need to have—at least—an appreciation of the problems associated with computers and of potential alternatives available to solve those problems. These problem areas include: (*a*) designing information systems; (*b*) gathering, organizing, and protecting data derived from business transactions; (*c*) preparing application programs; (*d*) processing the data and operating the equipment; and (*e*) protecting the installation from both fraudulent operation and physical damage.

If each student can be given the insight to understand how the computer will have an impact on both his professional and private life, a major goal will have been accomplished. Tying terminology, equipment, and systems together in the context of the business world of today can do much to eliminate the mystique surrounding computers.

Organization

This book's organization provides several major sections which are related but relatively independent of each other so that the teaching emphasis may be altered and stressed as desired. These sections are:

1. The *Data, Data Processing, and Business Information* section lays the basic groundwork for an emphasis on both the fundamental needs of an information processing system and on how relatively simple and inexpensive devices may, at times, serve to expedite the functions basic to such a system. The emphasis is on supplements to and on serving a computer system.

2. The *Computers* section deals with the growth of computers, computer characteristics and terminology, and how individual electronic devices serve in the preparation, input, storage, manipulation, and output of the informational data required in the business organization. The comparative tables of current equipment capabilities provide an insight into the devices and the alternatives that are available to make up a computer system.

3. The *Design and Development of Information Systems* section stresses: (*a*) how data and its flow may be represented pictorially and how programming software has evolved over time; (*b*) techniques available in controlling the integrity of data and in physically protecting that data and its processing equipment; and (*c*) how an integrated management information system can be used by management in planning and control functions.

4. The *Implementation of Information Systems* section is an overview of problems in and approaches to justifying and, if required, introducing a new computer system into the firm's data processing operation.

5. The *Computer Programming* supplement is designed to provide both an overview of and the essentials necessary to learn the fundamentals of the FORTRAN IV and COBOL programming languages.

6. An *Appendix* provides a historical background of computing devices and punched card equipment and an extensive glossary of computer associated terminology.

Alternative Ways of Using the Material

This book is being used in a variety of ways:

1. As a fundamentals book in business data processing. Most community colleges and universities have such a course as a three semester or four quarter hour basic requirement in the business program at either the freshman or sophomore level. By assigning Chapters 1 and 2 (possibly 3 and 4 also), then devoting considerable time to the discussion of computers (Chapters 5 through 11), the place of the computer in business can be well covered.

This can be followed by a discussion, with problems to be solved, in utilizing programming. Both FORTRAN IV and COBOL programming languages are provided. However, if the instructor feels that additional information is desirable, there are numerous paper-back books published on programming languages which can supplement what is available in this text. The course can be rounded out with a discussion of how the computer is being used in business today through assigning Chapters 15 and 16. It is suggested that once the programming material is covered students can continue to expand their programming capabilities through problem assignments while other material is covered in class.

2. Many short course programs are provided to assist people who are already employed in upgrading their knowledge base. This is particularly true in public accounting. This text can well fit the needs of such programs. The authors recommend Chapters 5 through 11 on computers, Chapter 12 on system analysis and flowcharting, and Chapter 14 on computer systems controls and security.

3. The book is also being used, along with supplements as a text on accounting systems and data processing which would probably be a senior level course for accounting majors. In this usage, the following sequence of Chapters is recommended: Chapters 1, 2, 12, 3 through 11, and 13 through 18 in that sequence. To supplement this approach, cases which are available through the Intercollegiate Case Clearing House at Harvard University are highly recommended. Extensive use should also be made of the references noted throughout the chapters by assigning groups of students to conduct panel discussions on various aspects of specialized subjects.

Acknowledgments

It must be recognized that in an undertaking of this magnitude the authors are greatly indebted to many individuals for their suggestions, help, and encouragement. To each of them we wish to acknowledge this indebtedness and to express our appreciation.

Professor Robert B. Fetter has been most cooperative in suggesting organizational and writing style improvements.

We are particularly indebted to all the major equipment manufacturers, and their local representatives, for their cooperation in furnishing data in general and information on their equipment in particular, and for permissions to use their illustrations.

December 1974

C. ORVILLE ELLIOTT
ROBERT S. WASLEY

Contents

Film Memory. Semiconductor Memory. Other New and Developing Memory Devices.

Part VI.   Appendixes

I

Data,
Data Processing,
and Business
Information

Data for Managing Resources

As FAR BACK in history as the Assyrians and Babylonians, we have indisputable evidence of commercial transactions. A large part of commerce centered in the temples. The scribes, who were the chief accounting officers, recorded all receipts and disbursements of property belonging to the local temple, the "corporate clearinghouse" of those early times. It is even evident that credit existed on an extensive scale.

The surviving facts which those early scribes recorded are meager. However, as trade and commerce expanded, the records of business ventures also became more detailed and extensive. There was increased interest and concern in the outcome of business ventures by different groups of people; owners, as well as the taxing authorities, had a vested interest in the venture, and it was important to them that adequate facts be made known or data be kept.

This need for information in our more complex society of today also applies to many other forms of group activity besides those of business and government, as each group must keep records of what has been done in the past, what is being performed currently, and what future plans have been proposed and adopted.

WHAT ARE DATA?

According to one source, "Data is something known or assumed as facts and made the basis of reasoning or calculation. The quantities, characters or symbols on which operations are performed by computer and other automatic equipment and which may be stored or transmitted in the form of electrical signals."[1] Another, equally well-known source states that "Data is information organized for analysis or computation."[2]

From these definitions it would appear that data are kinds of information which can be expressed in either alphabetic or numeric form, or both. Data, as applied to business operations, are expressed in terms of dollars and cents, as well as in numeric and alphabetic form.

As an example, any business which sells on credit today must maintain, at a minimum, a record of the name and address of the person to whom credit was extended, a description of what was sold, the amount of the sale, and the terms of credit. In addition, various types of tax may have been collected, interest charged, and so on.

As a governmental example of data, once every ten years the United States undertakes a census of its population. This involves not only counting people, but also records their sex, age, marital status, annual income, educational attainment, address of domicile, as well as many other personal details. All of this information is later used for purposes of analysis.

A city recreation department on the other hand must keep records of the amounts of money appropriated to it, expenditures which have been made, names and addresses of people enrolled in various sport programs, the teams to which they have been assigned, the schedule of each team, and the record of the wins and losses of that team within the league to which it belongs.

DEMAND FOR DATA

One of the first things to be considered in the study of data processing is, what brings about the need for data. Much of the need results from the necessity of those who must make decisions to know precisely where things stand at a given point in time.

As one of many examples where government utilizes data which has been accumulated, take the recent statement in the press that approximately six million people in the United States were not counted in the 1970 census. It was also estimated that most of these were in the very low income groups. Since much of the federal aid to states

---

[1] R. W. Burchfield, ed., *Supplement to the Oxford English Dictionary* (Oxford: Clarendon Press, 1972), p. 737.

[2] Peter Davies, ed., *American Heritage Dictionary of the English Language* (New York: Dell Publishing Co. Inc., 1970), p. 183.

is based on the annual income levels of the population within the state, there were going to be states that would not receive as much federal aid for poverty programs as they were entitled to.

College or university administrators have a host of facts which they must have available in order to run their institutions efficiently. For example: (1) They must know the number of students enrolled in a course the last time it was given. It is on this basis that the determination is made to offer the course again, as well as the number of sections to be offered. (2) They must maintain for future reference the grade record as well as the credit hours passed by each student. (3) They must have a record of the revenue derived and the expenses incurred in the operation of a dormitory constructed by the sale of bonds. In such a case the net income received from the dormitory operation is used to pay off the bond issue.

Managers of modern business enterprises also need to know facts about their operations frequently. They need to know such things as:

1. Amounts owed by customers.
2. The quantity of a certain item sold last week.
3. The size of garment sold to the last customer.
4. The amount of wages paid employees the last payday.
5. The sales tax collected and that owed to the state on sales made last month.
6. An analysis of sales by territory, by product, for the last three years.

How have the facts above been obtained? They certainly have not been able to accomplish this in a hit-or-miss fashion. Instead, they have accomplished it by having a carefully conceived plan and system whereby necessary types of data were gathered at a certain time, place, and/or in a given way over a period of time and were accumulated and processed in a manner conceived long before the first fact was ever gathered.

INTERNAL NEED FOR DATA BY DECISION MAKERS

An important function of administrators and managers is to decide upon courses of action which their organizations should follow. Some of these decisions must be made at frequent intervals; others need not be made as often.

Almost anyone who has had responsibility delegated to him or her for given functions or activities finds that he or she needs to have knowledge of what has gone on in the immediate past—what the system or way of doing things has been. Without this information or data, it is difficult, if not impossible, to make intelligent decisions of either a short- or long-term nature.

For example, take a laboratory or firm which devotes its energies to some kind of research. Suppose that the possibility for a large research contract arises in a new type of scientific endeavor. It therefore becomes very important to the management of the laboratory that a team of research workers make themselves as knowledgeable as possible about what has been written in scientific journals to this point in time so that they can make a proper proposal for the research grant.

An interesting new information retrieval system has been developed to serve a need such as the one above. This is known as Selective Dissemination of Information Libraries and requires a computer with massive storage capabilities to provide the files to be searched. The system first involves the selection of special key words for the identification of all types of scientific writing. Then ways are devised whereby the key words can be assigned to articles either by the authors or by the editors of the journals in which the articles are published. To make this system work as intended in searching out specific information from the files, many complex computer programs have had to be written. Information on what has been written on a certain subject, may, by using the proper access code, obtain a listing of the publications in which information of the type requested can be found.

Short-Run Decisions

Managers of all types of business are continually confronted with needing to know facts or data in order to make the best possible decisions concerning the immediate problems at hand. For example:

1. The cost of making our product is too high. (At what point, and why, did the costs become excessive?)
2. Sales have been very good for the last month, and it is important to have the merchandise needed to fill the orders. (What types of merchandise have been sold, and what quantities remain? Do we now need to order more?)
3. Business has been good, with even better potential. (Are we at the point where we can afford to add another salesman?)
4. The firm is badly in need of cash to meet current operating expenses. (What money is owed us, and when is it likely to be col-

lected? What course of action should the business follow to provide the needed funds?)
5. With the growth of the business, there are many new customers,
most of whom are seeking credit. (Which customers are good
credit risks and which are not?)

A business manager also has the problem of planning activities for
the business one month, three months, or six months in advance. Once
more, facts concerning the past are of vital importance in making decisions as to what should be done in the immediate future. An accurate
knowledge of the past can materially influence decisions affecting
future actions.

Long-Run Decisions

There are many decisions, however, which will affect the long-run
course of the business. These decisions should be made only after long
and considered thought by the board of directors and/or managers
of the business. For example, at what level of economic development,
or in what type of economic endeavor would they like to see the business involved 10 or 20 years from now?

Arriving at a Plan of Action

The act of planning may be quite informal in nature in a smaller
business, taking place largely in the head of the proprietor. In a larger
business, on the other hand, it may be much more formal and may
be largely in writing. In such a business, there may be an overall plan
which consists of a number of detailed plans covering various interde-
pendent activities. These activities include sales, production, purchasing, inventories in every phase of the business process, accounts receivable, investments in plant, equipment, and so on.

A complete business plan indicates not only the physical levels of
each of the various operations, such as the number of products to be
manufactured, held in stock, and marketed, but also the values to be
created and to be used in the business processes during a period of
time. This plan is the *budget,* simply another name for a formalized
program.

A formalized budget program provides a complete projection into
the future of the company's probable activities, capital requirements,
and profit. To enable management to be aware of deviations from the

planned program, the budget should be set up with the same corresponding structure as the financial reports, which will eventually show
the actual performance, so that a comparison of the budgeted and the
actual figures will reveal all deviations. An analysis of these deviations
should explain their causes and in many cases provide answers as how
to correct them.

For example, a manufacturing firm's approach to preparing a budget
for the next fiscal period would probably commence with the sales
budget and would consider the following facts in its preparations:

1. Anticipated sales both in dollars and by product, determined by —
    a. past experience and/or
    b. anticipation of business prospects for the future period
        (1) possibly determined by correlating demand for products
            with some other measurable form of business activity.
2. Anticipated sales in dollars and by products probably will also be
   determined by month, by salesman, and by territory.

Control

Control over operations is accomplished only by having a combination of factors present. There must be a fully understood delegation
of authority and responsibility for each manager of the division, department, or section to which each segment of the budget applies. There
must also be active, willing acceptance on the part of the individual
assuming the authority as well as the responsibility which has been
delegated. It is only when these conditions exist that control can possibly occur.

Attention is called to the need for control when the planned results
for one of these organizational subdivisions is compared with the actual
results for a comparable period of time and sizeable differences are
reflected. Control occurs only when a positive action is taken to explain
or rectify the factors causing the differences so that these same differences hopefully will not reoccur in the future.

In addition to comparing the planned or budgeted figures with the
actual occurred figures, several examples of ways to call attention to
the need for control are by using the following:

1. Ratios; that is, like ratios can be compared for a period of time,
   or ratios can be compared with like ratios in the industry;
2. Percentage relationships; that is, such percentages as those of operating expenses to net sales can be compared for a series of years,

both vertically and horizontally; and percentage relationships can also be displayed graphically with good results;
3. Return on investment analysis can be applied to divisions, territories, departments, or products.

Systems[3]

What have the managers of modern business enterprise done to assemble the data which they have felt that they needed?

They have had two sources to turn to—the existing accounting system which has always dealt with the traditional dollar-and-cent facts as they affected the business, and then they have had what has been called the "informal information system." This last includes the systems of data gathering carried on by various departments of the organization who have each felt they needed specific kinds of information, as it affected their work, which was not gathered in a formal manner by the existing accounting system. A few typical examples might be:

1. Analyses of sales. Which are the fast moving items? Which are the slow moving?
2. Quality-control information. The number of units rejected out of each 100 produced. This information may be necessary to determine whether bonus payments to workers are due because they produce higher than standard quality products.
3. Analysis of the reasons for employee absences. This could be used to determine necessary claims to be made under Workmen's Compensation Insurance.

With the advent of the computer with its capacity to accumulate, manipulate, store, and summarize many types of data, there is no longer any reason for the existence of numerous data accumulation systems within an organization. All of these systems can be merged together into what is often called a *Management Information System* (MIS).

EXTERNAL DEMANDS FOR DATA

Historical Background

The business records of the English trading companies in the 17th and 18th centuries show that many expeditions were joint ventures. Several people pooled their resources to outfit an expedition or trading mission. It was important to keep records of the resources which had

---

[3] A set of interrelated ideas, principles, rules, procedures, laws, or the like.

been committed, but very little additional information was required. When the trading mission returned, all the resources of the mission would be liquidated. But it was at this point that data and records became important once again, because each member of the joint venture wanted to be certain that he received his just share of the proceeds.

In the early business history of this country, detailed business records were not maintained. The prime requisite of the records was only that they provide confidential financial statements of the company's progress to the owners at periodic intervals, and most of the companies were either single proprietorships or partnerships.

As the corporate form of business enterprise became more prevalent (in the later 1800s), the interest of the public in the activities of particular businesses began to be recognized. Ownership of these corporations became more widespread. In fact, ownership in many instances became international in character with the investment of large sums of money in the industries of this country by foreign investors. With greater public interest in the financial activities of corporations, the need for more complete data about the activities of the corporations increased. It was not long before the governments of the respective states began to legislate (in many ways) how financial affairs and the records of corporations were to be maintained, and to set up specific requirements as to how and when these corporations were to report their financial activities.

In 1913 the first federal income tax law (after the ratification of the Sixteenth Amendment) was passed, and this enactment has probably had more to do with increased public interest in business data than any other one single event. All businesses, as well as all individuals, became more conscious of business transactions, and it was now mandatory that they keep adequate record of them so that they could be reported to the federal government on an annual basis.

The revenue acts and regulations of 1918 had an important effect on improving general accounting practices. The most significant provisions of the acts related to (1) depreciation and depletion and (2) inventory valuations. Federal income tax allowance for depreciation deductions caused many companies to make more systematic record-keeping provisions than previously thought necessary.

The Securities Exchange Act of 1934 (SEC), which created the Securities and Exchange Commission, gave the commission powers to obtain from registrants whatever detailed information it considered necessary and appropriate to protect the public interest of investors. It also required that all corporations with securities listed on a national stock exchange, or corporations desiring to offer the public an issue of securities in excess of $3 million, must file certified financial statements with the SEC.

One effect of all these government regulations was to heighten the interest of most businesses in statistical data.

Governmental Agencies

Today, the regulations and demands for data by state, local, and municipal authorities are almost as great as those of the federal government. Some of the demands of governmental agencies may be summarized as follows:

1. Income taxes on employer (federal, state, and local).
2. Withholding of federal and state income taxes, and federal social security taxes, from personal income of employees.
3. Social security taxes (federal and state) on employer.
4. Sales taxes (state and local) collected from customers and paid by the seller.
5. Manufacturer's excise taxes on sales of luxury goods.

Owners

As business units have increased in size and complexity, the trend has been for more and more business firms to become publicly owned. This has usually been brought about by increased needs for capital. In general, the easiest method of acquiring capital in quantity has been through the sale of shares of stock which represent individual shares of ownership of the firm.

With this trend, corporate management soon recognized the obligation—as well as the public necessity—of issuing periodic financial statements supported by considerable statistical data. These financial data are of utmost importance to prospective investors as well as to financial analysts, who are concerned with the financial outlook for the business as well as the industry.

In addition to regular balance sheets and income statements, there is a growing use of statistical analyses. For example, the recently published annual report of a nationally recognized corporation contained the following analyses to aid in judging the firm's financial condition and outlook:

1. Ten-year trend of amount of dividends paid per share of common stock plus one year projected.

2. Ten-year trend analysis of the consolidated sales of the company analyzing the part that different products played in the total sales each year.
3. Ten-year trend analysis showing the total invested capital of the company each year as well as the changes in those things in which invested capital was invested over the same period.
4. Ten-year trend analysis of the changes in total long term debt as a percentage of total capital.
5. A five-year picture showing the consolidated income after income taxes but before corporate overhead, interest on long-term debt and extraordinary items, of the principle income producing divisions of the company.

In a financial report such as the one described above, not only would the stockholders and financial analysts find information of interest but so would creditors, labor organizations, and the public at large. Each special-interest group can extract the material in which it is primarily interested for its own particular purposes.

The authors, however, would like to call the attention of the reader to the variety and quantities of business data which must be accumulated in some systematic manner in order to make such a report possible.

SOURCES OF DATA

In considering the sources of the data required in the typical organization, it will be found that here, also, data may originate from inside or outside the firm, depending on the type of data considered.

Internal Data

A business form is usually the medium on which data are first recorded at the time an event occurs: for example, a sales invoice, a time ticket, a production order, or a bank check. There are many types and designs of forms. In each instance, however, the form is designed to capture the facts, which management, owners or other outside agencies are interested or concerned with, as accurately and simply as possible. The recorded data may not have to be transcribed again throughout the entire data processing operation, depending upon the type of system used. The importance of minimizing the transcription of data, as well as the importance of keeping them in a form which can be readily processed, cannot be overemphasized.

When, however, it is necessary to transcribe data, it is important to plan the layout of the form so that it will clearly provide the data in the same order (on the page) in which it will be transcribed. The sequence in which information is transferred to a punched card versus the layout of the hard-copy form from which the information for the punched card is taken would be a typical example.

It might also be well at this point to stop and remember that data need not always be expressed in the form of dollars to be usable by those with management responsibilities; data may also include quantities and descriptions of items, man- or machine-hours, or data may be expressed in percentages, ratios, volumes, and other informational terms. For example, take a sales ticket from a retail clothing store and analyze its data with the view of recognizing the needs and uses for all the recorded data.

FIGURE 1–1. Example of a Sales Ticket

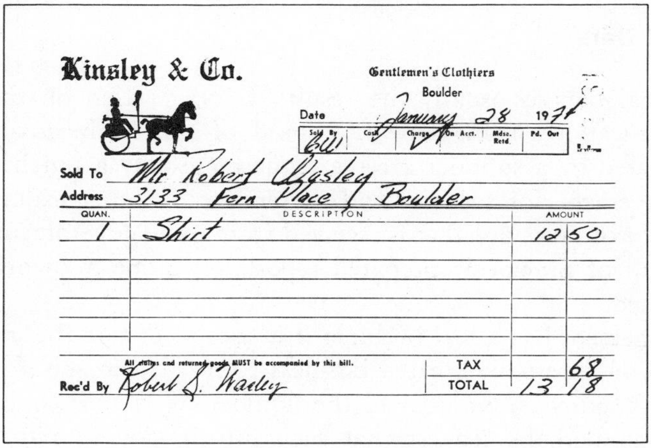

In Figure 1–1 the sales ticket identifies certain bits of data important to the operation of the store. These bits of important data could be identified as follows:

1. The name and address of the person who purchased the merchandise on open account. This information identifies the customer and indicates where the monthly bill should be sent.
2. The sales tickets are numbered in sequential order. Each night the tickets are filed in sequence so as to be able to account for all the sales transactions of the day.

3. The clerk making the sale is identified. This is done because the clerk is compensated, in part, on the basis of what is sold.
4. This same sales ticket would be used if the merchandise had been sold for cash. The sum of all of the cash sales tickets written during a day should be equal to the balance in the drawer of the cash register as counted that evening, less the amount of change which the cash register started with in the morning.
5. The amount of sales tax collected is clearly indicated. It is important that this be known because, in this particular illustration, there is a state sales tax and a city sales tax as well as a regional transportation authority tax levied on all sales which are made.
6. The person receiving the merchandise is asked to sign for it. Doing this protects the merchant from people coming in and saying that they had never purchased or received the merchandise at a later date.

External Data

External data is usually the result of some action on the part of the organization's management. Typical of this is the invoice which is originated by a supplier after a request (usually a purchase order) by management for supplies and/or services. Another example might be a notice of taxes due that is received from some governmental agency as a result of previously prepared reports on property owned or revenues earned.

Management has a real problem if it tries to dictate the information included on externally created business forms. It can specify items desired on a purchase order, and the number of invoice copies desired, and it can perhaps request that such information as purchase-order number, store number, or department number be included on the invoice, but it has no control over the arrangement of the data, the size of the document or its color, or the medium used in its preparation. The problem of verifying the accuracy of data is multiplied manyfold under these circumstances, yet just the possibility of these circumstances tends to slow up the entire data processing operation.

DATA FLOW

The flow of data is another important consideration. The techniques and equipment to be used in a given situation are directly dependent on the mass of data to be handled, on whether these data are produced at a constant level or in spurts, and on the urgency of timely action to record the data and produce the required output of statements and reports.

DATA VOLUME

Along with the problems of assembling the needed data, accumulating it in a systematic manner on a form, transcribing it as few times as necessary, and continually checking to verify its accuracy, there is also the problem of the quantities of data with which the organization will be concerned. This problem is of particular importance in considering the method of data processing to be used. The manual methods are slower, but they are also the least costly when the volume is low. The mechanical methods would logically follow next in line, and then the electronic methods, in terms of relative speed and cost.

Another facet of this problem of data volume is whether the flow of data is cyclical or whether it is fairly steady and even. If the data are cyclical in nature, the questions then posed are:

1. Is it necessary that the peaks of data be processed with great rapidity?
2. Or can the data wait until other, slower methods of data processing can absorb them?

TIMELINESS OF DATA

How timely must the data output be: within seconds, minutes, hours, days, weeks, or months? Management must be able to bill its customers for their purchases as quickly as possible in order to collect these accounts when they are due. Management must also be able to plan the financial needs of the firm if it is to pay its creditors when its obligations are due. If this is a governmental unit, management must know promptly the unencumbered balance of appropriated funds.

Other examples of the necessity for promptness in the processing of data to furnish information could be cited almost indefinitely. In each of these examples, management must have timely answers to its questions to avoid such consequences as the impairment of credit, over- or underproduction, excess or insufficient purchase of goods and supplies, or other actions that could have a serious effect on the well-being of the organization.

QUESTIONS

1. Why is it that data have become increasingly important through the years in the conduct of most of the institutions and organizations with which we are familiar?

2. Who or what determines what data are important or significant?

3. How is data used in the conduct of the affairs of an organization?

4. Give five examples of the form which data might take in different situations.

5. What do you understand the control function of management to be?

6. How is data used in the control function of management?

7. Of what importance is the "system" to the gathering and interpreting of information?

8. Why is it that all users of information today seem to need it so much more rapidly than they did in the 17th and 18th centuries?

9. Why are owners asking for so much more information to be included in published financial statements than they did 40 years ago?

10. Why is data originating within the firm so much easier to deal with than data which arises outside the firm?

11. Is there any relationship between the amount of data to be processed and the way in which it is processed? If so, explain.

12. What does the timing of the need for the data output have to do with the way in which the data is processed? Explain.

chapter

2

Information Systems for Planning and Control

IN THE PAST, systems for gathering information have been almost solely concerned with what has happened to the affairs of a particular business or institution. There has been little concern for "why" the affairs were as they were or for "what might be done about them." The designers of information systems have been oblivious to other basic needs of management, such as information for control by comparing actual performance with the predetermined plan. These faults cannot be blamed wholly on the systems in use at the time, however. Management personnel were not trained in the use of such information and did not ask that it be prepared.

Today, however, the modern computer system is becoming economically feasible for most organizations, and their managements are being trained in the use of new management decision-making techniques. Consequently, it is important that the information system be designed to provide not only the historical information, but also the planning and control features of a true management information system.

To state it a little differently, information managers are learning that they must be both interested and concerned with the basic management processes—those of planning and control. Unless they are intimately acquainted with the problems of management in these areas, they are not going to be able to fulfill this role.

BASIC MANAGEMENT PROCESSES

Planning

The planning function is a decision-making process because it is only done where possible alternatives exist. The information manager or management accountants' role in planning is to provide information to management to assist in the evaluation of alternative courses of action.

Business or organizational planning has often been described as being composed of four parts: formulation of objectives; setting of policies; preparation of long-range plans, which involves the selection of strategies as well as deciding among alternative courses of action; and preparation of operating budgets.

Objectives. There is probably no function of management which is dealt with less by management in general than is the function of setting objectives. Yet, in the long run, it is probably one of the most important managerial functions. Unless top management has a clear sense of mission and knows what it is trying to accomplish, decisions are going to be determined by personalities and by apparent opportunity rather than by objectives which should have a more enduring quality to them.

Business objectives might include the following considerations: (1) What direction should intended business growth take? (2) Which business opportunities should be considered as potential alternatives to existing ones? (3) What rate of growth should be sought for in sales, profits, assets, and so on? (4) What should be the profit objectives? (5) How should future expansion be financed? (See Reference 9.)

To spell out the role of the management accountant in assisting management to accomplish these objectives William N. McNairn of Price Waterhouse & Co. has the following to say: "Objectives are of practical value for scientific management purposes when defined in specific terms that enable their accomplishment to be measured. If left in abstract terms they are too formless for practical use."[1]

When the objectives are defined in specific terms, that is, a particular return on the investment or share of the market, the accounting function can be of great value to management through the internal reporting function comparing current results with the predetermined objectives.

[1] William N. McNairn, "Objectives," *Price Waterhouse Review*, Spring 1970, p. 37.

Policies. Policies may be defined as broad guides to future action. Expressed in another way, policies can be formulated only after objectives have been determined because policies constitute the broad means whereby objectives will be met.

Long-Range Plans. Plans which extend over a year in length are generally referred to as long-range plans. They have become more necessary because of (1) the growing scale and complexity of business operation, (2) the rapid transformation of many labor costs from variable to fixed, and (3) the tendency for qualified personnel to become a scarce resource.

Long-range plans often go wrong because of the unwillingness of financial managers to forecast. To combat this, some firms are asking for forecasts expressed in three ways: optimistic, pessimistic, and the most likely predictions to which varying weights of possibility may be assigned. This is being done to allow the forecaster a greater amount of leeway in his prediction and to permit the forecasts to be utilized in computerized mathematical decision-type programs to provide alternative projections which are available to management.

Operating Budgets. An operating budget is usually prepared on an annual basis and contains detailed projections of the anticipated revenues and expenses of the organization. (See Reference 1.)

Control

When narrowly defined, control means "to regulate, to keep within limits." This is an unduly restrictive connotation in many situations.

Instead, the point of view of William T. Jerome III is infinitely more constructive and useful. He says:

> The purpose of control is to set the stage for action; controls provide the best teaching or educational devices available to executives; effective control for managerial purposes requires flexibility rather than steadfast adherence to any given plan of action.[2]

The first point of view is static, while the latter is dynamic. In the typical organization of today, where change and flexibility in operation is a daily requirement, the later point of view is, of course, preferable.

Management should never lose sight of the fact that it is people that they are dealing with, and that it is only through people that any form of control can be effective. It is, therefore, of extreme impor-

---

[2] William Travers Jerome III, *Executive Control—The Catalyst* (New York: John Wiley & Sons, 1961), p. 30.

tance to communicate the comparison between a department's planned and actual activity in a way that the results will be clearly understood and with prompt action following when needed. (See References 2 and 7.)

ORGANIZATIONAL INGREDIENTS NECESSARY SO THAT PLANNING AND CONTROL CAN MORE READILY OCCUR

In order for management to deal with planning and control responsibilities effectively, there must be certain basic elements existent within the structure of their organization and within its information system.

Clearly Defined Organization Structure

In order that an information system may accumulate and interpret data in a meaningful way, there must be a clearly defined plan of organization where the functions and responsibilities of all levels of management are clearly defined. This becomes increasingly important as organizations grow in size and complexity.

Wherever possible, this information should be set forth in either an organizational chart or manual and should be available to all concerned. Conflicting responsibilities should be avoided.

Data must be accumulated by the information system in accordance with the defined areas of responsibility in order that the reports prepared can be pertinent and meaningful to the recipient and can reflect the financial responsibility and accountability of the individual concerned. In order for this to be accomplished, it will, in turn, require that the chart of accounts of the organization be designed and organized so that the data can be accumulated in the desired manner.

An important criterion of the adequacy of any plan of organization is the extent to which it provides for organizational independence as between operating, custodial, and recordkeeping departments. This is saying that it is not wise for the department which is doing the work to also keep its own records, nor is it wise for it to have custody over all of the materials and supplies which it is using.

Chart of Accounts

A chart of accounts is a list of the ledger accounts of a business which hopefully have been chosen by management to provide information in which they are interested and concerned. In each area of government controlled industries such a chart of accounts is prescribed by law while in the private sector it is not. In many ways, however, it is more than a list of accounts we are talking about. In using financial data to facilitate the planning and control functions, the accounts must provide relevant and significant information both to (1) give those responsible and accountable the information needed for planning and control over those operations for which they are responsible, and (2) provide those reviewing the operations with information of "how" the activity is doing.

Take, for example, Wages in Figure 2–1. Wages Sharemilker (account 4021) is a much more definitive account title than Wages by

FIGURE 2–1. A Segment of a Chart of Accounts for a New Zealand Sheep Rancher

	Expenses		*Expenses*
4010	Wages	4050	Cash Cropping Expense
4011	Wages Manager	4051	Windrowing
4012	Wages Permanent	4052	Heading
4013	Wages Casual	4053	Sacks and Twine
4014	Wages Wife	4054	Drying and Storing
4015	Wages Meals etc.	4055	Dressing and Certifying
4021	Wages Sharemilker	4056	Spraying
4030	Animal Health	4057	Potato Planting
4031	Bloat Control	4058	Potato Grading
4032	Dips Fly Control	4060	Cultivation
4033	Dockg Tags Gas	4061	Clearing and Bulldozing
4034	Drenches Vaccine	4062	Initial Work
4035	Footrot Control	4063	Final Work, Sowing
4036	Veterinary Fees	4070	Dairy Shed Expense
4038	Health Appliances	4071	Rubber Ware
4039	Dog Hydatid Control	4072	Brushes Brooms
4040	Breeding Expense	4073	Cleaning Materials
4041	Artificial Breeding	4080	Electricity
4042	Herd Testing	4081	House
4043	Pregnancy Tests	4082	Shearing Shed
4044	Service Fees	4083	Dairy Shed

Source: Lincoln College and University of Canterbury, Christchurch, N.Z., *Joint Project in Farm Management Accounting*, June 1966.

itself, as it helps to pinpoint the responsibility for the expense. Having an account with such a title will necessitate having procedures capable of capturing data in accord with this responsibility. The same would be said for Electricity Dairy Shed versus Electricity.

It is of the greatest importance—both to the planning and to the control function—that the accounts used are adequate and descriptive of what management is trying to do. Some charts of accounts are not planned; they just happen. They represent an accumulation of a number of persons' contributions over years of use. Each of these contributors had his or her own ideas as to account classification and, as a result, added his or her bit of logic to that of others.

An ideal chart of accounts is one that is flexible enough to permit new accounts to be added without changing the basic accounts or hindering the accurate and rapid consolidation of accounting and financial data. If the business under discussion has several divisions or separate organizations, it is vital to use homogeneous classifications for all parts of divisions in the corporate entity.

Natural Classification of Accounts. In order to facilitate the economical and speedy preparation of financial statements, the accounts should be arranged in the sequence which will be followed in the preparation of the balance sheet, income statement, and supporting schedules.

For example:

1.   Balance sheet asset accounts.
2.   Balance sheet liability accounts.
3.   Balance sheet owner's equity accounts.
4.   Sales income accounts.
5.   Manufacturing expense accounts.
6.   Selling expense accounts.
7.   General and administrative expense accounts.
8.   Research and development expense accounts.
9.   Other income accounts.
10. Other expense accounts.
11. Income tax accounts.

The caption of each account should be both brief and clearly descriptive.

Periodically the accounts being used should be reviewed as to their adequacy and relevance for the purposes intended. If there are accounts which are not being used, they should be deleted. On the other hand, if needed information is not presently provided, the chart should be sufficiently flexible to permit such accounts to be added with ease.

Account Coding. Definitions of the process of account coding vary, but most agree on the basic principles involved. Typical definitions include: "Account coding is the science of selecting and assigning account numbers to specific account lists."[3]

---

[3] Conan Doyle Whiteside, *Accounting Systems for the Small and Medium-Sized Business* (Englewood Cliffs, N.J.: Prentice-Hall, 1961), p. 217.

The National Association of Accountants in their Research Report No. 34 describe coding in this way:

> The assignment of numbers, letters or other symbols according to a systematic plan for distinguishing the classification to which each item belongs and for distinguishing items within a given classification from each other.[4]

Devising a Coding System. When devising a coding system, each digit of the code should have meaning. If one is to follow this idea, the next question is: How many digits are necessary for a particular coding system? The fewer digits there are in the code, the less likelihood there is of error in recording; speed in sorting is facilitated; and less storage space is required for the data on the document, in the punched card, or in the memory storage devices of computers.

The designer of the coding system must also ask himself or herself the following questions as to the use of the system. What is it that is being classified? For example: Is the coding system going to be used to identify the accounts of a small to medium-sized business which appears to intend to continue this same type of business into the foreseeable future? Or, is it going to be used to identify the many diverse areas of responsibility, as well as all of the corporate accounts, of a large corporation engaged in many activities? Or, is the coding system going to be used to classify items of inventory? In each of these instances the code will be constructed differently.

BLOCK CODES. This particular type of numerical sequence code reserves a block of numbers for a definite classification of items within that block. Each number within the block identifies the item itself.

5—Plant, Property & Equipment
  5–1 Land
  5–2 Building and
      Improvements
  5–3 Delivery Equipment

6—Prepaid Expenses
  6–1 Insurance Policy "A"
  6–2 Insurance Policy "B"
  6–3 Rent

This might be the coding system designed for the small- to medium-sized business, mentioned above.

GROUP CLASSIFICATION CODES. This code uses one or more of its numbers to classify the items into major and minor groups. In this code, all items of any group can be identified by selecting the one number of the code which identifies the group. The larger grouping

---

[4] NAA Research Report No. 34, *Classification and Coding Techniques to Facilitate Accounting Operations,* April 1, 1959, p. 3.

is always found on the left. Reading toward the right are found the smaller subdivisions of the group.

INCOME ACCOUNT

3111
 Revenue
  Government
   Cost reimbursable contracts
    Cost plus fixed fee subcontract

EXPENSE ACCOUNT

5461
 Expenses
  Advertising department
   Printing media
    Brochures

In the "expenses" classification above, those of printing brochures are classified under the advertising department, which has the responsibility for authorizing that expenditure. Other departments would each have their related expenditure responsibilities shown under their expense account classifications. This illustrates again the importance of having clearly defined areas of authority and responsibility.

This type of code could be an example of the coding system for the large corporation with many areas of diverse responsibility mentioned previously.

SIGNIFICANT DIGIT CODES. Within this code all or some of the digits represent the item information (such as weight, dimension, distance, and capacity). This system has most application in classifying items of inventory. It is not applicable to the classification of ledger accounts. Two examples:

31000 Files	13000 Electric Light Bulbs
31040—Files 4″	13020—20 Watt
31045—Files 4½″	13040—40 Watt
31050—Files 5″	13100—100 Watt
	13250—250 Watt

(See Reference 4.)

Cost Accounting System

If the firm under consideration manufactures what it sells, a cost accounting system becomes necessary in order for the management to be able to first plan and then control the operation. It is the function of the system and the persons working with it to account for and then assign the manufacturing costs which are being incurred to the units of product produced or to the operating processes to which they related. The cost accounting system, therefore, plays a direct part in the determination of the value of the ending inventory as well as the cost of goods sold, which in turn will influence the net income figure.

Any attempts to cope with the problem of assigning manufacturing costs to units of product or to operating processes must in turn recognize the fixed, semivariable, and variable nature of these costs. It is generally presumed that the management can first plan their pattern of expenditures for the period, and then in turn compare their plan with the actual results, thus making the function of control a greater reality. (See Reference 8.)

Operating Budgets

An operating budget compels all members of management to plan in advance precisely how each of their activities must be carried out in order that the objectives and plans which have been set can be met.

It should be pointed out that although a budget does not become a part of the data accumulation system, it is modeled directly from the accounting system. It is a plan of action. It spells out the responsibilities of all of the sectors of the business organization by year, by quarter, by month, and in some cases, even by the day. These responsibilities are spelled out not only in dollars and cents but also in terms of units of activity over which various individuals have authority and responsibility.

When a budget is prepared in this way, internal reports can be prepared at regular intervals, according to individual areas of responsibility, comparing planned activity with what was actually accomplished. The individual responsible for a particular area is regarded by top management as being responsible and must account to top management for any marked deviations from budgeted activity in that area. In this way, a budget is used not only as a planning device but as a control device as well. (See Reference 3.)

Internal Reports for Management

As businesses have become larger and more diversified, management has realized the necessity of knowing what is occurring in their respective areas of responsibility when it is occurring rather than waiting until the end of an accounting period. This has given rise to the preparation of internal information reports, which should be prepared on a more frequent basis than the annual financial statements and which contain only information directly pertinent to the responsibility of a particular member or segment of the management team.

It is customary to find that the higher up the management ladder an internal accounting report is submitted, the more summarized and "all encompassing" it will be. Also, the less frequently it will be submitted. In contrast, as one goes down the management ladder, one will find that the reports are more specific in nature and are more frequently submitted. This is because control can be more readily accomplished the closer one is to the actual operations. Also, each area of management at the lower levels is responsible for specific activities.

Some examples of the timing of internal reports might be that the report to the shop foreman is prepared daily showing such things as: hours worked by his crew, or pieces of production by his crew rejected by the quality control department versus the budgeted standard that particular day. On the other hand, the vice president in charge of marketing receives a report semiannually or annually showing his or her company's share of the market and its competitions' share. All of this might then be compared with the total market size.

Committed Top Management

The top management of any firm must be completely committed to the concept that a formal planning and control procedure is essential and that it intends to anticipate or detect errors in plans and correct them on a continuing basis. If this commitment does not exist, it won't take the other personnel of the firm long to detect it. From this point forward the value of the planning and control concept will soon deteriorate.

Responsibility Reporting System

A somewhat specialized adaptation of many of the ideas which have been brought forward in this chapter can be summarized in the concept of what is termed a responsibility reporting system. The idea behind this concept is the development of an accounting system directly related to the responsibilities of people rather than merely classifying items of cost as parts of a functional activity.

Basing the preparation of reports on responsibility assignments is not a revolutionary new idea. It merely recommends that costs be accumulated according to the various areas and levels of responsibility, as outlined and defined in the organization structure of a business firm. It also recommends that only costs which are controllable at the various levels of responsibility be reported to the responsible individuals.

In order to make such a concept workable, there are several other requirements which must be present within the organization and the information system.

1. The managerial reports with which we are concerned should tell us not only what has happened but also who is responsible for the occurrence. This means that the firm must have spelled out these responsibilities by means of a clearly defined organization structure well in advance.

2. In order that the majority of all costs be recognized as controllable by some member of the management team, any costs which vary over the period or from period to period must be identified and related to the responsible manager. This, in turn, will require that specific ledger accounts be created so as to relate these costs to those members of management who truly have control over them. To do this will demand not only a greatly enlarged chart of accounts but also an increased understanding on the part of the system designers of the basic nature of all of the costs incurred in the business organization.

3. A budget informs management as to what it is to account for. Each supervisor should have the right to participate in the preparation of the standard by which he is to be evaluated. A complete budget for the entire business organization must be constructed from the lowest echelon of management to the top and spelled out according to the responsibilities of each level of management. It is only in this way that the responsibility for the incurrence of controllable cost by any level of management will be sincerely assumed.

4. In order that control can actually take place, there must be frequent reports to all levels of management comparing, in the clearest possible manner, what had been budgeted for a particular level of management to what actually occurred. Such reports should suggest action, they should emphasize deviations from the budget plan, and they should direct thinking toward the business objectives.

Numerous ways have been conceived whereby management can be stimulated to keep the actual controllable costs in line with the budgeted controllable costs, and these ideas must be considered when the decision is made to implement a responsibility accounting system. Figure 2–2 is an example of a report which illustrates the points discussed.

FIGURE 2–2. Product Line Statement of Earnings

Manager, Radio Department

Month	Gross Sales Over (Under) Plan*	Gross Sales Actual Plan*	Standard Profit Contribution Amount Over (Under) Plan*	Standard Profit Contribution Amount Actual Plan*	Standard Profit Contribution Percent Over (Under) Plan*	Standard Profit Contribution Percent Actual Plan*	Standby Expense Spec.	Standby Expense Gen.	Pro-gram'd Exps.	Standard Product Line Earnings	Orders Received This Year	Orders Received Last Year	Order Backlog This Year	Order Backlog Last Year
Jan	(21)	2,534	(54)	937	(1.8)	37.0	35	310	44	548	2,653	2,760	92	173
Feb	(116)	2,540	(60)	968	(0.6)	38.1	35	312	56	565	2,598	2,795	113	216
Mar	79	2,901	49	1,142	0.6	30.3	36	312	42	752	3,113	2,961	301	258
Apr	33	2,922	3	1,131	–0–	38.7	35	312	39	745	3,016	3,003	275	219
May		2,889*		1,119*		38.7*	35	312	39			2,871		216
Jun		3,055		1,183*		38.7*	36	312	38			3,217		352
Jul		2,224*		862*		38.7*	35	312	39			2,219		171
Aug		3,088*		1 196*		38.7*	36	312	40			3,156		278
Sep		2,967*		1,157*		38.7*	36	312	39			2,991		207
Oct		2,822*		1,093*		38.7*	36	312	39			2,762		197
Nov		2,656*		1,028*		38.7*	35	312	36			2,461		101
Dec		2,556*		991		38.8*	35	312	48			2,333		71
Year to Date	(25)	10,897	(54)	4,178	(0.4)	38.7	141	1,246	181	2,610	11,380	11,519		
Original Plan		33,199		12,860	38.7			425	3,742	499	8,194				
Current Forecast		33,174		12,806	38.5			425	3,742	499	8,140				

Source· Max F. Sporer, Partner, Touche Ross & Co., "The Mechanics of Accounting under Profitable Accounting." (Company training materials.)

Companies which adopt a responsibility reporting system face certain problems when it comes to the preparation of the year-end financial statements because considerable data manipulation is required in order to translate data accumulated and analyzed by responsibility assignment into the typed profit-and-loss categories of manufacturing, selling, and administrative expense. Some companies also have the problem of reporting profits on a divisional basis, but both of these problems can be readily solved if the system is properly designed. (See References 5 and 6.)

REFERENCES

1. BOETTINGER, HENRY M.   "What Corporate Planning Can Do For You." *Financial Executive,* May 1971, p. 24.

2. COLBERT, BERTRAM A.   "Pathway to Profit—The Management Information System." *Price Waterhouse Review,* Spring 1967, p. 4.

3. CRANDALL, RICHARD E. "Key Steps in Profit Planning." *Management Controls,* January 1972, p. 7.

4. *Data Processing Techniques: Coding Methods.* White Plains, N.Y.: International Business Machines Corporation, Form F20–8093.

5. FERRARA, WILLIAM L. "Responsibility Accounting—A Basic Control Concept." *NAA Bulletin,* vol. 46, no. 1, September 1964.

6. HOLMES, ROBERT W. "An Executive Views Responsibility Reporting." *Financial Executive,* August 1968, pp. 39–42.

7. JEROME, W. T., III. *Executive Control—The Catalyst,* New York: John Wiley & Sons, 1961.

8. KRAMER, EUGENE H., and ATTSHULER, EDWARD A. "A Universal Distribution Number System." *Management Adviser,* November–December 1973, p. 25.

9. MORRISON, WILLIAM G. "Cost Accounting and Decision Making." *Management Controls,* March 1972, p. 42.

10. ROSS, TIMOTHY L., and JONES, GARDNER, M. "An Approach to Increasing Productivity: The Scanlon Plan." *Financial Executive,* February 1972, p. 23.

QUESTIONS

1. Can you think of any activity which one might become involved in which would not involve the planning function?

2. What are the four parts of the planning function? In what ways are the parts different and in what ways are they similar?

3. When the statement is made that the functions of management are to plan and then control, which concept of control is the most acceptable to you? Why?

4. What is the relationship between a clearly defined organization structure and the planning function? Explain.

5. When one is speaking or thinking about information systems, specifically describe the roll of the Chart of Accounts in this activity.

6. What purpose does coding serve in a Chart of Accounts? Explain.

7. What is a cost accounting system?

8. Under what circumstances does a cost accounting system become necessary? Explain.

9. Is an operating budget a part of the books of account? Explain.

10. In order for internal reports to be able to serve their purpose, what other factors must be present within the company?

11. What is the purpose of an internal report?

3

Basic Data Processing Functions—Originating and Recording

IN EVERY PROCEDURE involving the processing of business data, there are certain basic steps to be performed. These steps must be followed regardless of the data processing system employed—handwritten, mechanical, punched card, or electronic computer. These functions, which are basic to the processing of all data, are those of originating and recording (discuss in this chapter) and those of classifying, sorting, summarizing, calculating, and communicating (taken up in Chapter 4).

In manual (pen or pencil) data processing, all of the basic functions may be performed by hand. It is possible, however, for specialized forms, techniques, and even equipment to perform many of the required functions. In most instances, the work is not only speedier but also costs less per unit of work performed and—perhaps most important of all—gives more accurate results.

There is a seemingly infinite combination of equipment and techniques to perform the functions required in the processing of business information. In many instances, using a computer is neither the best nor the least expensive way to accomplish the required results. Some firms, usually either quite small or very highly specialized, should use traditional manual recording techniques. Many firms can and should perform certain phases of their data processing by equipment other than computers. Most firms—even with a computer—will utilize specialized data preparation and collection equipment, equipment to perform data manipulation functions in selecting and arranging data for computer processing, and, under some circumstances, use noncomputerized equipment in minor processing procedures. It is in connection with these varied needs that the typical alternatives available in the processing of business data are presented in conjunction with the basic functions they may perform. The type of business firm, the volume and flow of the data, the timeliness required in processing the data, and the costs which can be afforded all enter into the specific combination of equipment and techniques utilized by a given business firm.

In every instance, however, the procedural logic to be followed in the processing of business information is exactly the same—regardless of the methods used. Of course, as techniques are used which require this procedural logic to be processed at increasingly faster speeds, more complex equipment will be required and this, in turn, may alter the manner in which the functions are performed.

In electronic data processing (EDP) the data may either be originated manually, in which case it will be transcribed later into a coded computer-acceptable form, or it may be originated in one of the many machine-acceptable forms. The computer is then given a coded program of steps to follow, which is stored in the computer's "memory." Next, the data are fed into the computer, and all the remaining basic processing functions necessary to the procedures required are completed automatically, with the individual processing steps being performed in millionths or even billionths of a second.

Regardless of the equipment and techniques used, however, most business systems and procedures depend on business documents or forms to assist in their processing procedures (the actual steps or operations in a system which are required in getting the job done). Forms are the means through which, with or without the help of machines—typewriters, calculators, bookkeeping machines, or computers, the data is collected, the procedural steps may be performed on and also serve as the media on which the final results are reported. Therefore, the efficiency and economy of a procedure may hinge on the forms which make up that procedure.

ORIGINATING

Forms are basic to the data manipulation process, as they are the media on which the data are initially captured at the time a transaction occurs. It is from this point of origination, in most instances, that the act of processing data actually begins.

In most data processing operations today forms become the initial input into the system. It is imperative that the data assembled on them be clear and accurate and in a pattern which will make the transcription of the data from the form to the punched card, or other data processing media, as quick, easy, and accurate as possible.

First, it is important to ascertain the data required in a procedure. To do this, one must determine the output, or report, desired from the data processing operation. Take the sales invoice procedure as an example: Does the system require only that the name and address of the creditor be known along with the amount owed, or does the system require a detailed analysis of sales by salesman, by product, by size, and by color, in addition to the above information? If this additional information is required, the variety of data on the sales invoice will be considerably greater.

Another important consideration in the format of any business form is the sequence of data on the form. The data on the initial sales invoice should be arranged in the same sequence as is desired in the data transcription pattern of the punched card or other media. This sequence of data, on both of these business forms, should also follow the natural sequence required in the procedure.

The accuracy of the data is always of vital concern to anyone interested in the problems of data processing. Once an error is made, the accuracy of the data cannot be improved by any subsequent processing. A number of ways have been conceived as a means of alleviating this problem of being accurate in recording data in the originating document. None of these, however, completely achieve the end desired. Some of the methods recommended are:

1. As much of the basic data surrounding the transaction as possible should be preprinted on the form. If the data are not preprinted, they may be precoded on the form. In this way the accuracy of the data may be proven before use.
2. The forms should be designed so as to be easily prepared. This is facilitated when adequate space is provided for the insertion of data; when it is possible for the data to be arranged in a neat, orderly manner, and in logical groups; when the sequence of data flows smoothly from left to right and from top to bottom of the form and is consistent with data on related forms; and when instructions are properly located on the form and are so worded as to be easily understood.
3. A contrast should be created between the preprinted data and the inserted entries. The inserted data should stand out plainly enough to be easily read, and the preprinted data fade into the background.

Precoding and Originating Machine-Recognizable Codes

Various methods have been devised to assure the initial accuracy of data at the time it is captured. Where humans record the data in the first instance, there is a real likelihood of error. Efforts have been made, therefore, to devise ways of verifying the majority of data surrounding a transaction before the transaction occurs. This is done by the advanced recording of the fixed data concerning a transaction on the related form. In this way, the accuracy of this data can be predetermined. The data captured at the time of origination should also be machine processable from this point on. There has been a variety of innovations in this area.

Printed Characters. Machine-recognizable printed characters present one of the most interesting potentials for reducing data processing costs.

There are two types of character recognition equipment: optical and magnetic ink. The optical equipment scans the character, determines the presence or absence of ink or pencil lead in certain positions, and from this information, establishes the character. Because of this recognition technique, the type font used is somewhat stylized. A typical optical font is illustrated in Figure 9–16.

Magnetic ink character recognition (MICR), commonly used by banks, involves the recognition of differences in intensities of magnetism present in the ink used in the printing of the data. For this reason, portions of some characters are exaggerated to provide greater intensity and permit differentiation (Figure 9–20).

Printed Codes. The printed code is another medium involving optical scanning. The gasoline credit card is probably the best known example of this method. It is embossed with the customer's account number and name. An example of this code is shown in Figure 3–1.

When the customer makes a purchase, his or her credit card is placed in an imprinting machine (Figure 3–2) where the attendant, by adjusting some levers, can indicate the amount of the sale. This, along with the customer's name and number, will be imprinted on a sales invoice by means of carbon paper and the pulling of a small roller across the credit card over which the sales invoice form is superimposed. Later, the customer's name, account number, and amount of sale an be optically interpreted to prepare the data for computer input on punched cards, magnetic tape, or fed directly into a computer system.

A common type of point of sale (POS) printed code, used in department or grocery stores, utilizing color coded stripes or lines is

FIGURE 3–1. Gasoline Credit Card Code

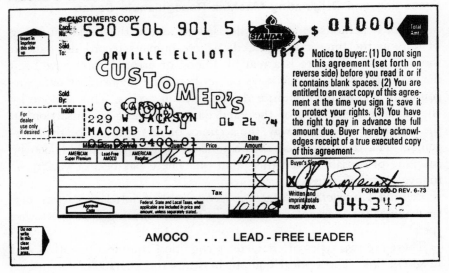

FIGURE 3–2. Imprinter

Courtesy of Addressograph Multigraph Corp

illustrated in Figure 3–15. This data is either fed directly into a computer or stored for later computer input.

Perforated Codes. There are several machine-recognizable perforated codes available to fit the requirements of a particular business or application. These include the perforated plastic card, perforated tags, perforated paper tape, and the very common punched card.

PLASTIC CARD. A perforated plastic card, which is the innovation of the National Cash Register Company is one answer to the problem of automatically collecting data in a credit sale transaction.

Every customer is provided with a card containing his or her name, address, and account number, all in embossed letters (Figure 3–3). The card also contains certain oblong-shaped holes which are the customer's account number in "automation" code.

FIGURE 3–3. Credit Card

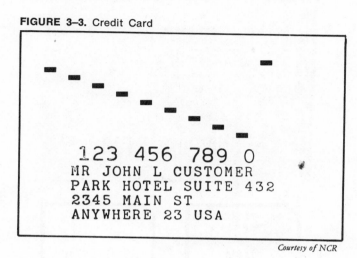

123 456 789 0
MR JOHN L CUSTOMER
PARK HOTEL SUITE 432
2345 MAIN ST
ANYWHERE 23 USA

Courtesy of NCR

The salesperson cannot forget to record an account number because the cash register, built to go with this system, will not operate unless the credit card is placed into the credit-card reader. The only exception is when a special button is used to release the register mechanism for a customer who does not have a credit card. In this event, the customer's account number can be entered through the register keyboard.

The information on the credit card is imprinted on the sales ticket. This information may also serve as a direct input to the computer.

TAGS. The perforated tag is a medium designed primarily for the retail industry (see Reference 1). Varying amounts of data can be punched into the tags, depending upon the needs of the user. For example, the manufacturer, department, style, size, class, color, season, fabric and price can be recorded automatically. The data punched into these tags can be interpreted by a reader and stored in punched cards or magnetic tape for computer processing. An example of a perforated tag is shown in Figure 3–4.

PAPER TAPE. A perforated code with an even broader usage than those above is the punched paper-tape code—actually several codes varying in the number of channels or positions used to represent a character (Figure 9–8 and 9–9). Many of the mechanical devices de-

FIGURE 3–4. Perforated Garment Tags

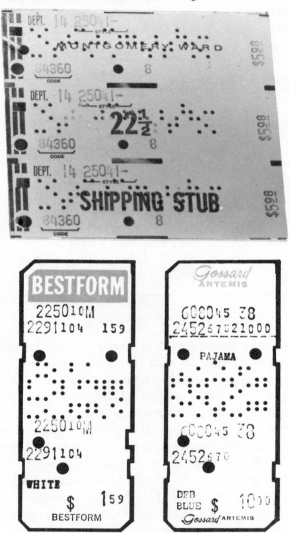

scribed in chapters to follow produce a punched paper tape as a by-product of their operation. The tape produced may then be used as input into a computer system.

PUNCHED CARDS.   The coding of the punched card (Figure 8–4) is also a perforated code. This is one of the most widely used form of input for computer systems and it may be coded at the time of data origination by many types of mechanical devices which produce it as a by-product at the time the data is captured. However, most punched cards are prepared by keyed-punching in a transcription recording procedure by a card punch operator who reads the data from a previously originated document.

MARK SENSING.   The mark-sensing technique was developed to provide a method of originating data that is easy to learn and simple to perform in which the end result is a perforated code. At the same time that the data are recorded, they are incorporated on a document that is machine processable, and once transcribed by machine into punched holes, there is no further necessity for retranscription, as the data are ready to be processed in a computer system.

Mark sensing (Figure 3–5) is a manual technique which is extremely portable. All that is required in recording data is a special type of

FIGURE 3–5. Mark-Sensed Card and Punching

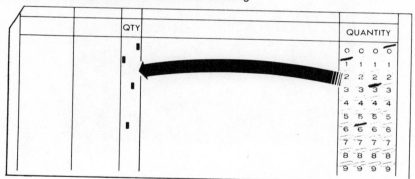

lead pencil and a stack of especially designed cards. The person recording the data merely places a pencil mark on the card in a preprinted designation. These preprinted designations are in the form of small horizontal or diagonal oblong ovals printed on the card in every position acceptable to marked data.

Care is required, of course, in marking the card, as an improperly placed mark, a short mark, or an extended mark may be interpreted by the machine equipment as a value other than that intended.

The marked cards are then assembled and passed through a piece of equipment known as a mark-sensing reproducer. Each pencil mark position on the card is read by three electrical contacts or "brushes." Through a series of timed electrical impulses in combination with an electrical impulse flowing down the outer brushes through the mark and out the middle brush, a hole is punched in a predeterminable position on either the marked or another card. The hole position represents the same numerical value that was indicated by the original pencil mark.

It should be noted that the marking space to indicate a single number requires three times that normally used to record the same data in punched hole form. This limits the capacity of the card to 27 mark-sense columns instead of the 80 columns normally provided.

PORT-A-PUNCH. The Port-A-Punch (Figure 3–6) is an effective and economical answer to a great many "on-the-spot" data originating operations, such as physical inventories, job and sales tickets, and statistical surveys. It is a manual means of punching cards generally

FIGURE 3–6. Port-A-Punch

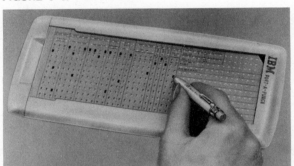

Courtesy of IBM

used at the scene of the transaction being documented to eliminate the preliminary writing or typing of a source document and to prepare a machine-processable document.

The card used with the Port-A-Punch is a standard-sized card but only contains 40 columns of prescored 12-row positions which may be pressed out with a stylus to leave a "punched" hole in the card. Only 40 columns are provided due to weakening the structural strength of the card. To be processed with normal 80-column standard cards, the 40-column cards must be reprocessed on punched card machines to make the columnar data compatible for a given unit of information.

DUAL CARDS. Another type of punched card is known as a dual card (Figure 3–7). This type of card is manually originated by writing data in blank spaces or marking labeled boxes provided on a standard punched card. This card is later inserted in card punching equipment

FIGURE 3–7. Dual Card

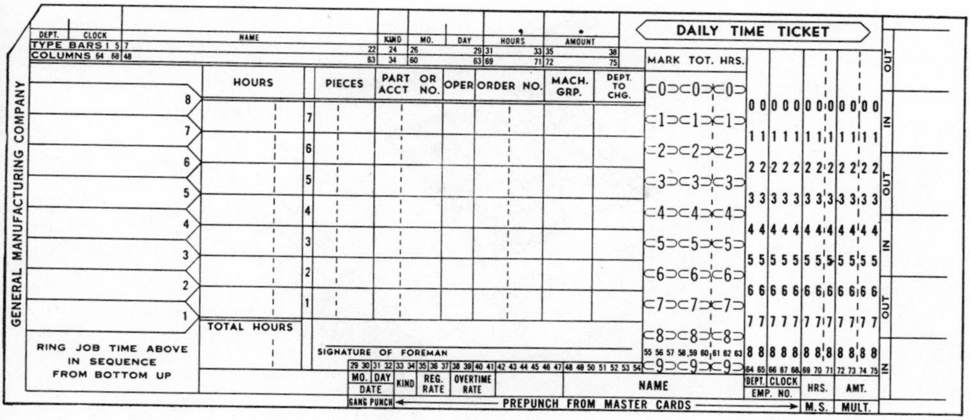

(Chapter 8) and the data is read by an operator who keypunches it into the card to produce a form that may be input into a computer system. The "dual" capability is in originating the data manually and recording it in a machine-processable form on the same document.

OPTICAL SCANNING PUNCH. IBM, Remington Rand Corporation, and others have developed punches which read normal pencil marks and translate them into punched holes. No special symbols need to be used. The numeral to be duplicated may be entered on the card, or it may be preprinted and be circled or have an "X" marked through it. The value of any mark is determined by its position on the card, rather than by the mark itself. An example of a punched card designed for this purpose is shown in Figure 3–8.

FIGURE 3–8. Optically Scannable Card

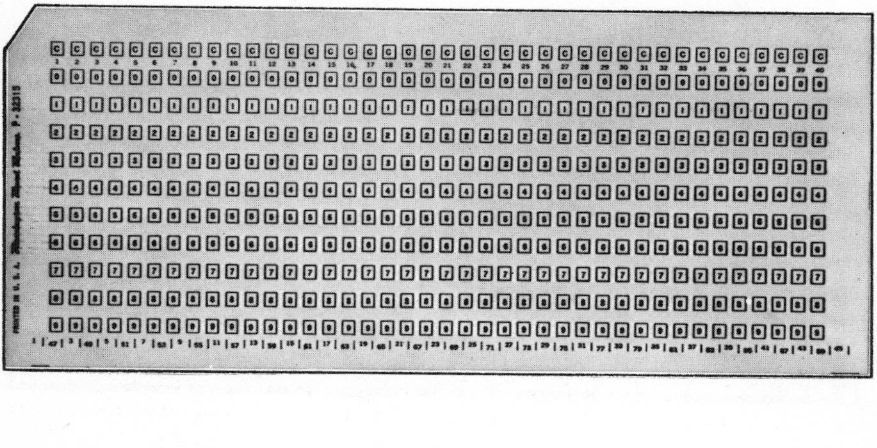

FIGURE 3–9. Source Record Punch Model 1740

Courtesy of The Standard Register Co.

Optical character reading from source documents which have been previously marked, printed, written or punched is also utilized as direct input into computer systems (Chapter 9).

SOURCE RECORD PUNCH. The source record punch is a desk-top electric data collecting machine (Figure 3–9) that originates information in both human-readable language (printed) and machine-readable code (keypunched) on the same document at the same time and place in one writing. The document employed is called a ZIPCARD set (Figure 3–10), which is a carbon-interleaved set of papers which includes a standard punched card (Chapter 8). The design of this set and the

FIGURE 3–10. ZIPCARD Set

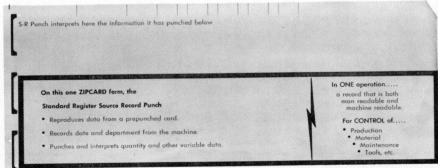

S-R Punch interprets here the information it has punched below

On this one ZIPCARD form, the

Standard Register Source Record Punch

• Reproduces data from a prepunched card.

• Records date and department from the machine.

• Punches and interprets quantity and other variable data.

In ONE operation.....
a record that is both
man readable and
machine readable.

For CONTROL of.....
• Production
• Material
• Maintenance
• Tools, etc.

Courtesy of Standard Register Co.

fixed information to be printed on the pages must be determined well in advance as an essential element of this system. By so doing, the recorded information is immediately ready for human use as well as for computer processing.

The source record punch is designed to merge three different types of information: (1) constant information which is either prepunched from a master card or imprinted from an embossed plate onto a ZIP-CARD set; (2) semivariable information, such as the date or department number, which is recorded by setting a mechanism in the machine which punches and prints this data on the same ZIPCARD set; and (3) variable information, such as identification codes, charges, quantities, and so forth, which is recorded through the use of a keyboard on the front of the machine by simultaneously punching the data into and printing it on the ZIPCARD set.

Cash Registers

One means of attempting to insure greater accuracy in originating data is to make certain that every transaction is recorded as quickly as possible. The cash register (Figure 3–11), if properly used, is a

FIGURE 3–11. Cash Register with Locked-In Audit Tape

Courtsey of NCR

device for recording cash and credit transactions easily, quickly, and accurately. It is designed to be of greatest assistance in a retail situation when large volumes of transactions need to be recorded and controlled.

The cash register is a device of such fundamental character that it is used by almost every retail business, regardless of size or type. It serves to speed up the data processing operations; it affords the owners or managers substantial control over cash, accounting data, and personnel; and it aids materially in recording transactions and in accumulating and storing management information.

These machines are built in a wide variety of sizes and capabilities. They are widely employed because of the various controls they provide over the receipt of cash. These controls are not only important in the protection of cash but are also essential in assuring accuracy in and control over the input of data into the data processing system.

Many of these controls can best be illustrated in a procedure which should be followed by employees who are handling the receipt of cash. In the first place, the procedure should require that cash receipts be recorded on the cash register immediately after the sale is made. As soon as the transaction is "rung up," the amount recorded is imprinted on the audit tape locked in the machine to provide a printed record of the transaction. This audit tape is visible in some makes of equipment, while in others it is not. At the end of the day, the register totals are available to be printed on the audit tape. Once these totals are added to the tape, it will then be removed from the machine by someone other than the person handling the cash. The total of cash received according to the tape must agree with the cash amount present in the drawer after taking into consideration the "change" money placed in the drawer at the beginning of the day.

On this same audit tape, the clerk who made the sale, the department in which the sale was made, and the item of merchandise sold may be identified by code number. This coded information can be of tremendous assistance not only in the control of cash but also in the control and handling of merchandise. This control can be accomplished by making an analysis of the sales in accordance with the coded information recorded on the tape. This permits management to determine the volume of sales each day and the items or types of inventory which are selling most rapidly, as well as the amount of inventory still on hand.

Certain models of cash registers print receipts (Figure 3–12) for the customer. This involves the customer as an auditor of the transaction as it is completed. The amount for each item sold is clearly indicated on the receipt along with the total due and perhaps the amount of change to be returned to the customer. This same information is visually

FIGURE 3–12. Cash Register Printed Receipt

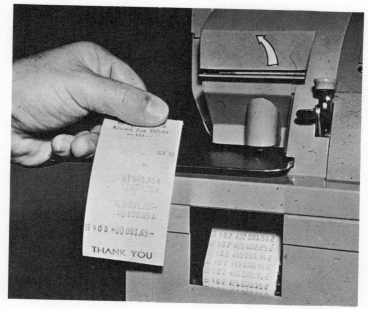

Courtesy of NCR

recorded for both the clerk and the customer to see in a window at the top of the machine as the items of sales are recorded. In this way, another audit of the recorded data is accomplished.

Individual cash drawers can be provided for each clerk using the machine. Each time a sale is made, it must be charged to a particular cash drawer. This information is recorded on the audit tape by drawer or clerk number, and each individual drawer can be checked against the balance of cash which should be in the drawer at the end of the day.

Certain models of cash registers contain multiple counters which enable them to sum up individually the amounts recorded each day on different keys of the machine (Figure 3–13). Note keys marked "meat," "produce," "dairy," and so forth. These amounts may represent total sales, total number of transactions, sales by department, sales by salesperson, or, possibly, sales by merchandise class. The counters enable statistical analysis to be accomplished much more quickly, as well as permitting financial responsibility to be pinpointed more accurately.

A model of cash register can also be procured which can perform

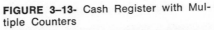

FIGURE 3–13- Cash Register with Multiple Counters

Courtesy of NCR

some of the functions of a bookkeeping machine. It can print on an itemized credit sales check, and it can also be used to post to an accounts receivable ledger. The sales check provides control over all charge sales, deposit sales, c.o.d. sales, employee sales, exchange sales, and deliveries. The customer's name and address would have to be imprinted on the sales check by the salesperson.

In the NCR sales register, a visible journal tape (Figure 9–16) is produced which provides a historical record of every sale in the order of its incurrence. Daily register totals are also printed on the journal tape. This tape is optically scannable, by specialized equipment (to be discussed later), as input to a computer, where the data will be processed and totals determined. These totals must check with the totals previously determined by the different registers of the sales register. Once again, another form of control is provided over input being fed into a data processing system.

A compact magnetic tape recorder may be attached to some cash registers to capture data entered into the register in machine language on reusable $\frac{5}{32}$ inch magnetic tape cassettes. Once captured on the cassettes, the data may be mailed or transmitted over telephone lines to a computer processing center. Larger-capacity models of the recorder attached equipment also include a 10-key numeric keyboard for manually keying in additional desired data into the tape.

An even more sophisticated data capturing system is the NCR 280 Retail System. A modern electronic recording cash register (Figure 3–14) is used to record the originating data at the time and point of

FIGURE 3–14. NCR 280 Retail System

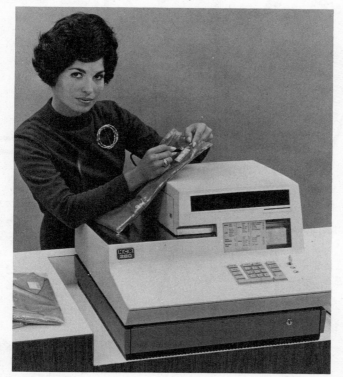

Courtesy of NCR

sale.[1] Data may be input by reading a precoded tag (Figure 3–15) attached to the merchandise, whose data is in the form of color-coded stripes of varying width. This reading is performed by a hand-held optical wand formed by a bundle of flexible optic fibers. Similar color-coded data may be scanned from the customer's credit card and any additional required data may be keyed in from a keyboard on the equipment.

As the information is captured it is automatically fed into a data collector and recorder or magnetic printer where the data are recorded in magnetic tape form which can then serve as input into a computer system.

---

[1] This type of equipment is often called POS or point of sale equipment.

FIGURE 3–15. NCR 280 Sales Tags

Data Recorders

Source data are written by a Data Recorder (Figure 3–16) on an 80-column-sized tab card form (Figure 3–17). Plastic cards stored in the Data Recorder can record fixed data on the tab card forms, while the key levers on the front of the machine control the recording of variable data. This data may be visually checked in registers on the front of the machine before the data are imprinted in bar code on the tab card forms. The card forms created in this way serve as machine-readable documents for data conversion to computer input languages. The conversion of bar-code data format to computer input language is done by means of the Optical Code Reader (Figure 3–18). The numeric values in bar code are electronically converted into an eight-channel

FIGURE 3–16. Data Recorder

Courtesy of Addressograph Multigraph Corp.

code which is punched into paper tape. The paper tape can then be used as input to a conventional computer system.

The hard-copy tab card forms provide an audit trail or track if it is ever necessary to trace the data back to the transaction after it has been recorded. The advantage of this particular system is that the cost of the Optical Code Reader is far less than other scanners currently on the market which read printed data and prepare data input in computer-acceptable form.

FIGURE 3–17. 80–Column Tab Card

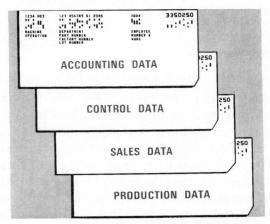

Courtesy of Addressograph Multigraph Corp.

FIGURE 3–18. Optical Code Reader

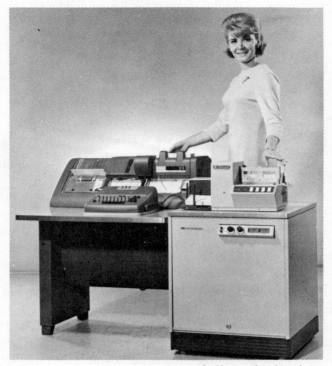

Courtesy of Addressograph Multigraph Corp

There are numerous possible areas of application of this type of system in hospitals, job time card procedures, the issuance of tools or materials, and many others.

Data Collection Systems

Data collection and gathering systems (Chapter 10) are also utilized in the origination of data. In these systems the data are captured by the input of various types of cards, badges, and tapes on which fixed data have been prerecorded in a machine-acceptable language. Variable data related to the recording of a specific transaction are recorded by dials, knobs, or other types of manual settings. In these systems the use of prerecorded and visually observed manual input data, along with available specific internal control checks (to be discussed later), provides a great deal of assurance that the data are accurate.

RECORDING

With the development of some of our modern recording devices, there are instances where it may be hard to delineate between the basic functions of originating and recording. As an example, the Port-A-Punch performs both functions by serving as an originating device in capturing the data at the time the transaction occurs and in recording the data in a machine-processable form.

The act of recording a transaction, however, has reference to the capturing of the pertinent data surrounding an economic event in reasonably permanent form. This is normally performed after data have been initially captured (originated) when the transaction occurred and recording is usually the second step followed in processing the data so captured. The simplest manual method of recording a transaction is provided by the journalizing of the transaction data. There are many techniques and types of equipment available to perform this function.

Time Clock

The time clock is a very useful piece of equipment in any transaction process involving timing procedures. Different models are available with varying capabilities which permit them to be widely used in manufacturing, wholesaling, and office-type situations.

Typical examples include their use in keeping track of the elapsed time an employee has spent on the job. One type of such machine will record on a card the "in" time, the "out" time, and the "elapsed" time of a job. You will note from the illustration (Figure 3–19) that the daily printed time card produced by this machine is also capable of being used as input media for a computer installation.

Another form of machine produces a time card which is suitable for a job cost situation. In such a situation, the accounting department needs to know the time spent on each job by each employee. The card which is produced (Figure 3–20) is capable of recording the time at which an employee begins work on each job during the day, as well as the time he or she leaves.

Time clock equipment is also available which is on-line to a computer system. As the "time" is activated from a card or identification badge by its insertion into the device, the data are input directly into computer storage. One advantage of this method of collecting time data is that it eliminates "human" transcription of the data. Also, it may be very important—especially in a production situation—to know who is not

FIGURE 3–19. Daily Printed Time Card

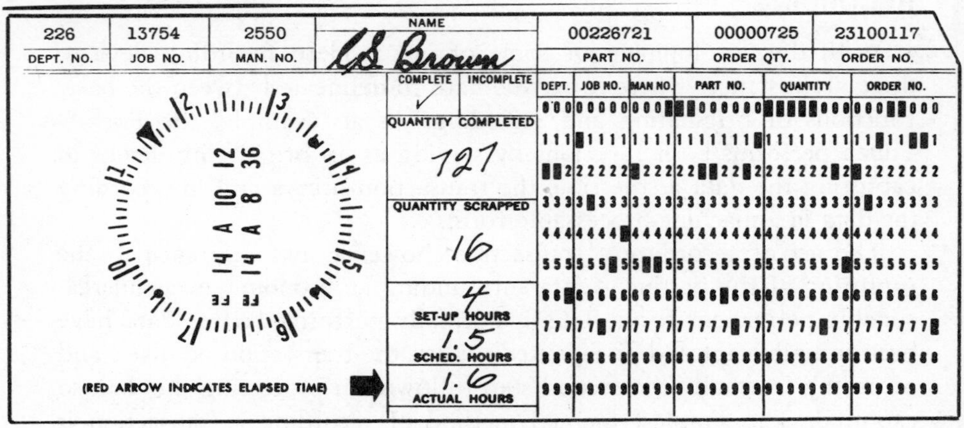

226	13754	2550	*C.S. Brown*	NAME	00226721	00000725	23100117
DEPT. NO.	JOB NO.	MAN. NO.			PART NO.	ORDER QTY.	ORDER NO.

COMPLETE   INCOMPLETE

QUANTITY COMPLETED
727

QUANTITY SCRAPPED
16

SET-UP HOURS
4

SCHED. HOURS
1.5

ACTUAL HOURS
1.6

(RED ARROW INDICATES ELAPSED TIME)

DEPT. | JOB NO. | MAN NO. | PART NO. | QUANTITY | ORDER NO.

on the job as well as who is there. If key personnel are missing, the production schedule may have to be modified or changed before production may start.

Special Adding Machines

Several adding machine manufacturers have devised equipment which may be used to prepare input media for computers as a by-product of their normal operation. Some of these machines produce both the conventional adding machine tape and a coded punched-paper tape or punched cards as output. The regular tape may be visually scanned to verify the accuracy of the recorded data before the punched tape or card is used as computer input.

Another type of adding machine prints a stylized type font on the tape output and the tape itself can be input to a computer through an optical scanning device.

Any of these machines above could be used by smaller business firms to record transactions or summarize results which could be processed— after conversion to computer acceptable input—by a computer service bureau to produce the accounting records needed by the firm.

This type of special recording aid and other equipment associated with integrated data systems involving the use of common-language equipment and the transmission of data from one geographical location to another are more fully discussed in Chapter 10 under Communication Techniques and Devices.

FIGURE 3–20. Job Cost Card

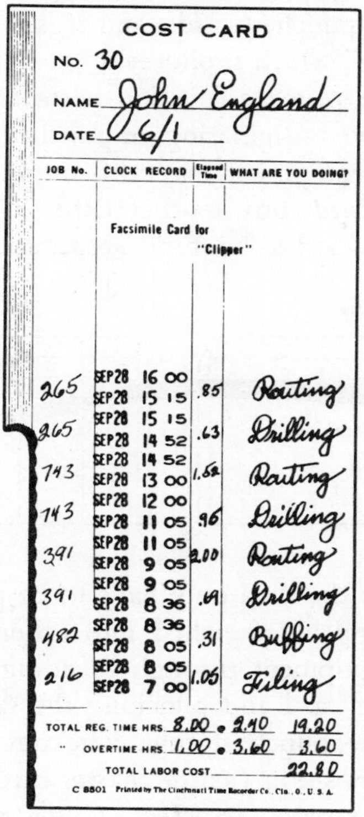

COST CARD

No. 30

NAME John England

DATE 6/1

JOB No.	CLOCK RECORD	Elapsed Time	WHAT ARE YOU DOING?
	Facsimile Card for "Clipper"		
265	SEP28 16 00 SEP28 15 15	.85	Routing
265	SEP28 15 15 SEP28 14 52	.63	Drilling
743	SEP28 14 52 SEP28 13 00	1.52	Routing
743	SEP28 12 00 SEP28 11 05	.96	Drilling
391	SEP28 11 05 SEP28 9 05	2.00	Routing
391	SEP28 9 05 SEP28 8 36	.49	Drilling
482	SEP28 8 36 SEP28 8 05	.31	Buffing
216	SEP28 8 05 SEP28 7 00	1.05	Filing

TOTAL REG. TIME HRS 8.00 @ 2.40 19.20

" OVERTIME HRS 1.00 @ 3.60 3.60

TOTAL LABOR COST 22.80

C 8501 Printed by The Cincinnati Time Recorder Co., Cin., O., U.S.A.

Data Transcription

Closely associated with the recording process is the transcription of data. Of course, in a manual system transcription involves the hand-copying of data from one business form to another. In punched card and electronic systems utilizing cards for input, transcription may be performed manually or it may be produced by a machine process.

New cards may often be required to replace those which have become worn or "frayed" as they are used over and over in processing procedures. In other instances new or additional data need to be added to existing cards. In yet other instances the same or partial data is used in a different application, but the pattern in which it is recorded in the card needs to be reorganized.

Transcript Cards. A card punch operator, who visually takes information from an originating document and manually keys the data into punched card form (to be described later in Chapter 8), produces a type of card known as a *transcript card.* Once a transcript card is completed it has no distinguishing features or characteristics to identify it as such from other punched cards, and it is known only by the technique of "transcribing" which produces it.

Duplicating. The primary function performed by card punches is that of recording or even originating, in punched hole form, the needed data. However, this equipment may also duplicate all or part of the information in one card into another card. This permits data, such as a date, in a master card to be duplicated into all the cards to follow

FIGURE 3–21. Duplicating

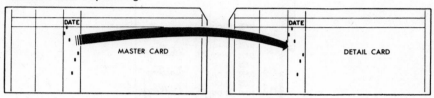

(Figure 3–21). Thus the data only have to be punched once and they are accurately and quickly punched into other cards. Duplicating is performed by the equipment through "reading," at the read station, what is in the master card and punching the same data into the card being punched in the punch station. The newly punched card then moves into the read position (as the master card is fed into the stacker position) where it becomes, in effect, a new master card to provide the data to be placed in the new card now in the punch position. This read-punch combination operation is performed one column at a time as the two cards move to the left, under their respective positions, from *column to column.*

The function of duplicating reduces the work to be performed on each card and, while assuring accuracy in the transferal of data, increases the productivity of the equipment operator.

Reproducing. This card punching function, like that of duplicating, causes data to be transferred from one card to another. However, where duplicating on the card punch transfers data from one card to another, which passes the data to the third and so on, is performed one punch at a time, reproducing is performed in various reproducing machines by transferring data from one deck (group) of cards to another, *card by card* (Figure 3–22). This transferal can be the complete copying of one card into another, or only selected data may be transferred. Also, if desired, the data in one card may be moved, as to its columnar placement, as it is transferred, through the use of wired control panels which serve to tell the machine what is desired.

FIGURE 3–22. Reproducing

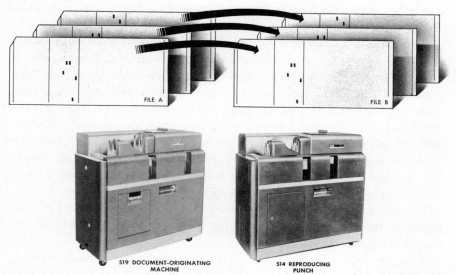

519 DOCUMENT-ORIGINATING
MACHINE

514 REPRODUCING
PUNCH

Courtesy of IBM

Gang Punching. Another function, somewhat similar to that of duplicating and reproducing, is that of gang punching. This is performed on basically the same equipment as used in reproducing and is like both duplicating and reproducing in that data are punched from one card to another. However, gang punching is punching all or part of the data in a master card into a group of succeeding cards (Figure 3–23). It is similar to duplicating in that a master card is used for all cards to be gang punched. It is also similar to reproducing in that

FIGURE 3–23. Gang Punching

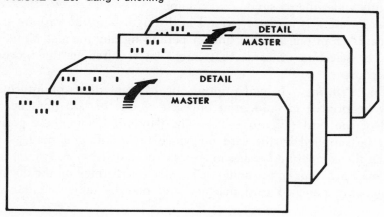

all or part of the data from a single card can be punched into other cards, but gang punching is the production of *one or many cards from a single card* rather than a one-for-one reproduction.

There are two basic types of gang punching. *Single master-card gang punching* uses one master card placed in front of a deck of blank or partially punched cards to produce all the other cards desired. Where groups of data decks are desired from a number of master cards containing different data, the function performed is called *interspersed gang punching*. In this form of gang punching, the master cards are interspersed into a deck of blank or partially punched data cards. As a master card is read, its data will be placed in all the cards which follow until another master card is read. This new master data is then placed in the cards following this second master card.

Gang punching may be performed separately or in combination with reproduction and summary punching (Chapter 8) for both alphabetical and numerical information.

Interpreting. Another form of data transcription is the interpretation of the data in the card and printing it on the same card for visual reference (Figure 3–24). Depending on the model of interpreter used, the data in the card may be printed on either of two lines near the top of the card or on various lines throughout the body of the card.

Printing data contained in the card on the card may also, as discussed later, be performed by the printing card punch as a by-product of the punching operation. Unlike the printing performed on the card punch, which may be 80-columns long with each character printed just above the related punched character, the 60 columns of printed characters on the interpreted card have no relationship whatsoever with the data punched directly underneath those printed characters. In fact, a careful study of the interpreter's printing will show each character to be slightly wider than a single-card column.

Interpreting is necessary to aid in distinguishing the various groups of cards from one another and in permitting any manual filing, sorting, or selection of cards that might be required in the processing procedure

End Printing. In end printing, up to eight digits of information may be printed in bold print on each of one or two lines near the end of the card (Figure 3–25). The data printed in these positions may be supplied by the card on which the printing is made, a card under the comparing brushes in the read unit, or from an emitter inside the machine. This end-printing operation is performed on the document originating punched card machine and may be done simultaneously

FIGURE 3–24. Interpreting

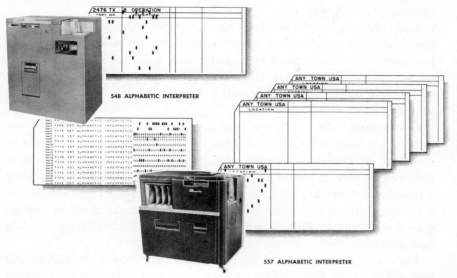

548 ALPHABETIC INTERPRETER

557 ALPHABETIC INTERPRETER

Courtesy of IBM

FIGURE 3–25. End Printing

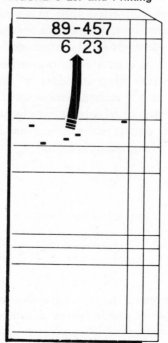

with gang punching, summary punching, reproducing, and mark-sensed punching procedures.

End printing is particularly useful in procedures in which prepunched cards are stored in racks or bins for convenient reference and selection. Personnel attendance cards, stored for insertion in a time clock, and inventory cards, stored for selection (picking) at the time of the sale of the items represented, are typical examples of the use of end printing.

Conversion. As mentioned earlier, punched paper tape may be produced as a by-product of the operation of a cash register, adding machine, or typewriter. This type of data capture, whether described as data origination or recording, serves a valuable function of producing a machine-processable medium at a very early stage of the processing procedure. In such a form it need never be retranscribed by people and this serves to eliminate the possibility of human error in data manipulation.

However, the medium in which the data is captured by this means may not be in the proper form to serve as input into the data processing system in use. When this is the case, it must be converted into the proper coded form. Examples of this are: data captured in punched paper-tape form would not serve as input into a punched card system and would have to be converted into punched card form; data in punched paper-tape form may or may not serve as input into a given computer system as it depends on the input devices available and this may require the data to be converted into punched cards or transferred onto magnetic tape or disk files; and data in punched card form may have to be converted into punched paper-tape form before it can be transmitted over telephone or telegraph lines by some types of transmission devices. Thus data conversion can be from any given type of medium to another form of recording medium.

REFERENCES

1. "Print-punch Tickets Keep Clothing Retailer Fashionable." *Infosystems,* March 1973, p. 66.

QUESTIONS

1. A businessman was heard to say that anyone could use the preprinted business forms which can be bought in a stationery store in a data processing system. Do you agree?

2. What are some of the means used to insure the accuracy of data captured in the business form?

3. Why don't all businesses capture the initial data for a transaction on business forms, rather than worrying over the possibility of which of the many different methods available ought to be used?

4. Explain in your own words how magnetic ink character recognition (MICR) works.

5. Give an example of where you have seen MICR in use. Explain.

6. Can you see any basic difference between the concepts behind printed codes and those behind perforated plastic cards? Explain. Why is it that we have them both?

7. Give three examples of where precoded data are widely used? Describe and explain.

8. Give three examples of control which are either built into the cash register or which are recommended in its use.

9. Can the cash register be used as more than a data origination or recording device? Explain.

10. Can you imagine the necessity of using more than one way to originate data in any one particular business? Explain.

11. What are the advantages of the NCR 280 Retail System over conventional cash registers?

12. How does the Data Recorder serve in the origination of data?

13. Can time clocks be used for other purposes besides the "clocking in" procedure for payroll purposes? Explain.

14. Using your imagination a little, list some pros and cons of a company purchasing a time clock, which would be kept at the main entrance, and allowing the employees to keep their own time.

15. Why may data have to be transcribed?

16. What is the process of conversion?

4

Basic Data Processing Functions—Classifying, Sorting, Summarizing, Calculating, Communicating

As THE FUNCTIONS of classifying, sorting, summarizing, calculating, and communicating are investigated, it should be recognized that some of the equipment described under originating and recording could be used for these functions as well. Also, as many of the items discussed in this chapter are multifunctional in nature, their discussion is usually based on their more common usage. Consequently, they may be utilized for one or more other functions in specific types of applications and procedures.

CLASSIFYING

Once business data have been originated or captured on a business document, the first step in processing them is to classify them as to what they represent. Classification has been defined as a process of identifying each item of a group or list and systematically arranging similar items together. They may be classified according to their common characteristics or even at times according to their fundamental differences. Classification is required in most data processing applications, however, it is always necessary to strike a balance between the amount of detailed classification that is desirable and the cost of providing such information.

Classification of business data can in part be accomplished when the data are initially recorded on a business form. Take, for example, the sales ticket which is written out when a sale is made in a department store on credit. The clerk, normally, will have been instructed to identify clearly certain items of data which management considers to be important, such as the name and address of the customer, a complete description of each item sold, the quantity of each item sold, the unit selling price, the total selling price, any state and/or federal taxes applicable, and the total amount of the sale to the customer. If this sales ticket form has been carefully prepared, much of the data classifying function has already been accomplished.

For another example, take the student who is working one of his or her first accounting problems. The problems gives some transactions, and the student is asked to journalize them. When the student decides what must be debited and what must be credited, he or she is, in effect, classifying the data.

The manner in which data must be classified will be largely determined by the way in which management intends to use the data and by the form in which the data will be presented in the business reports which management requires from the accounting system. The format of the reports can vary tremendously, depending upon the patterns of classification used in gathering and arranging the data. For example, cost data will be classified quite differently if the object of the system is that of planning and controlling cost rather than that of determining unit costs for inventory valuation purposes. In the planning and control of costs, the cost items will likely be classified, as nearly as possible, according to areas of individual responsibility. On the other hand, if the determination of unit cost is of paramount concern, the costs will probably be classified by functional groupings and then allocated to the products produced by the firm on the most equitable basis possible.

The coding activity, discussed in Chapter 2, is also an intrinsic part of the classification function. When one codes a series of accounts he or she is, in effect, making it possible to classify the same basic data in several different ways—for example, according to the plant, to the department, or to the departmental subfunction.

In data processing there is always the concern that an employee may not properly record, accurately classify or code the data, when they are first originated on a business form or when they are transcribed into some other more usable form for further processing. As a result of this problem, the technique of precoding certain types of business transactions has been devised. Much data are common to transactions of a certain type, therefore, it is often possible to identify certain transaction data before the events actually occur. In this way, the data is classified and verified before being put into process. Perforated garment tickets and credit cards are examples of ways whereby this is done.

Perforated garment tickets (Figure 3–4) are often used in clothing stores. All pertinent data identifying the items are prepunched into tickets and verified by the manufacturer of the garment. The tickets, in turn, are attached to each related item of clothing. When the garments are sold, one part of the ticket is retained by the salesclerk. When these tickets are accumulated and processed, a complete description of the items sold can be printed out, giving management up-to-date classified information on the items sold.

Data are classified in the keyed punching of cards or as data are keyed onto magnetic tape or disk (Chapter 8). Each field or group (class) of data must be carefully determined before the punching procedure can be performed. The assignment of specific codes to represent the pertinent information to be entered in some of these fields may also represent an additional technique related to this classification.

SORTING

Sorting can be defined as the process of arranging data into some desired order according to rules dependent upon a key or field contained by each item. It may be performed manually, mechanically, electromechanically, or electronically. The complexity of the sorting task will be determined both by the number of fields by which the items being sorted are identified and by the physical volume of items to be sorted. This complexity and the volume of items determine the sorting technique and equipment to be utilized.

Manual Sorting

Earlier it was established that the act of determining what was to be debited and credited in a transaction was an act of classifying data. Since this is true, the act of posting these data to appropriate ledger accounts represents an illustration of the sorting process. It is as though the ledger accounts were boxes like those in a post office, with each box representing an address, and the person doing the posting was in the process of sorting mail for each address.

This same process may be carried out by using multicolumn journals (Figure 4–1). The fact that a journal has numerous columns enables

FIGURE 4–1. Multicolumn Journal Forms

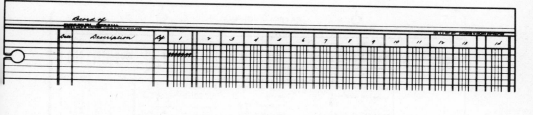

one to classify data and also sort it on a simultaneous basis. Of course, the posting operation still remains, but in this case the sorting has largely been accomplished, and postings are through totals rather than individual items.

Mechanical Sorting

The method used by the more simple bookkeeping machines in keeping business records is quite similar to that used in manual systems. However, the forms, journals, ledgers, and so forth (Figure 4–2) used are designed so that the given columns on each of them will match if they are laid on top of one another. Through the use of carbon paper, the recording of data can be completed simultaneously on these various forms through the combined use of the equivalent of both a typewriter and an adding machine. In this way, the classifying, recording, sorting, and even summarizing functions can be accomplished at the same time.

FIGURE 4–2. Bookkeeping Machine Forms

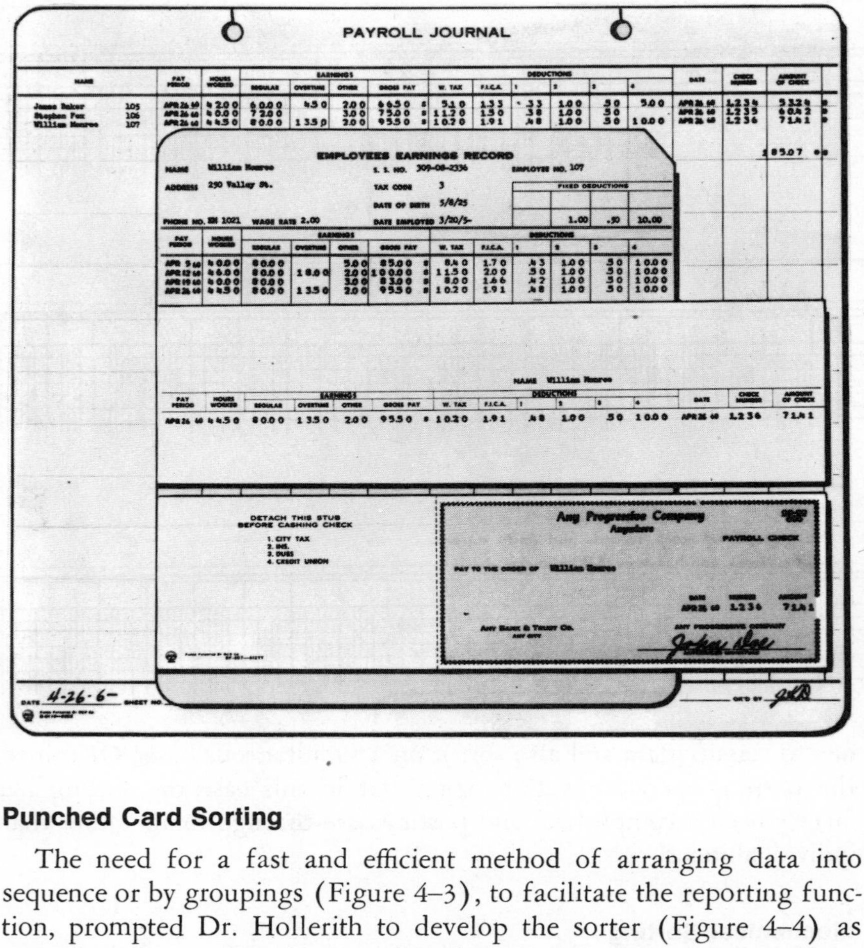

Punched Card Sorting

The need for a fast and efficient method of arranging data into sequence or by groupings (Figure 4–3), to facilitate the reporting function, prompted Dr. Hollerith to develop the sorter (Figure 4–4) as one of his first pieces of punched card equipment. The sorter was later followed by the development of the collator (Figure 4–5) which is a somewhat more sophisticated device and extends the sorter's capability in sequencing or selecting data by the matching and/or merging of two sets or decks of cards. These techniques will be discussed in more detail in Chapter 8.

Electronic Sorting

The function of sorting, as it is performed in electronic computers, involves the movement of coded electronic impulses within the equip-

FIGURE 4–3. Sorting

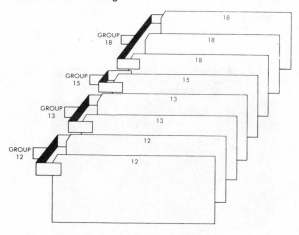

FIGURE 4–4. Sorters

82, 83, & 84 SORTERS

Courtesy of IBM

ment. Depending on the number of digits or letters contained in the data to be sorted and the type of equipment used, thousands of a given type of data may be sorted in a few seconds. You will become acquainted with this technique in your study of a programming language.

FIGURE 4–5. Collators

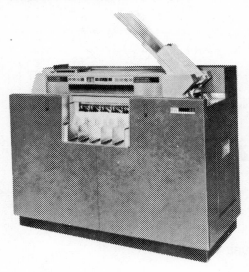

88 & 188 COLLATORS
Courtesy of IBM

In summary, sorting is an important part of the data processing activity. It is continuously being accomplished irrespective of the complexity of the data processing system being used. Normally, the sorting function is accomplished in conjunction with other basic functions, even though quite often it may not be specifically identified as being performed.

SUMMARIZING

The need for the summarization of data becomes more obvious when one realizes that the data discussed in this chapter have now been assembled, classified, and sorted as to classification. At periodic intervals, management needs to know where the business stands. In order to inform management on this point, the data which have been assembled by classification must be summarized.

If the accounting records are being maintained manually, the classified data have probably been posted to ledger accounts. If this is the case, it then becomes necessary to add up the sum of the debits and the credits and to find the balance in the account. Either an adding machine or one of the electronic calculators can be used to good advantage to facilitate this activity.

Punched Card Equipment

The function of summarizing may be performed by several types of punched card equipment. The accounting machine and calculating punches (to be discussed under the functions of communicating and calculating) both have internal counters or registers in which data may be accumulated and summarized.

Summary punching, however, is a technique of automatically converting data, read into or developed by one of the various accounting machines, into coded punched holes in a card. The actual summary punching is performed by a piece of equipment which is cable connected to an accounting machine. As the data is accumulated in the counters of the accounting machine and a point is reached where a total is desired, an impulse is sent to the summary punch where the data is punched into a card. Several types of summary punches, or equipment which perform this function, are available for use with the various types of accounting machines (Figure 4–6).

FIGURE 4–6. Summary Punching

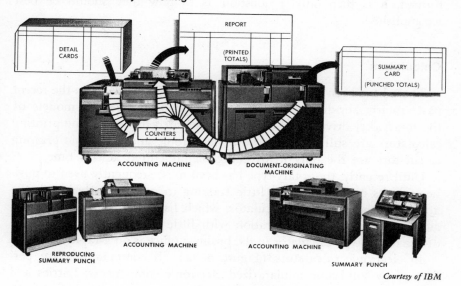

Courtesy of IBM

A major use of summary punching equipment is to provide summarized totals of large volumes of data to reduce the volume of card handling and the ensuing storage requirements where large masses of data must be held available for use. One example would be the use of a single card to represent the total sales for the day, week, or month which could serve as general ledger account data. Another use of summary cards would be to provide balance forward data such as the year-to-date information needed in a payroll procedure to determine if the payee is subject to a FICA tax deduction or if deductions have previously been made on the maximum requirement.

CALCULATING

The importance of the calculating function in data processing cannot be overemphasized. In a simple sales situation, it may be necessary to multiply the number of units sold by the unit price in order to find the total amount of the sale. This item may be added to other items sold in order to ascertain the total amount of the sale chargeable to a certain customer. The total amount may then be multiplied by a percentage which represents either the state or local sales tax.

All other data processing applications are just as full of possible calculating applications. Therefore, since calculations must be performed, it is then only a question as to how they should be best accomplished.

Calculators

There have been four basic types of calculators available in the recent past: rotary, key-driven, electronic, and printing. Though models of the rotary, key-driven, and electrically operated models of the printing calculators are still used, the newer electronic and electronic printing calculators are the only items being manufactured at this time.

Until recently, the rotary-type has been most frequently used in business offices because it takes little training to operate it, but with the advent of the electronic calculator, which has greatly increased speed and provided noiseless operation with little increase in cost, the use of the rotary-type calculator in the business office is on a rapid decline.

In electronic calculators (Figure 4–7a) all computations are performed by solid-state miniaturized electronic components. Entries and answers appear on a screen somewhat like pictures on a television set. Operating speed of this equipment is measured in a few milliseconds. In addition to the ability to add, subtract, multiply, and divide, many

FIGURE 4–7. Electronic Calculators

(*a*) Calculator

Courtesy of Victor Comptometer Corp.

(*b*) Programmable Calculator

Courtesy of Burrough Corp.

(*c*) Printing Calculator

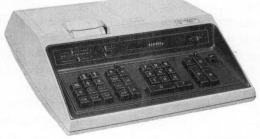

Courtesy of Monroe

of these units can also raise numbers to powers; calculate square root; provide automatic decimal points, rounding and constants; and do many other functions not previously available on this type of equipment. Also, most provide one to ten independent memories for data storage and some are even programmable (Figure 4–7b) to accept precoded logic cards to direct the performance of the given logic steps required in some specific calculating application.

The printing electronic calculator (Figure 4–7c) can perform all the arithmetic functions available on other calculators. However, instead of displaying the intermediate and resulting answers, these are printed on a tape similar to that found on adding machines. This tape is particularly valuable where a proof or permanent record of the procedure and its results are desired.

Punched Card Equipment

The computation of a result, through the use of one or more of the arithmetic techniques of multiplication, division, addition, or subtraction can be performed by a number of different punched card machines.

Counting. The accounting machines, calculators, electronic statistical machines, and sorters equipped with special devices are particularly adapted to keeping a count of the number of cards, or particular items punched in them, as they are fed through the equipment.

Accumulating. This function is that of gathering data, usually through addition and subtraction, pertaining to a common classification to provide a total of that class of data. This function is performed by a number of punched card machines of which the accounting machines, summary punches, accumulating reproducers, and calculators are typical.

Calculation. The techniques of multiplication and division are usually performed in calculators and calculating punches (as they are in adding machines, calculators, and even most electronic computers) through a process of multiple addition and reverse addition (subtraction) steps. Thus multiplication of 5 times 20 would involve the addition of the number 20 for 5 times to provide the answer 100. The division of the number 100 by 5 would involve the number of times the number 5 could be subtracted from 100 and would provide the answer, 20. The factors used in the calculations may be read from one or a series of cards, be emitted by a device within the machine, or may be developed as a result of a series of other calculations. The results obtained may be punched into the data cards fed into the equipment or into a blank trailer card which follows the data cards.

Of course, calculating can be a major function to be performed in any given computer processing procedure. In computers this function is performed at electronic speeds involving only microseconds or nanoseconds (millionths or billionths of a second), as the recorded magnetic characters are manipulated electronically. The techniques involved in electronic computer calculating will be discussed in detail later.

Computers

There are still many installations utilizing punched card equipment as peripheral devices (associated with or assisting) for a computer system. However, over the past few years card-oriented small-computer systems have begun to replace most punched card systems (Figure 4–8). In addition to the calculating capacity of the computer processor unit, it serves as a input/output device as well as providing the traditional punched card equipment functions of reproducing, gang punching, summary punching, collating, and sorting.[1]

COMMUNICATING

As is the case of several of the other basic data processing functions, communicating is closely related to, and predicated upon, the performance of other functions. However, the communicating function is primarily concerned with the assembly and transmission of data throughout the data processing system so that the data may be acted upon. (The techniques and devices utilized in this "communications" aspect of communicating with and between computers will be discussed in detail in Chapter 10.) It is also concerned with the distribution of the results, usually in the form of reports, to the users of the data. Many types of communication media are used to accomplish this.

Several differing aspects related to the communicating function must be considered. Only a few years ago, the major emphasis in communicating was in written communication, such as one traditionally thinks of when one is talking about accounting work. Information was recorded in the books by hand and classified in journals and ledgers, and the results were summarized and written out in the form of accounting statements for distribution. The preparation of written reports cannot

---

[1] IBM System 3 and System 360 Model 20, UNIVAC 9000, and Burroughs 1700 Series are examples of this type of equipment.

FIGURE 4–8. Multiple Function Card Units

(a)   UNIVAC 1001—Card Controller

Courtesy of UNIVAC

(*b*)   Burroughs 9419–6 96-column Multipurpose Card Unit

Courtesy of Burroughs Corp.

be belittled, as the need for written communication is as important today as in the past. In fact, it was the need for a faster, improved, and more extensive system of communicating information that resulted in the development of the techniques now used in our modern business information systems. Though business data may be communicated between various types of equipment systems, the ultimate end result of the communicating function will always be in some form of human-readable written communication.

Common Language Needs in Communications

In many modern computer installations (and in the future even more) communication serves as the bridge to connect points where data originate and points where the data are to be processed and used. Computer technology has, in the past few years, increased the operational speed and storage capacity of computers and has, at the same time, also increased their reliability and reduced their cost. As a direct result of these increasing capabilities, the demand for data to be processed has expanded. This in turn has created other problems, such as the need for the transportation of a continuous flow of data to the computer at a speed sufficient to keep the equipment fully utilized, if the gains from technological development are to be adequately achieved.

The demand for data has resulted in many improvements and developments in both communication facilities and equipment. Communications, as a computer-associated area, is rapidly becoming a more important link in the data processing operating pattern. This will be discussed in depth in Chapter 10.

One of the basic principles of integrated data processing (IDP—see Chapter 15) is to capture data automatically as a by-product of the initial recording in a "machine common language." This means that the data captured must be in a form in which they can be processed— free of human intervention—by other machines in the processing procedure. In order for this to be possible, all of the machines utilized must be capable of being activated by the data in the form in which they are initially captured. It is because of this that the term *common language* has been coined. This common-language concept becomes extremely important when one thinks of handling large volumes of data both quickly and accurately. Card code and channel code are the two "common-language" codes used, as both may be utilized to perform all the basic data processing functions in a modern computerized management information system. Communication is always a very important function in such a system, as data must be transmitted at high rates of speed from point to point.

Card Code. It will be emphasized in later chapters that the hole in the card may be used as a means of activating any of the basic pieces of punched card equipment and serve as input data in most computer systems. In other words, the hole—or holes—located in a particular position on the card constitute a code whereby either alphabetic or numeric data can be expressed. Today, card code is capable of communicating with practically any business machine, either directly or by going through a converter. This is one means of processing data automatically when it is initially captured in code form.

Channel Code.   Channel code derives its name from the fact that either holes or magnetized spots are made in imaginary channels which run the length of the recording medium. This medium may be in the form of punched paper tape or magnetic tape. Channel codes are widely used in both the manipulation and communication of data in computer systems.

Punched Card Communicating Equipment.   The typical reports required in a given business operation may be prepared for external use (customer statements, shipping notices, or purchase orders) or they may be strictly limited to internal usage (ledgers for record keeping or the many types of analyses which serve as management aids). In the punched card information system, the *accounting machine* performs by far the majority of the reporting functions required of the system.

There are several different accounting machines available, but in general they differ only in their input/output speeds, printing capability, and in their accumulating capacity. All the accounting machines operate automatically in both the feeding of cards and the printing of results. Information previously punched in cards can be read into these machines, and the functions of accumulating data by addition and subtraction, comparison, selection, programming, and detail data and group data printing can all be performed. The function of summary punching may also be performed if a summary punch is cable connected.

The automatic control of the functions performed by the accounting machine (Figure 4–9) is based on instructions given in the form of "point-to-point" wiring on a prewired control panel inserted into the machine.

Data Transmission.   As business evolved over the years, it became more complex, and better communicating systems became necessary to keep the various levels of management properly informed. As business became more widely dispersed geographically, it also became necessary that better systems of communication be developed.

Though for many years we have had what have proven to be "limited" techniques to transmit data over long distances, it is only in the relatively past few years that true communication systems have evolved.

Punched paper tape has been used in the transmission of data over

FIGURE 4–9. Accounting Machine

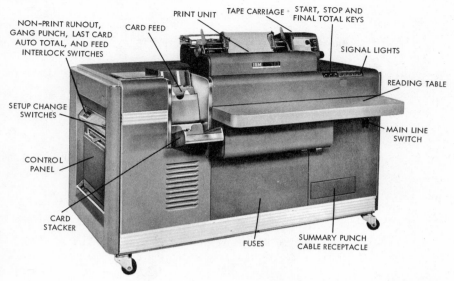

Courtesy of IBM

teletype or telegraph systems for nearly 200 years. However, the type of data normally referred to as business data has utilized teletype—in even a low-volume sense—only since the 1930s. Punched cards have utilized transceivers (a forerunner of today's terminal) to convert and transmit data over wires since the early 1940s, but only in the past decade has it become possible for magnetic tape to be used in the high-speed transmission of data. Even more recently, it has become possible for on-line devices to receive and transmit data directly from communication terminals to computers and for one or more computer systems to communicate directly with other computers.

Equipment and Media Originating Common-Language Data. Typewriters, adding machines, calculators, bookkeeping machines, and cash registers are probably the most frequently used equipment in making a record of data soon after it has been captured at its source. Several business machine manufacturers have produced equipment which can be used as attachments to these basic recording devices. Generally, these attachments produce punched paper tape or punched cards as a by-product of the operation of the recording device. The tape-producing machines are also capable of being activated at a later time by their own or other coded paper tape data.

FIGURE 4–10. Teletype® Model 33 ASR

® Registered trademark of Teletype Corp.

Courtesy of Teletype Corp.

The teleprinter (Figure 4–10) is capable of producing hard copy as well as five-channel tape in the same operation. Also note the FLEXOWRITER[2] (Figure 4–11), which is a typewriter with the capability of producing punched paper tape as a by-product of any typing operation. This tape can be used to activate any punched paper tape-oriented input equipment, including the FLEXOWRITER itself.

Looking at an example of a paper tape application, let us say a salesperson sends in a handwritten order to his or her company office. From it, a typist using a tape-punching typewriter prepares a production order. Part of the data needed to produce this order may be provided by a strip of punched paper tape or an edge-punched card stored in a customer master file. This tape or card contains data prerecorded in a channel code which is read by the FLEXOWRITER equipment

---

[2] A trademark of The Singer Co.

FIGURE 4–11. FLEXOWRITER* Automatic Writing Machine

*A trademark of The Singer Co.

Courtesy of Singer Business Machines

to provide such information as the customer's name and address, shipping instructions, and other standard data.

As the first tape is refiled, a second tape containing an organized description of the standard product ordered may be pulled from a product master file. The information coded thereon is also automatically reproduced on the order. All the typist has to add is the variable information (some 5 to 15 percent of the total) such as the current date and number of the order, quantity of material ordered, color, sizes or weights, and so on. When the typing of the order has been completed, it can, if desired, be automatically verified by the same tape-reading device or the order produced can be visually scanned.

As the data is typed, a complete by-product tape containing all the data from the standard tapes used, along with the variable information added, is automatically produced by the machine. This tape could be used as direct computer input or, if not, could by means of a tape-to-card converter be converted into punched cards for various bookkeeping and statistical reports. Since this last eliminates manual keypunching and subsequent verification, there can be a considerable saving in time and effort.

The common-language medium used in any particular application will be determined by the remainder of the data processing equipment which is to be used. A consideration of primary importance is the choosing of a common-language medium which is compatible with either the existing or projected data processing equipment.

Handwritten messages or sketches may be sent over transmission

FIGURE 4–12. Electrowriter and Data Set

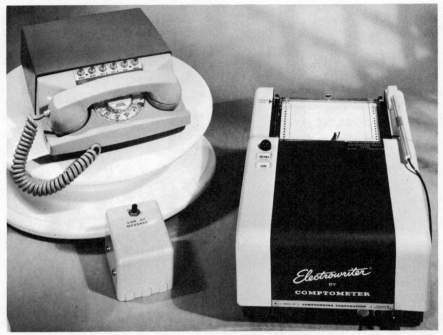

Courtesy of General Telephone and Victor Comptometer Corp.

terminals to provide a communication of this type of data between remote locations (Figure 4–12). A ball-point-type pen is used and varying tones are generated as it moves over the paper. These tones are sent through a converter out over telephone lines to the receiving point where they are converted back into tones and reproduced into the original line forms on the receiving machine.

Facsimile terminals (Figure 4–13) are basically duplicating devices except that the material is read in at one location and printed out at another many miles away. It is possible to transmit anything written, typed, printed, or hand drawn over telephone lines from one point to another. At the originating station, the document to be transmitted is fed into the scanner, which converts the image into electrical signals for transmission. At the receiving station, the electrical signals are reconverted into images, and a duplicate of the original document is reproduced. (See References 1 and 2.)

The machines which have just been described are typical examples of ways business data can be converted into the desired common-language medium.

FIGURE 4–13. Xerox 400 Telecopier

Courtesy of Xerox Corp.

BOOKKEEPING AND ACCOUNTING-COMPUTING MACHINES

These machines are discussed at this point under the communication function as the final output of all bookkeeping machines is either in the form of printed reports for communication to people or coded data to be communicated over transmission lines to centrally located computer systems. They are also operator controlled rather than program controlled, as in the case of computers.

The electronic era has had its impact on the bookkeeping machines for a number of years. Recent developments in their manufacture, however, have almost completely done away with electrical-mechanical equipment of this type. There are, of course, thousands of installations of such nonelectronic machines. These will continue to be in use for many years as they are well built and, in many instances, have high performance at a reasonable cost. New installations, however, will utilize the electronic models which provide even greater performance and reliability at a lower cost.

The equipment currently being replaced by electronic models include the rear- and front-feed carriage models and the automatic bookkeeping machines. As mentioned above, however, this equipment will still be in common use for some time yet, and so it is briefly described below.

The lowest-priced machines are essentially electrically operated adding machines with a *rear-feed carriage*. Such machines may or may not have a tabulating carriage and usually provide a single total. These are used primarily by smaller business firms or by branch offices of larger firms where activity is relatively light. The *front-feed carriage* machine is basically an adding machine with a typewriter-type carriage, which permits faster posting and provides one or two totals. They speed up form handling by guiding the forms into an exact columnar position and alignment for data entry. These machines are also in the low price range.

The *automatic bookkeeping machines* (Figure 4–14) incorporate many automatic features which eliminate operator decisions and man-

FIGURE 4–14. NCR 400 Electronic Accounting Machine

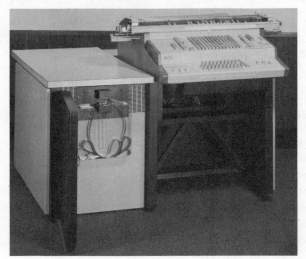

Courtesy of NCR

ual operations. These automatic features include: tabulation and carriage return, carriage opening and closing, totaling and subtotaling, punctuation, and ribbon color control (credits in red). They may also provide two or more accumulators for totals or subtotals. These features naturally make the posting operation simpler, faster, and less susceptible to operator error.

In the more simple automatic machines, built-in program control bars provide some automatic functions and cause positioning to a proper column following a prescribed sequence by depressing a key. The analogy might be drawn between the program control bar and the tabular stops on a typewriter.

In larger automatic machines, the programming (the directing instructions) of automatic functions may be performed internally by the machine. These machines can be instructed to accumulate, print, control the punching of a line total (where punched paper tape is a feature)—a zero line proof or balancing procedure to prove the accuracy of distribution—and take automatic totals from all memory units at the completion of a posting run.

With the addition of available data recording devices, some makes and models of equipment may be expanded to produce, as a by-product of their operation, punched paper tape, magnetic tape (cassette type), or punched card output. Where this type of feature is provided, it makes it possible for the by-product tape or card to be used as input into a computer system.

There has been considerable effort and many dollars expended in research in the *electronic accounting-computing equipment* area in the past few years. This has brought about changes which include larger capabilities, more sophistication, greater simplification in programming, and even lower prices. There are currently several different levels of capability within this grouping of equipment. Some only extend the capability of the previously described types, while those with more versatile input/output capability and larger memories may be classified as mini or desk-size computers.

The lower range of this equipment is an extension of the bookkeeping machine with some limited capabilities of the computer. These models have electronic memory, are programmable, and have a limited variety of input/output capabilities. Typical models are the NCR 299 and the Burroughs L5000 Magnetic Record Computers (Figure 4–15).

The features of this type of equipment includes a multi-form, split platen, carriage for hand-copy (printed) output; both typewriter and ten-key numeric keyboards; and limited magnetic disk memory which is used to store both the program of instructions and the data to be manipulated. Additional I/O capability is provided by a card reader/punch, paper tape punch, and magnetic ledger cards. These outputs may be utilized in providing input data for a computer system.

In such systems, the stripes on the ledger cards (Figure 4–16) store, in magnetic pulse form, pertinent alpha and numeric account data such as customer name and address, accounts receivable balances, part numbers, item descriptions, inventory balances, and minimum inventory levels. Some systems have the capability that, upon insertion of the

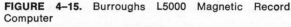

FIGURE 4–15. Burroughs L5000 Magnetic Record Computer

Courtesy of Burroughs Corp.

ledger cards, detailed headings and item descriptions (as an example) may be automatically typed on an invoice. When the operator lists the quantity to be shipped and other nonstandard data, the information from the magnetic stripes is able to fully complete the invoice and post the accounts receivable ledger and at the same time update the active inventory ledger accounts.

The upper range of the electronic accounting-computing equipment includes the compact *desk-size computers.* These machines are designed to retain the best features of bookkeeping machines along with the speed, memory, and computing capabilities of computers. In terms of data processing, these machines have both the capacity and the speed to handle and process relatively large volumes of paper work and most can also serve as a computer terminal for the input and output of data, from local or remote installations to a central computer system. All of the makes of these machines presently on the market emphasize simplicity of operation and programming along with a relatively reasonable rental cost per month.

These systems, basically designed for small business systems, will accommodate a variety of input and output devices—punched paper tape, edge-punched cards, punched cards, and the keyboard. Some models also utilize magnetic tape cassettes and others the magnetic striped ledger card as both input and outut. The feeling is, quite natu-

FIGURE 4–16. Magnetic Ledger Cards

Courtesy of NCR and Burroughs Corp.

rally, that business data will be in one of these forms in the medium-sized businesses for which these computing systems are designed.

Programming (instructions to operate the equipment) assistance is usually readily supplied to the user of the equipment. One manufacturer offers to do all of the necessary programming or provide programming application packages for the applications (various jobs) which a prospective user of the equipment envisions when he or she installs the equipment. Any future alterations to existing programs or writing of new programs will be done by the manufacturer for a small fee.

Storage in the different systems is accomplished in different ways. All, however, utilize some form of magnetic-type memory (such as magnetic cores, magnetic disk, or semi-conductor memory, to be described in later chapters) for data storage. In addition, some systems have additional storage capacity provided by magnetic tape cassettes (like home tape recorders) and magnetic ledger cards.

As an illustration of a typical system of this type, the basic NCR 399 Accounting Computer (Figure 4–17), designed around the NCR

FIGURE 4–17. NCR 399 Accounting Computer

Courtesy of NCR

605 minicomputer, sells in the $14,000 range. This basic system includes limited magnetic core memory, a magnetic tape cassette handler, an alphabetic and 10-key keyboard, and a ball-type typewriter printer. Additional core memory, a second cassette handler, and disk memory may be added for additional storage. The NCR 399 also has a communications capability which permits the equipment to serve as an intelligent terminal (able to process as well as transmit data) in transmitting and receiving information to and from a central computer system installation.

SUMMARY

In addition to pointing out the basic data processing functions, Chapters 3 and 4 have indicated that there are many individual types of equipment to assist the processing of data requirements in a given firm's data processing system installation. Some of these types of equipment capture data directly in machine language form or produce it indirectly (as a by-product of some other basic function), while other types serve in the alteration or manipulation of the data.

The needs of the individual firm for data will be conditioned by (1) the immediacy of the demands by management for information for decision-making purposes, (2) the variety of information desired, and (3) the volume and timing of the flow of data. In some instances only manual equipment will be necessary, in others some combination of manual and mechanical or electromechanical (punched card) equipment may suffice. In still others a computer of some type may be a necessity.

These chapters have tried to provide an overview of the more common equipment—other than computer systems—available to serve specific data processing needs. The major equipment items associated with computer systems will be described later in Chapters 9, 10, and 11.

REFERENCES

1. "Facsimile." *Telecommunications,* July 1973, p. 13.
2. "Facsimile—Two Who Are Satisfied." *Infosystems,* January 1973, p. 34.

QUESTIONS

1. What is meant by the classifying of data? Give two examples where data would be classified.
2. By what means is the classification function usually accomplished?
3. Classifying and sorting both serve to give data a pattern. How do these functions differ?
4. Discuss three different methods of sorting data, making certain to note the strengths and weaknesses of each method.
5. What is the purpose of summary punching?
6. Of what importance are all of the other data processing functions if adequate communications to transmit the data to those who are interested in them do not exist? Discuss fully.
7. Describe in as many ways as you can how the communication function is involved in the field of data processing.
8. Differentiate between the two basic types of common language.
9. In what ways can data be transmitted other than in common-language code?
10. What is the importance of the "common-language" concept when discussing the use of various pieces of equipment?

11. Describe two machines which produce as their output data in a common-language form which is acceptable as input by other pieces of mechanical or electronic computing equipment.

12. Under what conditions might you recommend a desk-size computer to a business client? Explain.

13. Which of the data processing functions discussed in this and the previous chapter is most important? Carefully support your answer.

II
Computers

chapter

5

Electronic Computer Development

AN AUTOMATIC COMPUTER was first conceived in 1786 by J. H. Muller, a German engineer. He proposed a device to generate data for functions from algebraic formulas involving their differences. Though Muller developed his ideas on paper in great detail, he did not attempt to produce the machine due to the tremendous engineering and technical difficulties that would have been impossible to surmount at that time.

Charles Babbage, the son of a banker in Devonshire, England, taught himself mathematics, and when he entered Cambridge in 1810 found that he knew more in this field than his teachers. In working with the logarithm tables available at that time in his statistical work, he discovered a number of errors and became intrigued with the idea of developing the series of numbers in these tables by some mechanical method. This, he felt, would eliminate the human errors seemingly always present in the calculations required in the development of such a complex series of numbers.

So in 1812, at the age of 20, Babbage conceived the idea of what he called his Difference Engine.[1] He presented these ideas to the societies of his day and was granted financial help from both the Royal Society of London and the English government to aid him in the development of his equipment.

The Difference Engine was basically a specially designed adding

---

[1] "The Cranky Grandfather of the Computer," *Fortune*, March 1964.

machine for the computation of polynomials (such as $x^2 - 2xy + y^2$) with an accuracy up to six decimal places. A working model of the Difference Engine was completed in about 1822. It used the concept of "state" (either the presence or absence of holes) in a type of punched card that had been used in controlling the Jacquard Frame Loom. The basic operational idea involved the constancy of the difference in the third power of a sequential series of numbers (Figure 5–1).

FIGURE 5–1.

X	X^3	1st Difference	2nd Difference	3rd Difference
1	1			
		7		
2	8		12	
		19		6
3	27		18	
		37		6
4	64		24	
		61		
5	125			
20	8,000			
		1,261		
21	9,261		126	
		1,387		6
22	10,648		132	
		1,519		6
23	12,167		138	
		1,657		
24	13,824			

Babbage later proposed and tried to build a similar machine with accuracy up to 20 decimal places. This work was also sponsored by the government, but engineering and other technical problems prevented it from being completed on schedule, and financial support was withdrawn in 1833.

A larger model of the Difference Engine was eventually completed in 1859 and was put to use in calculating life tables for insurance ratings in 1863. George Scheutz and his son, from Sweden, and an Englishman, each constructed Difference Engines several years after Babbage's death. Both of these gave good, reliable service for many years.

Babbage conceived the idea for an Analytical Engine to perform digital computations in 1833, about the time his finances were cut off on building the Difference Engine. This idea has since proven to be the fundamental basis for the development of modern computers, and the Analytical Engine is considered the ancestor of today's general-purpose electronic computers. Babbage is often spoken of as "the father of computers."

In his proposals for the Analytical Engine, Babbage utilized an input of data in the form of punched cards or handset dials. He described the punched cards used in his equipment as being somewhat similar to those used by the French inventor Jacquard. The holes in his cards, however, represented mathematical symbols rather than machine controls. He is quoted as saying it "weaves algebraic patterns" just as the Jacquard Loom weaves flowers and leaves.

The input data was processed by using flexible arithmetic controls which performed the calculations required in what Babbage called a "mill." Internal storage, which he termed a "store," was designed in the form of counters which provided 50,000 units of available information (1,000 numbers of 50 digits each). Output was also flexible, as it could be in the form of punched cards or a printed page (actually a mold from which type could be set). The development of the Analytical Engine soon ran into almost insurmountable engineering problems and financial difficulties. A model of the Analytical Engine was never completed, due to the mechanical production difficulties and the resulting costs, and the idea of automatic computing machines was to be forgotten for over four decades.

EARLY MODERN COMPUTERS

Dr. Vannevar Bush and some associates at Massachusetts Institute of Technology constructed a large-scale analog calculator in 1925. It was basically a mechanically operated computer, though some electric motors were utilized in its construction. In 1935 Dr. Bush and associates started to construct an improved model of their 1925 analog computer. This equipment had considerably greater capabilities. It was completed in 1942, but the project was kept secret until after World War II had ended.

Dr. George R. Stibitz started to work on the Bell Model 1 in 1937 at Bell Telephone Laboratories under the supervision of Samuel B. Williams. The Bell Model 1 was a semiautomatic computer which used telephone relays to perform its computations. It was completed in 1939 and was used in computing complex numbers used in the design of telephone transmission networks and transformers. Though in the true sense this was not an electronic computer, as it utilized electrical relays rather than electronic circuits, this equipment was used in the first public demonstration of an automatic computer. This demonstration was in conjunction with the September 1940 meeting of the American Mathematical Society in Hanover, New Hampshire.

Stibitz later, in 1942, developed under a government contract a "relay interpolator" at Bell Telephone Laboratories under the direction of E. G. Andrews. This equipment performed arithmetic operations under the control of a program recorded on paper tape.

A revised model was constructed in 1943, during the war, to be used as a "ballistic computer," which could be termed a general-purpose computer. In this same period, Stibitz also built an "error computer" to search files of paper tape for selected data. These models were also based on government contracts and were completed at Bell Telephone Laboratories.

Other early relay-type computers included the IBM Pluggable Sequence Relay Calculator, BARK (Sweden), Zuse, the Imperial College Computing Engine, and the ARC (Automatic Relay Computer).

In 1935, Dr. Howard Aiken, then a graduate student at Harvard University, studied Babbage's plans and ideas and decided that modern engineering capability would permit the development of equipment such as Babbage had envisioned. In 1937, after performing some initial work on his project, Dr. Aiken went to the International Business Machines Corporation (IBM) for both financial and technical help on his proposal. Both were forthcoming from IBM, and in 1939 IBM started to work on this project with Aiken serving as consultant to J. W. Bryce, C. D. Lake, B. M. Durfee, and F. E. Hamilton—all IBM engineers.

The Automatic Sequence Controlled Calculator (ASCC), also known as Mark 1, was the product of this combined effort and proved to be the largest of the relay calculating devices ever to be constructed. Its computational capability was close to that of the early electronic computing devices which followed.

The ASCC was completed in 1943—but not publicly announced until 1944 due to wartime security regulations—to become the first of a series of equipment that was to develop into the electronic computer as it is known today.

A second model of the ASCC, the Mark 2, was started immediately after Mark 1 and was completed in 1947. Both were basically electro-mechanical in nature. Later, models 3 and 4 were built, each an improvement on the others and, consequently, considerably faster in their calculating ability. In all models, instructions were fed into the machines by punched cards as they were needed, and the calculations necessary were automatically performed. These equipments were all designed for scientific work and were used by engineers, physicists, and mathematicians to compute long series of complex arithmetical problems.

ELECTRONIC COMPUTERS

It has long been thought that the first truly electronic computer was developed as a result of a proposal made in 1943 by Dr. John W. Mauchly and J. Presper Eckert, in conjunction with a World War II contract, at the Moore School of Electrical Engineering. However, a court ruling by U.S. District Judge Earl H. Larson on October 19, 1973, as a result of a 8-year court fight by Honeywell over patent rights claimed by Sperry Rand on the ENIAC computer (described later), has brought out that a Dr. John Atanasoff actually developed many of the ideas Mauchly and Eckert patented.[2] (See Reference 1.)

Atanasoff, then at Iowa State University as a mathematics and physics professor, conceived the basic idea in the winter of 1937–38. With the aid of an assistant, Clifford Berry, the ABC (Atanasoff–Berry Computer) machine was started in 1938 and completed in May 1942 (Figure 5–2). During this period Mauchly visited Atanasoff in Ames, Iowa, read his material, and corresponded with him.

As mentioned later, the firm established by Mauchly and Eckert was purchased by a forerunner of the UNIVAC Division of Sperry Rand. They acquired the contested patents at that time and since, up to the court decison, have been charging others for any usage of these ideas.

To return to what has been considered the historical development of the first electronic computer, Mauchly and Eckert entered into an Army contract to develop an electronic computer.

After a period of two years (1945), the first completely electronic, high-speed computer was produced as the Electronic Numerical Integrator and Calculator (ENIAC). Over 18,000 vacuum tubes were used in its construction. The ENIAC could perform 5,000, 10-decimal-digit calculations a second and multiply at a speed up to 300 calculations

---

[2] "Court: Computer Iowan's Idea," *DesMoines Sunday Register,* January 27, 1974, pp. 1A and 8A.

FIGURE 5–2. Atanasoff–Berry Computer (ABC)

Courtesy of Iowa State University of Science & Technology

a second (compared to a maximum of 1 per second on the fastest relay-type calculator), but it occupied a room over 100 feet in length (1,500 square feet) and used up to 100 kw. of electrical power.

One of the first problems assigned to ENIAC was one in nuclear physics which was solved in about two hours of computation over a two-week period of time. It has been estimated it would have taken about 100 man-years to have solved this problem using conventional techniques.

ENIAC was installed in the Ballistic Research Laboratory at the Aberdeen Proving Grounds, Aberdeen, Maryland, in 1946. It was used in ballistic research until October 1955, when it was retired. It is now in the Smithsonian Institution.

The Electronic Discrete Variable Automatic Computer (EDVAC), was the second computer designed by Mauchly and Eckert and built at the University of Pennsylvania. It was started about 1946 but was not finally completed until 1952. It was smaller in size (only 3,500 vacuum tubes required) but larger in capability than the earlier ENIAC. It utilized the binary system of number notation and was completely internally programmed (rather than using externally wired boards and other external input). Though other computers utilizing similar chatacteristics became operational before EDVAC, they were all based on ideas proposed for this equipment. Thus, the EDVAC is considered to be the prototype of serial-type computers which utilize internally stored, serially ordered, instructions.

Dr. John von Neumann of atomic energy fame had joined Mauchly and Eckert at the Moore School of Electrical Engineering in 1945 to learn more of their project and to determine if it might be applicable to the type of research he was involved in at that time. During his stay at Moore, Von Neumann attended a series of conferences held by Mauchly and Eckert on computers and discussed many ideas with them. The result was that Von Neumann wrote a paper on computers describing them in great detail. This paper was published soon after this period and sometime before Mauchly and Eckert developed their EDVAC. There has been considerable speculation as to whether Von Neumann obtained his information from Mauchly and Eckert or vice versa or if the ideas were a product of joint stimulation by discussions between them. However, there has been sufficient fame and other rewards resulting from the paper, the Institute of Advanced Study Computer (produced later), and EDVAC to satisfy all concerned.

As an outgrowth of Von Neumann's work with Mauchly and Eckert at Moore, the Institute of Advanced Study of Princeton University and the Moore School of Electrical Engineering proposed a study to produce, as a joint project, the IAS Computer for the U.S. Ordinance Department. This was completed by Princeton in 1952. It used a punched paper-tape input/output system, the binary number system, one-address instruction commands, asynchronous timing, and a cathode-ray-type storage tube in its design. Addition and subtraction were performed in 10 microseconds and multiplication in 300 microseconds (millionths of a second). The basic design of the IAS has been copied and improved upon many times in the production of a number of the single model and a few of the commercial-type computers produced since its development.

The Electronic Delayed Storage Automatic Computer (EDSAC) was completed in May 1949 as the first serially operating computer. This equipment used many of the ideas proposed for EDVAC and was constructed under the direction of M. A. Wilkes at the Mathematical Laboratory of the University of Cambridge in 1949. Mercury delay lines were used for storage, and depending on the size of the digit involved in the computation, it only took 34 to 70 microseconds to perform the addition and subtraction function. Input was in the form of five channel punched paper tape and output was to a tape punch or teleprinter.

A second English computer the Automatic Computing Engine (ACE), using EDVAC and Von Neumann ideas, was started in 1945 by Turing, Womersley, and Colebrook at the National Physical Laboratory, London, and was completed in 1950. The ACE used punched cards for its input and output, delay-line-type storage and less than 1,000 vacuum tubes in its operation. It was faster than EDSAC and more reliable. The ACE was the first computer to use the "two-address code" for instructions, with each instruction containing both the location of the number (address) to be operated upon and the location of the next instruction.

The Whirlwind 1 computer was produced at M.I.T. in 1950 under the direction of J. Forrester. It was the first to use the electrostatic cathode-ray tube, devised by Forester, for storage. One of the first attempts to use magnetic tapes for external storage was on the Whirlwind. Input and output were both normally performed by punched paper tape and teletype. However, output could be displayed on the face of a large cathode-ray tube for visual inspection or photographing. Addition or substraction required 5 microseconds and multiplication 40 microseconds in the Whirlwind.

PRODUCTION MODEL COMPUTERS

Mauchly and Eckert resigned their positions at the University of Pennsylvania in 1946 and organized their own computer company, the Electronic Control Company. Shortly thereafter, they procured a contract from the National Bureau of Standards and proceeded to develop what became the Universal Automatic Computer (UNIVAC 1) in 1951. This was the first truly commercial computer to be produced on the assembly line.

The Electronic Control Company was purchased in 1949 by the Remington Rand Corporation, which was quite active in the production of punched card and other electromechanical equipment. This firm, in turn, became the Univac Division of Sperry Rand Corporation, which today is Sperry Univac, one of the leading producers of computers and associated equipment.

The second commercial model computer, the CRC 102 (NCR 102) computer, was produced in 1952 by the Computer Research Corporation. This company was soon absorbed by the Electronics Division of the National Cash Register Company. The third piece of equipment to be produced for commercial distribution was the IBM 701, which was developed in 1952 by IBM. This was a successful computer but, as with most computers of its day, was strictly limited to scientific applications.

Business Applications

With the increasing use of computers in the scientific and engineering areas, considerable interest developed among business people as to how the computer could aid them in combating the expanding load of paper work in record keeping and in solving problems of data manipulation for managerial use. The first use of computers for processing business data was in a Bureau of the Census application on the UNIVAC 1 in October 1954.

Though IBM had aided Dr. Aiken in the development of the Automatic Sequence Controlled Calculator (ASCC) at Harvard University in the period 1937 to 1943 and had developed punched card calculators in the 1940s, it did not enter the computer field until 1952, when it produced the IBM 701. The IBM 701 was a scientific application computer, but it served to develop a staff which produced the IBM 702, a small commercially oriented computer, and the IBM 650, a general-purpose computer with special business capabilities, in 1953, and many others which followed. The IBM 650 was first used in Boston, Massachusetts, on a business application in December 1954; later it became the most popular of all the first-generation group of computers.

The IBM 650 was one of the first all-purpose computers (serving the requirements of both scientific and business applications). It utilized vacuum tubes in its electrical circuits, magnetic-drum-type storage, and punched cards for both input and output of information. The IBM 650 has been termed, by many, the "Model T" of computers because of its comparatively low price, broad usage application, general reliability, and wide acceptance. (All attributes of Ford Motor Company's early Model-T automobile.) With the development of the IBM 650 and its ability to adapt itself to applications of both scientific and business problems, IBM assumed the position of leading producer of computers by 1955—a position it has continued to consolidate as time has passed until it is now the "giant" in the field.

PROGRESSIVE CHANGES OVER TIME

Many different models of computers were constructed during the early period of development of computers. In nearly every instance each progressive development added new features to the design of the newer computers. In later equipment, increased capability—in both speed and storage capacity—and differing usage adaptability became the basic trend of development, but even here there was not always a clear-cut delineation or completely new equipment developed as changes occurred in what will be described as "the generations" in Chapter 6. Usually, the new techniques were introduced individually over time. It was only when they were consolidated and incorporated in a new series of equipment that the idea of a so-called new generation became accepted. In most instances this classification occurred only after the passage of time, when hindsight permitted looking back and observing that some accumulation of changes, now incorporated in a new system, was in reality a major departure from what had been done in the past.

Thus, to understand how the progressive changes took place to provide the various classifications of computers described in the next chapter, it is well to also look at the changes that have occurred over time in the various functionally related segments of the entire computer system.

Storage

By the early 1960s, only a comparatively few years after the first business application of computers, data storage devices of computers had passed through various stages utilizing relays, vacuum tubes, and mercury delay lines into the era of magnetic drums, cores, disks, tapes, and cassette tape units. In the late 1960s, several of the newer models of computers utilized magnetic film or integrated circuitry as limited but very fast buffer or read-only internal memory. Semiconductor memories were introduced in the early 1970s. They are slowly growing in usage. (These techniques will be described in later chapters.)

Storage capacities have advanced from a few hundred or thousand units of information stored internally in the computer to many thousands of units stored internally in conjunction with literally millions (in some instances even billions) more stored in external devices that are immediately available to the computer on its demand. Internal access speeds have advanced from thousandths of a second (milliseconds) to millionths of a second (microseconds), and—in most of the newer equipments—to billionths of a second (nanoseconds).

Input/Output

Input and output devices have changed from handset dials, paper tape, and paper cards to include cathode-ray tubes, magnetic tape, console typewriters, on-line analog computers, magnetic ink characters, optical scanning devices, microfilming techniques, and the use of cassette tape units. Some success has even been achieved in control by human voice commands and in output in the form of machine "spoken" words.

Input/output capability has changed from the time required to set or read a few dials on the face of the equipment to the computer's automatic acceptance of over two thirds of a million bits of numerical data per second from magnetic tape units.

Some of the more powerful processing units, used in systems involving centrally located computers with remote capability, have a wide range of completely different input and output units from which they will accept input data and to which they may feed output data. These larger computer systems have increased computational capabilities to permit the computers to be working on two, three, four, or more problems simultaneously. These utilize differing series or sets of internally stored instructions, external storage devices, and input/output units— all under priorities which may be assigned by the operator.

These multiprocessing systems may use several computers (probably remotely located) to feed a central computer and, in some instances, a system of several computers may not only interact with each other but actually utilize the memory, storage, and input/output capabilities of each other. In such systems, preassigned priorities are incorporated into complex executive-type programs which control the sequence of operations and the assignment of memory locations to prevent any overlap of usage.

Paper tape can now be read at speeds up to 1,800 and punched at rates up to 1,000 characters per second. Punched cards can be read as fast as 2,500 and punched at 800 cards per minute. In addition to devices that serve as both input and output, optical character reading can be performed at up to 2,000 characters per second and magnetic ink characters may be read at 1,200 characters per second. Also, the demand for business reports has led to the development of on-line printers which will print up to as many as 2,000 lines of data per minute.

Where the data need not be read directly from a printed report, it may be output onto microfilm at speeds up to 25,000 lines per minute. This data may be printed out in hard-copy page form later if it is desired, or the data may be scanned visually by using one of the many models of microfilm viewers.

Teleprocessing systems have brought about a wide usage of remote terminals of various types, which include not only the typical typewriter (teleprinter) input and output capabilities but also graphic units which present data in graphical form and visual display devices of various types utilizing cathode-ray tubes similar to those used in television (the output of which may be developed or changed by the use of light pens or beams). A few of these visual display devices are even beginning to present data in color. The use of intelligent terminals with processing capability, often involving minicomputers, seems to be one of the more rapidly expanding I/O techniques.

Though great strides have been made in developing and improving techniques for both the input and output of data in computer systems, the demands for faster and simpler techniques seemingly multiply in an exponential pattern with the passage of time. Just as in the early period of computer development, I/O capabilities continue to lag behind the computational capabilities of the processing equipment.

Internal Circuitry

Internal circuitry has changed from electromagnetic relays to vacuum tubes and on to transistors, diodes, other solid-state devices such as solid logic technology (SLT), and semiconductor integrated circuitry. The speed of operation has advanced from a few hundred closings of a relay per minute to speeds which are measured in terms of milliseconds, microseconds, and a few hundred nanoseconds.

Experimental circuitry is being developed that operates in billionths of a second (nanoseconds) and even in trillionths of a second (picoseconds).

To give some concept of how fast these speeds are, a space ship traveling at a speed of 100,000 miles per hour would only move 1¾ inches in one microsecond. Another comparison, in terms of time rather than speed, is that there are as many nanoseconds in one second as there are seconds in 30 years. Any illustration—either in terms of speed or time—of an operation involving picoseconds is almost beyond imagination and everyday comparisons.

Internal computer speeds now permit addition to be performed as fast as 6 million numbers per second, multiplication at 2 million numbers per second, and access to fast memory at 13.3 million numbers per second. In the ILLIAC IV, up to 64 computations can be performed simultaneously and 100 to 200 million instructions can be executed per second.

Space and Other Requirements

The first computers, which utilized vacuum tubes in their operation, were massive in size and often required the space of a number of average-sized rooms just to house the components.

The operation of the large number of vacuum tubes necessary for a typical computer brought a demand for not only considerable power requirements but also many differing levels of voltage. These electrical demands were supplied by separately housed power supply units. These power units, as well as the tubes themselves, generated a vast amount of heat—enough, in fact, to melt the components in some of the various units. This heat had to be offset by blower fans inside the units and by large-capacity air-conditioning equipment to keep the rooms and equipment at operable temperatures.

The computer, the associated power supplies, and the air-conditioning equipment all made heavy demands on the electrical service required. It was quite common to see heavy cables 2 or 3 inches in diameter laced across the floor from unit to unit. It naturally followed that this demand for large amounts of electrical power made the operation of the equipment quite expensive.

In the late 1950s, computers were developed to utilize the then newly developed solid-state electronic devices, such as transistors and diodes, to replace the vacuum tubes previously used. These computers have become known as the second generation of computers. The solid-state devices were quite small in size, relative to vacuum tubes, had low power requirements, generated only a small amount of heat in their operation, and proved themselves to be much more reliable than the tubes they replaced.

As the operational speed of the internal circuits of the computer increased, the distance along the wires and between the components became a critical factor in their performance. Electricity travels at the speed of light, which is about 186,300 miles per second. However, when you consider a circuit operating in billionths and even trillionths of a second, a length of wire a relatively few inches in length can slow up the time it takes the current to flow from one device to another. Thus, smaller and more compact components became a necessity for performance as well as for the size and weight requirements of the space program, where most of these developments evolved.

In conjunction with these solid-state devices, etched-circuit boards and the solid logic techniques of the 1960s involving monolithic and integrated circuits (Chapter 11) came into use and eliminated much of the conventional wiring previously used in electronic circuits. These further cut down on the space requirements. Now, even the larger business computers only require a good-sized room for their installation, and the smaller ones are installed in a desk-style cabinet.

The techniques available in the production of these devices, micro-miniturized circuit boards, and semiconductors also permitted mass production and assembly lines to be utilized instead of previous manual-type assembly techniques. This resulted in increased efficiencies, which reduced cost while at the same time providing a more reliable and standardized product.

Computer Operating Costs

With the advent of second- and third-generation computers, costs began to decrease. Relatively powerful systems became available for the smaller or the medium-sized firms at a price previously paid for punched card calculators and accounting machines.

Where the early computers were individually designed and hand-assembled, the new equipment now flows from the assembly line, where most of the components used are produced and assembled through automated techniques.

The performance capabilities and operating reliability of the solid-state components and etched-circuit boards are such that costs are minimal, in terms of both component replacement and the resulting nonoperating downtime, and are now at a new minimum level. Preventive maintenance checks, automatic within some equipment, have also been developed that test the operating level of the components to allow replacement of items that appear to be failing before there is any loss of operating efficiency.

Power demands of solid-state, integrated, and semiconductor circuitry are quite low, relative to that of vacuum tubes, and the costs associated with this lower demand for electrical power have decreased.

These lower power demands have also cut down on the need for special air-conditioning provisions so that the normal air conditioning provided in most modern offices is adequate to dissipate the small amount of heat generated by the computer system.

REFERENCES

1. "Recognition . . . 35 Years Late." *Computerworld,* March 13, p. 1; March 20, p. 15; and March 27, p. 9.

QUESTIONS

1. Why is Babbage often spoken of as the father of computers?
2. When was the first modern-day computer developed, where, and by whom?
3. When and where was the first electronic computer developed?
4. Describe the characteristics of the ENIAC computer.
5. Which well-known computer manufacturers of today are pioneers in this field of endeavor?
6. Has the development of computer capabilities been rapid? Explain. Give some examples.
7. For what purposes were the early computers used? Explain.
8. In general, what were the physical characteristics of the early computers?
9. Have the physical characteristics of computers changed through the passage of time? Explain.
10. It seems, at times, that we have heard of computers most of our lives; but just how long ago was it that computers were first used in business data processing?

6

Classifications of Computer Systems

COMPUTERS ARE REFERRED TO in many ways. This is frequently quite confusing to those who do not understand the various terms used in describing a given computer. The terms used may be associated with the family of computers, their areas of usage, their design as to the unit of information manipulated internally, or, in a broader sense, the name may be used in referring to the generation or period in which they were developed.

To a large extent much of the mystery of the computer (outside of its technical aspects, of course) can be cleared up by some conceptual understanding of the terms most frequently used in describing computers.

FAMILIES OF COMPUTERS

There are two distinct families of computers: analog and digital, each of which provides a unique contribution in the manipulation of data.

Analog Computers

The analog computer is used to solve problems that normally originate as physical realities. These problems are solved by substituting an equivalent or analogous relationship, generally in the form of electronic voltages, which may be manipulated, higher or lower, to correspond to the larger or smaller size of the variables in the physical problem. A much simplified example of this technique would be to let a volt of electricity be the equivalent of a degree of temperature (a pound of pressure or vacuum, a unit of volume, or some other measurement). As the temperature increased or decreased, this would be sensed by the equivalent of a thermometer which would, in turn, increase or decrease the voltage fed into the computer. As the voltage (temperature) reached predetermined levels, which had previously been stored in the memory system of the computer, the computer would activate a valve to either increase or decrease (as needed) the flow of fuel feeding the furnace serving as the heat source.

Data represented by the voltages can be assigned, by their very nature, any value between the maximum and minimum voltages permissible and are thus *continuously variable* over their range of operation. The accuracy of the analog computer is, therefore, limited by the precision with which these voltages can be controlled.

The most common method of describing physical problems is in the mathematical form of either linear or nonlinear differential equations and associated algebraic, transcendental, and perhaps arbitrary relationships.

Combinations of analog computing units may be needed in solving more complex problems by having each unit provide the equivalent of one of the various equations that may arise where a number of variables are present. In a typical problem these variables need to be assigned various values to provide alternatives for some type of optimum operation.

Typical output of the analog computer may be in the form of a graphical presentation of the relationship of one variable as a function of another variable, either in the form of plotted data or pictorial drawings prepared by printers or recorder traces, or electronically plotted by utilizing oscilloscopes or cathode-ray tubes.

Other outputs may be in the form of voltages or pulses which may be used to control temperatures, pressures, and flows by actuating the many differing types of control devices available. These electronic outputs may also be used as inputs to digital computers, where their storage and computational capabilities provide additional information that may, in turn, be used as input back into the analog unit originally providing the information or to another analog computer.

The more common usage of the analog computer is in areas where physical control is the end result. Typical is its wide use in industry to actuate various controls in many types of automatic processes such as those used for machine tools and in the flow of materials (both liquids and solids). Many uses have also been discovered for the analog computer in radar work, guided missiles, and the space program in general.

By referring back to the temperature-voltage example, previously used in describing the manner in which the analog computer operates, and adding similar analogies of pressure, volume, and physical properties of the input material, it is not hard to envision, in a very simplified manner, how these computers can be used in the automated control of an oil refinery. Here, the specific gravity and other physical properties of the crude oil being fed into the refinery system would be tested and checked at regular intervals. As the oil flows through the system, various stages of differing pressures, vacuums, and temperatures are required to break it down into the refined products required. By varying these factors, larger or smaller quantities of a given product, or combinations of products, may be produced as the demand for products changes.

For each set of products to be produced from a given volume of crude oil, with its specific physical properties, there is a series of required temperatures, pressures, and other factors to produce the optimum level of production of each of the end products desired. It would require many employees to perform all the functions needed and to adjust all the valves and controls necessary to do this refining process, and even then many of the tests and readings required could only be made periodically. Consequently, manually operated refineries do well to achieve more than 75 percent efficiency in attempting to reach optimum production levels. Through the use of computers, which can be continually "on line" checking all the factors, it has been possible to achieve 95 percent or better efficiency in automated plants.

As a word of caution, the automated refinery does not rely completely on analog computers for its operation. Many computers of the analog type serve to provide the input required for one or more digital computers where the larger memory capability allows all the inputs to be weighed against previously stored instructions and formulas. Computations are made to determine the optimum functional controls required, and this information is then sent back to the various analog computers which, in turn, make any necessary adjustments required of the control devices.

Digital Computers

Data are represented in the circuitry of a digital computer by a pattern of coded electrical pulses, or "spurts" of electrical energy. In the memory of the computer, these pulses may magnetize certain patterned spots on component parts of the computer (magnetic drums, disks, and films) or magnetize the component part itself (magnetic cores or integrated circuits). These data cannot be of a continuous nature as in the analog computer but must represent discrete (specific) numbers such as quantities and amounts. It is this ability to accept and manipulate discrete data that makes the digital computer so adaptable to business data and problems. Thus, where the analog computer "measures," the digital computer "counts."

Both the analog and digital computers can be used in making mathematical calculations, but as previously mentioned, the accuracy (in terms of data lost through rounding techniques) of the analog unit depends upon the precision control of voltages. In the digital unit, accuracy depends on the number of value positions available for the manipulation of data. Just as in the case of hand calculators the more place values available—the less rounding needed—the more accurate the answer to the computation. Thus you only need to add the electronic equivalent of additional place or value positions to increase the accuracy of the digital computer.

In as much as business data processing is the major concern of this text, the material to follow will relate to the characteristics and utilization of the digital computer.

Hybrid Computers

In addition to the two major families of computers there are also some computers that can best fulfill needs by combining the specifically desired features of both families. These computers, known as *hybrid* computers, are normally designed for a specific application where the process control features of the analog computer and the data processing capability of the digital computer are both required.

The previously mentioned oil refinery application would be a specific example where a hybrid computer would be utilized as gauges and thermometers need to be read and valves altered and set, depending on the results desired and the conditions found. These functions can best be provided by analog devices. The alternatives available and the files of information needed to determine the possible alternatives would be provided by digital devices. The alternative decided upon as best under the given circumstances would be relayed by the digital device to the analog devices where the desired combination of process control adjustments would be performed.

APPLICATION AREAS OF DIGITAL COMPUTERS

Computers are often described by names referring to the general application area for which they are designed. In digital computers the two major application areas are (1) scientific (mathematics or engineering) and (2) business (accounting and/or data analysis).

Scientific Computers

It was mentioned in the discussion of the development of computers that there are two different types of *digital computers*. These are those that are particularly adapted to the calculations needed in *scientific* work and those that have not only calculational ability but also can store the tremendous mass of data typical of the records necessary in a *business* firm of any size at all and print out the many types of reports needed by management.

The need for accurate calculations in the development of atomic energy, guided missiles, and other war-related projects puts increased emphasis on the development of digital computers suitable for engineering and mathematical research problems. Funds were made available by the federal government, and a number of universities and equipment manufacturers started to work and, as time passed, brought out continuously improved equipment models.

These earlier pieces of equipment were all specifically designed for their computational ability, and emphasis was placed on the computational speed and accuracy of their circuitry. Provision for the storage of data was not a great problem in scientific work. All that was needed was sufficient storage facilities to store the coded set of instructions necessary to tell the computer the logical steps it was to follow in solving a given problem, an area for the data that was to be manipulated and the data to be used in the manipulation, and a place to store the resulting answer. As an example: instructions for the machine to accept input of one number (say a 4) and a second (say a 2), an instruction for the second to be added to the first, and an instruction either to hold the resulting answer (now a 6) for further manipulation or display the answer, in one of many forms, to the operator.

Business Computers

Computers used in business have requirements that are distinctly different from those used in the scientific areas.

Speed Requirements. Computational ability is not nearly the problem in business data processing it is in scientific data processing. Much of the total computer time spent in business processing procedures is spent in reading data, in searching through masses of information in internal or external memory storage for the associated data to be processed, and in preparing detailed reports for managerial use.

Most of the computational need in processing business data involves very simple addition, subtraction, and, only occasionally, the techniques used in multiplication and division. The period required in searching out the associated data in the processing of a typical business transaction is usually of a long enough duration that any arithmetical application can normally be completed long before the next bit of data is found and prepared for processing.

Input/Output Requirements. In most scientific work, only a limited amount of input is required and, in many instances, only a resultant single answer is provided as the output of a given computational problem. In business information processing, every one of the thousands of transactions that occur daily in a typical business firm must be input into the system and hundreds of pages of reports and analyses are produced daily for historical records and for managerial use.

Storage Requirements. Where the scientific computer only needed modest amounts of storage for the computational work performed, the business computer has large storage requirements.

In a typical business firm, daily transactions will involve many areas of associated records. The sale of merchandise will touch upon records pertaining to sales, personnel (salesmen), payroll (commissions or salaries), cash or accounts receivable (customers), inventory (items in stock), and any number of other records in some individual firms. The purchase of merchandise affects purchases (requisitions or purchase orders), accounts payable (creditors) or cash, inventory (items in stock), and other associated accounts. Other transactions all have their impact on their associated records.

It should be obvious that any one of these typical business records may actually require the storage of hundreds or even many thousands of individual records for the processing of just a single day's transactions. Accounts receivable, accounts payable, and inventories are particularly demanding in terms of storage requirements. In fact, the demands are normally so great that it is not economically feasible for most firms to purchase a computer that has sufficient storage capacity to meet all their storage requirements simultaneously.

FIGURE 6–1. Major Computer Systems Characteristics

System or Model	Memory Capacity		Data Structure	Access Time in Microseconds	I/O Channels		Basic Price ($1,000) – 1974
	Min.	Max.			Std.	Opt.	
Burroughs							
700	16 KB	49 KB	8-bit byte	1/2 B	1	8	39
1700*	16	262	8-bit byte	.667/3 B	5	12	73.5
2700	30	300	8-bit byte	1, 2, or 3/2 B	6	20	236
3700	100	500	8-bit byte	.65	8	20	691
4700	150	500	8-bit byte	.5/2 B	8	80	1,177
6700	393	6,000	48-bit word	.5, 1.2, or 1.5/6 B	1	1	2,122
7700	786	6,000	48-bit word	1.5/6 B	3	18	3,668
Control Data							
1700	4 KB	65 KB	16-bit word	.60	1	4	N.A.
3170	49	131	24-bit word	1.75	2	6	N.A.
3300	16	262	24-bit word	1.25	2	8	N.A.
3500	32	262	24-bit word	.90	2	8	N.A.
Cyber 72	32	131	60-bit word	1.00	12	24	N.A.
Cyber 73	32	131	60-bit word	1.00	12	24	N.A.
Cyber 74	32	131	60-bit word	1.00	12	24	N.A.
Cyber 76	32 Sm. Core	65 Sm. Core	60-bit word	.275	7	13	N.A.
Cyber 76	256 Lg. Core	512 Lg. Core	60-bit word	.275	7	13	N.A.
Cyber 172	32	131	60-bit word	.40	12	24	N.A.
Cyber 173	49	262	60-bit word	.40	12	24	N.A.
Cyber 174	49	262	60-bit word	.40	12	24	N.A.
Cyber 175	49	262	60-bit word	.40	12	24	N.A.
Honeywell							
58	5 KB	10 KB	8-bit byte	1.2	4		31
2020	24 KC	65 KC	6-bit char.	2.75 or 2.5	3	1	64
2030	40 KC	98 KC	6-bit char.	2	6		100
2030A	41 KC	196 KC	6-bit char.	2 or 1.6	6	12	101
2040	49 KC	131 KC	6-bit char.	1.6	8	24	124
2040A	65 KC	524 KC	6-bit char.	1.6/C or 1.5/2 C	8	24	140
2050	98 KC	262 KC	6-bit char.	1.6/2 C	12	18	203
2050A	131 KC	1,048 KC	6-bit char.	1.6/2 C or 1.5/4 C	12	64	245
2060	131 KC	524 KC	6-bit char.	1.14/2 C	16	48	295
2070	131 KC	1,048 KC	6-bit char.	1/4 C	16	64	493
6025	81 KB	131 KB	36-bit word	1.2/2 W	?	?	500
6030 or 6040	65	262	36-bit word	1.2/2 W	8	16	521–585
6050 or 6060	98	262	36-bit word	1.2/2 W	8	96	877–950
6070 or 6080	131	1,048	36-bit word	.5/2 W	8	96	1,277–1,365
IBM							
3*	8 KB	66 KB	8-bit byte	1.5	1	3	16
7*	2	16	8-bit byte	.4	1	6	15
360–20	4 or 8	33	8-bit byte	3.6 or 1.0	1	2	11–44
360–22	25	33	8-bit byte	1.5	2		32
360–25	16	49	8-bit byte	1.8/2 B	1	2	68
360–30	16	98	8-bit byte	1.5	1	3	80
360–40	33	262	8-bit byte	2.5/2 B	1	3	171
360–44	33	262	8-bit byte	1/4 B		4	87
360–50	131	524	8-bit byte	.5	1	4	470
360–65	262	1,049	8-bit byte	.75†		7	546
360–67	262	2,097	8-bit byte	.75†	1 or 2	4	1,076
360–75	262	1,049	8-bit byte	.75/8 B*		7	1,223
370–115	66	98	8-bit byte	.48/2 B	2	1	143
370–125	98	131	8-bit byte	.48/2 B	2	1	232
370–135	98	246	8-bit byte	.275 to 1.49	1	5	281
370–145	164	2,097	8-bit byte	.202 to .315	2	7	658
370–155	262	2,097	8-bit byte	2.1/16 B†	2	4	1,091
370–158	524	4,194	8-bit byte	1.035/16 B	3	4	1,782
370–165	524	3,146	8-bit byte	.08		12	1,975
370–168	1,049	8,389	8-bit byte	.08		12	2,691
370–195	1,049	4,194	8-bit byte	.054/16 B		24	4,366

FIGURE 6–1. (*continued*)

System or Model	Memory Capacity		Data Structure	Access Time in Microseconds	I/O Channels		Basic Price ($1,000) – 1974
	Min.	Max.			Std.	Opt.	
NCR							
50	16 KB	33	8-bit word	.8	2		Mod. 1 47.0 / 71.5
100	16	33	8-bit word	.8	2		89.5
101	16	66	8-bit word	1.2/2 B	2	2	89.5
151	33	131	16-bit word	.75/2 B	2	4	134.0
200	33	512	28-bit word	.65/2 B	4	8	193.7
201	33	512	16-bit word	.65/2 B	8	8	300.0
251	96	2,097	48-bit word	.65/4 B	9	6	478.5
300	131	2,097	48-bit word	.65/4 B	11	4	591.5
UNIVAC							
9200	8 KB	32 KB	8-bit byte	1.20	0	2	42.5
9300	8	32	8-bit byte	.60	1 or 2	0 or 1	142.2
9400	24	262	8-bit byte	.6/2 B	1	2	N.A.
9480	65	262	8-bit byte	.6/2 B	2	1	267.7
9060	131	524	8-bit byte	.6/4 B	2	2	507.7
9070	131	1,048	8-bit byte	.6/4 B	2	5	625.4
9700	65	1,048	8-bit byte	.6/4 B	2	5	N.A.
418III	32	131	18-bit word	.75	8	24	550
494 R.T.	65	262	30-bit word	.75	12	12	1,000
1106	65	262	36-bit word	1.5 or 1.0/B	4	28	1,375
1108	65	262	36/72-bit word	.75/B	8	70	2,140
1110	32	262	36-bit word	.3 to .5	8	88	3,603
Xerox							
Xerox 530	16 KB	128 KB	16-bit word	.80	16	24	20‡
Sigma 5	16	512	32-bit word	.95	8	32	70‡
Sigma 6	128	512	32-bit word	.95	8	24	196‡
Sigma 8	64	512	32-bit word	.90	8	32	225‡
Sigma 9	256	2,048	32-bit word	.90	8	32	425‡
Xerox 550	64	1,048	32-bit word	.65	16	256	104.7‡
Xerox 560	64	1,048	32-bit word	.65	16	261	162.7‡

* 96-Column Card.
† Faster Read-Only Memory.
‡ CPV Only.

A listing of the characteristics of most of the major business and general-purpose computers available today from each of the major manufacturers are given in Figure 6–1. The input/output capabilities of each of these systems are shown in Figure 6–2. The individual characteristics of each of the types of input, output, and storage units are provided along with their description in Chapters 9 and 11. A listing of typical communication devices available is provided in Chapter 10.

General-Purpose Computers

Just as there has been some combination of the analog and digital computers to produce a hybrid system, there has also been a trend in the combination of scientific and business capabilities of these types of digital computers into what is commonly known as general-purpose

FIGURE 6–2. On-Line Equipment Available with Various Systems

	Card Reader	Card Punch	Card Reader Punch	Line Printer	Mag. Disk Drive	Mag. Disk File	Magnetic Tape	Paper Tape Reader	Paper Tape Punch	Magnetic Drum	Optical Char. Reader	MICR	Console	Communications	Mag. Tape Cassette	Magnetic Card	Multi.-Function Machine
Burroughs 700	X	X	X	X	X	X	X	X	X					X	X		X
1700	X	X	X	X	X	X	X	X	X				X	X	X		X
2700	X	X		X	X	X	X	X	X		X	X	X	X			
3700	X	X		X	X	X	X	X	X			X	X	X			
4700	X	X		X	X	X	X	X	X			X	X	X			
6700	X	X		X	X	X	X	X	X			X	X	X			
7700	X	X		X	X	X	X	X	X			X	X				
Control Data 1700	X	X	X	X	X		X	X	X	X	X	X	X	X	X		
3170	X	X	X	X	X	X	X	X	X	X	X	X	X	X	X	X	
3300	X	X	X	X	X	X	X	X	X	X	X	X	X	X	X	X	
3500	X	X	X	X	X	X	X	X	X	X	X	X	X	X	X	X	
Cyber 72	X	X		X	X	X	X	X	X	X			X	X			
73	X	X		X	X	X	X	X	X	X			X	X			
74	X	X		X	X	X	X	X	X	X			X	X			
76	X	X		X	X	X	X						X	X			
172	X	X		X	X	X	X	X	X				X	X			
173	X	X		X	X	X	X	X	X				X	X			
174	X	X		X	X	X	X	X	X				X	X			
175	X	X		X	X	X	X	X	X				X	X			
Honeywell 58	X	X	X	X	X	X		X	X		X		X	X			
2020	X	X	X	X	X	X	X	X	X		X	X	OPT.	X			
2030-2030A	X	X	X	X	X	X	X	X	X		X	X	X	X			
2040-2040A	X	X	X	X	X	X	X	X	X	X	X	X	X	X			
2050-2050A	X	X	X	X	X	X	X	X	X	X	X	X	X	X			
2060	X	X	X	X	X	X	X	X	X	X	X	X	X	X			
2070	X	X	X	X	X	X	X	X	X	X	X	X	X	X			
6025	X	X	X	X	X	X	X	X	X	X	X	X	X	X			
6030-6040	X	X	X	X	X	X	X	X	X	X	X	X	X	X			
6050-6060	X	X	X	X	X	X	X	X	X	X	X	X	X	X			
6070-6080	X	X	X	X	X	X	X	X	X	X	X	X	X	X			

FIGURE 6–2. (*continued*)

	Card Reader	Card Punch	Card Reader Punch	Line Printer	Mag. Disk Drive	Mag. Disk File	Magnetic Tape	Paper Tape Reader	Paper Tape Punch	Magnetic Drum	Optical Char. Reader	MICR	Console	Cummunications	Mag. Tape Cassette	Magnetic Card	Multi.-Function Machine
IBM																	
3	X	X		X	X	X	X	X	X		X	X	X	X			X
7	X	X		X	X	X		X	X				X	X			
360–20	X	X		X	X	X	X	X	X		X	X	X	X			X
360–22	X	X	X	X	X	X	X	X	X		X	X	X	X		X	X
360–25	X	X	X	X	X	X	X	X	X		X	X	X	X			X
360–30	X	X	X	X	X	X	X	X	X		X	X	X	X		X	X
360–40	X	X	X	X	X	X	X	X	X	X	X	X	X	X		X	X
360–44	X	X	X	X	X	X	X	X	X		X	X	X	X		X	X
360–50	X	X	X	X	X	X	X	X	X	X	X	X	X	X		X	X
360–65	X	X	X	X	X	X	X	X	X	X	X	X	X	X		X	X
360–67	X	X	X	X	X	X	X	X	X	X	X	X	X	X		X	X
360–75	X	X	X	X	X	X	X	X	X	X	X	X	X	X		X	X
370–115	X	X	X	X	X	X	X	X	X	X	X	X	X	X		X	X
370–125	X	X	X	X	X	X	X	X	X	X	X	X	X	X		X	X
370–135	X	X	X	X	X	X	X	X	X	X	X	X	X	X		X	X
370–145	X	X	X	X	X	X	X	X	X	X	X	X	X	X		X	X
370–155	X	X	X	X	X	X	X	X	X	X	X	X	X	X		X	X
370–158	X	X	X	X	X	X	X	X	X	X	X	X	X	X		X	X
370–165	X	X	X	X	X	X	X	X	X	X	X	X	X	X		X	X
370–168	X	X	X	X	X	X	X	X	X	X	X	X	X	X		X	X
370–195	X	X	X	X	X	X	X	X	X	X	X	X	X	X		X	X
NCR																	
50	X	X	X	X	X	X	X	X	X		X	X	X	X	X	X	
100	X	X	X	X	X	X	X	X	X		X	X	X	X	X	X	
101	X	X	X	X	X	X	X	X	X		X	X	X	X	X	X	
151	X	X	X	X	X	X	X	X	X		X	X	X	X	X	X	
200	X	X	X	X	X	X	X	X	X		X	X	X	X	X	X	
201	X	X	X	X		X	X	X	X		X	X	X	X	X	X	
251	X	X	X	X	X	X	X	X	X		X	X	X	X	X	X	
300	X	X	X	X	X	X	X	X	X		X	X	X	X	X	X	

FIGURE 6–2. *(concluded)*

	Card Reader	Card Punch	Card Reader Punch	Line Printer	Mag. Disk Drive	Mag. Disk File	Magnetic Tape	Paper Tape Reader	Paper Tape Punch	Magnetic Drum	Optical Char. Reader	MICR	Console	Communications	Mag. Tape Cassette	Magnetic Card	Multi.-Function Machine
UNIVAC 9060	X	X	X	X	X		X	X	X		X		X	X	X		
9070	X	X	X	X	X		X	X	X		X		X	X	X		
9200	X	X	X	X	X		X	X	X		X		X	X			X
9300	X	X	X	X	X		X	X	X		X		X	X			X
9400	X	X	X	X	X		X	X	X		X		X	X	X		
9480	X	X	X	X	X		X	X	X		X		X	X	X		
9700	X	X	X	X			X	X	X		X		X	X	X		
418III	X	X	X	X	X		X	X	X	X			X	X	X		X
494R.T	X	X	X	X	X		X	X	X	X			X	X			
1106	X	X	X	X	X	X	X			X			X	X	X		
1108	X	X	X	X	X	X	X			X			X	X	X		
1110	X	X	X	X	X	X	X			X			X	X	X		
XEROX 530	X	X		X	X	X	X	X	X				X	X			
Sigma 5	X	X		X	X	X	X	X	X				X	X			
6	X	X		X	X	X	X	X	X				X	X			
8	X	X		X	X	X	X	X	X				X	X			
9	X	X		X	X	X	X	X	X				X	X			
Xerox 550	X	X		X	X	X	X	X	X				X	X			
560	X	X		X	X	X	X	X	X				X	X			

computers. In fact, most of the computers produced today are termed general purpose and have characteristics which permit their usage in both scientific and business data processing applications.

The previously discussed requirements in capabilities of the two application areas should make it plain that a given system cannot do both jobs equally well and for a given optimum investment. Individual models of these larger computers will normally be particularly orientated toward meeting one of these requirements with the other need being provided at a somewhat less efficient level based on the hourly cost of its use. This comes about by either a concentration on computational capability, storage capacity, or input/output facilities.

It is possible to design a machine to do business applications that will also do scientific work, but probably in the latter case the computational speed will be slower than desired and, in addition, a lot of storage and input/output equipment may be idle when processing scientific data. On the other hand, a machine designed more specifically for scientific work will probably have limited storage and input/output capability when it is utilized in business applications. Each firm must, of course, carefully consider both areas of needs when deciding on the purchase or rental of a computer system.

BASIC PROCESSING METHODS

There are two basic methods of processing data on digital computers: *batch processing* and *random access processing*. At present the batch method is still, in number of applications, the most widely used method of processing business data. Until recently, lack of economical mass storage devices has limited the use of random access methods. There is, however, an ever-increasing trend toward the random access method. Fairly recent developments in internal memory devices and on-line (available to the processing unit of the computer) mass storage techniques have made it economically feasible for many business firms to enter into random access methods of processing data. This is particularly true of firms involved in time-sharing and multicomputer systems (to be described below).

Batch Processing

To limit the total storage requirements necessary in processing a firm's accounting transactions, the data for specific groups of similar transactions, in terms of the accounts they affect, will be accumulated. Each batch is then processed against the storage files provided for only one (or more) of the affected accounts in each processing run. Thus, batch processing lends itself to situations where the files of data to be used are kept in a systematic manner and access to these files is usually desired in the same manner. Examples include accounts receivable which are filed by customer number and payrolls which are filed by employee number.

As an illustration of batch processing (Figure 6–3), assume that the accounts receivable files are maintained on punched cards (these could be on magnetic tape or disk). The daily credit sales slips would be accumulated over a period of time until a sufficient quantity of sales data is on hand to make it economically feasible to process it on the

FIGURE 6–3. Batch Processing

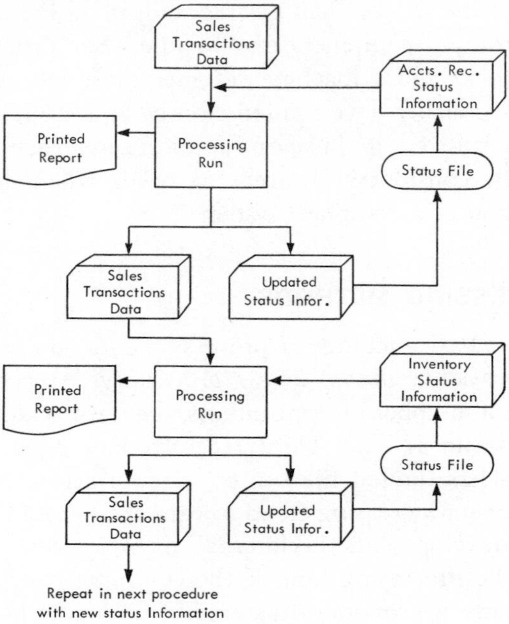

computer. (This might be a day, three days, or even a week in a given installation.) The data would first be key punched into cards, then it would be sequenced and collated with the accounts receivable records or cards of all the customers of the firm. In this way, the batch of credit sales cards read into the computer would be used to update the accounts receivable file. Where desired, the updated cards could be used as the basis for printing a report of the balances of the updated accounts receivable file or in preparing the customers' monthly statements.

In turn, the sales data would be processed with the inventory status data to update the inventory records to show the number of items still in stock on the store's shelves and in the warehouse. Other processing runs with these same sales cards could produce such typical reports as sales by salesman, by type of product sold, and by each store or department.

Note in Figure 6–3 that in the first processing run only a limited amount of computer storage is required for a given sales transaction and the related customers' account record (this entire file of customers might be in storage in some applications). In addition, the program of instructions to direct this processing procedure would also be stored in computer memory. Other batch processing runs would also require relatively little memory of on-line (part of the computer system) storage capability.

The most economical (in terms of processing time required) manner of processing batched data dictates—see Figure 6–3—that both the sales data and the receivable file first be sequenced by customer number. Otherwise, time would be required in searching the files to match customer sale and account together. Because of this requirement the terms batch and *sequential processing* are often used interchangably.

A modification of batch processing that has recently evolved is termed *remote batch processing.* This technique utilizes either geographically remote data gathering systems or the slack time (or otherwise unused time—at night for instance) on intelligent terminals or other small computer facilities to transmit data via telephone lines to a centrally located computer system. As in conventional batch processing, the data to be processed are collected over a period of time, but the input to the processing system is through the remotely located terminal rather than through local conventional card or tape input devices.

Random Access Processing

This method of processing follows much more closely the typical production of data and the pattern of processsing that would be preferred in most business firms. In the course of a period of time, a firm may make sales, order merchandise, pay accounts due, buy or sell assets, or do any of the many other procedural operations resulting from day-to-day business transactions. It is obvious these transactions would not occur in a patterned order but would be random in the nature of their occurrence.

In *batch* processing, the firm may have to wait for a sufficient number of each type of transaction to occur before it can economically process the data. In *random access* processing, the transactions are prepared for input to the data processing system in the random order in which they occur. This means that within a short span of time every account is updated to reflect the transactions which have occurred, rather than being forced to wait while batches of each given type of transaction have accumulated.

The requirements of a computer system capable of processing random data are considerably different from those used in batch processing. The major requirement is that the system have available a vast on-line memory storage capability.

Just as would be the case in any type of record-keeping system, any given transaction has to be processed with its respective status records. Consequently, if a firm is to be able to process (Figure 6–4) all transac-

FIGURE 6–4. On–Line Processing

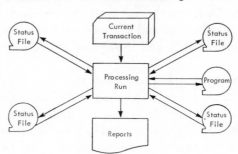

tions as they occur, it must have available, in storage, the status information pertaining to all aspects of the business. When you stop to consider the scope of information required to store all the data pertinent to employees, customers, creditors, merchandise inventory, and the many facets of business records, it becomes apparent that vast storage provisions must be made. In even a fairly small firm, the storage need for this status information may run into many millions of units of data.

In addition to the status information requirement, one would have to provide the instructions needed to tell the computer what to do with each unit of transaction data as it is fed into the computer system. These instructions would have to be made in such depth of detail that each logical procedure used in the processing of the transaction would need to be spelled out in individual steps. It is not at all unusual for a set of instructions, for a given processing procedure, to involve from several hundred up to several thousand individual steps. When these steps in a single procedure are multiplied by the many procedural applications necessary in processing any random transaction that may occur, one has to have many additional million bits of storage available.

In conjunction with the need for tremendous storage files, the equipment must have the facility to select, at high speeds (normally thought of as *access time*) any single unit of status information needed. The techniques involved in providing this ability in equipment will be discussed in the following chapter, but in general, the cost of high-access-speed equipment with very large internal storage capabilities has been economically prohibitive. Most equipment with vast storage facilities is currently in the form of *disk files*. Here the data are stored on stacks of disks, each of which resembles a phonograph record.

The design of disk-type storage is such that it usually requires some mechanical method of moving a read and/or write head from position to position and record to record. As a result, the access time to reach a given bit of information has been much slower than desired. However, some of the newer types of equipment have read/write heads for each disk and others have fixed heads for every position on the disk (Figure 11–12). This has reduced or eliminated much of the mechanical movement, increased data access speeds, and lowered processing costs per unit of data accessed.

VARIABLE AND FIXED WORD LENGTH COMPUTERS

Computers are also referred to as *variable word length* or *fixed word length* machines. The first is usually found in those specifically designed for business applications, while the second, found in scientific computers, usually includes those designed for general-purpose usage.

This classification method relates to the number of units or *bits* (*bi*nary dig*its*) of information handled by the computer in a single unit of data manipulation. The specific group or set of data acceptable as a unit of input into a given computer's memory is termed a *word* (of information), and the number of the units or bits involved is termed a *word length*. If the number of bits involved are always the same for a word, the computer is termed a fixed word-length machine. If the computer is designed so that the word may contain a varying number of bits, it is a variable word-length machine (Figure 6–5).

All of the early computers were fixed word-length machines as they were specifically designed for scientific usage. As the demand for business usage developed, it was found that fixed word-length machines

FIGURE 6–5. Fixed and Variable Word Lengths

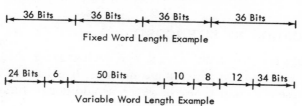

Fixed Word Length Example

Variable Word Length Example

were not efficient in the storage of business data. As an example, a sale of one dollar in merchandise would only utilize three memory locations when it had to be read in as a 32-, 36-bit, or some other fixed-length word. All the other unused positions took up memory locations but had no values stored in them. As memory is one of the most expensive components of a computer, the early fixed word machine was not practical for use in business data processing.

In the second generation of computers (page 127) some equipment was designed to use a variable length word. Thus, if the sale of $1.00 value was recorded, only three memory locations were used, instead of the 32 or 36 units of memory in a typical fixed word length machine. If the sale was for $10.00, only four memory locations were used, and so forth. Thus, an efficient and economical use of memory became available for processing business data.

Most of the third generation and our current computers are general-purpose computers. These utilize a fixed word input, however, the word may be subdivided and packed (Figure 6–6) with several separate units

FIGURE 6–6. A Typical Computer Word

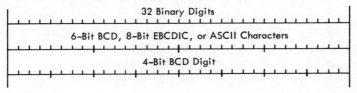

of data. Thus, even though it is a fixed word length, there will be few, if any, unused memory locations in recording business data. For instance, a 32-bit machine can read data in coded form utilizing 32 individual binary digits (for scientific work), as four coded alphabetic characters utilizing a 6-bit or an 8-bit binary coded decimal form, or as eight 4-bit binary coded decimal numbers. (See chapter 7.) Thus, our equipment is now fixed word length in design, but the fixed word may be variable in use depending on the type of data and application involved.

CLASSIFICATION BY SIZE (COST)

Computers are also classified as to size, such as large, medium, small, desk-sized, and more recently, minicomputers. It is hard to draw a line between these classes at times, however, as additional storage and I/O units can expand a given system into a higher classification. The class assignment is usually based on the monthly rental cost of the system.

Large computer systems (Figure 6–7) usually incorporate smaller peripheral systems (slave systems) for use in data preparation for

FIGURE 6–7. Large-Scale IBM System/370 Model 165 Computer System

Courtesy IBM

input and in the printing of the data output to conserve the very fast computing capability of these machines. There are many options available for I/O and large to very large storage capabilities are provided in these systems. Large-scale systems usually rent for over $20,000 per month.

The *medium* computer systems (Figure 6–8) include those falling in the $5,000 to $20,000 monthly rental price group. This class includes

FIGURE 6–8. Medium-Scale UNIVAC 1106 Computer System

Courtesy Sperry Univac

most of the more widely used systems. Computational speed is quite fast, there is a wide range of I/O equipment available, and storage may be increased until it is quite large. However, a combination of these features incorporated into the system may expand it into a *large* classification.

Now that more of the small- to medium-sized business firms are utilizing the computer in their operations, one finds a growing number of *small* computer systems (Figure 6–9) being installed. This group,

FIGURE 6–9. NCR Century 101, a Small-Sized Computer System

Courtesy NCR

in the $1,000 to $5,000 monthly rental range, may be a small card-oriented system or may incorporate some of the features of the *medium* systems.

Desk-sized systems (Figure 4–17) include some of the more sophisticated accounting and bookkeeping equipment up through the card-oriented systems mentioned above. The rental is usually in the $300 to $1,500 monthly range.

In the late 1960s, a trend to provide computerized data processing equipment to meet the needs of the smaller business firms led to the development of very small but true computers which have been termed, *minicomputers* (Figure 6–10).

Minicomputers—though not called by this name until fairly re-

FIGURE 6–10. Honeywell System 700—an Expandable Minicomputer System (basic system is typewriter connsole and central processor in center)

Courtesy Honeywell Information Systems

cently—have been around for a number of years. Until lately, however, these were generally special-purpose machines and most were analog-type equipment. The needs of the smaller business firms had not been adequately met, and the "mini" was a natural development in the evolution of the computer industry.

The purchase price of minicomputers varies considerably from model to model as does their capabilities, but the price ceiling classification seems to include those which sell for less than $25,000.[1] Once equipment of this type and price began to appear on the market, however, wider and wider usage needs began to develop. (See References 2 and 4.)

Most of this equipment has been produced by relatively unknown manufacturing firms rather than by the widely known computer manufacturers. By 1970 there were over 50 firms producing minicomputers with only Honeywell and General Electric (a multiprocess computer)

---

[1] Note that the price range for this class of computer is based on purchase rather than rental costs, as few of this classification are available for rental.

among the big computer firms doing so. By 1973 the overall number of firms manufacturing minicomputers had been reduced somewhat due to competition but production was expanding rapidly for the leaders in the field. IBM was producing their System/3 and System/7 line. Honeywell had purchased and absorbed G. E.'s computer manufacturing and distributing facilities and was producing a mini to small line. Both NCR and Burroughs were producing minicomputers as the top capability of their accounting-bookkeeping machine equipment lines. Other major manufacturers were manufacturing very small—though not quite minicomputers—as part of their regular series of computers.

Today, minis of many types and models are being utilized in processing business data in both small and large business firms. In the smaller firm they may serve in processing the entire set of business records as the major, if not only, data processing device utilized. In the larger firm the mini may process specific applications at remote (at least to the central computer) locations. Here, they probably also serve as intelligent—able to process as well as communicate data—terminals in sending and receiving data to or from one or more central computers.

There is a wide range of I/O and storage devices available for minicomputers. These include "add on" core and semiconductor memory; magnetic tape (both reel and cassette type), disk, and ledger card storage; line printers; card readers and punches; and paper tape readers and perforators (all discussed in detail in Chapters 9 and 11). Most of these are, of course, usually smaller in size and capacity and operate at slower speeds than those designed for use with regular computers.

There is little question but what the minicomputer is here to stay; in fact, it has been suggested that the mini computer may eventually replace most of the small-sized and even many medium-sized computers. This may indicate that as the trend for minicomputer costs goes down and performance goes up, the majority of computers may be typically either in the small or large range. The smaller units may serve as data collectors and concentrators feeding the large centrally located system or acting as a complete system for smaller firms.

INTENDED USE OF THE SYSTEM CLASSIFICATION

General-purpose computer systems designed to serve a large number of users who have a wide variety of problems are generally classified as *multiprocessing systems*. These systems are most commonly found in business data processing installations but may serve other users in a satisfactory manner. The three basic types of multiprocessing systems which have evolved to date are batch processing systems, time-shared systems, and multicomputer systems.

Batch processing systems, previously defined under "basic processing methods," may be traditional in that the central processor is integrally connected to a set of I/O devices. Each computer run is made in turn, with the data files associated with the input information.

Time-shared systems provide computer services to system users on a real-time basis, and several users may utilize the equipment simultaneously—at least it appears so to the user. The reaction time is so fast it seems that the user is the only one asking for data. In such systems, control over the programs and data manipulation are guided by executive and operating programming systems (Chapter 13) which schedule and assign priorities to the system's operation. The typical data entry or inquiry in such systems is via a remotely located terminal connected to the system by telephone lines. Any resultant reply is made over the same system directly to the user. (See References 1 and 5.)

Remote entry batch processing is a widely used combination of batch processing and time-shared systems where real-time service is not required. In this usage batches of data are collected at geographically remote locations and then transmitted to a central computer system in groups or batches of information. (See Reference 3.) This transmission is usually made at a time when the central system is not heavily used (at night for instance) and lowers the size and capacity requirements of the central system. If time is being purchased from a computer utility firm, the cost of the service is lowered considerably. Transmission of the data may utilize terminals, minicomputers, or even multicomputer systems.

Multicomputer systems may involve two computers which can communicate directly with each other in performing jobs which are generally special purpose in nature. An example could be where an analog process computer and a digital computer are utilized in an oil refinery or other process control application.

A second type of multicomputer system is where two or more computers not only communicate with each other but also utilize the memory, input, and output devices of each other without any restraint outside of that imposed by the executive programming system, which is usually provided by one specific computer of the group. This type of system is rarely found outside of extremely large systems.

A third and more commonly found multicomputer system is where one computer acts as the heart of a system of several computers. These serve to provide input/output interfaces in what is in reality a single system composed of several processors and associated equipment. This is the typical system found, where a centralized computer is fed by and serves geographically remote computer installations. An example would be a business with a headquarters and a number of regional offices with each having their own installation which is, at times, interconnected to the central headquarters installation.

CLASSIFICATION BY GENERATION OF DEVELOPMENT

Computers may also be classified into rough groupings which have been called generations. These generations usually are indicative of a significant scientific breakthrough or improvement in computer manufacturing technology. The first-, second-, and third-generation computers have been pretty well established and the present day may become known as the fourth-generation of development. Figure 6–11, showing pictorially the development of IBM computers, is typical of the developments which have occurred that justify the different generations of computers.

FIGURE 6–11. IBM Computer Development

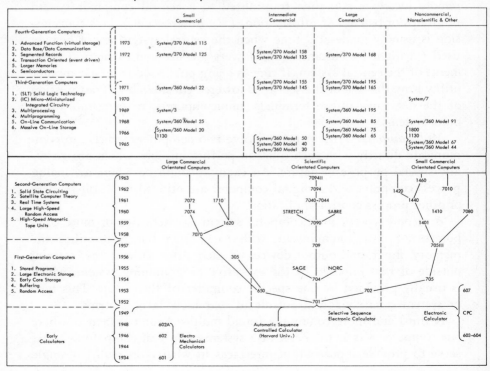

First-Generation Computers

Many of the forerunners of present-day computer manufacturing firms found their beginning in the development of one or more pieces of equipment in the late 1940s and early 1950s. Most of these were single units of a semispecial nature but later were improved and modified to become the ancestors of more general-purpose equipment. The know-how and staffs developed in this period provided the technical background and the leaders of many of the firms existing today.

The sequential development of computers in the initial development stage which produced the first-generation computer was, first, in the adoption of electromagnetic relays, which were then used in punched card equipment to provide control over the calculations performed. The sequential input of both instructions to the equipment and the data to be acted upon was generally through the use of punched paper tape or manually set dials or switches. In equipment produced in the intermediate stage, sequential contact was performed by externally wired plugboards similar to those used on punched card equipment. Later, the input of both instructions and data utilized punched cards and magnetic tape as input media.

Storage of data was minimal at first, but as needs arose and techniques became available, storage capability increased. At first, the relays themselves "held" or indicated the data, but as time passed, mercury delay-line storage, massive banks of vacuum tubes, and electrostatic memory using a cathode-ray tube (similar to the TV tube of today) were used. Finally, in the later part of this initial development stage, magnetic cores (discussed in detail in Chapter 11) were almost universally used to provide internal-type memory or storage. Magnetic tape was also introduced as a new external-type storage.

One of the more important developmental concepts of the first-generation period was that of the internally stored program. This utilized internal memory banks to store either part or, later, all the instructions to the equipment to perform the solution of the problem under consideration. The data on which the calculations were to be performed were also stored in memory and called for by the equipment as needed in the calculations. Intermediate results would be held in storage until needed, and final answers were either placed in storage or outputed in the form of punched paper tape, punched cards, dial settings, or light indicators to the operator of the equipment.

Another developmental concept of this period was that of buffering, which ordered the input, output, or movement of data and instructions through a type of priority system so that data, instructions, and calculations would not be commingled and become meaningless.

Buffers serve as temporary storage devices in that as data are fed to the computer they are held until the proper time (in terms of priority or nonuse of a given part of the system) and then fed into the operating system. In the case of outputs from the computer, the reverse procedure takes place in temporarily storing output information until the proper output device is available. An example of this last would be where a printer is currently busy on one set of output data but another set has also been prepared which is held in the buffer until the first job is completed.

Another important development of this first-generation period was that of random access to data. Most equipment of this period could only process data in some form of serial or sequential order. This was

FIGURE 6–12. Changes in Circuitry and Components

(a)   Vacuum Tube Circuitry, Transistorized Circuit Board, and
       Solid Logic Technology Chip

Courtesy of IBM

(*b*)   Second- and Third-Generation Components

Courtesy of IBM

usually satisfactory in the processing of mathematical or engineering data of that period but was very inefficient in the processing of business data.

Second-Generation Computers

With the development of the transistor and other solid-state components (Figure 6–12), along with techniques to mass produce circuit-board-type wiring components, the stage was set for the second generation of computers. This period is generally conceded to have started about 1958 with the introduction of the IBM 1620, IBM 1401, and UNIVAC solid-state computers. Of course, computers produced by other manufacturers and additional IBM and UNIVAC equipment were quick to follow the initial introduction of solid-state computers.

The previously used vacuum tubes (and thousands were used in early computers) were now replaced by transistors and diodes, which were much more reliable over long periods of time than were the vacuum tubes. These could be tested periodically to determine their operating level and could be replaced before this level fell to a point that would affect efficient operation. When computer users adopted testing schedules utilizing regular preventive maintenance techniques, they solved many of their problems relating to the upkeep and avoidance of downtime on their computer systems.

The concept of random access data processing was further developed by most computer manufacturers, and removable disk packs (see Chapter 11 for details) were developed which permitted machine-readable files to be stored nearby for quick insertion into disk drives when a given file of data (such as accounts receivable, inventory, or accounts payable) was needed to process current transactions. Magnetic drums, cores, and film were also made available for use in random access data processing. Through an extension of these techniques, the concept of "on-line real-time" data processing using remote terminals (see Chapter 15) began to be more than just a possibility.

Another major development in this second-generation period was that of high-speed magnetic tape units which made available reels of magnetic tape. These provided relatively cheap data storage which could be placed on tape drives as needed and utilized directly by the computer at high speeds. Even though this data had to be processed sequentially (serially), these magnetic tape units provided usable massive data storage at an economical cost.

Data transmission and communication devices were developed in this period to provide the capabilities necessary to develop fundamental techniques required in sending and receiving data from both local and remote data processing centers.

Manufacturers began to develop computer systems which could be expanded from a small- or medium-sized system to a large system. These computers were expanded by compatible equipment units utilizing what is often termed the "building block principle." Thus a system could expand with the growth and needs of the firm rather than being completely replaced by a new system.

The developments of this period resulted in a realization that the computer was not only here to stay but—to business in particular—it was to become more than just a device to replace the calculators and punched card machines. Its capabilities provided management with the means, for the first time, of having a true management information system capable of meeting most of their needs (through historical records, statistical data, forecasts, and management science techniques).

Third-Generation Computers

The third generation of equipment, developed in the early 1960s, brought about the utilization of miniaturized components which had been developed for use in the space programs. By the mid-1960s, these became microminiaturized and utilized what is now termed solid logic technology (SLT) to incorporate the components required in many circuits into small monolithic units or solid blocks (Figure 6–12a). These SLT components require low voltages, produce very little heat, are far more reliable than comparable components of the past, and are ultrasmall in size.

In the late 1960s, this technique became even more refined and dozens of components began to appear on integrated circuitry (IC) to further decrease the size, voltage requirements, and heat dissipation while increasing the reliability, efficiency, and speed of operation (Figure 6–13).

FIGURE 6–13. LSI Circuit Board

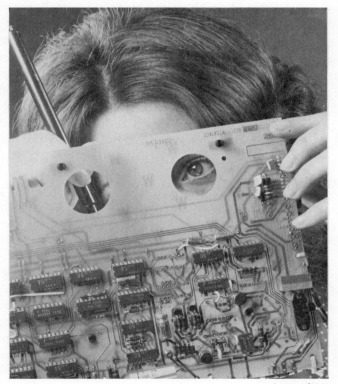

Courtesy of NCR

The IBM System/360 Model 85 and System/370 computers utilize a monolithic systems technology composed of chip-type components in what is now termed large scale integration (LSI). These components may be extremely densely packed at up to 53,000 components or more per square inch.

Massive on-line data storage capabilities are now available to provide reliable high-speed access to literally millions to billions of units of stored data.

There is almost an endless expansion and implementation of new techniques in data collection, data transmission, and data communication which permits the utilization of remote terminal and display unit facilities to be on-line with centralized computer installations.

On-line real-time systems' capabilities are now a reality through the use of remote facilities and newly developed multiprogramming and multiprocessing techniques. Executive control programs (see Chapter 13) have been developed which permit many individual operating programs to be processed in what, to the uninitiated, appears to be a simultaneous operation through multiprogramming. Not only can many operators using remote facilities communicate with the computer at one time, but it is now possible for computers to communicate with other computers through multiprocessing. This permits local computers, of a given firm, to communicate with the large centralized computers of that firm to provide and receive data and to utilize the additional processing capabilities of the large computer as they are needed locally.

Fourth-Generation Computers?

There is still some question as to whether we have entered into the fourth generation of computers. The changes which have taken place have mostly been in the rapid expansion in the use of minicomputers, the widespread use of terminals, and in the upgrading of what was known as the third generation of equipment (as in the case of the IBM/370 versus the IBM/360 systems). These changes include: (1) Faster and more extensive but smaller-sized memory devices (Figure 6–14); (2) improved capabilities in switching to and communicating with peripheral, remote I/O equipment and other computer systems; and (3) large capacity on-line storage systems. These last include add-on core memory devices, larger capacity and faster disk files, and higher density and faster magnetic tape units.

Though it had been widely predicted, there is still no widespread use of semiconductor type memory devices. However, the IBM System/360 Model 85 introduced a small "cache" type semiconductor memory and the System/370 Model 135 and 145 followed with more extensive memory capacity of this type. In each case though the semi-

FIGURE 6–14a. Silicon Chip Smaller Than Eye of a Needle

FIGURE 6–14b. Magnified Chip and Circuitry Equivalent to That in 300 Portable Radios

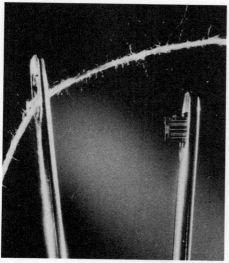

Courtesy of NCR

Courtesy of NCR

conductor memory (2 and 5 million bits respectively on the 370 models) supplemented larger magnetic core memory (18 and 27 million bits respectively). A growth in the use of semiconductors (Figure 6–15) in both integrated circuitry and in memory devices seems fairly assured as the seemingly ever-increasing demand for smaller, faster, and less costly memory continues.

These above changes may well prove to be distinctive enough to classify this equipment as fourth generation even though they seemed to have evolved over time (rather than being marketed as a breakthrough or something radically different) in the period in which these changes took place. Only time itself and the extension of these techniques, along with public acceptance and approval, will determine if this equipment is classified as fourth-generation computers.

However, regardless of what generation our present computers represent, the "hardware" developments of the currently available equipment are such that the capabilities of these machines have now become so extensive and complex that the only limitation—now and in the foreseeable future—seems to be in the imaginative and creative ability of humans in devising new usage techniques and developing the "software" to implement them.

FIGURE 6–15. Thin Film and Semiconductor Circuit Boards

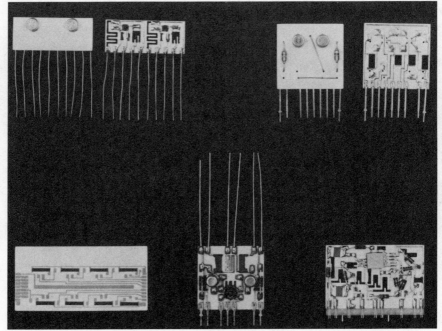

Courtesy Burroughs Corp.

REFERENCES

1. ARNDAHL, LOWELL D.   "Computers and Communications—New Trends and Applications." *Telecommunications*, January 1974, p. 32.

2. DAVIS, SIDNEY.   "A Fresh View of Mini- and Macrocomputers." *Computer Design*, May 1974, p. 67.

3. GALLAGHER, VINCENT E.   "Best of Two Worlds: Local Processing but With Centralized Files." *The Data Communication User*, March 1974, p. 119.

4. GARDNER, W. DAVID.   "Those Omnipresent Minis." *Datamation*, July 1973, p. 52.

5. SCHIFF, FREDERICK S.   "The Use of Time-Sharing in the CPA Firm." *Journal of Accountancy*, January 1974, p. 62.

QUESTIONS

1. Differentiate and clearly explain two basic differences between analog and digital computers.

2. Why is it useful and necessary to have these two basically different kinds of computers?

3. In what type of situations are analog computers most frequently used?

4. In what types of situations are digital computers most frequently used?

5. What type of computer is primarily used in accounting and data analysis work?

6. How do hybrid and general-purpose computers differ?

7. What do you see as the primary difference between the scientific computer and the business computer? In answering this question be certain to point out the differences between the problems with which these two computers are dealing.

8. Give three examples of business data processing activities which you would consider should be batch processed. Explain why you chose each example.

9. How does remote batch processing differ from batch processing? Explain.

10. What capability does random access processing of data provide management which is not possible when batch processing is used?

11. Give a business-type example in which you think random access processing would be the most desirable. Explain why you think so.

12. Do you think the programming problems for performing random access processing would be any different than for batch processing? Explain carefully your reasoning.

13. Are the physical equipment needs for the company doing batch processing going to be any different from the company doing random access data processing? Explain what some of these differences might be.

14. What does "word length" have to do with the problems of data processing for a businessman.

15.. What makes a large computing system large and a small one small? Explain.

16. Explain some of the principle advantages a third-generation computer user has over a first-generation machine user.

7

Computer Organization and Codes

IN EVERY TYPE of business information processing system, certain basic elements must be present. These elements must achieve the required basic concepts of originating, recording, classifying, sorting, summarizing, calculating, and communicating.

COMPUTER ORGANIZATION

Input must be provided, as instructions, data, and information must have some way of getting into the system. Then, there must be some provision for the *storage* of the information so that it can be used later. It may be reclassified, manipulated arithmetically, or recalled for presentation in its original form. There must also be some provisions for the *control* of the data processing operations, for the *processing* of the data to meet the requirements of given procedures, and an *output* in the form of reports or analyses.

In the electronic computer processing system the *input* of data is performed by various types of input devices which also frequently serve as output devices as well. Typical input devices (described in Chapter 9) include those accepting punched cards, magnetic tape, punched paper tape, magnetic ink, films, analog computer output, optically scanned data, and typewritten material, and there is always the provision for data to be entered into the system through the switches and buttons on the console of the computer itself.

The *central processing unit* of the computer system is made up of three distinct sections which perform different functions. First, the unit provides a control section for the *control* of all the operations performed by the computer through predetermined instructions (programs) stored internally in the machine. This control section directs and coordinates the entire computer system as a single multipurpose machine.

Second, this unit provides an *arithmetic-logic* section. The arithmetic part of this section performs the operation of addition, subtraction, multiplication, division, shifting, transferring, and storing. The logic part of this section provides the machine's ability to test comparisons and various conditions found during processing procedures and to take any action required as the result of the test. Such a test might be one to determine if one number is larger than, equal to, or less than another number. The next procedure to be performed would then vary depending on the condition found in the test.

The third and last section provides the *memory* or storage facilities required for the retention of the input information, the program which directs the processing, and the files of data needed for reference or additional processing.

Storage consists of two distinct types: *internal memory,* which is contained in the central processing unit itself; and *external on-line storage,* which is contained in separate storage devices external to the central processing unit but which is available, on demand, to the computer when it is requested by the control section. A third type of storage is that of *off-line storage,* which provides data storage in some form that is not interconnected to, or directly usable by, the computer. An example of this last is that of punched cards filed in a storage cabinet. Data stored in both the internal and external on-line storage devices must, of course, be filed in some machine-acceptable form which is understood by the particular computer in use. Off-line storage data may or may not be in a machine-acceptable form, depending upon the need of the system.

Output devices in a computer system record, write, or display information as directed by the computer. This output may be presented in some coded form (such as punched cards, punched paper tape, magnetic tape, magnetic disks, or console lights), it may be printed out on paper (by typewriters or various types of printers), displayed on some form of graphic or CRT (cathode-ray tube similar to television) display, or even presented in the form of electrical impulses used to direct other computers (particularly to analog computers which direct various physical control devices).

STORED PROGRAMS

It has long been the desire of people to have machines lighten their load. As mechanical devices were developed, they did this to some extent, but such devices still required the personal attention of people in the performance of each function, such as in turning wheels, twisting knobs, pulling handles, and depressing keys. With the invention and development of the computer, however, much of the old dream began to be realized. For the first time, a person could "write out" a set of instructions which could be used to direct the computer in an extensive procedural operation, which could be stored in memory, and which could provide the data necessary to the procedure. All the person had to do was punch a button telling the machine to "get started" and literally wait while the work was completed at a fantastic speed.

This self-directing ability of the computer is centered in the control section of the central processing unit. This unit acts upon a series of prepared coded instructions which have been fed into the memory section of the computer—usually in internal storage—to direct the computer in performing its data processing task.

The series of coded instructions used in directing the computer in performing a given procedure is known as a *program*. The fundamental ideas necessary to the preparation of such a program (programming) are presented in Chapter 13. The individual steps of the program are those logical steps necessary to complete the processing procedure. These will, of course, vary with the computer in use and the procedure under consideration but would normally direct the various devices under the control of the computer in the manipulation of the data. Data would be read into the computer, stored, processed as directed, and the results indicated in some output form. The possible variations of such a stored program provides the data processing system with almost unlimited flexibility.

COMPUTER DATA CODES

Just as data must be communicated between people in the form of spoken words or written words or symbols, so must data be communicated from humans to computers. Though experimental efforts are being made in directing the computer in its work by voice communication, the many complexities of human languages have, to date, restricted this means of instruction to a limited number of commands. Consequently, almost all computer instructions have been in some form of writing. As you will learn in Language Supplement B, the more modern program languages can be written in the English language, and these are acceptable to the machine. However, since the English language is very inefficient for internal computer usage a provision has been made for the computer to convert the English language instructions to some form acceptable to the computer. The codes and symbols acceptable vary with the computer and the associated input, output, and storage devices in use, and the conversion to these language forms is an almost automatic operation. Consequently, there may be some question as to the necessity of people being able to "speak" the language of the computer. However, in the course of writing, testing, and correcting a program, it is sometimes necessary to determine what—and where—data are contained in storage and what are the individual operations as they are performed on the data. This, plus the fact that most input forms of data are also in some form of code, makes it necessary for those associated with computer systems to get acquainted with some of the various forms of data representation used. Also, it should be a point of interest to have a little understanding of how the computer operates internally.

Binary Codes

Nearly every code form utilized in computer communication is based on some adaption of the binary number system, as this has proven to be the most efficient system for use in computers. This system differs from the decimal number system, which is based upon tenths and the digits 0 through 9, in that data can only be represented by two digits in the binary system; 0 and 1. These binary notations are also called *bits* (a contraction of binary digits), with the 0 condition described as *no bit* and the 1 state described as a *bit*.

The representation of two possible conditions or states, termed a binary mode, can be expressed in many ways, and many different forms of binary modes are found in computer coding (Figure 7–1). In the punched card the 0 state is expressed by the absence of a hole in the card and the 1 state is the presence of such a hole and indicates the presence of data. In the magnetic core, a small unit of storage used in computers, current flows either in one direction or the other. In the case of relays or switches, the circuit is either open or closed. In electronic tubes or transistors, current either flows or it doesn't flow. And, for continuous electrical currents, there is either a pulse (surge

FIGURE 7–1. Binary Indicators

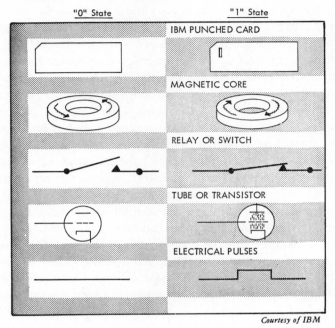

Courtesy of IBM

of current) present or there is not a pulse. These are only typical binary mode representations and certainly do not exhaust the many conditions which might also indicate a 1 or 0 state.

Once the 1 and 0 state is understood, one needs to progress to an explanation of how the presence of such a bit or no bit can be utilized

FIGURE 7–2. Place Value of Binary Numbers

etc. ←	2^6	2^5	2^4	2^3	2^2	2^1	2^0	*Power of 2*
etc. ←	7	6	5	4	3	2	1	*Place Position*
etc. ←	64	32	16	8	4	2	1	*Place (Bit) Value*

in the representation of data to the computer. If there were a series of such states (Figure 7–2) and each bit position were assigned a progressive value of powers of the number 2, the first place position would represent 2 (two to the zero power) and have the place value of

1, the second would represent 2^1 or a place value of 2, the third 2^2 or a place value of 4, the fourth 2^3 or 8, and so on until our series of place positions are all assigned a place value. It is also interesting to note that as you progress in the series from right to left, each place position is double the value of the previous. Thus with the first position assigned a place value of 1, you double this and arrive at the place value of 2 for the second position, double this for a value of 4 for the third position, again for an 8 in the fourth, and so on for the series.

These place-positioned values (Figure 7–3) indicate that if there is a 0 or no bit condition in each of the place positions in a series,

FIGURE 7–3. Binary Place Value Addition

64	32	16	8	4	2	1	Bit Values
0 +	0 +	0 +	0 +	0 +	0 +	0	= 0
0 +	0 +	0 +	1 +	0 +	0 +	1	= 9
1 +	0 +	1 +	1 +	0 +	0 +	1	= 89

there is no data representation. If there are 1s or bits in the first and fourth place positions (with no bits in the other positions), there is a binary coded representation of the decimal number 9. $(1 \times 2^0) + (1 \times 2^3) = (1 \times 1) + (1 \times 8)$ which, in turn, equals the decimal number 9. If there are bits in place positions one, four, five, and seven there is the binary representation of $(1 \times 2^0) + (1 \times 2^3) + (1 \times 2^4) + (1 \times 2^6)$ or $(1 \times 1) + (1 \times 8) + (1 \times 16) + (1 \times 64)$ which equals the decimal number 89.

To obtain the binary equivalent of a decimal number, select the largest binary place position (highest power of 2) whose value does not exceed the decimal number. Deduct its decimal value from the decimal number and repeat until there is no remainder left. For example, to obtain the binary equivalent of the decimal number 86, the largest power of 2 which does not exceed 86 is 2^6 whose decimal value is 64. Deducting 64 from 86 leaves 22. Next would be 2^4 or 16 which is deducted and leaves the decimal 6. Then deducting the decimal value of 2^2 or 4 one obtains a 2 whose binary equivalent is 2^1. Thus, $2^6 + 2^4 + 2^2 + 2^1 = 86$. However, to write these in binary form one must assign binary values "0" or "1" to each of the series of place positions affected, or $(1 \times 2^6) + (0 \times 2^5) + (1 \times 2^4) +$

$(0 \times 2^3) + (1 \times 2^2) + (1 \times 2^1) + (0 \times 2^0)$, which binary values, in turn, becomes the binary number 1010110.

The above method is not difficult when you are accustomed to working with binary numbers or the binary number is not too large a value. Where this is not the case, however, another method is available to aid in conversion. This method is to make a continued division of the decimal number by 2 and record any remainder not divisible by 2. Reading the remainders from bottom to top and placing them in order from left to right the binary equivalent desired is obtained. Using the same example above:

		Remainder
2	86	0
2	43	1
2	21	1
2	10	0
2	5	1
2	2	0
2	1	1
	0	

Reading upward we obtain 1010110 or 86.

Now that you have seen how the equivalents of decimal numbers are represented in the binary number system, you need to consider how the arithmetical operations of addition, subtraction, multiplication, and division are accomplished using binary numbers. First, recall one of the things which must be remembered in the decimal number system. If one is adding a column of decimal numbers, there is no problem if the total of the units position does not exceed the number 9. However, if the total is 10, 11, or more you have to put down the unit number of the answer and "carry" the 10s, or larger, portion of the answer over to the next, or 10s, column of the numbers you are adding and continue until all colunms are added.

In binary addition the same general rule of "carry" holds except that now there are only two possible numbers (0 and 1) to add. Thus a set of rules can be developed which may be followed in the addition of binary numbers by using a matrix of numbers to array the data as illustrated in Figure 7–4. However, it is important to understand that a computer only adds two numbers at a time and then adds the product to a third number and so on.

To follow a practical example of binary addition involving "carry" conditions, take the numbers 0011 + 0100 + 0101 as shown in Figure

FIGURE 7–4. Binary Addition Matrix Array

	0	1
0	0	1
1	1	0

0 + 0 (column 1, row 1) = 0
0 + 1 (column 1, row 2) = 1
1 + 0 (column 2, row 1) = 1
1 + 1 (column 2, row 2) = 0, carry 1*

* If a series of 1s are to be added, each time a 1 is added to a 1 a carry results. Thus you may have several "carrys" to start with when adding the next column.

FIGURE 7–5. Binary Addition

8	4	2	1		Bit Values
1	1	1		"Carry" values	
0	0	1	1	= Digit	3
+ 0	1	0	0	= Digit	4 to be added
+ 0	1	0	1	= Digit	5 to be added
1	1	0	0	= Answer 12	

7–5. In the first, or units, column add the 1 in row one to the 0 in row two, and following the rules above obtain an answer of 1. Then adding this 1 to the 1 in row three obtain an answer of 0 with 1 to carry. In the second column, add the carried 1 to the 1 of the first row to obtain a 0 with a carry of 1. This 0 when added successively to the 0s in the second and third rows provides an answer of 0 for this column. In the third column, add the carried 1 to the 0, the answer 1, this added to 1 provides an answer of 0 with one to carry. This 0 is added to 1 for a column total of 1. In the fourth column, the carried 1 is added to the successive 0s for a column total of 1. Thus, the complete total is 1100 which is equivalent to the decimal equivalent total of the three binary numbers $(3 + 4 + 5)$.

In decimal arithmetic, if a larger number is subtracted from a smaller number, a unit digit must be "borrowed" from the first column to the left which contains a decimal digit. This rule also carries over into binary arithmetic and follows in the rules for subtraction developed from the binary subtraction matrix array in Figure 7–6.

An example of binary subtraction is shown in Figure 7–7 where the number 00101 is subtracted from 11001. In the first column, 1 is subtracted from 1 leaving 0. In the second, 0 − 0 = 0. In the third, 0 − 1 (following the rule above) = 1. (In effect, what has happened is that an eight is borrowed as two 4s, and when one 4 is subtracted,

FIGURE 7–6. Binary Subtraction Matrix Array

	0	1
0	0	1
1	1	0

0 – 0 (column 1, row 1) = 0
0 – 1 (column 1, row 2) = –1, or 1 with 1 borrowed
1 – 0 (column 2, row 1) = 1
1 – 1 (column 2, row 2) = 0

FIGURE 7–7. Binary Subtraction

	16	8	4	2	1	Bit Values
			1			"Borrowed" values
		0	1			(2–4's for the 1–8)
+	1	1̸	0	0	1	= +25
–	0	0	1	0	1	= – 5
	1	0	1	0	0	= 20 Answer

there is a balance of 4 left.) In the fourth column, 0 — 0 (the 1 was borrowed for the previous column) = 0. And in the last column, 1 — 0 = 1 for a complete total of 10100. Converted to decimal equivalents, 25 — 5 = 20.

If the subtraction problem above was reversed, that is, 11001 from 00101, where a larger number would be subtracted from a smaller, the numbers would be arrayed just as they are above (with signs reversed) and the resulting answer would be a negative number.

Rules for multiplication can be developed from the binary multiplication matrix array as shown in Figure 7–8.

FIGURE 7–8. Binary Multiplication Matrix Array

	0	1
0	0	0
1	0	1

0 × 0 (column 1, row 1) = 0
0 × 1 (column 1, row 2) = 0
1 × 0 (column 2, row 1) = 0
1 × 1 (column 2, row 2) = 1

To multiply in the binary system, you follow the same procedure as in the decimal system. First you multiply the multiplicand by the multiplier. If these numbers each contain two or more digits, there will as a result be two or more rows of numbers forthcoming which need to be totaled before the answer is obtained. Thus, both the rules of multiplication and addition must be applied. Multiplying 1101 (13) by 1011 (11) thus produces the answer 10001111 (143) as shown in Figure 7–9.

FIGURE 7–9. Binary Multiplication

128	64	32	16	8	4	2	1		Bit Value
				1	1	0	1	=	13 Multiplicand
				1	0	1	1	×	11 Multiplier
				1	1	0	1	=	13 First operation
	1	1	1						"Carry" values
				1	1	0	1	+	26 Second operation
	1	1	0	1				+	104 Third operation
1	0	0	0	1	1	1	1	=	143 Answer

The rules for division in binary numbers follow exactly the same rules for long division in decimal numbers. When determining how many times the divisor will go into the dividend, the rules of multiplication are needed, and when you are determining if there is a remainder, the rules of subtraction are required. As an example, follow the division of 10001111 (143) by 1011 (11) to obtain the resulting answer 1101 (13) in Figure 7–10.

FIGURE 7–10. Binary Division

	8	4	2	1		128	64	32	16	8	4	2	1			Bit Values
								1	1	0	1			=	13 Answer
Divisor 11 =	1	0	1	1		1	0	0	0	1	1	1	1		=	143 Dividend
						1	0	1	1					−		88 First operation
						0	1	1	0	1	(1	1)		=	55 Result balance
						1	0	1	1					−		44 Second operation
						0	0	1	0	1	1			=	11 Result balance
						1	0	1	1					−		11 Third operation
								0						=	0 Remainder

It must also be remembered that subtraction can be performed by using the complement of the number to be subtracted and adding to produce the proper answer.

$$
\begin{array}{ll}
25 & 25 \\
\underline{-13} & \text{or} \quad \underline{+99987} \text{ Complement of 13} \\
12 & 100012 \text{ (always ignore the last carry)}
\end{array}
$$

Multiplication may be performed by the repeated addition of the multiplicand the number of times indicated by the multiplier.

$$
\begin{array}{cc}
10 & 10 \\
\underline{\times\ 5} & +10 \\
50 & +10 \\
 & +10 \\
 & \underline{+10} \\
 & 50
\end{array}
$$

Division can be accomplished by determining how many times the divisor can be subtracted from the dividend.

$$10 \div 5 = 2 \qquad 10 - 5 = 5 - 5 = 0 \ (\text{Answer 2})$$

These last methods of subtraction, multiplication, and division are all used in some different makes and models of computers, and the use of binary arithmetic is equally applicable to these methods. This presentation of how arithmetical calculations are performed in computers is to develop "just a glimmer" of the technical aspects involved and to allow the reader to have some understanding of how these "electronic brains" perform.

Binary Coded Decimal System (BCD). Once the binary number system is grasped, it is easy to understand the binary coded decimal system of numbers. If you use only four positions of place values—8, 4, 2, and 1—it will be seen that these four positions can provide the binary equivalent of the decimal digits 0 through 9 (Figure 7–11).

FIGURE 7–11. Binary Representation of Decimal Digits

8	4	2	1	Bit Value	
0	0	0	0	=	0
0	0	0	1	=	1
0	0	1	0	=	2
0	0	1	1	=	3
0	1	0	0	=	4
0	1	0	1	=	5
0	1	1	0	=	6
0	1	1	1	=	7
1	0	0	0	=	8
1	0	0	1	=	9

Then, if these groups of four bit values are assigned the units, tens, hundreds, thousands, and so forth, designation (as is done in a series of digits in a number in the decimal system), one is then able to express the decimal number 6,452 in binary coded decimals (BCD) as

Thousands	Hundreds	Tens	Units	
6	4	5	2	Decimals
0110	0100	0101	0010	Binary Coded Decimals

instead of 1100100110100 as in binary code.

The BCD system is subject to the same procedures used in performing arithmetical calculations as was the binary system of numbers. In addition it is possible to adapt the binary coded decimal system to provide, in addition to numbers, the alphabetic letters and characters needed in processing business data.

In the Hollerith punched card code, named after the developer of the card code, numbers were expressed by a single punched hole in the digit punch area. Letters and characters were provided by the addition of a zone punch(s) in combination with a digit punch (chapter 8). Now to return to the binary coded decimal system. If four binary bit positions provide the numeric digit needed, one can add two additional binary bits to the bit array and assign them A and B zone designations to provide the zone bit(s) required in combination with a digit bit in the designation of letters and characters (Figure 7–12). Where three

FIGURE 7–12. Bit Positions, Seven-Bit Alphameric Code

Check Bit	Zone Bits		Numeric Bits			
C	B	A	8	4	2	1

zones—12, 11 and 0—are provided in punched card code the B bit can be the equivalent of the 11 zone, the A bit can be the equivalent on the 0 zone, and a combination of both the A and B bits can be the equivalent of the 12 zone (Figure 7–13). Usually a seventh bit position (in 8-bit codes a ninth bit) is added and checked, by the equipment involved, to provide what is called a "check" bit. This permits computers to check automatically the data as entered into the machine for valid data codes. This procedure is termed a *parity check,* which in some equipment is an even number of bits (even parity) and in others an odd number of bits (odd parity). As data are transmitted, each character is automati-

FIGURE 7–13. Comparison of Zone Bit Usage

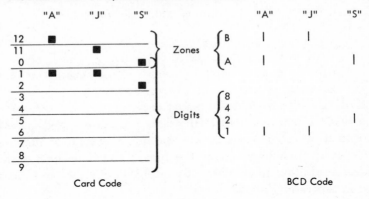

Card Code   BCD Code

cally checked to determine if the correct parity condition exists (Figure 7–14). In the illustration, check bits are added for the letters *A, B, L, T,* and the numbers 1, 2, 8. If this had been an odd parity device, check bits would have been added for *C, J, K, S, U,* and 3. As data is moved from one device to another, the parity is checked and modified as required.

FIGURE 7–14. Even Parity, Horizontal Check

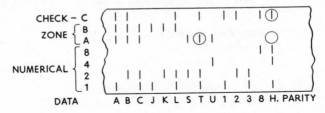

Bits may be lost or added to the data code in several ways. Typically, in the loss of bits the tape may have a flaw or a dirty spot on it that prevents a bit being recorded, a severe impact may shift or destroy data on magnetic tape or disks, or they may even be subjected to a magnetic field (unknowingly or intentionally). Undesired bits may be acquired by an undesired magnetic field from a magnet, an electrical circuit in a nearby coil as in a motor, or even from lightning striking transmission wires as data is transmitted.

In some equipment there is also a horizontal parity check performed on each channel at the end of a given unit of data where bits are added for the parity condition found in each channel. If a bit had not been recorded, such as the circled item above the letter *T,* there would have been a horizontal parity bit necessary, see blank circle, and the horizontal parity bit for the *A* channel would not have been required. However, the parity needs for the *C* channel would not be in the agreement with the parity needs for the horizontal parity column. This would be sensed automatically and a check made as to where the error might be by a reread procedure.

Some equipment recently developed is so sophisticated that once it has determined where an error, such as the above, exists, it can automatically make a decision to correct the error and insert the missing bit or bits required. Not all bit errors are this simple, so only certain types of errors are automatically corrected.

Hexadecimal Code. To offset the disadvantages of the long strings of zeros and ones in the binary code representation of large numbers, a base 16, rather than a base 2, number system is utilized in several computer systems, which includes the widely used family of computers in the IBM System/360.

In the hexadecimal number system each hexadecimal digit represents four binary digits (Figure 7–15). Just as in base 10 number systems, 10 numerical symbols are required, and in base 2, or binary, 2 symbols are necessary, the base 16 hexadecimal system utilizes 16 symbols. These symbols include the familiar 0 through 9 numbers and in addition use the letters *A* through *F* to provide a total of 16 symbols, whose place values 1 through 16 are assigned in ascending order, first to the 0 through 9 and then to *A* through *F* symbols.

In Figure 7–15, the hexadecimal representation of the decimal num-

FIGURE 7–15. Decimal, Hexadecimal, and Binary Notation

Decimal	Hexadecimal	Binary	Decimal	Hexadecimal	Binary
0	0	0000	16	10	10000
1	1	0001	17	11	10001
2	2	0010	18	12	10010
3	3	0011	19	13	10011
4	4	0100	20	14	10100
5	5	0101	21	15	10101
6	6	0110	22	16	10110
7	7	0111	23	17	10111
8	8	1000	24	18	11000
9	9	1001	25	19	11001
10	A	1010	26	1A	11010
11	B	1011	27	1B	11011
12	C	1100	28	1C	11100
13	D	1101	29	1D	11101
14	E	1110	30	1E	11110
15	F	1111	31	1F	11111

bers 16 through 31 is provided by a 1 in the "carry" position. Other decimal numbers are provided by using larger hexadecimal values in carry positions.

To convert binary numbers to hexadecimal notation, simply divide the number into groups of four binary digits, starting from the right, and replace each group by the corresponding hexadecimal symbol. If the lefthand group is incomplete, fill in zeros as required. For example, the binary number

$$
\begin{aligned}
111110011011010011 &= 0011/1110/0110/1101/0011 \quad \text{BCD} \\
&= \quad 3 \quad \quad \text{E} \quad \quad 6 \quad \quad \text{D} \quad \quad 3 \quad \quad \text{Hex} \\
&= (3E6D3)_{16}
\end{aligned}
$$

If the binary number is a fraction or a mixed number, care must be taken to mark off groups of four bits from each side of the decimal mark. Thus the binary number

$$
\begin{aligned}
1011001010.1011011 &= 0010/1100/1010.1011/0110 \quad \text{BCD} \\
&= \quad 2 \quad \quad \text{C} \quad \quad \text{A} \ . \ \text{B} \quad \quad 6 \quad \quad \text{Hex} \\
&= (2CA.B6)_{16}
\end{aligned}
$$

Similarly, to convert hexadecimal numbers into binary, substitute the corresponding group of four binary digits for each hexadecimal symbol and drop off any unnecessary zeros. For instance, the hexadecimal number

$$
\begin{aligned}
(6C4F2E.7B8)_{16} &= \quad 6 \quad \text{C} \quad 4 \quad \text{F} \quad 2 \quad \text{E} \ . \ 7 \quad \text{B} \quad 8 \quad \text{Hex} \\
&= 0110/1100/0100/1111/0010/1110.0111/1011/1000 \quad \text{BCD} \\
&= (11011000100111100101110.011110111)_2 \quad \text{Binary}
\end{aligned}
$$

The meaning of hexadecimal numbers is made clear by expansion in powers of 16. For example, the hexadecimal number 2CA.B6, above, means (when decimals are substituted for hexadecimal symbols)

$$
\begin{aligned}
&(2 \times 16^2) + (12 \times 16^1) + (10 \times 16^0) + (11 \times 16^{-1}) + (6 \times 16^{-2}) \\
&= (2 \times 256) + (12 \times 16) + (10 \times 1) + (11 \div 16) + (6 \div 256) \\
&= 512 + 192 + 10 + 0.6875 + 0.0234375 \\
&= 714 + 0.7109375 = (714.7109375)_{10}
\end{aligned}
$$

In working out an example of this type, it is best to arrange the products in a vertical column for convenient addition.[1]

Binary Codes with Expanded Capability.   Other terminology, closely associated with computer coding, which will be used in conjunction with various equipment in illustrations to follow, is "words" and "bytes." As previously described, a "word" is a varying group of bits representing characters or numbers (the number of bits required depends on the computer system involved) which is acceptable to the

[1] International Business Machines Corporation, *A Programmer's Introduction to the IBM System/360 Architecture, Instructions, and Assembler Language* (White Plains, N.Y., 1966), p. 28.

equipment as a unit of input or internal manipulation. In some of the general-purpose computers currently in use the "word" may be sub-divided into several "bytes" (an 8-bit unit) each of which, in turn, may be divided again into two four-bit units. Currently most computers use a word of 32 binary bits (Figure 6–6). This word may be subdivided into four 8-bit bytes each of which may be used to record a single alphabetic letter or special character (four zone bit positions and four digit bit positions with place values of 8, 4, 2, 1). Each byte may be divided into two 4-bit units to record two digits (four bits each with place values of 8, 4, 2, and 1).

The 8-bit byte can be used to record in the 6-bit BCD code or it can be utilized in one of the newer expanded capability codes which provide a possible 256 bit combinations including codes for upper and lower case letters, digits, symbols, machine controls, and a number of, as yet, unassigned codes. The first of the 8-bit codes was called the Extended Binary Coded Decimal Interchange Code, commonly called "eb c dic" (EBCDIC). This is illustrated in Figures 7–16 and 7–18.

FIGURE 7–16. Extended Binary Coded Decimal Interchange Code

Bit Positions → 01	00				01				10				11			
4567 \ 23 →	00	01	10	11	00	01	10	11	00	01	10	11	00	01	10	11
0000	NUL				BLANK	&	-						>	<	‡	0
0001							/		a	j			A	J		1
0010									b	k	s		B	K	S	2
0011									c	l	t		C	L	T	3
0100	PF	RES	BYP	PN					d	m	u		D	M	U	4
0101	HT	NL	LF	RS					e	n	v		E	N	V	5
0110	LC	BS	EOB	UC					f	o	w		F	O	W	6
0111	DEL	IDL	PRE	EOT					g	p	x		G	P	X	7
1000									h	q	y		H	Q	Y	8
1001					.		,	"	i	r	z		I	R	Z	9
1010					?	|		:								
1011					.	$	,	#								
1100					◄	*	%	@								
1101					(	)	⌐	'								
1110					+	;	−	=								
1111					‡	¢	±	✓								

Courtesy of IBM

A more recent attempt to develop a universal or standard code for all uses has resulted in the American Standard Code for Information Interchange (ASCII—pronounced "askey") shown in Figures 7–17 and 7–18.

FIGURE 7–17. American Standard Code for Information Interchange

4321	00/00	00/01	01/00	01/01	10/10	10/11	11/10	11/11
0000	NULL	DC_0	b blank	0	@	P		P
0001	SOM	DC_1	!	1	A	Q	a	q
0010	EOA	DC_2	"	2	B	R	b	r
0011	EOM	DC_3	#	3	C	S	c	s
0100	EOT	DC_4 STOP	$	4	D	T	d	t
0101	WRU	ERR	%	5	E	U	e	u
0110	RU	SYNC	&	6	F	V	f	v
0111	BELL	LEM	'	7	G	W	g	w
1000	BKSP	S_0	(	8	H	X	h	x
1001	HT	S_1	)	9	I	Y	i	y
1010	LF	S_2	*	:	J	Z	j	z
1011	VT	S_3	+	;	K	[	k	
1100	FF	S_4	,	<	L	\	l	
1101	CR	S_5	-	=	M	]	m	
1110	SO	S_6	.	>	N	↑	n	ESC
1111	SI	S_7	/	?	O	←	o	DEL

Identification of Control Symbols and Some Graphics

NULL	Null/Idle	V TAB	Vertical tabulation	$S_0 - S_7$	Separator (information)
SOM	Start of message	FF	Form feed	b.	Word separator (space, normally non-printing)
EOA	End of address	CR	Carriage return		
EOM	End of message	SO	Shift out	<	Less than
EOT	End of transmission	SI	Shift in	>	Greater than
WRU	"Who are you?"	DC_0	Device control ① Reserved for data link escape	↑	Up arrow (exponentiation)
RU	"Are you . . .?"			←	Left arrow (implies/replaced by)
BELL	Audible signal	DC_1 -		\	Reverse slant
FEo	Format effector	DC_3	Device control	ACK	Acknowledge
HT	Horizontal tabulation	DC_4 (stop)	Device control (stop)	②	Unassigned control
SK	Skip (punched card)	ERR	Error	ESC	Escape
LF	Line feed	SYNC	Synchronous idle	DEL	Delete/Idle
		LEM	Logical end of media		

Courtesy of IBM

FIGURE 7–18. A Comparison of Typical Data Input Coding

Letter or Digit	Punched Card Zone Digit		Binary 8421	BCD BA 8421	EBCDIC 01234567	ASCII 76×54321
a	NA		NA	NA	10000001	11100001
A	12	1	NA	110001	11000001	10100001
j	NA		NA	NA	10010001	11101010
J	11	1	NA	100001	11010001	10101010
t	NA		NA	NA	10100011	11110100
T	0	3	NA	010011	11100011	01110100
1		1	0001	000001	11110001	01010001
3		3	0011	000011	11110011	01010011
8		8	1000	001000	11111000	01011000

QUESTIONS

1. Briefly describe the functional components of a computer installation.

2. What purpose do each of these components (described in question 1) serve?

3. Assume that a program for a particular application was in punch card form. What would be done with these program cards before the actual program could become operative?

4. Why is it possible for the outputs of a computer system to be in so many different forms?

5. Why is it that digital computers all use some variation of the binary numbering system? Why isn't the decimal numbering system good enough?

6. Express the number 387 in a straight binary numbering system. Express the number 387 in a binary coded decimal form.

7. Does the binary coded decimal system possess advantages over the straight binary numbering system? If so, what?

8. Explain how a parity check works.

9. Does the parity check assure the accuracy of the data to the user of the equipment? Explain.

10. Explain how alphabetic letters may be expressed in binary coded decimal.

11. How does the hexadecimal code differ from the BCD code?

12. Express 23 in hexadecimal code.

13. Take the numbers 57, 21, and 94, express their binary equivalents and add them to provide the answer in binary form. Show carries.

8

Computer Input/Output— Data Preparation

THERE IS A WIDE RANGE of input/output equipment combinations available with most computer systems. These vary as to type of unit (for the various and differing needs of individual systems); as to the speed and capability of each unit (as smaller or slower units are less expensive); and as to type of data I/O media required by the given unit. The typical I/O units and their characteristics and capabilities are discussed in Chapter 9. A discussion of the preparation of the data media for the more common I/O units and the input preparation equipment available follows in this chapter.

There are a number of techniques utilized in the coding and preparation of input data to be used in computer systems. As to which is best for a given system depends on the overall data processing system. A decision to use a given type of input may rest on many differing circumstances such as the type of business (at times), and even the whims or biases of the individuals recommending and purchasing the equipment for the system.

If, for example, the firm is a bank, it is almost certain that magnetic ink character-recognition equipment will be involved, as this form of input has been universally adapted by the American Banking Association and the Federal Reserve banking system. A savings and loan association or a credit union may utilize magnetic ledger cards as at least one type of input equipment, as they not only need machine-processable data for processing purposes but also need an inexpensive "hard copy" human readable document to refer to. Very small retail firms may not be able to afford a computer system, but they may utilize a service bureau to process their data which will specify the type of input they desire. In such instances the bookkeeping machines, adding machines, typewriters, and even cash registers may produce some type of computer acceptable input as a by-product of manual operations. The type of input produced may involve punched cards, punched paper tape, or optically scannable tape, characters, or forms. Almost all of these and many other forms of input may be converted into another form, such as magnetic tape or disk, before being utilized in a given system as computer input.

When a large-scale computer system is under consideration, with its tremendous manipulation and calculation capabilities, it would probably dictate that some fast input capability be provided, and this means that probably either magnetic tape or disk would be the input medium. However, in most computer systems and in terms of total volume usage, the most commonly found input form has traditionally been the punched card. Even here, though, changes are taking place in the capturing of data from originating documents. Keyed tape and keyed disk data recording (described later in this chapter) have been expanding rapidly the past few years until they probably come close to equalizing in volume of data recorded that which is key-punched into cards. Optically scanned data input has grown slowly over time in volume but, except for specialized instances, this technique has not been able to compete economically with keyed-type data input systems.

INPUT MEDIA CODING

Each type of input media has its own, often unique, method of presenting data in coded form. The immediately following segment of this chapter will be concerned with the characteristics of the coding and the placement of data in the punched card. The other input media codes will be discussed in later chapters in conjunction with the overall description of those individual types of equipment.

Punched Cards

The punched card is one of the many media forms which can be used as input into a computer system. As each card is designed to contain certain facts concerning a single business transaction (one line of an invoice, for example), it is sometimes referred to as a *unit record.* One way to visualize typical unit records would be to think of the individual debits and credits to ledger accounts. Thus, each of the individual sales cards would serve both as a "debit" to the customer's account and a "credit" to the sales account for the merchandise sold. A payment made by a customer recorded on a card would be a "debit" to the cash account and a "credit" to the customer's account receivable. Other items such as purchases, payments on what the firm owes, returns of merchandise, and so forth would each be recorded on a single unit record punched card.

Punched cards were one of the early forms of input utilized in electronic computer data processing systems because of their wide usage in unit record (punched card) systems. The card quickly became and probably still is the most commonly used input form for computers.

The punched card is a thin piece of cardboard 7⅜ × 3¼ inches in size (Figure 8–4). These particular dimensions were those of our paper currency in the period of development of the punched card and were arbitrarily chosen to also be the standard size for the punched card. This type of card has become accepted as the standard card for use with most data processing equipment utilizing the punched card for either the input or output of information.

A new size and type of punched card was introduced, however, by IBM late in 1969 to be used as input to its then newly announced System/3 computer system. This card (Figure 8–1) is 3⅜ inches long and 2¾ inches high and contains three rows of 32 columnar positions to provide 96 units of recorded data. The holes are round and quite

FIGURE 8–1. 96-Column Card

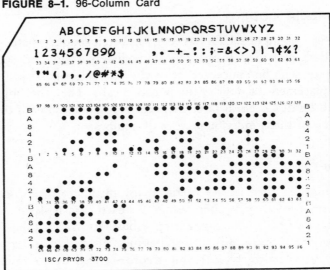

small in diameter. The punching code utilizes a 6-bit alphanumeric Hollerith code with *B* and *A* Zone positions and the BCD 8,4,2,1 digit representation as described later in Chapter 8. This card is now being used by other companies as well as IBM, and it appears it will have heavy usage in some of the smaller computer systems.

Special Features Available. Though the standard card is the most common card size used, it is far from being the only size that can be used. Special cards are all the same height as the standard card, but they may vary in length from one third the size of the standard card to a document 16 inches in length. These are "special" in that they are used for special or particular purposes in certain machine installations where there is a need for a card shorter or longer than the size that has become the standard. The shorter than standard card may be used as both input and output, however, the longer card is only used as a form or document on which output data may be printed.

The basic or standard color for cards is off-white, but many other colors and color combinations are available where there is a need for color identification for the various types of information punched in cards or for special preference requirements. These colors may be in the form of stripes or bands across the card, solid-color cards, partial or overall tinted cards, or even combinations of colors, stripes, and tints to provide an almost infinite variety of combinations that can be secured by special order.

Other special features available on cards include:

1. Prenumbering and prepunching of repetitive or consecutive series of numbers for tallying and control purposes.
2. Special scoring and creasing of cards to facilitate tearing or folding.
3. Corner cuts, notches, holes, and perforations for identification purposes.
4. Tabs or stubs that extend beyond the general area of the given-sized card which may serve as receipt stubs or evidence of some action taken.
5. Special printing on the face of the card so that it may be used as an invoice, check, and so forth.
6. Cards attached in the form of books or continuously folded cards.

Many other types of special features are also available as required for special purposes but are not used in sufficient quantity to deserve mentioning here.

Punched Card Coding. The standard card is commonly called an 80-column card as there are 80 vertical columns available for punched holes. These vertical columns are numbered from left to right on the card from number 1 through 80.[1] Any one, several, or all of the punched columns can be selected and read or interpreted as individual alphabetical letters, numbers, or characters representing pertinent information. In addition to the vertical columns there are also 12 horizontal rows in which the position of the punched hole or holes indicates to the machines whether the information in a given column is a letter, a number, or some special character such as &, $, #, %, and so forth. These horizontal rows are numbered from top to the bottom of the card by zones and digits. (Figure 8–2). The first three rows are the

FIGURE 8–2. Zone and Digit Rows

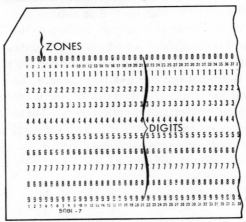

12, 11 (sometimes called "X"), and 0 zones. The third row from the top down through the bottom row are the digit rows and are numbered for the digits they represent: 0 through 9.[2] Thus, by a given punched hole, or set of holes, in the horizontal rows of a certain vertical column it is possible for the machine to read the information represented.

---

[1] Some early Remington Rand Univac punched card equipment utilized the same standard-sized card, but the punching was in a 90-column arrangement made up of columns 1 through 45 in the upper half of the card, and columns 46 through 90 in the lower half of the card. Round holes were punched in the six punching positions of a single column in both the upper and lower halves of the card for data representation. Numbers were represented by a single hole or a combination of two holes punched in a single column. Alphabetic characters were represented by a differing series of combinations of two or three holes punched in a single column.

[2] It should be noted that while there are specified rows representing 3 zones and 10 digits, there are only 12 rows in the card. This results from using the third row as both the "0" zone and the digit zero.

Data to be processed in punched card or computer systems must be punched in the card according to a predetermined standard arrangement. This arrangement or card design as it is usually called, is generally preselected for each individual business unit, as almost every firm has its own peculiarities as to the information pertinent to its general type of business and the arrangement in the orginating documents of that firm.

This standard arrangement or grouping of information in the design of a card is made possible through the use of *fields* of information. A field of information is the designation given to any single unit, or group of information, punched into a column, or succeeding columns, in a card. Typically, this would be the data needed to represent the recording of each fact concerning a business transaction and would include such items as an address, name, invoice number, amount of a sale, and so on. After the card has been punched and checked (verified), it is a permanent *unit record* which can be used to provide the information required in the many phases of data processing.

If a field consists of a single zero or number, it is punched into the card by a single rectangular punch in a predetermined column of the card (column 11, Figure 8–3). However, a field consisting of a

FIGURE 8–3. Field Punching

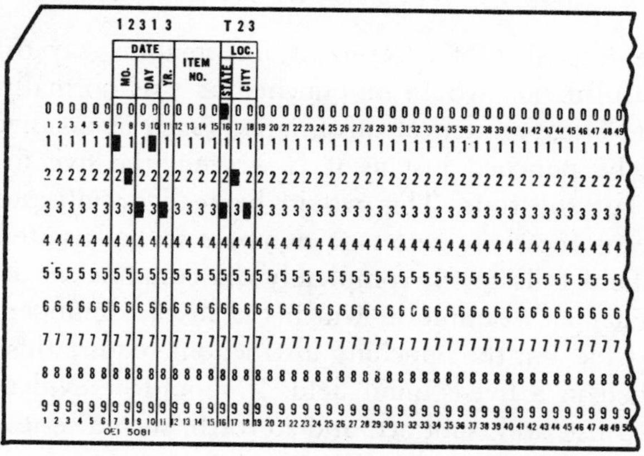

single letter of the alphabet requires two holes to be punched in a given column of the card (column 16). Two holes are required as there are 26 letters of the alphabet, but only 12 possible positions in the card to record a letter. The combination of a high or zone punch (12, 11, or 0) with a low or digit punch (0 through 9) is used to provide the coded language of punched cards that represents the letters of the alphabet and most special characters. Figure 8–4 illustrates the punches required for the alphabet, digits, and special characters of the Hollerith code (46-character keyboard), as well as additional special characters provided for by other codes (64-character keyboard).

FIGURE 8–4. Card Code Punches

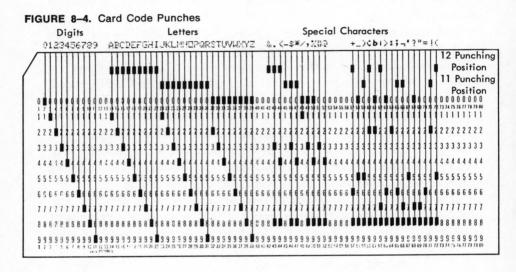

If the field consists of a series of information, say three columns wide, the information would be punched as it is normally read, from left to right. Thus, numerical information, such as an invoice number 574, would be punched just as it is written, the five first, then the seven, and last the four. This would be read or interpreted as 574.

In many instances the series of numbers to be inserted in a given designated field fails to fill completely the columns set aside for that entry. Consider an example in which the invoice number 574 is only three digits wide, but the punching instructions require this information to be punched in a five-column field. It should be evident that if the machine is to list, add, subtract, and so forth, such a series of numbers, the significant digits must be aligned to provide a meaningful report or answer in exactly the same manner as if they were being written down by hand preparatory to adding up a series of numbers. The "unit" digits would all be in the same column, the "tens" digits would be in another column, the "hundreds" digits in still another, and so on through all the significant digits.

The alignment of a field containing alphabetic information of variable length is handled in a manner similar to that for numeric data except that the alignment of data is made from the left position of the field. Blank columns are allowed in alphabetic fields to signify the spaces between words and to space over otherwise unused columns where the information is of shorter length than the field space allowed.

INPUT MEDIA PREPARATION

As previously mentioned, there are many methods and techniques involved in the preparation of input data for a given computer system. Many of these, however, produce only a small fraction of the total input data utilized in most systems. There are optical scanning devices (Chapter 9) which hold great potential as semiautomatic data preparation or accumulation devices, but to date their cost has delayed their widespread adoption. Punched paper tape, as mentioned earlier, may be produced as a by-product of the operation of a typewriter, adding machine, bookkeeping machine, or other device and used as input into a computer system. Magnetic ink character recognition (MICR), described later, also serves as computer input but its usage is almost entirely restricted to the banking and related fields of business operations. However, keyed data preparation is the leading source of input data for most computer system installations. (See References 2 and 3.)

The major keyed-data entry systems are those which produce punched card, magnetic tape, and magnetic-disk recorded input data. Also included in this general classification would be keyed terminals, console typewriters, and several keyed manual devices whose output is in a machine usable form. Most of this last group of equipment has previously been discussed in Chapters 3 and 4.

The use of keyed magnetic media recorders has grown considerably since the very late 1960s. However, the actual number of units installed is about 100,000 units as compared to well over 500,000 card punch installations. There is little question but what the growth trend of this form of capturing data input will continue as the need for faster and more economical methods of input preparation is an ever-expanding demand.

Card Punching

To prepare punched cards on a card punch (Figure 8–5) an operator reads the data to be punched from a source document. Keys on the

FIGURE 8–5. Card Punching

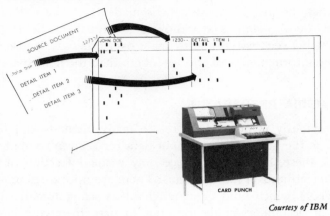

Courtesy of IBM

FIGURE 8–6. Card Punch 64-Character Keyboard

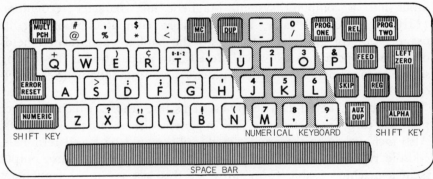

Courtesy of IBM

keyboard of the equipment (Figure 8–6) are depressed and coded holes representing the data are punched into selected vertical columns of the card. Depending on the model of the equipment, numeric, alphabetic, or a combination of numeric and alphabetic information may be punched. If a printing card punch is used, the data punched may also be printed, column by column, at the top of the card and directly above the coded punch in the card.

There are five basic card positions on the card punch (Figure 8–7). First, the *card hopper,* where the input cards are stored until they are fed downward to the punch bed in *feed position,* where they are held

FIGURE 8–7. IBM 29 Card Punch

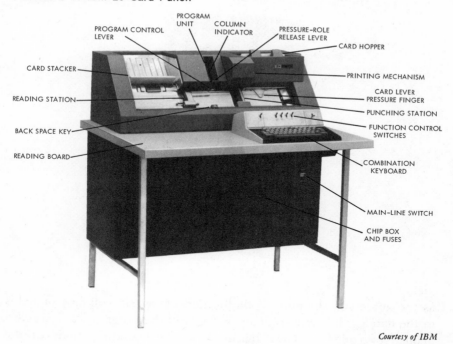

Courtesy of IBM

under the *card level pressure finger.* Cards are advanced from the feed position under the *punching station,* where they advance column by column as data are punched or the column skipped because no data are required. Once the card is punched or fed through the punching station, it moves to the read bed and is positioned under the *reading station* as a second card is positioned under the punching station. This card advances synchronously with the card in the punching position and may, if so instructed, be "read" by the brushes at this station so the data may be transferred (duplicated) into the card under the punch to perform the duplication function below. As cards advance through the reading station, they are eventually "stacked" in the *stacker position* until either the punching operation is completed or the stacker position acquires sufficient cards to push the toggle-type switch to "off" position, which cuts the electrical power to the equipment.

The *program unit* at the top center of Figure 8–7 is controlled by a program card wrapped around the program drum (Figure 8–8). This program card has coded holes punched in it which are read by the program unit and instruct the machine in such automatic operations

FIGURE 8–8. Program Drum

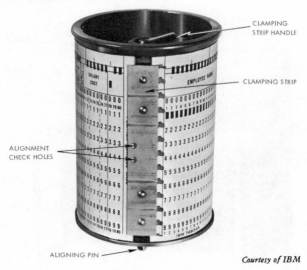

Courtesy of IBM

as the automatic skipping or duplication of certain columns or fields in the data card. These columns or fields in the program card are also defined by coded punches. Inasmuch as the operating mode of the equipment is always numerical when it is under program control (alphabetic when under manual control), there is a provision for an automatic shift to the alphabetic mode provided by a punched hole code. An illustration of a typical program card and the operation controlled is shown in Figure 8–9.

A word of caution to the student is always necessary at this point

FIGURE 8–9. Program Card

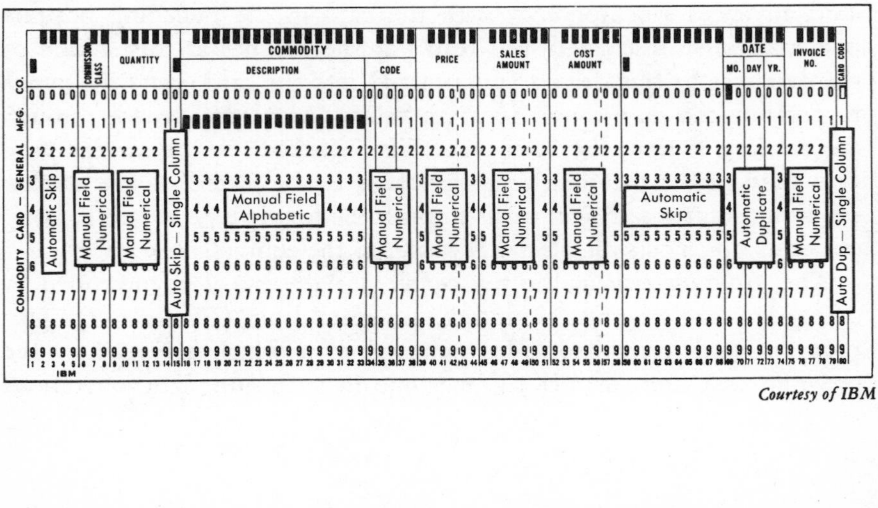

Courtesy of IBM

regarding the coded holes in the program card. This code is not in any manner related to the coded information to be punched in the data cards. The program card code is only used to control certain automatic operations which may be performed on the card punch.

Verification

Once data has been punched into a card it is in computer input acceptable form. However, it is normally advisable to check the accuracy of the data recorded (Figure 8–10). Incorrect data may have been

FIGURE 8–10. Verifying

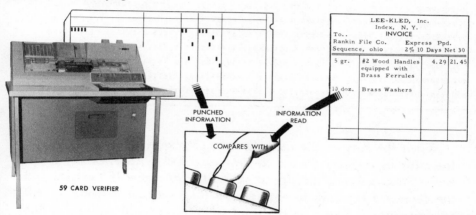

Courtesy of IBM

keyed into the card by the operator as the wrong data may have been read from the originating document or the wrong key may have been depressed in error. This verification function is usually performed on a card verifier (some models of the card punch may also perform this function).

The card verifier is similar in appearance to the card punch and is essentially different only in the function performed. An operator (usually one other than the punching operator) follows the same procedure as in card punching in reading data from an originating or source document and depressing keys on a keyboard. Instead of punching holes, however, the previously punched holes in the card are verified as being the proper coded punches for the data keyed. If the coded holes are satisfactory, the card moves to the next column, where the operation is repeated, and continues until the data check of the entire card is completed. As the card is checked and is moved into the next operating position, a notch is cut in the upper right edge of the card to indicate that verification is completed (Figure 8–11).

FIGURE 8–11. Verified Card

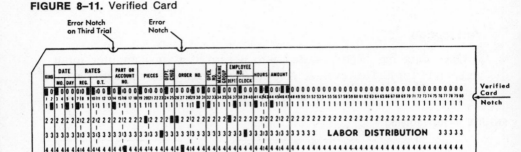

When the data in the card do not agree with the key depressed, the error light comes on and the keyboard locks. An error key is depressed and a second attempt at verification is made. If the data and the depressed key still do not agree, a third attempt is made. If still no agreement is found on the third try, the card will advance to the next column in the card, but an error notch will be cut in the top of the card above the column error. This provides a ready identification of cards with errors and of the column in error after the verification of a deck of cards is completed.

In most of the standard card punches, holes are physically cut into a card as data is keyed. Consequently, a card which has an error punched into it can be corrected only by punching the correct data into another card. Most of the data on a card containing an error is usually correct, however, and may be duplicated—by the card punch— into the new card with only the errors being manually corrected.

Verifying Punches. To offset some of the above difficulty in error correction of cards some of the newer verifying punches (Figure 8–12)—which were first marketed in the very late 60s and early 70s— have memory capability. This permits the data entered for two 80-character record lengths to be held in storage. Errors may be corrected any time before the data is entered into a card by backspacing

FIGURE 8–12. UNIVAC 1701 Verifying Punch

Courtesy of Sperry UNIVAC

to the error position and keying in the correct data. Some special editing features are also available in this equipment.

The features available in this equipment provide a data entry system that is nearly as flexible as some of the key-to-tape and key-to-disk systems to be described below. This flexibility has permitted card punching to hold its own to a great extent against the competition of these newer techniques in keyed data entry. (See Reference 1.)

Keyed Magnetic Tape Input

Punched cards are read rather slowly—compared with other forms of input—and have proven to be an input bottleneck to most computer systems. Since the late 1960s, a number of manufacturers have followed the 1965 introduction of the Keyed Data-Recorder by Mohawk Data Science Corporation with models of their own keyboard-to-magnetic tape recording equipment.

There are two distinct types of keyed tape equipment. The most common type at present is that which records the data on full-sized reels of magnetic tape compatable with those utilized on computer tape drives (Figure 8–13). These may be mounted on those drives and

FIGURE 8–13. NCR   735–101   Magnetic   Tape Encoder

Courtesy of NCR

read directly by the computer system. The other type utilizes magnetic tape cassettes (Figure 8–14) which may or may not be computer compatible as only a few computer systems have cassette input capability at present. The cassette may be utilized at remote locations for use there or to capture data for later conversion by communication devices which may be used on-line to transmit the data to a central computer system.

In basic equipment of either type of keyed tape recorder, an operator depresses keys on a keyboard, similar to that of a card punch, but instead of producing punched cards, the equipment records the data onto magnetic tape. The keyed data may be entered directly onto the tape in coded form, but most keyed tape units provide for the data to be accumulated, by record lengths or blocks, in storage before entry onto the tape. This permits the operator to visually observe the data keyed and to make any error corrections required before the data is

FIGURE 8–14. Magnetic Tape Cassette

Courtesy of NCR

entered onto the tape. However, the tape data may be verified independently by another operator in much the same manner as that used in the verification of punched cards. In keyed tape verification it is not necessary to have separate recording and verifying devices as the basic recording unit can be switched to perform this function. Errors on tape are corrected by writing the correct information over the incorrect rather than by producing a new tape.

The keyed-tape recording devices were developed to permit data to be recorded directly onto magnetic tape as magnetized spots rather than into punched cards as punched holes. This permits the utilization of a much faster form of data input (magnetic tape) into the computer system. There is also an advantage in keyed tape recorders in that some limited memory is provided so that the data may be held and, if necessary, corrected before it is entered onto the tape (in punching cards the hole is punched as the key is depressed and corrections involve punching a new card).

The use of keyed tape and keyed disk (described in detail later) recorders, to replace keyed card punching units, involve a number of factors which must be considered by management in making such a decision. Foremost, of course, is the requirement that the computer system have magnetic tape drives as input devices. Other factors involve the volume of data to be captured and the location or locations where the data is to be captured.

If the volume is small, then the computer system will probably be small and the use of cards will either be more appropriate or will not present any particular problem as to the input time requirement. If the volume is large and the keying is performed in a central location, then either keyed tape or disk recording should certainly be considered. However, if data is prepared for computer input in various departments or regional locations and the volume is not too large at any one point, then there may be some question as to what would be best. Also, if these areas are at remote locations, the type of communication facilities available will be a factor to be considered.

This keying method of recording data directly onto magnetic tape has been further expanded to (1) permit data to be remotely input and transmitted to a key tape recorder, where the data would be received and fed onto tape; (2) permit data recorded on punched paper tape or punched cards to be converted to magnetic tape records; (3) permit data to be fed into the recorder through an adding machine, which also produces a hard-copy tape; (4) permit data to be read from magnetic tape by the recorder and printed out either on line printers or on typewriters to produce a printed copy of the recorded information; (5) permit data recorded by many operators on short tapes to

FIGURE 8–15. Singer 4300 Magnetic Data Recording System

be consolidated onto standard magnetic tape reels; and (6) permit data to be recorded by many operators—some systems up to 64 operators—onto a single shared tape or individual tapes (Figure 8–15) which are then "unloaded" at high speed onto magnetic tape reels.

There are a number of verifying and operating features which may be available, depending on the equipment selected, to assist in error control and to increase through-put which are not available on competing card punch units.

Keyed Magnetic Disk Input

Data preparation devices involving key-to-disk systems (Figure 8–16) are usually recommended where a number of operators are used

FIGURE 8–16. Honeywell Model 5500 Keyplex System

Courtesy of Honeywell Information System

in providing input data for a computer system. There is normally a central control unit made up of a processor unit (actually a small computer), a magnetic disk (similar to phonograph records) unit, a magnetic tape recording unit, a supervisory control station, and a number of individual operator "keystations." In larger systems there may also be printing devices and a communications capability to permit the system to serve as a terminal or direct input device to either a local or remotely located computer.

The processor unit serves to organize and manipulate the data as it is fed into the system. The data is then fed onto the magnetic disk file for temporary storage. This disk file also contains the programs (instructions) and routines which direct the internal operation of the system. After a given volume or a specific set of data are eventually collected on the disk, the data are then transferred onto magnetic tape for later use as computer input or they may, if the communications feature is available, transfer and input the data directly to a computer.

The supervisory control unit serves the operator in charge in controlling the operation of the entire system. This operator determines which instruction programs are to be used and how the data are to be accumulated on the disk and tape units. The output of each of the individual keystations is also under the supervisory control as to the format or pattern in which the data are to be captured and where the output of each station is to be stored on the central disk file.

A recent expansion of the keyed disk system has been in the incorporation of optical character-recognition capabilities along with keyed input in the capturing of data. The OCR capability includes data from one or several type fonts and from handprinted data according to Recognition Equipment, Inc. which developed the system. Up to 22-keystations, each with its own video-display terminal, may be provided with the system.

Keyed Data Terminals

Terminals, as the word suggests, are usually remotely located and serve as either an input and/or output device. They may be used in the input of data to, in inquiries from, or output from a computer system. There are, of course, many types of terminals available. Most of these will be discussed in Chapter 10 as the concern here is in the manually keyed input of data from a remote location (the extent of the distance involved is not necessarily a factor).

Remotely located keyed terminals (Figure 8–17) are generally part of or associated with various input and output units such as tele-typewriters, visual display devices, intelligent terminals (processing as well as I/O capability), console entry devices, or some types of communication devices. In each instance, though, the keying of data is performed

FIGURE 8–17. Bell System Dataspeed 40 Terminal

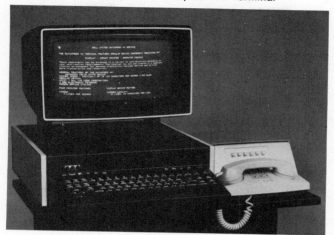

Courtesy of AT&T

by an operator on a typewriter-like keyboard. Depending on the associated equipment, the data may be entered into various types of storage devices (for later transmission to a computer system) or it may be directly communicated to a computer in an on-line (part of a computer system) or even real-time (able to communicate by inquiry of and receiving information from a computer in a manner similar to a human conversation) mode.

Data Collection Devices

Devices to collect data in remote locations come in many models but all serve in gathering data (Figure 8–18) at the point of origination in a computer-acceptable form. On-line data collection devices will be discussed in more detail in Chapter 10 but, regardless of whether the device is on- or off-line, the input procedure will probably require that a few keys (either numeric, alphabetic, or both) be provided to permit variable information, such as number of pieces or machine station number, to be entered manually. In addition, preset data such as a date, device location, or clock time, may be preentered into the device to be recorded with each entry. Precoded punched cards may be another form of input for such data as a job or part number. Badges or other precoded input, such as an individual's employee number, are additional forms of input often available on such devices.

FIGURE 8–18. IBM 2797 Data Entry Unit

Courtesy of IBM

In Summary

The type of input data system best suited to the needs of the information system of a given firm requires considerable investigation. The needs may be such that computer input data may be in the form of punched paper tape or cards produced as a by-product of a manual operation, as mentioned in early chapters. Or, only a few operators may be required to produce the input media which may be prepared by card punches or single unit key-to-tape equipment. In other installations, many operators may be required and here it may be advisable to utilize shared key-to-tape or key-to-disk systems where many operators work with the same data recording system. In still other systems, one may be able to utilize keyed terminals, data collection devices, MICR encoding, or even other techniques to best serve the data input needs.

DATA MANIPULATION

In addition to equipment which actually prepares the data in a computer input acceptable form, there is a need at most installations for peripheral devices which are used to rearrange or alter the input media or data into a more usable form.

Sorting

There are several punched card sorting techniques available to arrange the data into a given required pattern or sequence.

In a *numerical sort* the selection switches on the sorter must first be set for numerical sorting, then the data must be sorted on each column of the field to be arranged. If there is only a single column in the field, a single pass through the sorter will put the data in the desired order, if it is removed from the sorter's stacking pockets properly. However, if there is more than one column in the field of data, the procedure is usually to sort first on the units position of the data, then the tens, hundreds, and so forth, until all the columns have been sorted.

In an *alphabetic sort,* where it is necessary that there be two coded holes in each column to represent a letter, two sorts must be performed on each column in the field before progressing to the next. The first sort in each column of data would be a numerical sort, as described above. The second sort in each column would be a zone position sort with the selection switches on the sorter set for this type of sort. When the two sorting runs are completed on the units position (right-most or last column of the field), one progresses from right to left until all columns are sorted for the field.

A procedure used where large volumes of data are to be arranged, or where more than one sorter is available for use, is that of *block sorting.* This usually involves breaking the card deck down into blocks of data by sorting on the largest significant digit first. Then other sorters may be used to continue the sorting process. Even if only a single sorter is available, block sorting may be advisable, as the first block may be sorted and processing started on other equipment while the sort of the second and following blocks of data is completed. The value of block sorting depends entirely on the need or ability to utilize other equipment to speed up the information processing.

When the data are to be classified, in sequence, by several fields of information for a given procedural run, the importance relationship of the fields must first be determined. The sorting procedure starts with the least important or minor field and proceeds through the increasingly important intermediate and major fields of data.

Collating

Punched card collators are also available to arrange or rearrange data into some required pattern. This may involve only a single deck of cards or it may be necessary to intermix two decks of cards.

Punched cards containing coded data representing certain particular quantities or other characteristics may be *selected* (Figure 8–19) from data decks on sorters and collators.

FIGURE 8–19. Selecting

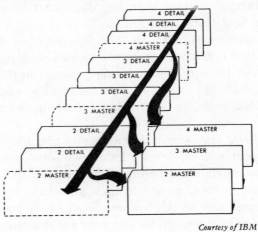

Courtesy of IBM

The collators aid in the major data processing problem of filing and file maintenance where the records must be kept accurate, up to date, and accessible. The principal use of these machines is in feeding and comparing two decks of cards simultaneously and either matching them against each other or merging them together in some order. The functions performed include those of selection, sequence checking, merging, merging with selection, matching, and limited editing in the form of either, or both, blank-column or double-punch detection.

A test to determine if cards are arranged in either an ascending or descending order is that of *sequence checking.* This procedure is performed on any of the collators by comparing each card fed into the machine with the previous card. As long as the proper sequence is maintained, normally in ascending order, the operation continues through the deck of cards. If a card is discovered out of order, an error condition exists, the error light comes on, and card feeding is automatically stopped. Sequence checking may be performed independently or in conjunction with a matching, merging, or selecting procedure.

The procedure to determine if the cards in two files are exactly the same, regarding specific data, is termed *matching* (Figure 8–20) and is performed on the collators. This involves a series of checks on pairs of cards previously arranged in a given sequence. After the check is completed, the two matched decks of cards are stacked separately. If desired, this procedure may be combined with a selecting procedure in which the unmatched cards in each deck are pulled from their respec-

FIGURE 8–20. Matching

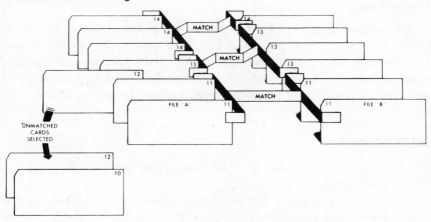

tive decks and filed separately in two additional stacker pockets of the machine.

When two decks of cards, already arranged in sequence, are to be combined to produce one deck of cards, then they are *merged.* Merging is performed on any of the collators by placing one of the two sequenced decks in each of the primary and secondary feed hoppers on the equipment. As the procedure is started, the card in the first file of cards is compared with that in the second file. If the first primary feed card is the lower in sequence, it is fed into a stacker where the two decks will be merged. If the card in the second file is the lower, it will be placed in the stacker hopper first. If the cards are both of equal value, the card from the primary file will be fed to the stacker first. From this last it will be seen that it may, in some procedures, be quite important as to which deck of cards is placed in the primary feed file of the equipment.

Listing

Data may be needed in listed or printed form to serve as an internal control check—usually by totals—which can be checked against computer processed results (described more fully in Chapter 14).

Interpreting

The data contained in punched cards may need to be interpreted and printed on the card, so that people—as well as machines—may be able to read the data.

Converting

As mentioned earlier, a given form of input media may not be an acceptable form for a particular computer processing system. It may be necessary, for example, to convert punched paper tape to punched cards or magnetic tape cassette reels to standard-sized tape reels. There are many types of conversion or reproduction devices available.

REFERENCES

1. FEIDELMAN, LAWRENCE A. "All Keypunches Aren't Alike." *Modern Data,* August 1973, p. 26.
3. FEIDELMAN, LAWRENCE and BERNSTEIN, GEORGE B. "Advances in Data Entry." *Datamation,* March 1973, p. 44.
3. SALZMAN, ROY M. and NISKANEN, ANTHONY S. "Data Entry Systems." *Modern Data,* February 1973, p. 28.

QUESTIONS

1. Discuss four factors which undoubtedly have a bearing on the type of coding and input techniques used.
2. Why should the type of business which happens to be under consideration have considerable bearing on the technique used in preparing input data?
3. Why is a punched card referred to as a unit record?
4. Are there particular advantages to using the System/3 punched cards?
5. What purpose is served by using punched cards with colored stripes on them or punched cards of different colors?
6. Why is it recommended that data be punched into a card according to a predetermined standard arrangement?
7. How should a three-digit number be punched into a card which contained a five-column field for this type of data?
8. Briefly describe three different types of keyed data entry systems?
9. Why do you suppose this many keyed data entry systems exist? Shouldn't one be enough?
10. Describe the function of the *program unit* in the keypunch machine.
11. How is verification accomplished in a keypunching operation? Describe how it works.
12. How can an error in a punch card be corrected?
13. Has the verifying punch eliminated the problem of having to correct punching errors in cards? Explain.

14. How does a Mohawk Keyed Data-Recorder differ from an IBM Card Punch? Explain.

15. Why would anyone want or need to use keyed magnetic disk input?

16. In what type of situations would you imagine *data collection devices* might be used?

17. If you have 1000 cards each with a number on it somewhere between 1 and 1,000 and you had to get the cards sorted into numerical sequence, how would you go about doing it? How does a sorter do it?

18. What purpose is served by the collating function in a unit record-media data processing system?

9

Computer Input/Output—
Typical Devices

THE PARTICULAR EQUIPMENT utilized in a given computer system is dependent upon a number of factors, which are considered in detail in Chapters 17 and 18. However, to perform a given set of applications, there may be a wide variety of equipment available—each grouping of which has its own desirable characteristics.

For instance, in the case of speed requirements, it is certain in nearly every installation that at some point in acquiring fast access and computational capability, the costs associated with speed must be reconciled against this need for speed.

In other instances, where there are many I/O devices available, they must all be carefully analyzed to determine which will best serve the purposes desired. Factors weighed in this consideration must not only include the processing system itself but also the place where the data originate. For example, is the place near or far from the central processing unit? The type of business, the originating sources of the data, the transmission distances to be involved, and the type of output data to be provided are other factors to be considered.

The above discussion only scratches the surface of the many decisions which must be made in selecting specific equipment for a given system. However, it should indicate some need to be familiar with the many types of equipment available and the capabilities of each.

Almost any classification of computer equipment requires some arbitrary decision as to the specific category of use for a given device. An example of this is the magnetic tape unit which serves both as an I/O device and as an on-line memory device. To alleviate this classification problem, the discussion to follow will classify these devices as those which are (1) strictly input and/or output units; (2) direct access storage devices, which serve either as an extension of internal memory or as an on-line storage device; (3) internal memory devices, whose components are more commonly found as a part of the central processing unit; (4) communication devices; and (5) data collection systems. Both of the last two classes are on-line-type units which may be isolated from the computer area and operated from another area many miles distant.

INPUT AND/OR OUTPUT UNITS

The class of device which either inputs and/or outputs data assumes many and quite differing forms. Some of these have been in use since the development of the first computers, while others have only recently been perfected to the point where they now have practical and acceptable usage. (See Reference 7.)

Punched Cards

It has been mentioned earlier in Chapter 8 that the punched card is one of the major forms of input (Figure 9–1) into the typical com-

FIGURE 9–1. IBM 3505 Card Reader

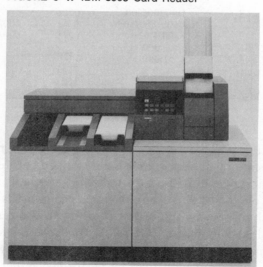

Courtesy of IBM

puter systems which make up the small- and medium-sized range of equipment. The punched card is also used as output from a computer but volume-wise, its use as output is relatively small when compared to its use as input. However, most computer systems will have card output capability in either the form of a Card Punch or as a combination Card Reader/Punch.

The Card Reader of today generally uses a photoelectric (electric-eye-type) sensing mechanism. This permits cards to be fed much faster, more accurately, and with less danger of card jams. Typical card reading speeds are from 600 to 800 cards per minute, however, various models are available (Figure 9–2) which range from 100 to 1,600 cards per minute.

FIGURE 9–2. Card Reader Characteristics

Model	Cards/Minute	Model	Cards/Minute
Burroughs		*IBM*	
124	800	2501	600/1,000
9110	200	2502	150/300
9111	800	3504	800/1,200
9112	1,400	3505	800/1,200
9115/9116	300/600	*NCR*	
9119–1 (96 Col)	300		
Control Data		680–201	1,200
		682–100	300
415	1,200/1,600	686–201	750
Honeywell		*UNIVAC*	
58	100/200/300	0706	900
123	400/600/800/1050	0711	400/600
223	800/1,050	0716	600/1,000
CRZ 201	900	*Xerox*	
CRZ 301	1,050		
		7121	200
		7122	400
		7140	1,500

The Card Punch (Figure 9–3) is a slower device than the Card Reader as the card must be positioned and stopped before the punching die can produce a hole in the card and then the hole is checked for accuracy by a photoelectric sensing device. Card punches (Figure 9–4) range in punching speeds from a few cards up to 500 cards per minute for a standard 80-column card. Of course, the speed is increased when a shorter than standard card is punched or only a few columns are punched in a card. Punching may be. performed either serially or in

FIGURE 9–3. Burroughs 9319–2 96-Column Card Reader/Punch

Courtesy of Burroughs Corp.

FIGURE 9–4. Card Punch Characteristics

Model	Cards/Minute	Serial/Parallel	Stackers
Burroughs			
9210	100	S	1
9212	150	S	3
9213	300	S	3
Control Data			
415	250	S	1
Honeywell			
214	100/400	S	1
CPZ 201	300	S	1
CPZ 300	100/400	S	1
IBM			
1442/5, N2	160	S	1
2520	300/500	S	1
3525	100/200/300	P	1
NCR			
684–301	100/460	S	1
686–302	82/240	S	1
686–311	60/180	S	1
687–301	100	P	1
Xerox			
7165	100/300	S	1

parallel. In serial punching (the more commonly used method) a single column (a character) is punched at a time. In parallel punching all the data to be punched in a given card is stored in memory or in buffer storage and the actual punching is performed row by row in the card for all characters to be punched.

In some instances combination Card Reader/Punch units are utilized (Figure 9–5). These serve both to read cards for input into the system

FIGURE 9–5. Card Reader/Punch Characteristics

Model	Read Cards/Min.	Punch Cards/Min.	Print Cards/Min.	Stackers
Burroughs				
9319* (96 Col)	300/500	60/120	60/120	2/3
9419* (96 Col)†	300	60	60	2/6
Control Data				
430	500	100	—	1
Honeywell				
214–2	400	100/400	—	—
IBM				
1282 (Optical)	200	200	—	—
1442	300/400	80/160	—	—
2520	500	500	—	—
2540	1,000	300	—	—
2560	310/500	65/91	140/sec	4/5
2596* (96 Col)	500	120	120	4
5424* (96 Col)	250/500	60/120	60/120	4
NCR				
684–101	500	100/460	—	—
686–102	800	83/294	—	—
686–111	560	60/180	—	—
UNIVAC				
1001*	1,000 (2 feeds also sorts, edits, and proves)			
0600	300	300	—	—
0603 (Serial)	200	75/200	—	—
0604 (Row)	250	250	—	—

* A multifunction machine (reads, punches, prints, collates).
† Also serves as an independent recorder.

and to output punched cards from the system. Some of these units, depending on the model, may perform other punched card manipulation functions, such as collating, limited sorting, interspersed gang punching, reproducing, editing, or proving. In addition, some of the 96-column card equipment also prints the punched characters on the card. In a few instances, some Reader/Punch models may also be switched off-line and used as an independent keyed data recorder, as discussed in Chapter 8.

Punched Paper Tape

Paper tape readers (Figures 9–6 and 9–7) serving as input to computer systems operate at speeds up to 1,500 characters per second. Paper

FIGURE 9–6. UNIVAC 920 Paper Tape Subsystem

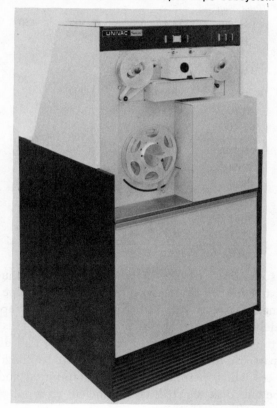

Courtesy of Sperry UNIVAC

tape punches, as with card punches, are slower than their readers and most operate in the range of from 100 to 240 characters per second. The major use of punched paper tape in computer systems today is where data may be originated in this form as a by-product of another operation (typewriters, adding machines, bookkeeping machines, and

FIGURE 9–7. Punched Paper Tape Reader and Punch Characteristics (all 5-, 6-, 7-, and 8-channel codes)

Model	Type	Characters/Second Read	Punch
Burroughs			
9120	Reader	500/1000	
9220	Punch		100
Honeywell			
PTS–200	Reader/Punch	500	150
IBM			
1012	Punch		150
1017	Reader	250	
1018	Punch		120
2671	Reader	1,000	
NCR			
662–100	Reader	1,000	
662–101	Reader	1,500	
665–101	Punch		200
UNIVAC			
0920	Reader/Punch	300	110
Xerox			
7062	Reader	300	
7063	Punch		120

so forth), as described earlier, or where data is communicated from one location to another by teletype or other paper tape device.

Though many systems still utilize punched paper tape as input it is not as widely accepted as it has previously been. This has partially been due to the advent of the keyed magnetic tape and disk data entry devices and partially to the development of more sophisticated communication devices which permit data to be transmitted and received on magnetic tape and disk which is more efficient as input to a computer system.

The actual tape used in paper tape devices may be oiled or dry paper or plain or aluminized Mylar tape. Its width depends on the number of channels (described following) available: $^{11}\!/_{16}$-inch for 5-channel, $\frac{7}{8}$-inch for 6- or 7-channels, or 1-inch for 8-channel tape. In actual usage the tape may be in short lengths (strips) or stored on reels. Typical reels are the 8-inch reel with a capacity of 700 feet and the $10\frac{1}{2}$-inch reel with a capacity of 1,000 feet. The typical recording density (characters or frames per inch) of 10 frames per inch thus would provide storage for up to 84,000 and 120,000 frames, respectively, for the 700- and 1,000-foot reels.

Paper tape may be punched as unchadded (where the hole is only partially cut out and a flap extends at each hole punched) or as chadded (where the hole is clean cut and the chad is punched out). With our modern photoelectric readers, however, you will rarely find unchadded tape used in computer installations.

The coding techniques used to record data on paper tape are often referred to as 5-, 6-, 7-, and 8-channel codes. The term *channel* stems from the fact that the impressions or holes representing data are made in imaginary channels which run the length of the tape. The numbers referring to the channel codes refer to the actual number of channels used in recording the data, sometimes called channel widths.

The 5-channel tape utilizes the Telegraph Code developed by Jean Maurice Emile Baudot of the French Ministry of Posts and Telegraph in 1870 (Figure 9–8). This code has been used so extensively in teletype

FIGURE 9–8. Baudot Paper Tape Code—5-Channel

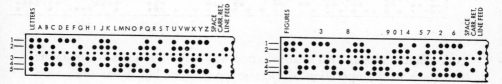

transmissions that you will often hear it referred to as the Teletype Code. A close analysis fails to reveal any apparent relationship between the pattern of punched holes and the number, character, or letter presented. However, the code was developed on the basis of using fewer holes for the letters and numbers most frequently used at the time. When you recall that the frequency of use of the letters was based on the French language, it is easy to understand why the code has no apparent relationship to our English letters.

The number of pulse and no-pulse code combinations in a 5-channel paper tape code provides a maximum number of 2^5 or 32 available combinations. Six of these are set aside as signals to the equipment to execute basic machine functions such as space and carriage return. The teletype keyboard is similar to that of the typewriter and has the ability to "shift," with a given key depression, to produce either of two type characters. This feature is utilized in the basic machine function to provide signals to instruct the machine to either print letters or figures. This permits the remaining 26 basic code combinations to be extended to 52 positions and provide a total of 58 positions.

The 6-channel code is often termed the Press Code because it is used almost exclusively in newspaper press data transmission. It differs from the 5-channel code only in that the additional channel permits the transmission of both upper- and lower-case letters.

The 7-channel code, a binary coded decimal code, is used mainly in electronic computer systems and utilizes the four bottom channels for 8, 4, 2, and 1 valued binary bits to represent a digit. These are used in combination with zone bits to represent letters and characters. The remaining channel serves as a check or parity bit.

The 8-channel code (Figure 9–9) is similar to the 7-channel code in regard to data representation. The eighth channel provides additional

FIGURE 9–9. Punched Paper Tape—8-Channel Code

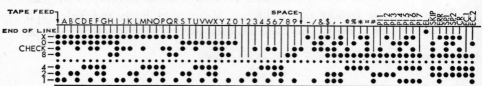

code combinations. This channel code was originally used for machine functions in the operation of electric typewriters, but it has since been adapted for use in wire transmission.

The parity check available in both 7- and 8-channel codes is particularly important in data transmission as it permits an automatic check, by the receiving station, on the parity of each character received to determine if the bit combinations represent valid data.

The 8-channel code is also widely utilized in recording data in the EBCDIC and ASCII 8-bit codes. However, all eight channels are utilized in the coding of the characters and the vertical parity check feature is not available. This does not cause much concern in an "in house" installation as punched paper tape is usually produced as a by-product of some other operation in which a human readable tape or document is produced at the same time and it may be checked visually.

In the transmission of data over telephone and telegraph lines each vertical segment of the character or frame of data is transmitted serially from top to bottom rather than as a multi-channel frame (vertically across the tape) and the sending equipment adds the parity bit as required. In most computer communication situations today, the receiving unit will not be a paper tape punch but will be a magnetic disk, tape, or other storage device and the parity will be recorded and checked as the data is received.

Line Printers

One of the major characteristics of a business information processing system is that it provides large masses of "human-readable" output. This is normally provided by printing devices (Figure 9–10). The char-

FIGURE 9–10. Control Data CDC 512 Printer

Courtesy of Control Data Corp.

acteristics of such printers vary considerably from manufacturer to manufacturer and even in the different computer systems furnished by a given manufacturer (Figure 9–11). Printers are described in several different ways as to (1) lines of print per minute; (2) the print positions (columns of print) on a line; (3) the various sets of characters which are available for printing; and (4) the type of printing mechanism utilized. (See Reference 6.)

FIGURE 9–11. Line Printer Characteristics

Model	Lines/Min.	Char. Set	Print Positions	Type
Burroughs				
9243–N	1,100	64	120/132	Drum
9246	475	64	120	Drum
9247	440/610/750/1,100	96/64/48/16	132	Chain
9249	90/180	48	132	Chain
Control Data				
222	300	63	136	Drum
501	1,000	48, 64	136	Drum
512	1,200	48, 64, 94	136	Train
580	1,200/1,600/2,000	48, 64, 94	136	Train
Honeywell				
58	100/200/300/450/600	40/64	96/128	Drum
112	300/650	63	120/132	Drum
112–2A	392/450	63/53	132	Drum
122	450/650/950/1,100	63	120/132	Drum
222	300/450/950/1,100	63	120/132	Drum
239	670	86	132	Chain
PRT 200	1,200	43/64	136	Drum
PRT 300	1,200	48/63	136	Chain
IBM				
1403	210/1,100	48	120/132	Train and Chain
2203	230/750	63/13	120/144	Bar
2213	66 (Char./Sec.)	64	132	Matrix
2222	80 (Char./Sec.)	64	220	Matrix
3203	600/1,200	48	132	Train and Chain
3211	2,000	48 & OCR	132	Chain
5203	100/200/300	48	96/120/132	Train and Chain
5213	85/115 (Char./Sec.)	64	132	Matrix
NCR				
640–102	450/900	64/52	132	Drum
640–122	200	64	132	Drum
640–132	300/600	64/52	132	Drum
640–200	1,500/3,000	64/52	132	Drum
640–205	750/1,500	64/52 OCR	132	Drum
640–210	1,500/3,000	64/52	160	Drum
640–215	750/1,500	64/52 OCR	160	Drum
640–300	600/1,200	128/64 $\left(\begin{array}{c}\text{U. \&/or}\\ \text{L. Case}\end{array}\right)$	132	Drum
649–300	300	64	132	Split Drum
646–201	2,500/1,500/1,200/ 952/679/365	255	132	Train
647–201	3,500/3,000/2,000/ 1,608/1,156/625	255	132	Train
UNIVAC				
0758	1,200/1,600	63	132	Drum
0768–00	900/1,100/1,200/1,600	63	132	Drum
0768–02	840/1,000/2,000	94	132	Drum
0770	800/1,400/2,000	24–384	132	Band

FIGURE 9–11. (continued)

Model	Lines/Min.	Char. Set	Print Positions	Type
Xerox				
1200	4,000	95	132	Xerographic
3451	350	56	132	Drum
3461	300	64 ASCII	132	Drum
3463	700	64 ASCII	132	Drum
3464	500	95 ASCII	132	Drum
3465	1,250	64 ASCII	132	Drum
3466	925	95 ASCII	132	Drum
7440	600	56	132	Drum
7441	1,100	64	132	Drum
7442	1,100	91	132	Drum
7446	1,500	64	132	Drum
7450	225	63	128	Drum

Typically today most of the printers used in systems of any size will print data at some rate around 1,000 lines per minute. However, where the need does not justify this or requires faster printing speed, there are printers which print from as low as 200 or as high as 4,000 lines per minute (depending on the model and the character set used). The normal length of the print line is usually 132 characters per line, but here also, if need demands, shorter and longer printer lines are available.

Speeds quoted in printer descriptions are not necessarily actual speeds to be expected in a given installation as these are ideal or optimum speeds and the ideal or optimum situation rarely—if ever—exists in actual practice. Thus, in selecting equipment the important consideration is what can be expected under the circumstances found in that particular installation. The major variables to be considered include typical printing on a line, both as to characters used and number of print positions used, and the amount of spacing required on the form. Limited usage of characters would save time but extensive spacing would slow the printing operation up.

Perhaps the widest variation that occurs in describing printers is in the set of print characters to be used. This may be as small as just the ten digits themselves and a few special characters. The printing mechanism will probably contain multiple sets of these 13 or 14 characters and will not have to move very far for the character to be available for printing in a given column position. Thus, the more limited the available number of characters in the set, the faster the unit will be able to print. The most commonly used character set in use today is the ASCII set of 64 letters, numbers, and special characters. Other commonly found sets include the older Hollerith 48-character set, and an ASCII set which contains both lower- and upper-case printing capability. The ease with which these sets may be switched or interchanged on given printers is often a consideration in making a purchase of this equipment.

There are about four major types of printing mechanisms in use today with the drum- and chain-type printers dominant, with bar printers being phased out, and with matrix printers usually being provided for terminal operations. The *drum-type* printer uses an elongated drum slightly longer than the print line to be used. The selected character set is provided around the drum in each print position. Data to be printed is fed into memory or buffer storage and, when the entire line to be printed has been determined, it is fed to the printing mechanism. Then, as the drum rotates and given characters are positioned and available to print positions on the line, print-hammers strike the paper against a ribbon which, in turn, is pressed against the type font on the drum and the character is printed. In a few pieces of equipment a split-drum is used in which the drum is literally sliced into segments for each character set, but the basic principle of operation is similar.

The *chain-type* printers include those of several patented techniques (Chain, Train, and Band) but the general operating principle of all can be classified under a single type. In this technique a series of characters—usually a multiset of characters—are mounted on an endless flexible chain (Figure 9–12). This chain is mounted horizontal to the printing line and is rotated at a fast speed. As the given character on the chain, to be printed in a given print column, goes by the printing position, the print-hammer strikes and the character is printed. It may be that several such characters are positioned simultaneously across the page and all would be printed at the same time. Then, as the chain rotates the other print positions would be printed. The pattern involved in this type of printing relies on the logic of either a buffer or software (a program) control and the speed of printing rests on the logic used. Thus, buffer logic—designed for the specific unit—usually provides more nearly optimum results.

Bar-type printers were widely used in the past as the technique was carried over from the printing mechanism of the punched card accounting machine. There are not too many printers currently using this method as the speed is definitely limited and the action is entirely mechanical. Each character set is mounted on a bar for each print position. The bar raises vertically until the given character desired for printing

FIGURE 9–12. Printer Chain

Courtesy of Burroughs Corp.

is in position to be printed on the print line and then a print-hammer strikes the bar and drives the character against a ribbon and the paper for printing to occur. In most instances all printing bars are raised into position and the print-hammers are all struck at the same moment.

To date the use of *matrix printers* has been limited to relatively low-speed printing devices and this most common usage has been in conjunction with terminal type of miniprinters. Matrix printing involves the printing of data in the form of a printed series of dots whose outline follows the contour of a given character. The size of the dots and the number of dots used will vary from model to model. The basic idea is that a matrix of potential dots is provided and then specific dots in the matrix are used to provide the printed character. (See Reference 8.)

Console Units

Almost every computer system has a device (Figure 9–13) which permits some form of manual entry into, and control over, the central

FIGURE 9–13. NCR Century 300 Console

Courtesy of NCR

processing unit and, in turn, there is usually a need for some type of output unit from the central processing unit to permit the system to answer back to instructions or to advise the operator when some need arises.

The typical input unit is either a typewriter or a typewriter keyboard terminal (discussed later in Chapter 10). In either case the input speed is limited to the ability of the operator to utilize the typewriter keys. Output, however, may be in the form of the typewriter printing capability, a CRT display unit, or one of the smaller limited capability line printers. Thus the output speed will vary from around 10 characters per second on the typewriter to up to 200 characters per second on some of the printers. If the CRT visual display device is used for output, the volume of data displayed will depend on the capability of the display tube and will be rated in terms of characters per lines and the number of lines available on that device.

The various types of terminals available for use with computer systems are discussed in Chapter 10. They are used in the remote communication of data in so many instances today that it was thought best to describe terminals as part of the available communications devices.

Optical Character Recognition (OCR)

There has been a steady improvement in the capability and reliability of optical scanning devices (Figures 9–14 and 9–15) over the past few

FIGURE 9–14. IBM 1231 Optical Mark Page Reader

Courtesy of IBM

years. These devices provide a sophisticated input technique that can serve many types of business problems in converting source data from originating documents directly into a machine-recognizable form.

There are two basic types of OCR readers: (1) those that handle individual documents in the form of paper sheets or cards and (2) those that accept continuous rolls of paper such as cash-register or adding-machine tape. These types can both be subdivided into those that read a single-print font style and those that are multifont readers which can read from a few up to hundreds of printing styles, including hand-printed characters. The capability of these machines can also be described as those which can only read a single line for each insertion of a document, those which can read an entire document at a single insertion, and those which read lines progressively as the role of paper

FIGURE 9–15. Optical Document and Character Reader Characteristics

Model	Type	Documents Per Hour Max.	Pockets or Stackers
Control Data			
915	Page Reader	370 Char./Sec.	2
921	Document Reader	1,200 Doc./Min.	1
936	Document Reader	750 Char./Sec.	3
955	Page and Document Reader	750 Char./Sec. / 300 Doc./Min.	1
Honeywell			
243	Document	1,100	3
IBM			
1230	Mark Scoring	1,200	—
1231	Mark Page	2,000	—
1232	Mark	850 to 2,000	—
1288	Page	Variable	—
3881	Mark	3,700 to 5,000	—
1287	Character	100 to 655	—
3886	Character	330 to 5,580	—
NCR			
420–1	Character	52 L/Sec., 32 Ch./Line, NOF font	—
UNIVAC			
2703	Document	300 to 600	3

feeds past reading heads. Some readers also provide a sorting capability in outputting the scanned document into a few or as many as 12 different stacker bins.

OCR problems not only include the wide variety of methods of recording data and the many type fonts used but also include document sizes and the mechanical aspects of moving and positioning the documents so that the data may be read and interpreted correctly. Data to be read by OCR must also be carefully prepared and handled, as marks, smudges, creases, stains, and so on may appear to be data to the scanning device.

Single-line, single-font readers can be purchased for as low as $5,000, but the demand for these in business applications is quite limited. Page and document readers—depending on their capabilities and the fonts used—cost between $50,000 and $500,000. Where multifont reading is desired at speeds of 500 to 14,000 characters per second, the price increases to near the $2 million level.

OCR can be used in almost any type of business input data situation as equipment is available to read garment tags, punched cards, bar-coded cards, marks and characters of many types, as well as hand- and machine-printed letters, numbers, and characters. There are somewhere around 1,000 OCR installations today, and the predictions are that while this form of data input will continue to expand, its growth will be slow for some time to come. The rapid growth in the use of the direct keyboard-to-magnetic tape and disk recording techniques over the past few years has had a decided impact on the expansion of OCR usage as up to this time OCR is considerably more expensive.

NOF Optical Font. Many smaller business firms have sufficient volume of operations to make their record keeping system fairly expensive and usually they also need the results of their operations recorded faster than their present system provides. Where this is the case, it may be practical to rent computer time from a computer service bureau (Chapter 15). However, the preparation or cost of preparation of the data into acceptable computer input form is often prohibitive.

To meet this need and demand from small business firms the National Cash Register Company (NCR) has adapted a particular-shaped type font (Figure 9–16) for use as an input to its optical reader. This

FIGURE 9–16. NOF Optical Type Font

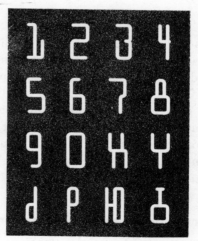

Courtesy of NCR

type font may be attached to NCR adding machines, cash registers, and accounting machines so that, as a by-product of the operation of the machine, a printed paper tape is produced by the equipment which may be read as a human-language record or fed directly into an optical reader at an NCR service bureau. This reader scans the printed paper tape at speeds of up to 31,200 characters per minute and the data read are used to either produce punched paper tape or serve as direct input into a computer system.

Optical scanning is achieved, using this font, by assigning five vertical channels (Figure 9–17) which are "read" by the two horizontal

FIGURE 9–17. Scanning the NOF Optical Type Font

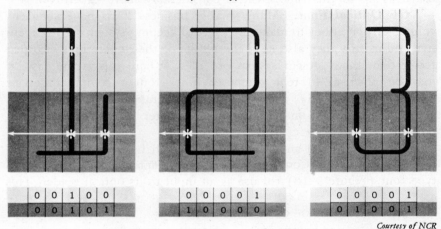

Courtesy of NCR

heads (represented by arrows in the illustration). As these heads sweep across the character, the type print lines encountered are recorded. This recording is in binary form and is shown below the figure in the illustration. The top binary line represents the findings of the top scanning head and the bottom binary line that of the lower head. The binary combinations found as the character is read are then interpreted into a computer system code if it is to be used as on-line input to a computer system or into a paper tape code if punched paper tape is to be produced.

Magnetic Ink Character Recognition (MICR)

The use of special type font characters printed on checks, deposit slips, and other documents by using an ink which has special magnetic qualities was developed through the joint efforts of the banking profession and computer manufacturers. The shape of the characters permits easy visual interpretation, and the special magnetic ink permits reading or interpretation by machines.

The use of MICR has grown rapidly since its development in the 1960s. Its general usage is in banking and related fields in reading the data on checks and other banking documents directly into summarizing devices or computers for calculations and processing, and then sorting the read documents into stacker bins for classification and storage. Most banking installations now utilize at least some form of MICR in the handling or processing of their customer-prepared documents— checks and deposit slips.

MICR devices (Figures 9–18 and 9–19) all have similar reading char-

FIGURE 9–18. Burroughs 9134 MICR Reader Sorter

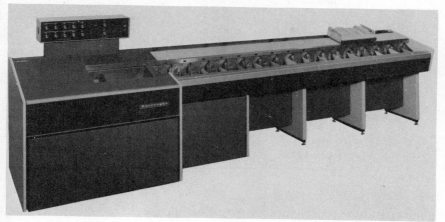

Courtesy of Burroughs Corp.

acteristics, as the first models were designed around a single set of specifications. These were produced, however, by a number of manufacturers, and each firm built in its own unique ideas in fulfilling the requirements of the specifications.

The standardized set of adopted characters (Figure 9–20) includes the ten digits (0 through 9) and four special symbols. These symbols include an "amount symbol" to indicate that the digits following represent an "amount"; and an "on us" symbol which indicates the next data are applicable to the local bank on which the check is drawn and includes two sets of digits—first the type of transaction (deposit, withdrawals, and so forth) and then the customer account number— separated by a symbol representing the equivalent of a "dash"; and a "transit number" symbol which indicates the data following are codes representing the local bank's assigned American Bankers Association

FIGURE 9–19. MICR Reader/Sorter Characteristics

Model	Documents Per Minute Max.	Stackers or Pockets
Burroughs		
9130	1565	13
9131	1565	13
9132	1565	16
9134	1625	16 to 32
9135	900	8 to 12
9136	600	8 to 12
Honeywell		
232	600	11
234	830	7
236	1625	16 to 32
MRS–200	1200	12
IBM		
1255	500 or 750	6 or 12
1259	600	11
1419	1600	11
NCR		
670–101	600	11
671–101	1200	18

number and the routing necessary to clear the check through the Federal Reserve Bank check clearing system.

Magnetic ink character recognition (MICR) has been adapted to some special purpose uses, but it is almost exclusively used in the banking industry.

The characters are printed at the bottom of the document in three carefully defined and prescribed areas (Figure 9–21). The amount field, to the right of the document, contains the dollar amount of the check (or other document) and contains space for ten digits and two amount-field symbols.

The on us field is located in the central area of the document. This area contains 20 spaces for characters, but only 18 are normally usable due to differences in preprinted and postprinted (printing inscribed at the bank after document is used in a transaction) tolerances. The on us field is usually divided into two areas, one for the transaction code (to the right) and the other for the customer account number.

The transit number field is positioned near the left edge of the document. Space is provided for 11 characters; four digits for the transit

FIGURE 9–20. E13B Type Font Characters

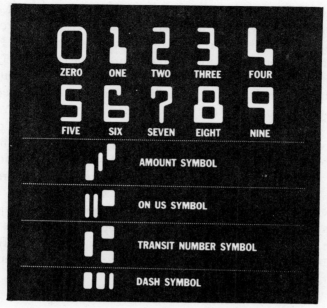

Courtesy of Burroughs Corp.

FIGURE 9–21. MICR Bank Check Encoding

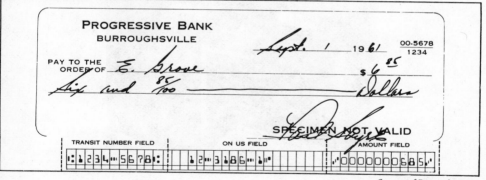

Courtesy of Burroughs Corp.

number, four digits for the American Bankers Association number, a separating dash symbol, and a beginning and ending transit number symbol.

A special auxiliary on us field may be used on extra-wide documents and is found at the extreme left edge of the document. As many as 16 characters plus an ending symbol can be placed in this special field.

MICR Encoders. Data which are to be read by magnetic ink character recognition equipment must, of course, be preencoded onto the document. Normally, the American Banking Association routing or transit number field is preprinted as the document is printed. However, the balance of the information cannot be supplied at this time, as it is not known which customer will use the form or for what amount it is to be prepared. The on us field containing the customer number and the transaction code (either a withdrawal or deposit in most instances) can be pre-encoded as the forms are delivered to the customer. The amount field, however, must be encoded onto the document after the customer provides the amount data. This is usually performed by the first bank—either local or Federal Reserve bank—to process the check.

MICR encoding equipment is produced by most of the major manufacturers of computer equipment and, of course, the features provided with the various models will be somewhat different. The Burroughs Series S100 MICR Proof Recorder (Figure 9–22) permits any one or

FIGURE 9–22. Burroughs S100 MICR Proof Recorder

Courtesy of Burroughs Corp.

all fields to be encoded with one pass of the document and in addition provides a "proof" tape for audit totals and batch controls as well as endorsing the back of the check to indicate it has cleared through the bank.

Microfilm

The use of microfilm in serving as another form of computer output was a newly expanding development only as recently as 1969. It was first used as computer input in an actual application by the Census Bureau in 1970. Though computer input usage has not expanded very rapidly there are now over 100 different manufacturers involved in microfilm-associated equipment. Many of these items are not directly tied to a computer but all assist in the capturing, copying, storing, handling, and display of microfilm.

Microfilm is a term which is broadly applied to several types of film including: 16 mm microfilm which currently is the most popular size roll film; 35 mm microfilm which is normally cut up into individual frames and inserted into aperture cards or slides for viewing purposes; and microfiche which is available in many sizes of which the 4-inch × 6-inch card is generally accepted as standard. Microfiche is a single semi-rigid film-type card on which many frames of data are recorded for ease of handling, storing, and display.

Microfilm may be produced on-line as a direct output from the computer but, though the speed is very fast, it still is slow compared to some other forms of computer output. Consequently, many systems prepare their microfilm off-line from magnetic tape which has been recorded at a computer output speed which is many times faster.

Computer-Output Microfilming (COM). A number of equipment suppliers have developed equipment to directly output computer data in microfilm form (Figure 9–23 and see References 1 and 5). Line printers have been an almost traditional impediment to computer output, as the mechanical speed of the printer is far below the electronic speed of the computer. Where around 1,000 lines per minute is normal for many printers, the use of COM permits the recording of data at speeds of up to 26,000 lines per minute. This is accomplished by feeding the computer's coded digital information into one of several electronic microfilm printers where it is converted to a "human-type" language form or a graphical display. As the data is displayed on a cathode-ray tube (CRT) or, in some systems, through a matrix of fiber optics (without benefit of an expensive CRT display), a camera is triggered to take the picture on film. There are some experimental techniques which will use laser beams to record the data directly onto the film.

Techniques have also been developed which permit typical business forms (invoices, ledger pages, and so forth) stored on glass or film

FIGURE 9–23. Burroughs Computer Output-to-Microfilm (BCOM)

Courtesy of Burroughs Corp.

slides to be projected as an overlay to the data being recorded. Thus, when the microfilm is viewed it appears as a photographed business form complete with its data.

A considerable amount of the data printed out from a typical business computer system serves as historical records for audit or tax purposes and requires large data storage facilities to retain these data for the several years required. The large volume of data printed out for the reports and analyses required by management also requires massive storage facilities. Microfilming consolidates data so that relatively little storage space is required and in addition provides the data in a form that can be easily, quickly, and inexpensively retrieved and scanned by the user. Thus, COM provides a readily available source of easily updated data which can be utilized by various levels of management in reviewing historical data files, current operating situations, and in analyzing data for decision-making purposes. (See References 2 and 4.)

It was estimated that this rapidly growing field of computer output equipment reached around 400 systems by the end of 1972 and that an even greater use will be made of this method of capturing data in the near future.[1]

Computer-Input Microfilming (CIM). A new approach to data input for computers was utilized by the Census Bureau in processing the data collected in the 1970 census. This was the first commercial use of CIM and possibly ranks in importance with the Census Bureau's first use of the punched card in 1890 and their first usage of a computer in a commercial application in 1954.

A modified FOSDIC SS (Film-Optical Scanning Device for Input to Computers) using a special system developed by the bureau provided the hardware that processed the mass of census data. This equipment was previously modified for the 1960 census to process the equivalent of eight hours of card-punched data in about one minute of processing time. The new modification permitted this same amount of data to be processing in about 12 seconds.

The forms were fed into a unit which automatically positioned the page and photographed it onto microfilm at a rate exceeding 3,600 frames per hour. The 70 million forms gathered were microfilmed in about 100 days of operation.

Once the form was photographed and developed, it was fed into the FOSDIC scan unit which "read" the data and converted it to a binary code format on magnetic tape. Six scan units were able to read about 700,000 microfilmed items per minute and record these on magnetic tape at a rate of 90,000 characters per second. These magnetic tapes were then, in turn, processed at electronic speeds on the computer.

Magnetic Ledger Cards

As mentioned in Chapter 4, some of the desk-sized computers utilize ledger cards or pages which have stripes or strips of magnetic receptive material on the back side (Figure 4–16). These cards or pages are usually hand inserted for reading or entering data. Readers (Figure 9–24) are now available, however, which automatically feed cards and read data from the card at approximately 50 cards per minute. This data may be fed directly into a computer system or it may be used to prepare a punched paper or magnetic tape for later entry into a computer.

These cards are also used by some of the more advanced accounting machines (which have evolved in capability until they are now classified

---

[1] Mark Flomenhoft, "Computer Output Microfilm," *Modern Data,* December 1972, pp. 32–33.

FIGURE 9–24 Burroughs A 4005 Magnetic Record Reader

Courtesy of Burroughs Corp.

as small desk-sized or minicomputers). The major use of magnetic ledger cards, in computer systems of any size, is in banking, savings and loan, and credit union applications, where a hard-copy ledger page is desired but computer processing is a must to handle the volume of individual customer accounts to be processed.

Voice Recognition and Response

Voice recognition as a source of input to the computer exists only in experimental systems. It has been estimated that the output of one second of human speech provides data that is the equivalent of around 180,000 bits per second, and when you also consider the infinite variation in vocal tracts, intensity of output, and the phrasing of words and sentences produced by any group of individuals it is "almost possible" to get a slight insight into the problems facing researchers in this area of study. Some limited success has been made experimentally, however, in applications involving a limited number of commands provided by a specific individual.

Cognitronics, IBM, RCA, NCR, Burroughs, Honeywell, Datatrol, and a few other manufacturers have introduced voice response systems in the past few years. The early models were the IBM 7770 Audio Response Unit (February 1965), IBM 7772 Audio Response Unit (July 1966), and the RCA 70/510–11 Voice Response Unit (October 1966).

There are two basic approaches to producing the human voice in voice response systems: a prerecorded voice made up of sentences, words, or segments of words which are quickly assembled to produce the response and a truly synthesized audio output. Most systems in use today provide voice response from a previously voice-recorded vocabulary which is stored in analag form on a drum. The range of the word output is limited to the capacity of the drum, and in typical commercial units this varies from 31 to 255 words on a given unit.

A few commercially available units, however, utilize a digitally controlled voice synthesizer as its output. Each word is produced by a series of phoneme (a basic unit of speech) commands, each of which requires a set of eight bits. In at least one system, this 8-bit binary word is broken down into a 6-bit component for the phonetic part of the output and these are converted from digital to analog form in the simulation of muscle commands to which are added simulated tones for phonetic articulations. The remaining 2-bit component of the word is used for voice inflection and to simulate the vocal cord and certain sound sources. The two sets of sounds are then recombined in a simulation of the vocal tract to produce the audio output.

Typical uses of the audio response system are in stock price and status from the New York Stock Exchange; the status of an account in a bank-teller application; the balance due from a customer's account or the confirmation or refusal of credit relayed to a station in a retail store; and the determination of the flow of material, progress in the assembly of a part, or inventory status in a manufacturing application. (See Reference 3.)

By far the most common form of input in a voice response system is the push-button-type Touch-Tone telephone (Chapter 10) where, first, the computer number is dialed and then the inquiry keyed in as the computer asks for it. The inquiry is forwarded—usually over some type of communication device—to the central processing unit of a computer system. Once this information is interpreted and the files have been contacted for the answer to the query, the data are put in the form of a coded message and returned to the response unit which, in turn, selects the proper set of "words" and relays them over the telephone to the inquirer.

REFERENCES

1. "Guide to COM Recoders." *Government Data Systems,* November/December 1973, p. 24.

2. HARMON, GEORGE W. "Functions of COM Equipment." *Information and Records Management,* July/August 1973, p. 38.

3. McCALMONT, ARNOLD M. "Communications Security for Voice—Techniques, Systems, and Operations." *Telecommunications,* April 1973, p. 35.

4. "Microfilm . . . Its Bigger Than You Think." *Infosystems,* April 1974, p. 24.

5. "Microfilm—Readers, Reader-Printers and COM." *Infosystems,* April 1974, p. 31.

6. MURPHY, JOHN A. "Line and Serial-Ro Printers." *Modern Data,* January 1974, p. 52.

7. ———. "Plus-Compatible Miniperipherals." *Modern Data,* December 1973, p. 30.

8. ZAPHIROPOULOS, RENN. "Nonimpact Printers." *Datamation,* May 1973, p. 71.

QUESTIONS

1. How are the holes in the card sensed or read by the typical card reader today?
2. Why are card punches and paper tape punches slower than their respective card and tape readers?
3. How many different paper-tape channel widths are in use today? Name and state their most common type of usage.
4. Which paper tape channel codes provide a parity bit for checking purposes?
5. What characteristics are used in describing typical printers?
6. Name the major types of printing mechanisms in use today.
7. Are console I/O units limited to a typewriter-type keyboard and printer?
8. What are the two basic types of OCR equipment?
9. Why isn't OCR used more frequently as it is a direct form of input that can be fed into the computer without punching or transcription by humans?
10. Differentiate between the NOF optical font and magnetic ink characters. In which ways are they the same and in which ways are they different?
11. What is the principal use of MICR equipment?
12. When might MICR Encoders be needed?
13. Describe the principal advantages of using microfilm as a medium of output.
14. In what fields of business are magnetic ledger cards most commonly used in computer systems?
15. Name the two techniques used in voice response systems.

10

Communication
Techniques and Devices

COMMUNICATIONS SERVE to link together the data producing and processing operations which go on at separate, and often geographically scattered, locations in such a way that the data produced at the various sources are expressed in a common-language form so that they can be read by other machines in the system. (See Reference 8.) In what is often termed integrated data processing (IDP) systems, communication devices connect the points where data originate and the points where the data are to be used or processed.

Computer technology took tremendous strides a few years ago (see References 5 and 7) by greatly increasing the operational speed and storage capacity of computers while, at the same time, reducing their cost. This greatly increased capacity at a lower cost, brought about a heavy demand for remote usage of the computer and resulted in a tremendous strain on communication facilities. If the technological gains were to be utilized adequately, the necessary quantities of data had to be transported to the computer at a speed sufficient to keep it fully utilized. Communication equipment, therefore, is now the most important link of all in this chain of operations for processing data.

Data can be transported manually or transmitted by means of electrical circuits. If a business has come to the conclusion that it can afford and can adequately use a computer, it is quite unlikely that it will consider transporting data manually from the location where it arises to the central location of the computer. There was a time when the invoices might have been sent by airmail or when the punched cards were sent by special delivery, but this time has passed. With computer systems costs as high as they are, it is imperative that adequate data be available and on hand at all times to be processed by the computer. In addition, competition demands that operational data be processed quickly to provide management with the timely information it requires in its decision-making. The speed and capacity of the means of data transmission, thus, have become all important.

DATA TRANSMISSION SERVICES

The quality and speed of data transmissions varies with the type of carriers and the equipment over which it travels. The type of communication channel used has a direct bearing on the directional (one-way or two-way) capability of the service. In addition, the channels are divided into grades or bands of service. The significance of the widths of the bands is that as the bands become wider, the greater is the frequency range. As the frequency range becomes greater, the clarity and speed of transmission increase.

In ordinary telephone conversation the vibration of the voice causes the telephone transmitter to change the acoustic energy supplied into an analogous electrical energy which is carried over the telephone line. As this electrical energy is received at the other end of the line, the telephone receiver converts it back to acoustic energy which one is able to hear as a reproduction of the voice spoken at the other end of the line.

FIGURE 10–1. Data Set

Courtesy of General Telephone Co.

Transmission of data is accomplished by utilizing what is known as a modem (a Data Set if designed by General Telephone [Figure 10–1] or a DATA-PHONE if designed by AT&T and furnished by the Bell System) to convert the direct-current electrical pulse of a bit (binary digit) from a computer—or other data processing device—to a tone modulated frequency to be transmitted over the telephone wires. At the receiving end another modem receives the tone and converts it back to a direct-current pulse which is fed to a computer device and read or stored as data.

Mode of Transmission

Terms which are often used in connection with the manner in which data is transmitted are asynchronous and synchronous. In *asynchronous transmission* start and stop bits precede and follow each character sent.

In *synchronous transmission* there are synchronizing and start of message characters preceding a large block of information characters which are, in turn, followed by a end of message and some error-checking characters.

Types of Communication Channels

There are three basic types of communication channels or circuits available in terms of directional capability. These are the *simplex, half-duplex,* and *duplex* channels. The simplex type of channel provides for one-way transmission of data, and its ability to carry information would be comparable to the ability of a doorbell. The half-duplex channel can carry information in both directions but in only a single direction at a time. The duplex channel, sometimes called a full-duplex circuit, is the most versatile of all in its ability to transmit information in both directions simultaneously.

The speed with which data may be communicated over these circuits is often expressed in terms of bits or bauds per second. *Bits per second* have been used in describing the flow of binary digits of information in a computer system and are used in the same sense here. *Bauds per second* refer to a communications standard which, though related to bits per second, is somewhat different. In certain equipment bauds and bits will be used interchangeably as they are the same in these instances, but in other equipment a baud of time may provide for the movement of two, three, or even four bits of data.

Grades of Circuits

In addition to types of circuits, there are also bands or grades of circuits whose capacity is in terms of basic line speed expressed in characters per second, bits per second, or words per minute. *Telegraph* grade channels have transmission speeds in the 45 to 75 bits per second range. This grade is utilized in data transmission by the various types of teletype equipment and data transceivers, along with other equipment.

Industry has used the teletypewriter for data transmission for many years. It not only can produce hard copy at the time the transaction is recorded but also it can produce and can be activated by five- or eight-channel paper tape. Since it utilizes paper tape, it is readily integrated into a data processing system.

The *narrow-band* grade, like the telegraph grade, has a slower speed than needed for voice transmission and is also called a *subvoice* grade channel. Generally, the transmission rate for this grade is within the range of 150 to 600 bits per second. The TWX or Teletypewriter Exchange Service utilizes this band and has over 60,000 subscribers in the United States who transmit data via five-channel paper tape at the rate of 60 words per minute. Many of the newer data collection and data communication systems also utilize this grade channel as it is relatively inexpensive.

The *voice-band* grade channels carry information over a range or band width of from 300 to 3,000 cycles per second providing a band width of 2,700 cycles (often referred to as 2,700 Hz or 2,700 Hertz). This channel may be subdivided for certain usage into subvoice channels composed of bands of 150 to 200 cycles. The 100-Speed TWX Service uses the voice-band grade for reading, transmitting, and punching eight-channel paper tape at the rate of 100 words per minute. The Bell Telephone system's DATA-PHONE and General Telephone's Data Set equipment and many other data transmission systems use this grade of channel to transmit data encoded on punched cards, punched paper tape, and magnetic tape. The cost for the use of this grade channel is similar to the cost of a voice long-distance call.

These specialized telephones, with the ability to change from a voice transmission to a data transmission capability and vice versa, may utilize almost any form of data—punched card or paper tape holes, magnetic spots on tape or disk, lines or handwriting on facsimile, or medical or other telemetric data. As an example, a DATA-PHONE may convert electrical signals picked up from punched cards fed one at a time by means of Transceiver, a Data Transmission System, or from punched paper tape by means of a Dataspeed Tape Sender (Figure 10–2), and

FIGURE 10–2. Dataspeed Sender and Receiver

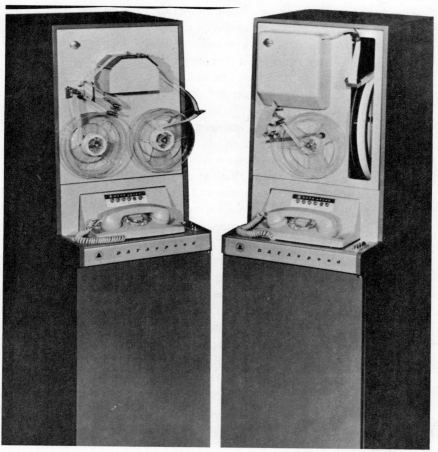

Courtesy of AT&T

transmit them at the rate of 1,050 or 1,200 words per minute to a distant receiving point. In receiving the data, Dataspeed Tape Receivers produce an exact duplicate of the material transmitted.

An interesting example of how this equipment has been put to work is in the trucking industry. This industry has found that improved data communication has not only facilitated the processing of data but has also improved shipping service. Trucks are loaded and sent on their way without waiting for the time-consuming preparation of bills of lading. These bills are recorded on paper tape and transmitted to the distant terminals concerned while the truck is en route. This not only permits the trucks to pull out faster but also provides the unloading terminals with advance information to be used in operations.

The *broad-band* grade of circuit, sometimes called the wide band, involves a microwave or radio-relay communication system operating at superhigh frequencies above 4 million kilocycles per second. Data transmitted over this band must be continually amplified and repeated by stations which use dish-like antennas. These stations can be seen on many high buildings and on towers spaced at intervals of 20 to 35 miles along highways. AT&T's Telpak is a private-line service carrying 60 or 240 voice channels connecting two or more points. It can accommodate the transmission of data, telemetering of information, and facsimile as well as telephone conversations.

Radio frequencies are very efficient carriers of data. They are also the fastest and the most expensive. On a test basis, 20 million bits (3.3 million characters) per second were transmitted over a TV circuit.

There are several radio frequency carriers, including radio bands themselves. Another is microwave. Generally, microwave signals have a short range and must be amplified and retransmitted on the average of every 50 to 90 miles, depending on the terrain. Line-of-sight transmission, such as microwave, is affected by weather disturbances, birds flying through the signal path, low cloud formations, and so on.

One of the newer means of transmitting messages is tropospheric forward scatter propagation. This technique sends out multiple signals, as from the large end of a funnel. These signals scatter and bounce off the troposphere, which ranges from five to eight miles above the earth's surface. One or more of these signals are picked up by a distant terminal.

Types of Service

Any of the above grades of circuits can utilize either local or long distance regular telephone line service (often termed switched-line service) for data transmission. However, there are also private-line and two special switched-line services available. The *switched-line service* is so named because it may be switched from one party to another as desired. In *private-line service* the line is leased between two points and it belongs to the leasor for unlimited use, with no switching involved, 24 hours a day.

A *foreign exchange line* is for usage by people outside the regular exchange area of the receiving telephone. As an example, a firm located in a given city might desire that their customers in a neighboring city could call—what to them is a local number—and be connected toll free as if making a call in their immediate city.

Another special type of switched service available is *Wide Area Telephone Service* (WATS), which is similar to regular long-distance telephone service in that it provides two-way conversation between a large number of telephones. However, it has a more economical rate treatment than long distance for larger volumes. WATS permits a customer to contact a large number of telephones within a specified area at a fixed monthly rate and is basically designed for the customer who has widespread large volume telephone traffic.

I/O DATA CHANNELS

In addition to data being communicated by transmission devices from one geographical location to another, the computer must be able to send and receive data to and from many other types of I/O devices besides the communication devices. To do this there must be a connector and this is usually found internally in the computer in the form of *data channels.* In small and most medium-sized systems these channels are physically integrated with the CPU. However, in some larger systems these may be provided as stand-alone (separate) units. Figure 6–1 indicates the actual number of I/O channels that are standard or optional for each model of computer shown. To determine how many there are of each specific type of channel (as described later) references would have to be made in individual systems manuals.

The concept of time-sharing (Chapter 15) is predicated on the ability of numerous data users at remote locations to have access to the data at will. This means that inquiries from various locations can be made almost simultaneously.

During the earlier stages of the development of the computer, the channel along which the data flowed to the computer could only accommodate data flowing in a continuous stream, and the speed of the channel constituted the speed by which data could be directed to the computer.

With the advent of the IBM System/360 (and other third-generation computers), a completely new concept in data channels was developed. Two different channels were provided, and they were of two general types: multiplexor channels and selector channels.

The *multiplexor channel* separates the operations of high-speed devices from those of lower-speed devices. Operations on the channel are in two modes: a "multiplex" mode for lower data rates and a "burst" mode for the higher.

In the multiplex mode, the single data path of the channel can be time-shared by a large number of low-speed input/output devices operating simultaneously; the channel receives and sends data to them on demand. When operating in the burst mode, however, a single input/output device captures the multiplexor channel and does not relinquish it from the time it is selected until the last bit of data is serviced.

Examples of low-speed devices that can operate simultaneously on the multiplexor channel are: printers, card punches, card readers, and terminals.

Examples of input/output devices that operate in the burst mode are: magnetic tape units and disk, drum, or data cell storage (Chapter 11).

The *selector channel* is used with high-speed I/O devices and operates only in burst mode. Each selector channel permits up to eight I/O Control Units to be attached and can address or communicate with up to 256 different I/O devices. A typical CPU of a computer system may provide several selector and multiplexor channels. The use of several channels permits data to be read, written, or computed on a number of devices all in the same time period.

Front-End Processors

Front-end processors are often referred to in communication installation conversation. To define a front-end processor—in perhaps far too simplified terms—is that it is a specialized communications processor that, regardless of the number of remote devices it controls, still appears as a single channel device to the host processor equipment. (See References 4 and 17.) All of the polling, error recovery, and code conversion techniques related to the remote devices are performed in the front-end communications processor rather than in the central processing unit of the computer. Also, to truly fit this classification there is a special set of software programs provided the host system which assists in performing the host machine functions (similar to those provided by operating systems software programs) in conjunction with the regular operating system to tie the host and front-end together in a unit-type operation.

The combination of these features should result in a much more efficient system by serving to save up to a third of the host storage regularly used in line handling, by providing much faster service throughout for remote location users, and by providing a possible extension to the number of devices that are normally limited to a multiplexor channel.

COMMUNICATION DEVICES

There are many different types of communication devices available. (See Figure 10–3 and References 11 and 16). These range from units which serve as connectors between devices and concentrators of data serving as buffers to a wide range of terminal-type devices and a number of data collection, transmission, and communicating systems and subsystems to fit many varying types of needs.

Terminals

The late 1960s and early 1970s saw a tremendous swing to the use of time-sharing and remote systems and a consequent wide growth in the utilization of data terminals at widely dispersed locations. There is now almost a bewildering array of terminals of various types to choose from as dozens of smaller firms as well as the major computer firms are producing several models of one or more types of equipment. (See References 3 and 6.) This, of course, makes the problem of equipment selection for a given firm or application one that requires a great deal of consideration.

There are two basic approaches to the use of terminals if the word is used in its broad connotation. First, in teleprocessing, the terminal is essentially used in the input and/or output of inquiries or data. These terminals have developed into several distinct types—many of which are interactive in that you may both send and receive data in a real-time context. These terminal types include: (1) keyed data input and either visually displayed or printed output, (2) graphical displays of data, (3) information retrieval systems, and (4) data collection or gathering systems (these last may also be multiprocessing systems).

FIGURE 10–3. Typical Terminal and Communication Equipment

Model	Type
Burroughs	
TC 500/3500 Series	Terminal computer system
TC 600/3600 Series	Terminal computer system
TC 700	Teller terminal computer
TC 1500	Terminal computer
TC 1700	Financial supervisor terminal
TD 700/800	Input and display system
TU 100	Data collection and inquiry terminal
TU 300	Credit authorization terminal
TU 500	Commercial teller terminal system
TT 100	Banking transaction terminal
DC 1200	Concentrator/Controller
B 771	RJE Terminal
B 9352/9353	Input and display terminal
Honeywell	
5	Remote terminal system
765/775/785	Visual information projection system
7340	Bank-teller terminal
7500	Remote programmable terminal
7700	V.I.P. with cassette capability
Datanet 700	Remote batch terminal
IBM	
1001	Data transmission terminal
1050	Data communication system
1627	Plotter
2250	Graphic display unit
2260/2265	Display station
2721	Portable audio terminal
2730	Transaction validation terminal (mag. stripe credit card)
2740/2741	Communication terminal
2770/2790	Data communication system
2780	Data transmission system
2922	Programmable terminal
3270	Information display system
3670	Brokerage communication system
3735	Programmable buffered terminal
3780	Data communications system
3790	Data communications system
NCR	
—	Plotter (Calcomp graph plotter)
260	Thermal printer
270	Hospital terminal
275	Financial terminal
279	Financial terminal
280	Retail system
399	Accounting computer
736 Series	Magnetic tape encoders
760	Punched tape transmitter
765	Punched tape receiver
795	CRT display system
796	CRT display terminal
798	Voice response terminal

FIGURE 10–3. (continued)

Model	Type
UNIVAC	
Uniscope 100/300	Visual communication terminal
DCT 500/1000/2000	Data communications terminal
DCS 1/10/14/16	Data communications subsystems
1004/1005/9200/ 9300/9400	Subsystems
CIC	Communications intelligence channel
Xerox	
AD 51	High speed analog to digital converter
CD 50A and 51A	Controller digitizers
DA 40, 41, 42, 50	Digital to analog converter
MD 40	Multiplexor/Digitizer
MD 51	High accuracy multiplexor/digitizer
SS 50	Sample-and-hold subsystem
7601	150 Word/min. message-oriented data set controller
7605	150 Word/min. procedure-oriented data set controller
7611	240 Char./sec. character-oriented data set controller (up to 64 multiplexed asynchronous lines)
7907/7908	Remote computer adapters
7910	Analog output controller
7916	Analog input controller
7923	Analog/digital adapter
7930/7935	Digital I/O subsystems
7970	Timing/control system

Second, terminals are used in multiprocessing systems, but here the terminal consists of a computer processor unit and some typical array of other input/output and storage devices. In this second instance the interaction is between computer systems (two or many), with some systems interchangeably utilizing each others memory, I/O, and storage capabilities and other systems in which only one of the systems utilize the others capabilities. Smaller, desk-size, accounting, and even mini computers may serve as the terminal equivalent and often are termed intelligent terminals.

Keyed data terminals are also commonly used as an inquiry device to request data from the central computer. They come in many types of models designed for either general or special types of applications. Portable models about the size of a briefcase have been developed, and only a standard telephone receiver (fed through a built-in acoustic coupler) is required to permit the terminal to become on-line with a computer (Figure 10–4).

Another type of keyed data terminal is the *push-button telephone* (Figure 10–5). The first set of this equipment was the Touch-Tone

FIGURE 10–4. Execuport 300 Series Portable Terminal

Courtesy of Transceiver Systems

FIGURE 10–5. Touch-Tone Card Dialing Telephone

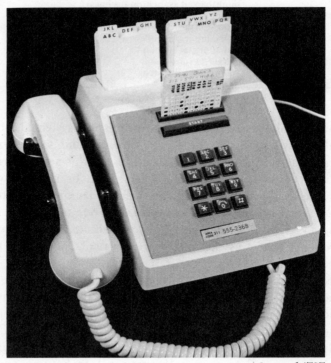

Courtesy of AT&T

telephone introduced by the American Telephone and Telegraph Company Bell System and was later expanded by the Touch-Calling telephone introduced by the General Telephone Company. Both of these push-button telephones utilize buttons for manual entry, and some models make available a prepunched plastic card for automatic dialing information entry. It is predicted that the combination of the push-button telephone and a central public utility-type of computer system (Chapter 15) will eventually serve homemakers in record keeping, grocery ordering, and other shopping; students in solving homework problems; and office workers in their business applications.

Graphical Display Terminals. Some graphs, of course, can be presented—in a limited sense—by teleprinters, and material of this type can also be displayed on visual display devices. Some of the visual display devices also permit the entry of data by using a *light pen* (Figure 10–6). The pen is moved slowly—point to point—across the face of the CRT display, and the computer-displayed information is altered

FIGURE 10–6. IBM 2250 Display Unit

Courtesy of IBM

by the operator. These new data are then returned to the computer to update the graph or drawing displayed.

Data displayed on the CRT may be, for instance, the presentation of a drawing. If desired, only a segment of that drawing may be displayed in expanded form, or if the drawing is a two- or three-dimensional (or more) drawing, the display may be rotated on its axis so that various dimensional views—from any viewing angle desired—may be displayed.

Extensive print-outs involving such complicated items as maps, engineering drawings, and multigraph presentations, however, require spe-

FIGURE 10–7. DP–3 Digital Plotter

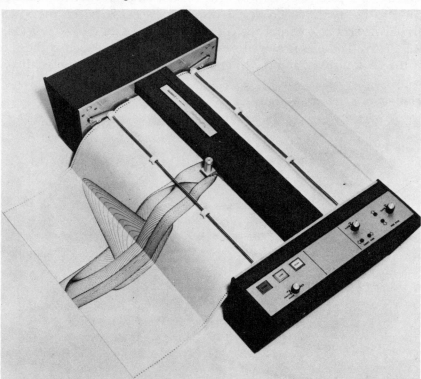

Courtesy of Houston Instruments, Division of Bausch and Lomb

cial techniques, and these are now being provided by digital incremental plotting terminals (Figures 10–7 and 10–8 and Reference 2).

Information Retrieval Terminals. Data which have been stored on microfilm, microfiche, and so on may be retrieved through newly

FIGURE 10–8. DPS 7 Digital Plotting System

Courtesy of Milgo Electronic Corp.

developed interactive information retrieval systems. (See Reference 9.) Most of these present the data in black and white, but others will even provide the display in color. These systems operate through either a direct or remote control interface with a computer processor.

Also, in both the above system classifications there has evolved a wide range of terminals (Figure 10–9) serving to receive and/or store data from a given system and to hold and relay information to a system. These include magnetic reel and cassette tape units, disk units, printers, card readers, and punched paper-tape send and receive units. Many of these have been designed to function with the expanding demand for minicomputer equipment and most are small compact units, limited as to speed or capability, that serve the same function of a similar standard or full capacity unit as has been described in this chapter or will be discussed later.

When any of these terminals are located at remote locations, they must utilize some type of communication device (previously described) to provide the interface required with the central processor of the centralized computer system.

FIGURE 10–9. Typical Terminals

(a) Burroughs 9491–2 Magnetic Tape Drive

(b) IBM 2721 Portable Audio Terminal

Courtesy of Burroughs Corp.

Courtesy of IBM

(c) Communications Terminal with Cassette

(d) Burroughs 9115/9116 Card Reader

Courtesy of Techtran Industries

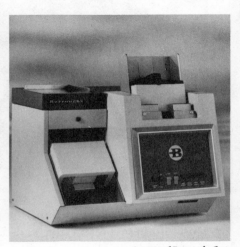

Courtesy of Burroughs Corp.

(e) Dataspeed 40 Printer Terminal

(f) Burroughs 9480–2 Disk Cartridge Memory Subsystem

Courtesy of AT&T

Courtesy of Burroughs Corp.

Keyed Data Terminals. The most commonly found type of terminal is one which permits data to be fed into the system through the manual keying of a keyboard similar to that on a typewriter. The data are, as sent or received, either printed out on the typewriter teleprinting device (Figure 10–10 and see References 10 and 14) or displayed on a cathode-ray tube (CRT) visual display device (Figure 10–11 and

FIGURE 10–10. A Teletypewriter in Use with Control Data Equipment

Courtesy of Control Data Corp.

FIGURE 10–11. Burroughs TD 700 Input and Display System

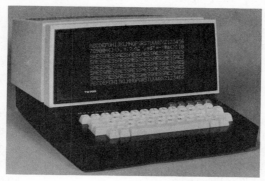

Courtesy of Burroughs Corp.

see Reference 1)—at least one model also produces a hard-copy photo-print of the displayed data if desired.

Color display units, similar to color TV sets, are available and are particularly desirable in certain types of applications where there is a need to distinguish between the various levels or importance of categories of information. In information retrieval systems the "keyword" calling for the data may be in one color, a given number of words each side of the keyword another color for emphasis, the source of the data yet another color, and so forth. In the case of air traffic control utilizing computer-driven radar, aircraft on a collision course may be indicated in one color, with various distance ranges displayed in colors, or even certain altitudes indicated by specific colors. These color terminals may even be used in management board rooms or training areas to provide multicolor displays of graphical or line drawing presentations.

An illustration of how a CRT/Keyboard reporting system might serve management is shown below:

First, an executive activates the CRT unit by inserting an instruction code through the keyboard. An index of subreporting systems which are available to him is flashed on the screen as in Frame I.

Frame I

	Code
Sales	100
Production	200
Personnel	400
Financial	600
Equipment	800
Profit control and analysis	900

Each subreporting system has numerous computer-stored reports that provide information in increasing detail about the general topic. Assume that the executive wants to review financial reports. He inserts Code 600 into the CRT and Frame II appears. The data at the bottom of the frame indicates that the last update was on August 21.

Frame II

	Thousands
610 Cash	4,820
620 Receivables	16,830
630 Inventories	20,100
640 Fixed assets	40,082

Frame II (*continued*)

	Thousands
645 Other assets	8,921
650 Current liabilities	20,921
655 Long-term liabilities	30,112
660 Equity	39,720
100 Sales (Net of C.G.S.)	90,821
680 Budget controlled expenses	71,020
690 Fixed expenses	10,200

U. D. 8–21–70

The executive is interested in the company's cash position. He inserts Code 610 into the CRT and Frame III appears showing a breakdown of cash in Frame II. The total of cash in Frame III does not equal cash in Frame II because the fomer is updated daily and $400,000 has been added since August 21.

Frame III

	Thousands
611 Cash budget 6-month projection	—
612 Demand deposits	3,320
613 U.S. securities	1,400
614 Time deposits	500
615 Source and application STMT	

U. D. 8–24–70

The executive can review the projection of cash needs by inserting Code 611 or review the prior twelve months' source and application of funds statement by inserting Code 615. If he wants a breakdown of maturities of U.S. Securities, he inserts Code 613 and Frame IV appears. By inserting 613.2, a detail listing of securities maturing within 15 days would appear on the screen.

Frame IV

	Maturities	*Thousands*
613.1	7 Days	—
613.2	15 Days	100
613.3	30 Days	300
613.4	60 Days	400
613.5	90 Days	200
613.6	120 Days	400

U. D. 8–24–70

The CRT reporting system allows the manager to browse through each subsystem picking and choosing the information he needs for decision making. The information is always up-to-date and can be displayed as fast as the keyboard can be activated. If desired, a hard copy can be printed of any report appearing on the screen.[1]

It should be realized that there are, at the present time, very few such reporting systems in actual use. Such a system would require an extensive on-line data file, a fairly complete set of operating programs available at call, and a considerable outlay in communication and display equipment in addition to other expenditures. The equipment, programming, and training costs for such a system are usually too great for most firms to consider at the present time. They will, however, with current trends in communications and usage needs be considered practical in the not too distant future.

Data Collection Systems

Automatic data collection implies the recording of the pertinent data about a transaction, in machine-readable form, at the time the transaction occurs. Some data collection systems collect and record the transaction data in batches in machine-readable form for later processing. (See References 12, 13, and 15.) Other feed the data directly into real-time computer systems to provide up-to-the-minute information for operational decisions. All such systems are designed to assist management to cope with changing conditions, and to do so they must have facilities which will make management constantly aware of any deviations—and the reason for such deviations—as soon as they occur.

Data collection systems consist of various types of input devices, a central receiving and processing device, and the necessary interconnecting communication links.

The input devices accept and transmit data from a keyboard, prepunched cards, badges, dials, levers, or some combination of these. Communication facilities (described earlier) transmit the data from the input units to the off-line output units or to a computer system. Output units generally record the transmitted data on punched cards, punched paper tape, or magnetic tape.

Data collection systems are widely used and are found in such diverse areas as manufacturing, retail merchandising, service firms, libraries,

---

[1] Bruce Joplin and James W. Pattillo, "Computer Displays for Management," *Management Controls,* Peat, Marwick, Mitchell & Co., July 1970, pp. 142–147.

and in education. In manufacturing, typical applications might involve purchasing; shipping and receiving; inventory, production, maintenance, and tool control; and many areas of personnel reporting and status-change records. In retail firms you might find telephoned sales, collections of accounts, and inventory changes to name a few applications. Each of the other applications areas have their own unique needs that may utilize the features of some type of data collection system.

In banking and related services a special Financial Terminal (Figure 10–12) has been developed to permit a teller or clerk to enter inquiries

FIGURE 10–12. NCR 270 Financial Terminal

Courtesy of NCR

concerning the status of an account, to determine interest earnings or charges, and to update an account by entering data on such items as deposits and withdrawals. A similar Hospital Terminal has a modified keyboard which permits inquiries on patient status, charges for services and drugs, credits for payments, and other entries typically related to hospital record keeping.

Systems such as those described above should—like computers in general—never be installed without a detailed systems study to determine the need and to develop the possible application usage. An automatic data collection and/or transmission system in and of itself will not solve problems. It will only create more of them if it is not properly implemented.

Although there are a number of manufacturers of equipment of this type, a typical piece of equipment is the IBM 2790 Data Communications System. It is a two-way, in-plant data collection and communication system composed of a network of individual data entry and area terminals linked by a system controller. Information is entered by badges, cards, and keyboard into area stations at primary locations. These data are transferred from the data entry units to the area stations (Figure 10–13) to the system controller and then to the computer processor.

FIGURE 10–13. IBM 2791 Area Station

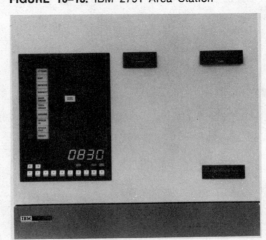

Courtesy of IBM

The framework of the IBM 2790 system is provided by its unique two-wire data transmission system; a high-speed pulse transmission system which links as many as 100 area stations to the system controller and a low-speed pulse system for communication between each area station and up to 32 data entry units.

An illustration[2] of how off-line data collection devices could be applied in a production and material control application (Figure 10–14) starts with data processing (the computer) preparing a *list of materials* arranged in order by production schedule date. (Or it could be arranged in Stores picking sequence.) This information comes from the master

---

[2] "A Standard Register Data collection System," Form 4904, The Standard Register Co., Dayton, Ohio.

STORES   STAGING AREA   MOVE   PRODUCTION (First Operation)   INSPECTION CONTROL

LCT or SRP Data Collection Station

MASTER CARD
One for each item of material

STORES ISSUE
4-PART ZIP/CARD FORM

Part Number –
Lot Number
Location
Unit of Measure
Vendor Code
Move To
Quantity
Date
Shift
Recording Station

PART 1

to Data Processing. Material issued, ready to move from staging area to Production.
A

PARTS 2, 3 & 4
stay with material

PART 2

to Data Processing; inspected parts to Stores or next production location.
B

PARTS 3 & 4

PART 3

to Data Processing; first production operation begins.
C & D

PART 4

with material as ID copy. Marked operations completed and material ready for inspection. Filed in Parts History File.

MASTER CARD

Master card from Parts History File tells inspection to be performed.

LCT or SRP Data Collection Station

4-PART CREDIT MOVE ORDER ZIP/CARD FORM

Part Number
Quantity Produced
Quantity Accepted
Types of Inspection
Move To
Group Number
Type of Container
Inspector's Number
Date
Shift
Work Center Number

PART 1

to Data Processing when inspection completed and material is ready to move.
E & I & J

PARTS 2, 3 & 4

PART 2

to Data Processing; inspected parts to Stores or next production location.
F

PARTS 3 & 4

PART 3

to Data Processing; acknowledge parts have arrived next location.
G

PART 4

remains with parts for ID purposes.
H

MASTER CARD
One for each item of material

List of Materials from Data Processing to Stock Room

DATA PROCESSING CENTER

PRODUCTION STATUS REPORT

RELS FROM STORES READY TO MOVE	AVAILABLE TO DEPT.	IN DEPT. BEGIN 1ST OPER.	+ –	QTY DUE	RELS FROM DEPT. READY TO MOVE	AVAILABLE TO DEPT.	IN DEPT. BEGIN 1ST OPERATION	REWORK IN DEPT. ESTIMATE TIME DEL.	HELD FOR INSPECTION REVIEW	RELS FROM INSPECT. REV. REWORK OK SCRAP REORDER FROM STORES
A	B	C		D	E	F	G	H	I	J

Courtesy of Standard Register Co.

production schedule listing stored in the computer file. The list of materials is sent to Stores where materials are withdrawn (picked) and distributed.

At the point of materials distribution in Stores, a Data Collection Station (Figure 10–15) or a Source Record Punch (Figure 3–9)

FIGURE 10–15. LCT 100 Data Collection Station

Courtesy of Standard Register Co

utilize a Zipcard[3] Stores Issue form. Master item cards kept on file at Stores contain part number, unit of measure, vendor code, and distribution. After inserting the proper master card for each item of material and a *Stores Issue* Zipcard form into the data collection machine, the materials issuer then enters through its keyboard the quantity of material issued. From another point in the machine, such semivariable information as date, shift, and recording station number is automatically entered. Upon activating the machine, the Stores Issue form is punched in Hollerith code with all the data from the information on the master card as well as the variable and semivariable information. The punched numeric data is also interpreted across the top of all copies of the form. A Stores Issue form is thus prepared for each item of material issued relating to the production order.

---

[3] Trademark, The Standard Register Company.

The Zipcard form (Figure 3–10) has four copies—the first three are standard-sized cards; the fourth is paper. Copy one is sent from Stores to Data Processing as notification that the material has been issued and is ready to move from the staging area to production. The rest of the set accompanies the material.

When the material is ready to be moved from the staging areas to a production location, the second card copy is sent to Data Processing as notification of its new location. At the time the first production operation is begun, Production sends the third card copy of the form to Data Processing. The fourth paper copy stays with the material as an identification copy. This copy is marked when all required operations within a given department are completed and the material is ready for inspection.

When the material is to be inspected, master cards relating material and the type of inspection to be performed are pulled from the Parts History File. Again an SRP or LCT data collection unit is used to record results of inspection. A Credit Move Order Zipcard set is punched with input from the master card and also variable and semi-variable information from the machine. When all the information has been punched into the *Credit Move Order,* copy one is sent to Data Processing as notice of the number of parts which have been inspected and are available to move to furnished stores or further production. Copy two is sent to Data Processing when the material is moved to Stores or to the next production location and copy three is used to inform Data Processing that the material has arrived in Stores or at the next production location.

REFERENCES

1. BRADDOCK, BRENT D. "Characteristics of Visual Display Terminals." *Telecommunications,* November 1973, p. 31.

2. "Can Computer Graphics Extend Business Infosystems?" *Infosystems,* April 1974, p. 72.

3. CIOLFI, P. K. "Communications Terminals." *Modern Data,* April 1973, p. 44.

4. "Communications Processors—Who, What, and Why?" *Telecommunications,* May 1973, p. 16.

5. "Current Status in Data Communications." *EDP Analyzer,* March 1973.

6. "Data Communications Terminals." *Telecommunications,* November 1973, p. 23.

7. "Developments in Data Transmission." *EDP Analyzer,* May 1969.

8. "Distributed Intelligence in Data Communication." *EDP Analyzer,* February 1973.

9. EXELBERT, RODD S. and BADLER, MITCHELL in collaboration with Alfred Tauber. "Automatic Information Retrieval." *Information and Records Management,* February 1974, p. 23.

10. "Focus on Hard-Copy Terminals." *The Data Communications User,* April 1974, p. 24.

11. HOPEWELL, LYNN. "Trends in Data Communications." *Datamation,* August 1973, p. 49.

12. "IBM Thinks P.O.S.-itively." *Modern Data,* November 1973, p. 28.

13. KROUT, DICK. "On-Line Data Collection a Must When Sales Mean Knowing Your Stock." *Paperwork Simplification,* Winter 1973, p. 2.

14. McLAUGHLIN, RICHARD A. "Alphanumeric Display Terminal Survey." *Datamation,* November 1973, p. 71.

15. MURPHY, JOHN A. "Point-of-Sale Systems." *Modern Data,* June 1973, p. 54.

16. "New Products in Data Communication." *EDP Analyzer,* May 1969.

17. O'BRIEN, BRADLEY V. "Keys to Low-cost Remote Data Entry." *Infosystems,* October 1973, p. 50.

QUESTIONS

1. What is the difference between the types of communication channels?
2. How is "grades of circuits" different from "types of channels?"
3. Why are different types of circuits available?
4. How do I/O data channels differ from the types of communications channels?
5. Describe several means of data communication.
6. What types of terminals are available?
7. Describe some of the purposes for which terminals can be used.
8. Describe two applications for which you feel a graphical display terminal should be capable of being used.
9. In what kind of business situation do you suppose a data collection system would be helpful?

11

Direct Access Storage and Internal Memory Devices

ALMOST ANY CLASSIFICATION of computer-associated devices requires some arbitrary decision as to the category assignment of a given item of equipment. The most glaring examples of this are in the classification of magnetic tape and disk-pack equipment, which in this text will be described under direct access storage devices.

As mentioned earlier, most of the larger computer systems utilize magnetic tape and disk-pack equipment as input and output devices as well as for both off-line and on-line storage, as the input speed of the other peripheral devices inhibits the full usage of the computational capabilities of these large systems. In smaller systems, most of the input today is still in the form of punched cards, and the magnetic tape and disk-pack units are utilized as data storage or for the output of information which will, in turn, be fed into a larger system as input data. (See Reference 6.)

Data storage files—as well as the computer word length (Chapter 6)—may be classified as being fixed or variable record length files (Figure 11–1). Data files may, for some types of information, be utilized rather inefficiently by the manner in which data are stored. In some equipment, the number of characters available in a given data record is specified. If more space is needed for a given data record—personnel data on an employee for example—then two or more record lengths are required. If the recorded data requires just one additional character to be stored in the second record length area, then the balance of that particular record length is unusable for other data. In some storage

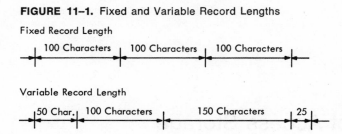

FIGURE 11–1. Fixed and Variable Record Lengths

Fixed Record Length

100 Characters | 100 Characters | 100 Characters

Variable Record Length

50 Char. | 100 Characters | 150 Characters | 25

files—both direct access and internal memory—record lengths may be flexible to permit the recording of variable lengths of data records and to provide a more efficient usage of the costly storage space in these files.

DIRECT ACCESS STORAGE DEVICES

The need for fast access storage devices to serve as an extension of the internal memory of the central processing unit brought about the development of several forms of mass data files. The design of these is such that under certain circumstances they must be directly accessed by the computer and become an integral part of memory, though their general usage is to provide large files of on-line storage of data.

Magnetic Tape

Nearly all the computer manufacturers have a series of magnetic tape units compatible with their computers. The individual models differ basically in two ways: one is in the density in which the data are packed on the tape (characters per inch) and the other is in the speed with which the mechanism can read and write data on the tape. A listing of the tape units produced by the major computer manufacturers is found in Figure 11–2.

The magnetic tape unit (Figure 11–3) serves both as an on-line input and output device. It performs the function of transferring the tape on one reel to another, past a read, write, or read-write head where data are read from the tape to the computer system or written on the tape from the computer system. Speeds vary with the tape unit used but data may be read or written on the fastest unit at the rate of 1.25 million alphabetic or 2.5 million numeric characters per second.

This speed has made magnetic tape one of the more widely used

FIGURE 11–2. Magnetic Tape Drive Characteristics

Model	Channels	Speed Inch/Sec.	Density Char./Inch	Transfer Rate K Char./Sec.	Recording Technique
Burroughs					
9380 (4 Units)	7	45	200/556/800	9/25/36	NRZI
9381 (4 Units)	7 or 9	22.5/45	800	18/36	NRZI
9390	7	90	200/556	18/50	NRZI
9391	7	90	200/556/800	18/50/72	NRZI
9392	9	45	1600	72	Phase
9393	9	90/150	1600	144/240	Phase
9394–1	7	120	200/556/800	24/66/96	NRZI
9394–2	9	120	800	96	NRZI
9495 (Self-loading)	9	75/125/200/250	1600	120/200/320/400	Phase
9496	9	25/50	1600	40/80	Phase
Control Data					
657–1	7	37.5	200/556/800	7.5/20.8/30	NRZI
657–2	7	75	200/556/800	15/41.7/60	NRZI
657–3	7	112.5	200/556/800	22.5/62.5/90	NRZI
657–4	7	150	200/556/800	30/83.3/120	NRZI
659–1	9	37.5	800/1600	30/60	NRZI/Phase
659–2	9	75	800/1600	60/120	NRZI/Phase
659–3	9	112.5	800/1600	90/180	NRZI/Phase
659–4	9	150	800/1600	120/240	NRZI/Phase
667–2	7	100	200/556/800	20/55.6/80	NRZI
667–3	7	150	200/556/800	30/83.4/120	NRZI
667–4	7	200	200/556/800	40/111.2/160	NRZI
669–2	9	100	800/1600	80/160	NRZI/Phase
669–3	9	150	800/1600	120/240	NRZI/Phase
669–4	9	200	800/1600	160/320	NRZI/Phase
Honeywell					
204B–1 or 2	7	36	200/556	7.2/20	NRZI
204B–3 or 4	7	80	200/556	16/44.5	NRZI
204B–5	7	120	200/556	24/66.7	NRZI
204B–7	7	36	200/556/800/1200	7.2/20/28.8/43.2	NRZI
204B–8	7	80	200/556/800	16/44.5/64	NRZI
204B–9	7	120	200/556/800/1200	24/66.7/96/144	NRZI
204B–200	7	18	200/556	3.6/10	NRZI
204B–300	7	36	200/556	7.2/20	NRZI
204B–400	7	54	200/556	10.8/30	NRZI
204C–13 or 14	9	36	800	28.8	NRZI
204D–1	9	35	800/1600	37.3/74.6	NRZI/Phase
204D–3	9	70	800/1600	74.6/149.3	NRZI/Phase
204D–5	9	105	800/1600	112/224	NRZI/Phase
204F–1	9	35	800/1600	37.3/74.6	NRZI/Phase
204F–3	9	70	800/1600	74.6/149.3	NRZI/Phase
204F–5	9	105	800/1600	112/224	NRZI/Phase
MTH 200	7	37.5	200/556	7.5/21	NRZI
MTH 201	7	75	200/556	15/42	NRZI
MTH 300	7	37.5	200/556/800	7.5/21/30	NRZI
MTH 301	7	75	200/556/800	15/42/60	NRZI
MTH 372	7	150	200/556	30/83	NRZI
MTH 373	7	150	200/556/800	30/83/120	NRZI
MTH 402	9	37.5	200/556	10/28	NRZI
MTH 403	9	37.5	200/556/800	10/28/40	NRZI

FIGURE 11–2. (*continued*)

Model	Channels	Speed Inch/Sec.	Density Char./Inch	Transfer Rate K Char./Sec.	Recording Technique
Honeywell					
MTH 404	9	75	200/556	20/56	NRZI
MTH 405	9	75	200/556/800	20/56/80	NRZI
MTH 492	9	150	200/556	40/111	NRZI
MTH 493	9	150	200/556/800	40/111/160	NRZI
MTH 501	7	75	200/556/800	15/42/60	NRZI
MTH 502	9	75	200/556/800/1600	20/56/80/160	NRZI/Phase
MTH 504	7	125	200/556/800	25/70/100	NRZI
MTH 505	9	125	200/556/800/1600	33/93/133/267	NRZI/Phase
IBM					
2401	7	75	200/556/800	15/41.7/60	NRZI
	9	37.5/75/112.5	800	30/60/90	NRZI
	9	37.5/75/112.5	1600	60/120/180	Phase
2415	7 or 9	18.75	800/1600	15/30	NRZI/Phase
2420	9	100/200	1600	160/320	Phase
3410/11	7	12.5	200/556/800	2.5/6.9/10	NRZI
	9	12.5	1600	20	Phase
3410/11	7	25	200/556/800	5/13.9/20	NRZI
	9	25	800/1600	20/40	NRZI/Phase
3410/11	7	50	200/556/800	10/27.8/40	NRZI
	9	50	800/1600	40/80	NRZI/Phase
3420	7	75/125/200	556	41.7/69.5/111.2	NRZI
	9	75/125/200	800	60/100/160	Phase
	9	75/125/200	1600	120/200/320	NRZI
	9	75/125/200	6250	470/780/1250	Group Encoded
NCR					
633–111/121	9	50	1600	80	Phase
633–117	7	50	200/556/800	10/28/40	NRZI
633–119	9	50	800	40	NRZI
633–211	9	90	1600	144	Phase
633–311	9	150	1600	244	Phase
634–107	7	25	200/556/800	5/13.9/20	NRZI
634–109	9	25	1600	40	Phase
634–117	7	25	200/556/800	5/13.9/20	NRZI
634–119	9	25	1600	40	Phase
634–209	9	50	1600	80	Phase
634–219	9	50	1600	80	Phase
635–109	9	100	1600	160	Phase
635–209	9	200	1600	320	Phase
UNIVAC					
Uniservo VI–C	9	42.7	800	34.2	NRZI
	7	42.7	200/556/800	34.2 (at 800 bpi)	NRZI
Uniservo VIII–C	9	120	800	128	NRZI
	7	120	200/556/800	96 (at 800 bpi)	NRZI
Uniservo 12	9	42.7	800/1600	34.2/68.3	NRZI/Phase
	7	42.7	200/556/800	8.5/23.7/34.2	NRZI
Uniservo 16	9	120	1600	192	Phase
	7	120	200/556/800	24/66.7/96	NRZI
Uniservo 20	9	200	1600	320	Phase

FIGURE 11–2. (concluded)

Model	Channels	Speed Inch/Sec.	Density Char./Inch	Transfer Rate K Char./Sec.	Recording Technique
Xerox					
3322	9	45	800	36	NRZI
3332	9	45	800/1600	36/72	NRZI/Phase
3345	9	75	800/1600	60/120	NRZI/Phase
3347	9	125	800/1600	100/200	NRZI/Phase
7316	9	75	800	60	NRZI
7322	9	75	800	60	NRZI
7332	9	75	1600	120	Phase
7333	9	150	1600	240	Phase
7362	7	37.5	556	20.8	NRZI
7372	7	75	200/556/800	15/41.7/60	Phase

forms of data input in the larger computer systems. In such systems the processing speed is so great that the computer's processor would actually be standing idle (waiting for data to work with) in between the time it would take to feed in punched cards from a card reader.

Magnetic tape does have a disadvantage in that it must be read serially, rather than randomly, but once the data has been accessed it may be read in or out of the system at a rate that is much faster than possible on most other data forms. The tape reels are also relatively inexpensive when compared to other fast I/O devices.

Physically, magnetic tape may come on reels, which may contain up to 2,400 feet of the ½-inch-wide tape, or it may come in cassettes which contain about 300 feet of ⁵⁄₃₂-inch tape. In either case the tape looks much like the tape seen on home tape recorders. Data are recorded as magnetized spots or bits in the metallic oxide found on one side of the tape. Once recorded, information on tape is permanent unless new data are written over the old (the old is removed as the new is added) or a special effort is made to erase the data. This ability to write new information over old means that tape can be used over and over again with significant savings in recording costs.

Data are recorded on the tape in the form of small magnetized spots (Figure 11–4) in either 7- or 9-channel form. Both utilize the binary coded decimal system in recording digits, letters, and characters in conjunction with a check bit. However, the 7-channel code is a modification of the 7-channel paper tape code, and the 9-channel code is either in the form of the Extended Binary Coded Decimal Interchange Code or the newer American Standard Code for Information Interchange. The number of channels used, however, may vary with the computer

FIGURE 11–3.

(a)   IBM 3420 Magnetic Tape Subsystem

Courtesy of IBM

(b)   Tape Cassette Units

Courtesy of Burroughs Corp.

FIGURE 11–4. Magnetic Tape Data Formats

(a) Seven-Track Tape

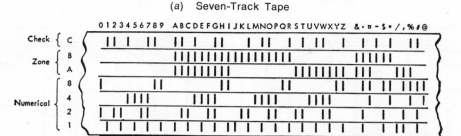

(b) Nine-Track Tape (EBCDIC Code)

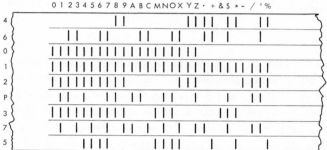

manufacturer and the computer system with which the tape is to be used. Magnetic tape is normally an even parity device. Data are read from the tape as it is moved past the read gap of either the two-gap head or the read-write gap of a one-gap head (Figure 11–5). As the magnetized spots on the tape move past the gap, small currents are generated in the read coil of the head. The presence and absence of these induced pulses of current is interpreted into data by the computer circuitry. Writing data is accomplished by small pulses of electrical current furnished by the computer circuitry, flowing in the write coil of the head which, in turn, through induction causes data previously written on the tape to be removed and the new data recorded.

Magnetic Disks.

Magnetic disks are very similar in appearance to the phonograph records used in the popular juke box. These "records" are metallic disks which are coated on both sides with a ferrous oxide recording material. They are permanently mounted, one above the other, on a

FIGURE 11–5. Read-Write Heads

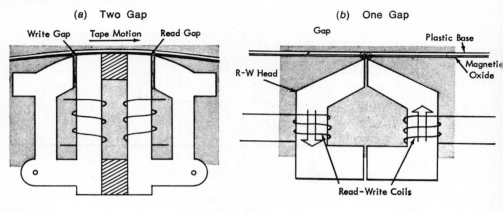

(a) Two Gap

Write Gap   Tape Motion   Read Gap

(b) One Gap

Gap   Plastic Base

R-W Head   Magnetic Oxide

Read-Write Coils

shaft which rotates at high speeds to spin the disks and permit mounted read and write heads to obtain or record data. In some equipment a single pair of read and write heads move in and out between the records and up and down on a shaft from record to record as they read from or write on the disks. In other equipment, two or more heads or a series of heads are used to perform the read and write functions. Of course, the greater the number of heads, the faster the data may be read or written but, as might be expected, the more expensive the unit.

Though quite similar in the function performed, disk memory files have developed in two distinct types. At first all disk files were permanently mounted in a case, with usually 25 or 50 disks in a module and one or two modules to file (Figures 11–6 and 11–7). More recently, disk drives have been made that are more compact and mobile (Figure 11–8). These are mounted, in a covered carrying case, in units of one to eleven disks, which provide a variable number of recording surfaces with the top and bottom surface of the multi-disk packs normally not usable (Figure 11–9). These disk packs may be quickly mounted in a disk storage drive unit (Figure 11–10) for processing purposes or replaced with another disk pack and placed in a file cabinet for storage until the recorded data are needed again.

Data may be addressed, or located, on the disks by the disk number, the sector on the disk, and the track number (Figure 11–11). The disks are numbered consecutively from bottom to top of the file, with the bottom number being 00, the next 01, and so on. There are five assigned sectors on each side of each disk. These are assigned sector

FIGURE 11–6. UNIVAC 8460 Disc File

Courtesy of Sperry UNIVAC

FIGURE 11–7. Disk File Characteristics

Model	No. of Spindles	Capacity per Spindle (Million Bytes)	Read-Write Heads/Spindle	Avg. Seek or Access (Millisec.)	Transfer Rate (K Bytes/Sec.)
Burroughs					
9372–12	1 to 5	10	1/track	20	208
9373–3	1 to 5	20	1/track	23	353
9375–4	1 to 5	20	1/track	40	228
Honeywell					
DSU 270	—	15.3	—	26	333

addresses 0 through 4 for the top of the disk and 5 through 9 for the bottom of the disk. There are usually 200 tracks of recorded data on each side of the disk which have addresses 000 through 199. The number of characters available, per sector per track, varies with the density of the data stored.

FIGURE 11–8. Disk Drive Characteristics

Model	No. of Spindles	Capacity per Spindle (Million Bytes)	Read-Write Heads/Spindle	Avg. Seek or Access (Millisec.)	Transfer Rate (K Bytes/Sec.)
Burroughs					
9480–1	1	2.3	2	80	193
9480–2	2	2.3	2	80	193
9481–1	1	4.6	2	80	193
9481–2	2	4.6	2	80	193
9484–3	2	60.5	20	30	312.5
9484–4	2 to 12	121	20	30	625
9485–3	2	60.5	20	30	312.5
9485–4	2 to 12	121	20	30	625
Control Data					
821	1 or 2	419 K Char.	1	100 Char.	420 KC
841	3 to 8	35.7 K Char.	1	75 Char.	420 KC
844–21	2 to 8	118 K Char.	1	30 Char.	1,130 KC
844–41	2 to 8	233 K Char.	1	30 Char.	1,070 KC
Honeywell					
171	1	4.6	10	80	147.5
172	1	9.2	10	50	208.3
274	8	147.2 K Char.	20	62.5	208.3 KC
275	1	18.4 K Char.	10	57	208.3 KC
276	1	37.4 K Char.	20	50	208.3 KC
277	1	64.0 K Char.	20	34	712.0 KC
278	5 to 8	175–280 K Char.	20	62.5	416.0 KC
279	2 to 8	133 K Char.	40	38.3	1,067.0 KC
DSS 058	1	3.5	10	60	156
DSS 167	1	15.3	20	75	208
DSS 170	1 or 2	15.3	20	34	416
DSS 180	1	27.6	20	34	416
DSS 181	1	27.6	20	34	416
DSS 190	1	133	19	30	1,074
IBM					
1810	1	512 (16-bit words)	2	70 or 520	36
2305	1 or 2	5.4 or 11.2	50 to 200	2.5 or 5	3.0 or 1.5 (MB)
2310	1	512 (16-bit words)	2	520	36
2311	1	2.7, 5.4, or 7.25	10	60	156
2314	1 to 8	29.176	20	60	312
2319	1 to 8	29.176	20	60	312
3330	1 or 2	100	19	30	806
3333	1 or 2	100	19	30	806
3340	1	34.9 or 69.8	12	25	885
5444	1	2.45 or 4.9	2	153	199
5445	1	20.48	20	60	312
NCR					
655	2	4.6	12	43.7	108
656	1 or 2 (1 Fixed Head)	4.98	1	47.5	312.5
657–101	1 or 2	29.8 or 59.6	1	60 or 30	315 or 500
657–102	1 or 2	96	1	30	500
658–101	1	100	1	38.3	806

FIGURE 11–8. *(continued)*

Model	No. of Spindles	Capacity per Spindle (Million Bytes)	Read-Write Heads/Spindle	Avg. Seek or Access (Millisec.)	Transfer Rates (K Bytes/Sec.)
UNIVAC					
8405	1	3.0	Fixed Head	8.3	624
8410	1	1.6	2	145	312
8411	1	7.25	10	87.5	156
8414	1	29.18	20	72.5	312
8424	2	58	20	42.5	312
8425	1	58	20	41.5	312
8430	1	100	19	35.3	806
8440	2	119.2	20	42.5	624
8460	2	46.5 (36-bit word)	40	80	75/95
Xerox					
3203	1	1.31	128	8	755
3204	1	2.62	256	8	755
3214	1	2.88	256	8	755
3215	2	2.88	512	8	755
7202	1	.75	128	17	188
7203	1	1.5	256	17	188
7204	1	3.0	512	17	188
7212	1	5.3	512	17	2,470
7232	1	6.2	512	17	384

FIGURE 11–9. Disk Pack

Courtesy of Burroughs Corp.

FIGURE 11–10. Disk Drive Unit with Disk Pack

Courtesy of NCR

FIGURE 11–11. Information Storage in Disk Units

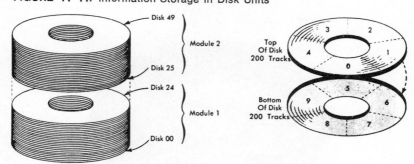

Courtesy of IBM

Data are usually recorded in BCD form in disk files; however, some computer systems use other forms of binary representation. The speed with which data may be read or recorded is directly dependent upon the speed of rotation of the disk, the density with which the data are packed on the disk, and the number of read and write heads available for the transfer of data. Most common makes of equipment have one or two read and write heads which move up and down to individual disks and in and out to the tracks on the disk. Some models of equipment, however, have read and write heads for each track on the disk (Figure 11–12). Typical transfer speeds for disk files would be a trans-

FIGURE 11–12. Multiple Read-Write Heads on Disk

Courtesy of Burroughs Corp.

fer rate ranging from 36,000 (36K) alphabetic characters (72,000 digits) up to 3 million alphabetic characters (6 million digits) per second.

The volume of storage provided by disk files is usually dependent on the number of disks available in the file and the density of the data packing, and on whether the record lengths are fixed or variable. Disk packs are small and portable and provide a maximum range of 2 to 500 million characters or 4 to 1,000 million digits per pack. However, disk packs may also be mounted in multiple drive modules (Figure 11–13) which provide many millions of characters of storage. Disk

FIGURE 11–13. IBM 3330 Disk Storage Subsystem

Courtesy of IBM

files provide up to approximately 20 million characters or over 100 million digits per file unit and some subsystems, utilizing several disk drives, provide up to 100 billion characters (200 billion digits) available on-line.

Magnetic disk memory has two major features which makes it such a desirable form of data storage. First, it provides for a tremendous volume of data to be stored in its disks. The need for this large volume of data in business information processing systems was previously described in contrasting the requirements of such a system with those of a scientific·data processing system. The second major feature is its ability to search the mass of stored data and retrieve any given bit of this data at random and to make it immediately available for processing. Data processing that makes use of this ability to select any given bit of data from the mass during the processing procedure is known as random-access data processing. This random access to data in magnetic disk memory files contrasts with the necessity of selecting data in sequence from magnetic tape files (where any selection of random data requires the serial reading of all data stored on the tape in between the desired units of data).

Magnetic Drum

Drum storage (Figure 11–14) is normally an internal type of memory which provides stored data. The data may be entered or recalled at a very fast access rate compared with other mechanical types

FIGURE 11–14. Magnetic Drum Characteristics

Model	Capacity (Million Bytes)	Read/Write Heads	Avg. Seek or Access (Millisec.)	Transfer Rate (K Bytes/Sec.)
Control Data				
865	8.3 M Char.	768	17 Char.	1,000 KC/S
Honeywell				
270A	4.2	1,024	8.6	1,200
IBM				
2301	4.09	800	8.6	1,200
2303	4.09	800	8.6	303.8
UNIVAC				
FH 432	1.5	384	4.3	1,440
FH 1782	12.5	1,536	17	1,440
FASTRAND II	132	64	92	153.6
FASTRAND III	198	64	92	230.4

of memory. Drums are also used as external on-line storage devices (Figure 11–15) where fast access memory is required. The physical size of the drum limits it as to the quantity of information available relative to the cost of such a unit, but some external storage units provide up to 200 million characters or 400 million digits of data.

Data are normally represented in binary coded decimal form on magnetic drums with a check bit. The drum is a round cylinder, which rotates at very fast speeds. Its surface is plated with a material which will become magnetized when exposed to a magnetic field. Data storage is in the form of invisible rings or tracks around the cylinder which have been divided up into sections; these sections are, in turn, subdivided into character locations (Figure 11–16). The number of these tracks, sections, and characters will vary with the make and model of equipment but, in general, the number has a direct dependence on the physical size of the particular drum considered.

Reading and writing data on the magnetic drum is accomplished by one or more read, write, or read-write heads. In some instances, where very fast speeds are desired, a separate head is used for each

FIGURE 11–15. CDC 865 Drum Storage Unit

Courtesy of Control Data Corp.

track. These operations are performed in essentially the same manner as those described for magnetic tape. Once placed on the drum, data are permanent until written over, as the magnetism is retained indefinitely. A few milliseconds are normally required for access to data on magnetic drums. However, as soon as the data are located, the act of reading and writing data records can be performed at rates up to 1,440,000 characters or 2,880,000 digits per second.

Magnetic Card

There are currently two types of magnetic card storage devices (Figure 11–17). Both utilize a thin plastic card which is coated with a magnetic receptive surface and resembles a wide, but short in length, strip of magnetic tape.

FIGURE 11–16. Typical Drum Storage Schematic

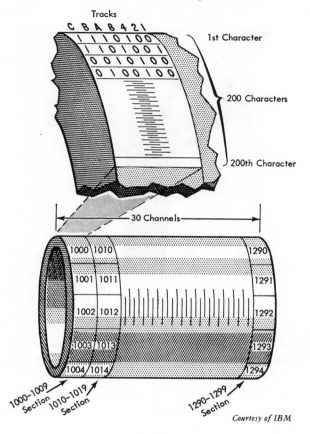

Courtesy of IBM

FIGURE 11–17. Magnetic Card Device Characteristics

Model	Type	Capacity (Million Bytes)	Access Time (Millisec.)	Transfer Rate (K Bytes/Sec.)
NCR				
653–101	CRAM	145	125	83
IBM				
2321	Data Cell	400	175 to 600	55

Card Random Access Memory (CRAM). CRAM is an on-line storage device which reads and records data on a mylar magnetic card 14 inches long and 3¼ inches wide (Figure 11–18). Each card

FIGURE 11–18. CRAM Card

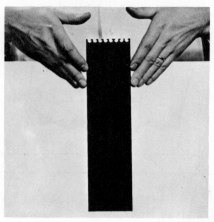

Courtesy of NCR

has seven invisible data recording tracks which can be individually addressed for reading or writing data. Each track has a storage capacity of 3,100 alphanumeric characters, so each card has a maximum storage capacity of 21,700 characters.

Two hundred and fifty-six (256) cards are stored in a cartridge (the equivalent of 69,000 punched cards) which may be inserted in or removed from the CRAM unit (Figure 11–19) in approximately 30 seconds. Any one of the 256 cards and any position of data on that card may be selected independently at a speed which allows the transfer of data at a rate of 100,000 characters per second. The cards are held suspended from rods inside the cartridge which move, on orders from the computer system, to allow the card to fall into a vacuum, which pulls it in position to be wrapped around a rotating drum turning at a speed of 400 inches a second (Figure 11–20). Read and write heads are positioned so that data may be read in a similar manner to that of reading magnetic tape. The data code used on CRAM cards is the six-bit alphanumeric binary coded decimal code with a check bit and an eighth channel, termed a clock channel, which is used for internal circuitry timing purposes and has no relation to the data represented.

Data Cell. The IBM 2321 Data Cell Drive (Figure 11–21), which is an on-line direct access storage for the IBM System/360, offers an

FIGURE 11–19. NCR 633 CRAM Unit

Courtesy of NCR

economical solution to the storage of large, sequentially organized data records requiring random reference. The Data Cell Drive houses 10 removable and interchangeable data cells each of which contains 200 strips of magnetic tape 2¼ inches wide and 13 inches long. Each of these strips provides 100 tracks for data, and each track provides 2,000 eight-bit bytes of data. The total storage capacity of the 10 removable cells in a Data Cell Drive is 400 million characters or 800 million digits of data. The transfer rate of this data is 55,000 alphabetic characters or 110,000 digits per second.

INTERNAL MEMORY DEVICES

The memory devices used as internal storage for data in conjunction with the central processing unit of the computer generally utilize the

FIGURE 11–20. CRAM Feed Diagram

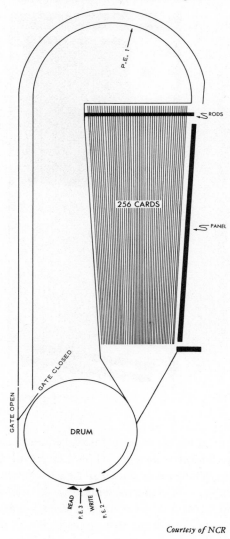

256 CARDS

GATE OPEN
GATE CLOSED

DRUM

READ   WRITE
P.E.3   P.E.2

P.E.1

RODS

PANEL

Courtesy of NCR

fastest and most capable type of such device available at the given stage of development. Thus many of the devices previously used as internal memory have been replaced by faster and more efficient devices. Also, some of the previously discussed direct access storage devices may be found to have been used for internal storage at times in the past and may even still be utilized, in a few instances, in computers for this

FIGURE 11–21. IBM 2321 Data Cell Drive

Courtesy of IBM

purpose today. The particular devices most commonly used for internal memory today, however, are the items which follow.

Magnetic Core

Magnetic core memory is composed of a large number of tiny rings or cores of ferromagnetic material, each threaded at the intersection of a fine lattice of wires. Each core is only a small fraction of an inch in diameter, and because of this size, core memory is very compact. Inasmuch as its operation is based on the flow of electricity, it is very fast, stable, and reliable.

The binary states of "on" and "off" are determined by the direction of the polarity or magnetic state of the core. If a wire is threaded through the center of the core rings, and a current of electricity sent through the wire, the core will become magnetized. The polarity of the magnetism is determined by the direction of the flow of this electricity (Figure 11–22). If the direction of the current flow is reversed, the polarity of the core will be reversed. In any instance, once the core is magnetized it will retain that polarity indefinitely or until reversed.

Inasmuch as it takes a specific amount of current flow through the wire to magnetize the core, all of a series of cores strung on the wire will have the same polarity. To permit the selective magnetism of a given core, two wires, each with their own string of cores but having a single core in common, are placed at right angles to one another. If only half the current needed to magnetize a core is sent through

FIGURE 11-22. Polarity of Magnetic Cores

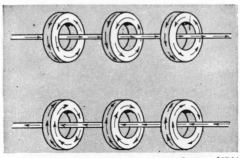

Courtesy of IBM

each wire, only the core at the intersection of the wires will be magnetized. To permit all cores to be selectively magnetized, the cores are placed on a screen or lattice of wires to form a magnetic core plane (Figure 11-23).

FIGURE 11-23. Magnetic Core Plane

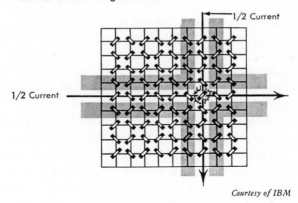

Courtesy of IBM

If several planes of cores are placed one above another and the same position in each of these planes is designated as part of a binary coded decimal character location, the cores in this position may be selectively magnetized to form, as an example, the binary configuration for the letter A, 1 11 0001 (Figure 11-24). All the other core positions also serve to represent individual BCD character locations. The number of cores in a plane vary with the equipment make and model, and many use several stacks of such planes to provide a magnetic core stor-

FIGURE 11–24. BCD Character Locations

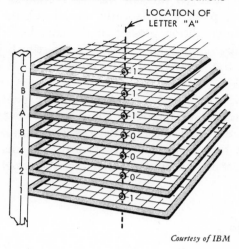

Courtesy of IBM

age unit. A given core position, in the stack of planes, provides a computer "word."

A third wire, termed a "sense" wire, is run diagonally through every core in a given plane. When a given position is to be tested, or read, for its magnetic state, current flows through the two wires previously described, and if the item stored is a 1 and is changed to a 0 by the test, this will be sensed by the sense wire (Figure 11–25), and the computer will "know" what was in this core position.

FIGURE 11–25. Core Sense Wire

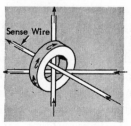

Courtesy of IBM

It should be noted that in the test the core tested was changed from a 1 to a 0. This, of course, changes the data stored in this core, and this is not desired in a read operation, as it may be necessary to read this same data many times before the data are written over in the recording of different data. To prevent the destruction of data in a read operation, the computer automatically reproduces, or regenerates, the same binary state condition present in the core before the test. This is accomplished by sending an "inhibit" pulse, which is reverse to the current flow of the "read" pulse, to regenerate the data which was "read out."

Until recently, core storage has been quite expensive and limited in its use for internal storage only. There are, however, some external on-line directly addressable storage devices which utilize magnetic core memory. Access time is always very fast for magnetic core memory and may be so fast as to provide an effective cycle time[1] of 125 nanoseconds per character.

Thin-Film Memory

Thin-film memory may vary in form somewhat from manufacturer to manufacturer, but basically such an element consists of a deposit on an extremely thin film of some base material which contains a uniform deposit of magnetic storage materials having high packing density.

The National Cash Register Company (NCR) introduced a unique form of thin-film memory in its NCR 315 Rod Memory Computer a number of years ago. This memory rod was a beryllium-copper wire electroplated with a thin film of nickel-iron material and wrapped with a ribbon of copper. Each rod was 0.015 inch thick and 6 inches long and was capable of storing 40 binary digits to serve in random, sequential, real-time, and remote inquiry processing. A 12-bit word could be transferred in 800 nanoseconds (4-bit word in 200 nanoseconds).

The NCR Century Series of computers uses a new thin-film short-rod memory in which the rod is $\frac{1}{10}$-inch-long piece of wire (Figure 11–26a) which stores one bit of data that can be retrieved in 800 nanoseconds. Two windings of copper wire around each rod (Figure 11–26b) serve in the reading and storing of data in magnetic form in the rod. These small rods are imbedded in plastic in a plane similar to that of core memory (Figure 11–26c). These planes are then stacked to provide a basic rod memory unit (Figure 11–27). Depending on the model of the Century Series, memory may be expanded in 16K (16,000) modules up to 2,097K 8-bit bytes.

The Burroughs Corporation is utilizing a planar thin-film memory

---

[1] The interval of time required for the completion of one operation of a set of repetitive procedures.

FIGURE 11–26. Rod Memory Elements

(a)   (b)

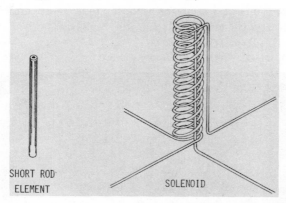

SHORT ROD ELEMENT   SOLENOID

(c)   Memory Plane Segment (enlarged)

Courtesy of NCR

FIGURE 11–27. Rod Memory Module

Courtesy of NCR

(Figure 11–28) in some of their larger units for main memory and as "read only" memory in other units. This memory has a cycle time of 600 nanoseconds and memory modules may be expanded from 16K to over 6,000K 52-bit words of storage.

FIGURE 11–28. Thin-Film Memory Planes

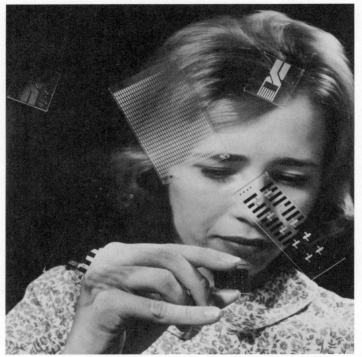

Courtesy of Burroughs Corp.

Sperry UNIVAC is also utilizing a limited amount (262K 36-bit words maximum) of thin-film plated-wire memory (Figure 11–29) in several of their computer systems. The access time of this memory is 300 nanoseconds. The core memory used in conjunction with this memory in at least one of these systems can be a maximum of 1,024 36-bit words depending on the customer's needs.

Semiconductor Memory

Burroughs has been using semiconductor memory in the form of large-scale integrated (LSI) memory chips (Figure 11–30) for some time now in several of its computers. IBM (as mentioned in Chapter

FIGURE 11–29. Plated-Wire Thin-Film Memory

Courtesy of Sperry UNIVAC

FIGURE 11–30. LSI Memory Module

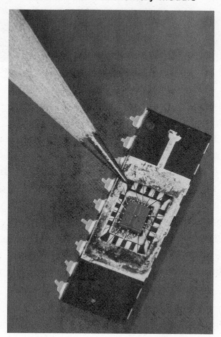

Courtesy of Burroughs Corp.

5) is using some microminiaturized monolithic semiconductor memory in conjunction with core memory to provide a very fast internal operating-type memory. NCR (Figure 11–31) and others have used this type

FIGURE 11–31. Monolithic Integrated Logic Circuit

Courtesy of NCR

of circuitry in their equipment and most—no doubt—will soon be adding this type of memory to their systems.

Semiconductor memory does have the drawback in that a loss of power may, in many instances, result in a loss of data as it does not always provide a permanently magnetized binary indicator as do magnetic cores, tapes, and disks. However, it is very fast due to the spacing of components (in Burroughs equipment up to 2,500 electronic devices—1024 bits of memory—are stored in little more than a relatively minute spot—Figure 11–32) and, as its production is fully automated, it will probably be a less costly memory, per unit of storage, than most others in use today once a larger production level is achieved. (See Reference 4.)

Other New and Developing Memory Devices

General Automation, a minicomputer manufacturer, has recently announced (Reference 3) what they call a "microcomputer" which uses

FIGURE 11–32. Memory Circuitry (magnified approximately 50 times)

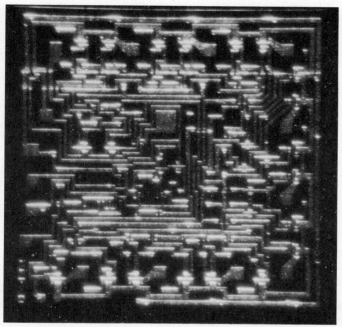

Courtesy of Burroughs Corp.

a silicon-on-saphire (SOS) technology. SOS has permitted them to place 2,000 gates, or the equivalent of 4,000 to 5,000 transistors, on a single semiconductor chip approximately one eighth inch square.

It has been predicted that thin films would continue to improve and expand in usage over magnetic cores. (See Reference 10.) Others have forecast that the use of semiconductor memories would overtake all other types of memory in usage as soon as their performance/cost basis would excel that of other types. In reality though, while the use of both thin-film and semiconductor memories have increased considerably, the use of core has expanded even more. It is now anticipated that—unless other experimental memories are developed to upset current usage—the trend toward thin film and semiconductors will continue and perhaps increase slightly but not involve any radical change in trends in the near future.

Bell Telephone Laboratories discovered a laser technology in 1969 which used electro-optical crystals (Figure 11–33) to interrupt the flow of light from a laser beam. This had the potential of permitting lasers

FIGURE 11–33. Testing a Laboratory–Grown Crystal of Magnetic Material

Courtesy of NCR

to serve as an optical type of computer memory by utilizing flashes of light on film to replace the electrically recorded spots of data on magnetic memory devices. (See Reference 9.)

This technique has been further explored by several other firms as well as Bell Labs. RCA, now out of the computer business but heavily involved in communications and the storage of information from communication satellites, has recently displayed what may be the first practical application of laser storage. (See Reference 7). The method used involves the transfer—by laser beam—of data (to and from a CPU) which is stored on holographic[2] photographic plates embedded in heat-sensitive plastic. Varying intensities of the laser beam serve to write and read the data. It is estimated that storage files at least as large as current disk files are practical and the access speed should be 1,000 times faster.

---

[2] A technique used in producing images, especially by using laser beams to record varying intensities of light and dark patterns on a photographic plate which, when projected, produce a three-dimensional image.

An even newer technique, also first proposed by Bell Labs back in 1969, is bubble memory. This involves magnetic bubbles found in certain minerals whose polarity can be magnetized to form the equivalent of the "1" and "0" bits in core memory. It has been forecast that Bell Labs will soon have an operating 16-million bit bubble memory and that North American Rockwell's Microelectronics Company and Sperry UNIVAC will also soon have models. (See Reference 1.) IBM has a very small experimental model using slightly different techniques in operation. It is estimated by Bell Labs that 10-million bits per square inch is feasible but IBM says their method may provide 1-billion bits per square inch.

Also, IBM has recently displayed an 8K semiconductor memory on a single-cell chip that is only 145 by 201 mils (.001 of an inch) in size. (See Reference 8.) This is the smallest of this type to date and provides 280,000 bits per square inch.

If any of the above developments become feasible from a production standpoint, there should be a big shift to larger and faster memories that are much less expensive and more efficient than current memories. Only time will provide the answer to this possibility. (See References 1 and 5.)

REFERENCES

1. BRUUN, ROY J. "When Will Core, Drum, and Disk Systems Be Just a Memory?" *Infosystems,* May 1973, p. 40.

2. CARSON, ROBERT W. "Minicomputer Removable Storage." *Modern Data,* March 1973, p. 46.

3. An advertisement. *Computerworld,* March 13, 1974, pp. 16, 17.

4. DAVIS, SIDNEY. "Selection and Application of Semiconductor Memories." *Computer Design,* January 1974, p. 65.

5. HOUSTON, GEORGE B. "Trillion Bit Memories." *Datamation,* October 1973, p. 52.

6. MURPHEY, JOHN A. "Plug-Compatible Miniperipherals." *Modern Data,* December 1973, p. 30.

7. "RCA Demonstrates Laser Memory: Core, Drum, Disk Replacement?" *Computerworld,* May 9, 1973, p. 21.

8. "RCA Uses Holgaphic Approach, IBM Puts 8K on Chip." *Computerworld,* February 28, 1973, p. 43.

9. "When Lasers Get the Message." *Business Week,* March 2, 1968, p. 11.

10. WITHINGTON, FREDERIC G.   "Trends in MIS Technology." *Datamation,* February 1970, p. 108.

QUESTIONS

1. Magnetic tape now comes in two major forms as well as in the magnetic card used in the Data Cell and CRAM. Describe these three forms? Compare both in physical size and in the extent they are used.

2. Would magnetic tape be more or less desirable than a magnetic disk as a direct access storage device? Carefully explain.

3. Describe the relative merits and shortcomings of the following three forms of storage: (*a*) magnetic drum, (*b*) data cell, and (*c*) magnetic disks.

4. Briefly describe how a card random access memory (CRAM) system works.

5. How can you differentiate broadly between on-line memory devices and internal memory devices?

6. For what use is the magnetic core form of storage frequently used? Why?

7. Name some of the types of thin-film memory.

8. How does the size of core and semiconductor memory compare?

9. Name some of the newer types of internal memory now in development.

10. Why are there so many different types of internal memory devices being developed?

III

Design and Development of Information Systems

chapter
12

Systems Analysis
and Flowcharting.

THE READER, at this point, should recognize that a data processing
system for any organization is made up of a host of subsystems. Each
subsystem is probably designed at a different time to take care of a
particular need at that time. It does not necessarily follow that any
one of the subsystems was planned with the others in mind. This, in
turn, often means that the procedures as well as the data do not cor-
relate together as well as they should.

As a typical set of examples, there is probably a set of procedures,
or a subsystem, to handle credit sales. In all likelihood, there is also
a different set of procedures to handle sales returns and allowances,
sales analyses, and cash sales. When all of these subsystems are put
together, they are referred to as the sales system. When the sales system
is combined with all of the other systems in the organization the result
is referred to as the data processing, accounting, or information system
of the business or organization.

Such a system is made up of forms, procedures, records, and reports.
Presumably, the system would have been planned in such a way that
it would assist the management to meet more adequately the objectives
of the business, which, among others, would certainly include (1) making a satisfactory return on the investment, and (2) conservation of
the business assets.

A complete system, such as is presumed in the above statement, will
probably not have been developed until the business entity has grown
to considerable size and until its organization is no longer simple but
represents a complex distribution of authority and responsibility. It
is also quite likely that management will not have thought through

and spelled out its objectives until the business has become reasonably large, has plants in numerous locations, deals with large sums of money, and has responsibilities delegated to a number of levels of executives.

In short, it is typical that as a business organization increases in size and becomes more involved in its operations, the data processing system must, as a necessity, be better formulated as well as more complex. However, it is also typical that the growth of the data processing system will lag behind the corresponding growth of the organization. The analysis of an existing data processing system will rarely be recognized as needed until serious problems arise and come to the attention of management.

Such problems might involve a lack of internal control, processing bottlenecks, or management's dissatisfaction with the information it is presently receiving. This dissatisfaction could be due to inadequate information, reports not timely enough, or a combination of these conditions.

Once management recognizes a need for systems reorganization, it must then decide whether to use company personnel to analyze the problem and to recommend a solution or to seek the assistance of outside consultants who may be representatives of either a certified public accounting or management consulting firm. Either alternative will require an analysis, in detail, of the existing system and will result in specific recommendations to correct the problems found.

The situation described in the preceding paragraphs may well lead to the decision that electronic data processing equipment should be introduced, or, if it has already been introduced, that the system needs to be modified. In either eventuality, it is paramount that the persons attempting to rectify the problems understand thoroughly the existing system and how the business operates. They must also understand what the inputs (forms), outputs (reports), resources, and procedures being practiced may be. It is only when all of these facets of the problem are clearly understood that a meaningful solution may be worked out. The new system must, at the very least, perform as well as the existing system. Therefore, an understanding of the existing system becomes the logical foundation for design of the new system.

ANALYZING THE PRESENT SYSTEM

The task, therefore, which confronts the group that analyzes a system is to decide whether they should review all of the existing system or whether they should regard this as too drastic an action and limit the review to an attempt to eliminate the current problems and bottlenecks in the system. Many people have found that the most effective compromise is for the systems review group to obtain permission to review, analyze, and design a total system, but to implement it on a building-block basis—piece by piece—over a period of time. The financial outlay to install anything close to a total system is extensive, and this is one of the reasons why many prefer to introduce the system in stages.

If the ultimate aim of the study is to provide a creative reconstruction of the data processing capabilities of all areas of the business, then the group (1) must probe deeply into management goals and methods of accomplishment, (2) determine the major policies and practices which are being followed, (3) recognize and understand current operating problems, (4) understand government regulations as they affect the business, both present and anticipated, and (5) determine the information which management needs to enable them to meet these problems.

Sources of information to provide answers to these questions would include:

1. Interviews with top management.
2. Annual reports.
3. Copies of management speeches about the business.
4. Employee orientation handbooks.
5. Investment house reviews and registers.

A system is designed by first determining what specific information is desired from the system, for what purpose it is needed, and on what time basis it must be furnished. It is only after the needs of the system have been ascertained that the inputs to the system—the procedures, records, and method of data processing—should be examined. At this point, the importance of the people who would be involved in making the proposed system work must be emphasized. All people involved with the system must be trained and educated so that they will understand and know how to deal with the proposed system when it is introduced.

Lastly, internal controls, which must be a part of all computerized systems, must be carefully thought out and included in the system.

Outputs—Reports

Broadly speaking, there are three types of financial reports with which any business is going to be concerned. First, there are the external financial reports, which include the income statement and the balance sheet. These are fundamental to any business organization. They are necessary to meet the requirements of stockholders, the public, labor unions, the Securities and Exchange Commission, and the various stock exchanges. Second, there are internal financial reports which are prepared to meet the requirements of management at varous levels within the business. Third, there are the reports required by governmental agencies—local, state, and national. The number, variety, and complexity of the reports required in a given business firm will, in addition to the needs of its management, also be determined by the type of business and the amount of supervision it receives from various agencies of government.

In many ways, the requirements and needs of the people or agencies which use these reports will dictate the data to be accumulated and the manner in which the data are to be summarized.

The firm's existing reports should be analyzed from the point of view of how adequately they are meeting the needs of the three groups of users of these reports. Normally, the area in which the most work will probably need to be done, due to the fact that it is often the least developed of all, is the area of internal control reports.

Factors to consider in deciding what reports are needed are:

1. Who needs information?
   a. Each person responsible for a function, an operation, a property, or for supervising a group of persons.
   b. The information needed will depend on the unit of output of the function; how each individual personally carries out his or her responsibilities; how he or she personally manages and controls in relationship to this unit of output.
2. What information is needed?
   a. Only details necessary for control. Supporting details should be available upon request.
3. When and how frequently is the information needed?
   a. Information may be needed in case of specific operations daily, weekly, or monthly, according to the several strata of management.

All internal reports should have the following characteristics in common:

1. Usefulness.
2. Simplicity, accuracy, and adequacy.

3. Timeliness.
4. Economy of preparation.
5. Conciseness.

Inputs—Business Forms and Records

It was pointed out early in Chapter 3 that "forms are basic to the data manipulation process." They are "the media on which the data are initially captured at the time when a transaction occurs." The analyst must certainly make himself or herself aware of all of the sources of business information and of the forms and records on which it will be captured.

Typical detailed original records are:

Cash receipts and disbursements

Sales invoices and records of customers

Purchase orders and records of vendors

Shipping reports

Receiving reports

Vendors invoices

Production orders and reports

Time tickets or reports

Store requisitions

Stock records

Salesmen's and distributors' reports

Personnel records

Plant and equipment records

Financial transactions

Credit information

Cost estimates

Standards

Corporate records

Correspondence

Insurance and tax records

In order for the analyst to understand the function of each of these forms and records, and since each of them is a part of the total data processing system, he or she will need to know the following about each item:

1. The nature of the form and its contents.
2. Where the form is prepared.
3. How it is prepared.
4. By whom it is prepared.
5. When it is prepared.
6. The number or volume of such forms prepared.
7. The frequency of reference made to any one record.
8. The reports and other records which are affected by these original forms and records.

The object of the analyst in securing the above information is to learn how these forms and records fit into the total data processing system.

Procedures

A procedures survey is a critical review of the methods by which a job is done, the tools used, and the physical location of operations. The objectives of such a review are to eliminate unessential activities, to coordinate the methods of conducting essential activities, to improve the physical location of work, and to determine staff requirements.

A management analyst uses many tools in such a procedures survey. She or he may interview employees and supervisors, prepare flowcharts of work, and analyze the design and use of forms and reports.

He or she will probably turn to the "Manual of Procedures," first of all, if one has been written. In it the analyst should find a description of all of the procedures currently in use. However, she or he may not find the manual reliable because (1) conditions may have changed without the manual being rewritten, or (2) existing practices may have gotten out of line with prescribed procedures without management being aware of it.

If a computer system is being reviewed, the Manual of Procedures takes on added importance because in addition to the information normally included in such a manual it should include information describing how the inputs are to be prepared and how to interpret the outputs. These facts would be indispensable to anyone reviewing the existing system.

The best way to learn what is going on is to go out and talk directly with the people who are doing the work.

The analyst should begin in a clerical department by obtaining an introduction to a supervisor by the superior, thereby demonstrating management's endorsement of the project. The tone of the meeting should be friendly and informal. The supervisor should be asked to outline briefly the functions of his or her work and how these are related to the functions of the other departments or units of the firm. The supervisor should be questioned about the major flow steps of the paper work. This information should be obtained in broad outline form at this point, and the supervisor should be assured that all findings and questions will be discussed with him or her first before any changes are recommended or made.

As soon as the analyst has learned the activities of the supervisors, attention should be turned to departmental employees and their work. It is not until this has been done that a procedure survey can be considered to be complete.

Resources

What does the systems analyst of the business firm under consideration have to work with in the way of resources? This becomes a basic consideration when one talks about changing a data processing system. Resources involve such things as manufacturing plants, office and communication equipment, data processing equipment, a resourceful executive group, and adequate financial resources. What the physical facilities are and where they are located in relationship to each other can have a lot to do with the type of system proposed. The same can be said for the talent and intellectual capacity of the executives, as well as the amount of money which may be available to carry out the design and operation of a new system. All of these elements must be considered and will have a bearing on the design of the system to be proposed.

Unforeseen Benefits

When the analyst has come to feel that he or she understands the problems of the business and what it is trying to accomplish and when he or she has studied the inputs, procedures, methods of processing data, available resources, and the outputs of the system, he or she is then in a position to have a good overall view of the role the data processing system should be performing in that particular business. Having gained this overall knowledge, the analyst is often in a position to make positive recommendations for improvement. Such recommendations may include:

1. Reduction in the number of steps in a procedure.
2. Elimination of unnecessary functions.
3. Elimination of duplication.
4. Combination of operations to reduce paper handling and get acquainted time, and thereby speed up the flow of work.
5. Elimination of unnecessary reports.
6. Improvements in methods.
7. Improvements in layout.
8. Revisions and redesign of forms.

It is quite possible that many such improvements, as enumerated above, could be accomplished with relative ease and little additional cost. When one has a broad, overall view of a problem, solutions which were not recognized previously often became obvious. (See Reference 4.)

FLOWCHARTING

Flowcharting, as a technique, is widely used as a means of better understanding existing or proposed data processing systems. It is a diagrammatic representation or map of the flow of events.

In general, the flowchart illustrations to follow will use standardized symbols. Any additional symbols used in actual business illustrations will be noted so that their usage will be brought to attention.

Flowcharts are constructed to conform to our natural tendency to read from left to right and top to bottom. Variations are, however, sometimes desirable in order to achieve symmetry and to emphasize certain points. Within this framework, flow lines can be drawn horizontally, vertically, and diagonally. The primary considerations are neatness, uniformity, and clarity. Explanatory footnotes are encouraged and are frequently used.

Some symbols are used almost universally in identifying particular events in the flow of data. The flow of data itself is usually indicated by a line, and the direction of flow by an arrowhead (Figure 12–1).

FIGURE 12–1. Direction of Flow

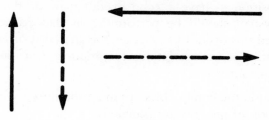

In flowcharting, solid lines are normally used to indicate the direction of flow, but occasionally it is desirable to differentiate between the physical movement of work and the mere transfer of information. This can be done by using solid lines in the first case and dotted lines in the second. For example, dotted lines are often used to illustrate accounting control functions.

Also, in order for one symbol to have a meaningful relationship to other symbols in a chart, it is necessary that it be connected to one or more other symbols in such a way as to indicate the sequence in which the operation occurs.

There are a variety of ways which can be used to flowchart an existing or proposed system so that it can be more clearly understood. Each method has a particular area of applicability. These major areas of applicability include (1) flowcharting for an informal series of steps and logical decisions; (2) flowcharting to represent symbolically the flow of documents through an organization; (3) flowcharting to show the development of the procedural steps to be followed in manually performed procedures; and (4) the technique of representing the flow of data through a punched card or electronic data processing system.

As a Series of Steps and Logical Decisions

This approach might be used where the objective is to understand the various activities, decisions, and alternatives required to achieve some required objective. The flowchart in Figure 12–2 illustrates the decisions a student must make when preparing his or her homework assignment.

In this type of flowcharting, the symbols may either be standard or nonstandard. In the illustration there is not to be a formal implemen-

FIGURE 12–2. Flowchart

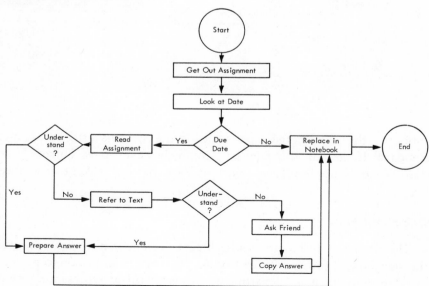

FIGURE 12–3. Flowchart of Document Flow

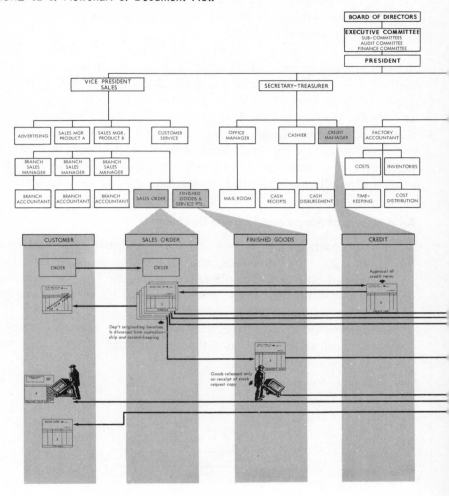

tation of the steps noted, and some of the symbols utilized are not standard. If desired, this flowchart could, however, have utilized standard symbols applicable to machine flowcharting (to be described later).

Document Flow

The flowchart technique applicable to document flow demonstrates the way various forms or other documents move from person to person, or from department to department, and is useful in representing sym-

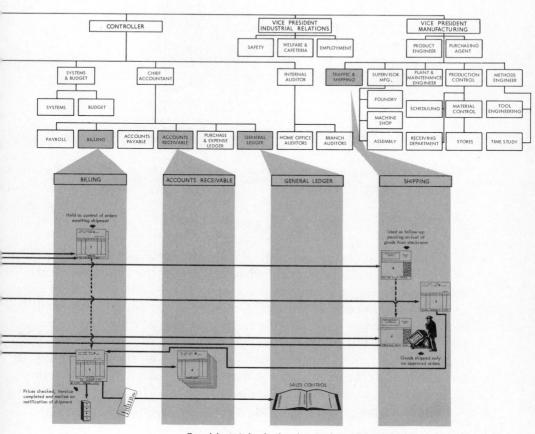

bolically the flow of paper work for a particular transaction or department. No special symbols are necessary, but it is useful to list the people or departments who are concerned across the top of the sheet. An illustration of flowcharting document flow is shown in Figure 12–3.

Manual Procedural Flow

Procedural operations which are to be performed in a manual system utilize five standardized symbols to represent the typical clerical operations normally found in such a system. These symbols are:

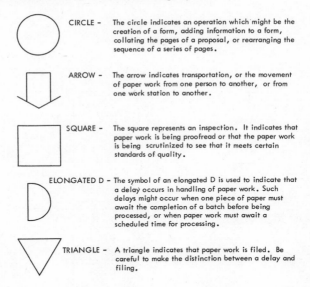

CIRCLE – The circle indicates an operation which might be the creation of a form, adding information to a form, collating the pages of a proposal, or rearranging the sequence of a series of pages.

ARROW – The arrow indicates transportation, or the movement of paper work from one person to another, or from one work station to another.

SQUARE – The square represents an inspection. It indicates that paper work is being proofread or that the paper work is being scrutinized to see that it meets certain standards of quality.

ELONGATED D – The symbol of an elongated D is used to indicate that a delay occurs in handling of paper work. Such delays might occur when one piece of paper must await the completion of a batch before being processed, or when paper work must await a scheduled time for processing.

TRIANGLE – A triangle indicates that paper work is filed. Be careful to make the distinction between a delay and filing.

Frequently, in conjunction with a manual flow chart, each step of the operation is carefully analyzed and notes of the action involved are recorded along with the symbols representing the action. An illustration of this practice is shown in Figure 12–4 in the partial procedural work sheet used in analyzing the steps involved in withdrawing stationery from central plant supplies.

In this illustration the component parts are (1) described in sequential order, (2) charted in symbolic form, (3) measured in the distance to be traveled in performing the operation, and (4) timed in terms of the elapsed time required to perform each operation.

Flowcharting for Computer Systems

It would be difficult to exaggerate the crucial importance of the system's study phase in the development of an electronic data processing installation. It is at this point that the real challenge of data processing is first met. A systems study provides an opportunity for a comprehensive examination of an organization's information-handling procedures. The objective is to make the organization run more efficiently. In this connection it is well to keep in mind that the uses of data processing systems have only begun to be explored. The processing ability of today's computers has thus far exceeded man's ability to utilize them

FIGURE 12–4. Procedure Analysis Work Sheet

Before   Exhibit 2 (Page 1)

SUMMARY	PRESENT		PROPOSED		SAVINGS		PROCEDURE CHARTED
	NO.	HRS.	NO.	HRS.	NO.	HRS.	Withdrawing Stationery from Central Plant Supplies
○ OPERATIONS	21	.57396					
⇨ TRANSPORTATIONS	8	.19128					CHART BEGINS
☐ INSPECTIONS	3	.167					In Ordering Office
D DELAYS	1	.167					CHART ENDS
▽ STORAGES	2	–					Distribution of Charges
DISTANCE TRAVELED	741 ft.						CHARTED BY / DATE

☒ PRESENT   ☐ PROPOSED

LINE NO.	STEPS IN PROCEDURE	OPER.	TRANSP.	INSPECT.	DELAY	STORE	DISTANCE IN FEET	TIME	ELIMINATE	COMBINE	SEQUENCE	PLACE	PERSON	IMPROVE
1	A. Section Clerk inspects stock	○	⟳	■	D	▽	5	.167						
2	A. Writes one copy of Form 1772	●	⟳	☐	D	▽		.083						
3	A. Carries Form 1772 to Supervisor	○	◼	☐	D	▽	40	.0167						
4	B. Supervisor signs Form 1772	●	⟳	☐	D	▽		.033						
5	A. Section Clerk takes Form 1772 to Stationery Stores	○	◼	☐	D	▽	225	.083						
6	C. Plant Stationery Clerk fills requisition	●	⟳	☐	D	▽		.167						
7	A. Section Clerk waits for Stationery	○	⟳	☐	●	▽		.167						
8	A. Takes Stationery back to section	○	◼	☐	D	▽	225	.083						
9	C. Checks each item as it is filled	●	⟳	☐	D	▽		.0167						
10	C. Initials Form 1772	●	⟳	☐	D	▽		.0042						
11	C. Delivers Form 1772 to Stationery Storekeeper	○	◼	☐	D	▽	75	.0083						
12	D. Stationery Storekeeper checks each item against Kardex file	●	⟳	☐	D	▽								
13	D. Determines if Stationery was originially charged to M&R or Engr. from Kardex	○	⟳	■	D	▽		.167						
14	D. Prices each item if credit must be developed and change made	●	⟳	☐	D	▽								
15	D. Places red check opposite each item to be credited to Engineering	●	⟳	☐	D	▽								
16	D. Extends Quantity x Unit Price	●	⟳	☐	D	▽		.083						
17	D. Totals cost for each requisition	●	⟳	☐	D	▽		.0167						
18	D. Sorts Form 1772 to Requisition Dept.	●	⟳	☐	D	▽		.00056						
19	D. Runs adding machine total by Dept.	●	⟳	☐	D	▽		.00028						
20	D. Runs adding machine total for All Engineering Credits	●	⟳	☐	D	▽		.0014						
21	D. Runs adding machine total of Dept. totals	●	⟳	☐	D	▽		–						
22	D. Writes out distribution of charges and credits	●	⟳	☐	D	▽		.00056						
23	D. Types letter – three copies – to Accounting Dept. to make entry	●	⟳	☐	D	▽		.00056						
24	D. Attaches bundle of requisitions to letter	●	⟳	☐	D	▽		–						

APPROVED BY   DATE

| TOTALS | 17 | 4 | 2 | 1 | | 570 | 1.09896 |

PAGE 1 OF 2 PAGES

Source: From *Systems Education Monograph # 1* (Detroit: Systems and Procedures Association, 1962), p. 19.

in their most sophisticated manner. At the present time the only real limit to the information-handling work that they can perform is the limit which may exist in people's ability to investigate a problem, reduce it to its basic elements, and reassemble these elements in a pattern which such a system can handle.

The significant feature of all business data processing problems is the fact that each seemingly complex problem can be broken down into combinations of elementary operations. This is the reason that such problems are readily handled by computing systems. Each of the present-day computing systems has the ability to do high-speed elementary operations such as simple addition, multiplication, and comparison. Utilizing the computer to attack a complex processing problem requires that the problem first be reduced to a series of logical elementary operations.

Since most data processing problems are complex, it is desirable to create a pictorial representation, a flowchart, showing the logical elementary steps in the solution of an overall complex situation.

In this chart, data provided by a source or originating document are converted to final or reporting documents.[1] A flowchart, then, provides a precise picture of the sequence in which operations are to be executed. Such a picture gives primary emphasis to the documents involved as well as to the work stations through which they pass.

Until about 1965, the symbols utilized previously for punched card machine applications were generally used in conjunction with computer applications. These symbols varied somewhat with given equipment manufacturers but were basically those suggested by IBM, the largest such manufacturer. With the rise of specific needs for standardized symbols for computer systems and programs, it was generally felt that such standards should be developed.

In 1966, the American Standards Association's X3 Sectional Committee on Computers and Information Processing Standards defined a standard set of flowcharting symbols for information processing problem description which are described as basic, specialized I/O, and specialized processing symbols (Figure 12–5).

In general, there are two types or levels of flowcharts used in punched card and electronic data processing. The first type is called *system flowcharts,* and the second is called *operations or program*

---

[1] It should be noted that in its broadest meaning a document is "any instrument conveying information." Such a definition is used in this discussion in order to include punched card, magnetic tape, paper tape, and magnetic disk in the same category as printed forms.

FIGURE 12–5. Flowchart Basic Symbols

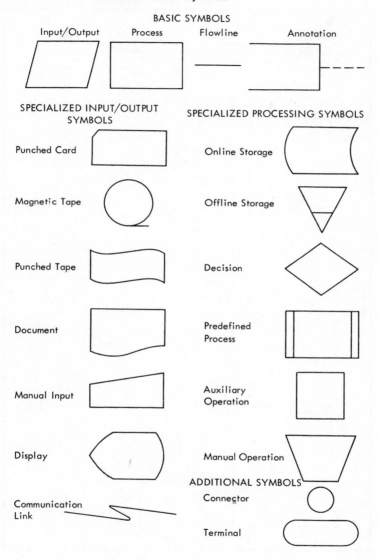

BASIC SYMBOLS

Input/Output   Process   Flowline   Annotation

SPECIALIZED INPUT/OUTPUT SYMBOLS

Punched Card

Magnetic Tape

Punched Tape

Document

Manual Input

Display

Communication Link

SPECIALIZED PROCESSING SYMBOLS

Online Storage

Offline Storage

Decision

Predefined Process

Auxiliary Operation

Manual Operation

ADDITIONAL SYMBOLS

Connector

Terminal

flowcharts or *block diagrams.* The symbols used for each type have specific usage. However, as some functions represented are common to both types of flowcharting, the same symbols will be used in both cases. Also, in both types of flowcharting, flowchart work sheets similar to that of Figure 12–6, will usually be used to facilitate the placement and arrangement of the symbols.

FIGURE 12–6. Flowchart Work Sheet

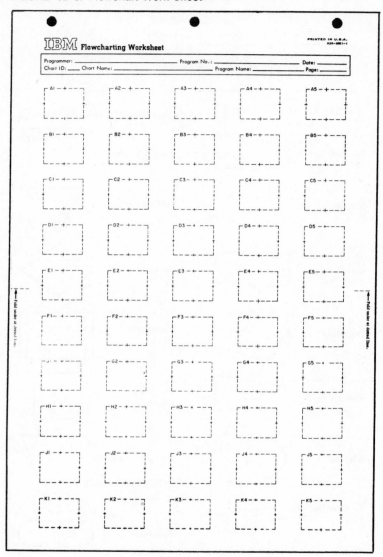

System Flowcharts. Flowcharts that are designed to show the sequence of major operations and that normally summarize a complete operation are known as *system flowcharts.* These are usually prepared as aids to management and systems analysts to permit them to understand some specific operation and to get an overall viewpoint of the operation.

The first step in system flowcharting is to define the data processing problem itself. In doing this, answers must be found to the following questions:

1. What information is required from the system in the form of reports?
2. What is required from this portion of the system to integrate it into the overall data processing system?
3. Where does the input information arise?
4. What exceptions can arise and under what circumstances?
5. How many transactions and how many exceptions of each type are involved?
6. How should each transaction and each exception be handled?
7. What files are involved and what information is involved in them?
8. Are results required on schedule or on demand?

Answers to the above questions will supply much of the necessary information for the preparation of the initial flowcharts of the system.

From the initial flowcharts, other flowcharts should be drawn so that each procedure is broken down into simpler subprocedures which may be related to each other and the entire system by the flow of information between them. Each subprocedure or subsystem must be analyzed in the same way as the entire system.

An example of a simple system flowchart is illustrated in the pictorial presentation of the major considerations in processing a payroll problem (Figure 12–7).

This figure also illustrates the use of the four basic symbols. The general representation symbol for any type of *input* or *output* is used in this flowchart. However, in this illustration, it is known, because of the *annotation symbol* and its information, that the input must be in the form of punched cards. The *output symbol* and notation at the end of the procedure indicates the preparation of typical payroll checks. Input and output can, of course, also be represented by any of the specialized symbols used to pictorially present the actual form of input or output to be used. In the illustration the *punched card symbol* could have been used as the input symbol and the *document symbol* used to represent the printed checks as output.

The *process symbol* is used to represent each of the series of calculations involved in calculating the payroll. First, is the determination of the gross pay amount, then the various payroll deductions required or agreed upon are developed, and last, the calculation is made of the net pay amount for which the check is to be written.

FIGURE 12–7. System Flowchart

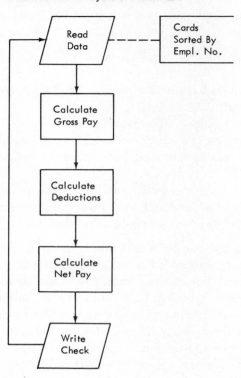

In each symbolic representation in this systems flowchart illustration, the symbol provides only general information and even the notations are in summary form, but the flowchart does provide an overall view of the procedure necessary to prepare the checks for a payroll.

Also in Figure 12–7, note the arrow leading from the output symbol back up to the input symbol. This represents a *looping* procedure. Without this loop notation, the application would indicate that only one payroll check is to be written. The loop, however, indicates to the coder writing the computer program that as one check is written another data card (or set of cards for a given employee) is to be read and the process continued until all the payroll cards are processed and the resulting checks are written.

Normally, a computer goes through a stored program in sequential steps, instruction by instruction in the order in which written, unless it is directed by the program itself to alter the sequential pattern. This is often necessary in a typical business program as there are certain segments of a procedure that may need to be repeated a number of times before progressing in the program. In other instances there may be circumstances which arise in the processing of the data where decisions must be made and, depending on the answers found, alternative sets of steps may need to be brought into the normal program or certain steps may need to be omitted entirely. Altering the sequence of instruction execution is known as a *transfer of control* and may involve *looping, branching,* or *jumping* within the program. Such a transfer of control is usually presented in a flowchart as a loop (illustrated above) or in connection with the use of the *decision symbol.*

Normally, most decision questions can be symbolized by the standard decision symbol, which provides two or three possible condition representations. This usage is illustrated in Figure 12–8 where (*a*) is a com-

FIGURE 12–8. Decision Branching

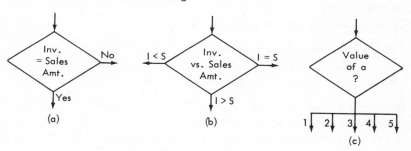

(a) (b) (c)

mon *yes* or *no* condition illustration in answer to a comparison question and (*b*) illustrates a comparison which has equal to, greater than, and less than conditions to be considered. In an occasional type of decision, however, there may be more than three conditions resulting from a comparison and this is illustrated in (*c*) where there are five possible answers.

In conjunction with the decision symbol, a set of commonly used arithmetic characters (Figure 12–9) are utilized to indicate the type of comparison desired to arrive at a decision to possibly alter the sequential pattern.

Program Flowchart. The program flowchart (sometimes referred to as a block diagram) is used to portray the various specific arithmetic and logical operations or steps which must be accomplished to solve the complete application problem. These charts or diagrams display specific operations and decisions and their sequence within the program. Generally, the programmer will use this flowchart to translate the elementary steps of a procedure into a program of coded instructions

FIGURE 12–9. Arithmetic Characters

Character	Description	Example	
:	Compare	A : B	Compare A with B
>	Greater than	A > B	A is greater than B
<	Less than	A < B	A is less than B
=	Equal	A = B	A is equal to B
≠	Unequal	A ≠ B	A is not equal to B
≥	Equal to or greater than	A ≥ B	A is equal to or greater than B
≤	Equal to or less than	A ≤ B	A is equal to or less than B
Σ	Sum	Σ A	Total of A

which will direct the proper machine operations to accomplish the processing operation.

Three important uses of program flowcharts are:

1. As an aid to program development.
2. As a guide in coding.
3. As documentation of a program.

In the development stage of preparing an application program, the first step is to determine the output desired. From this information the data needed to provide this output can be determined. Once the input data and its media form and format are known, the basic procedural steps to process the input data to obtain the results desired can be analyzed. At this stage, the flowchart representation of the procedures to be followed are usually general in nature and presented in system flowcharts (previously illustrated) showing the overall or general logic pattern to be followed. This pattern will provide information on the input and output functions with steps illustrating the identification and selection of records along with the decision functions required.

Once the general procedure is established—and this may involve a series of system flowcharts with each containing more detail—each element or block of the system flowchart will be broken down into the most basic steps and logic possible. This detailed breakdown is symbolized to the extent possible by utilizing the specialized input, output, and processing symbols shown in Figure 12–5. In addition, extensive notations may have to be provided to describe the data and its format, the specific items to be manipulated, and how they are to be manipulated in each logic procedure, any deviations from normal logic patterns by branching and looping procedures, and the output data and its format.

When such a detailed picture of a flowchart is prepared it is known as a *program flowchart* or *block diagram*. The coder, who is writing the actual computer program, can take the program flowchart and translate it into a language acceptable to the computer available. If the program flowchart is properly prepared and documented, the coder, in his or her translation of the flowchart, will not even have to be familiar with the application or procedure involved or have any knowledge of the needs of management in order to perform this language translation.

A typical program flowchart, Figure 12–10, illustrates the pattern of logic steps to be followed in a program to prepare a rather simple payroll check writing procedure. As mentioned above, additional documentation would be necessary to define or describe the abbreviated words (variable names) used. The description to follow will, in this instance, perform this function so this part of the documentation will be omitted.

Step (1) in the illustration uses the *process symbol* to show the storage space requirements for an overtime (OT) hours calculation and an overtime amount (OTAMT) and to set both storage locations to a zero value along with storage for a given value for the current social security rate (SSR) and the current maximum pay amount applied (CM). In each of these instances, as well as for other amounts to follow, the size of the values would have to be noted so that a provision for adequate space in storage could be made.

Step (2) indicates, by using the *punched card symbol,* that the time card employee number (TCENO) and the total hours worked (HRS) are to be read from a set of time cards. These would need to be in sequential order by the employee number. The *annotation symbol* shows the information to be read from each time card.

Step (3) is an *on-line storage symbol* for input from a disk storage device on which is stored the Payroll Master File. Data to be read from this file includes the payroll master employee number (PMENO)—and these also would have to be in sequential order, rate of pay (RATE), the amount of the social security taxable amounts used up-to-date for the year in computing social security tax (SS), the withholding tax factor (WTF)—based on the number of exemptions of the employee and the current withholding tax rate, and any other deductions (ODED)—such as insurance premiums, union dues, united fund, and so forth—which are either required by contract or law or have been requested by the employee.

Step (4) involves a *decision symbol* as the first time card employee number read may or may not be the same as the first payroll master

FIGURE 12–10. Program Flowchart

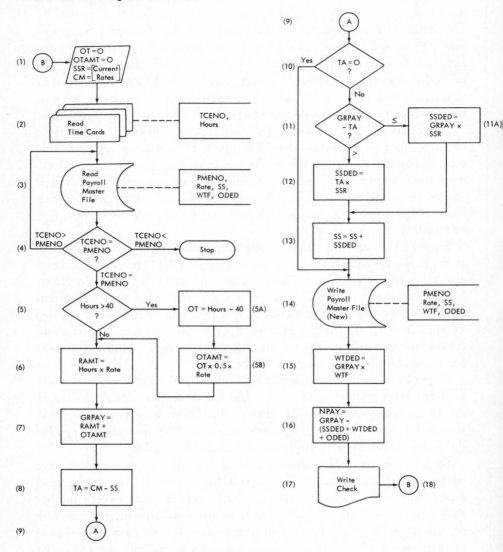

employee number read. These must be in agreement before the procedure can continue. If TCENO is less than the PMENO, something
is in error as to the sequence on the master file or the wrong disk
may have been mounted on the disk drive unit. The only recourse here
is to stop the procedure, as indicated by the *terminal symbol,* and investigate. If the TCENO is larger than the PMENO, then the machine
is to loop back to step (3) and read another record until the employee

numbers are in agreement. Of course, if the numbers are the same all is well and the machine continues to the next step.

Step (5) is another decision symbol and the question involves possible overtime work which, in this instance, is based on over 40 hours work in the week. If the hours worked are less than 40 the procedure continues to the next step. However, if the hours worked are greater than 40 the number of overtime hours are calculated in step (5A) and the incremental amount of overtime pay is determined in step (5B) (assuming overtime is one and one-half times regular pay).

Notice that the arrow from (5B) to (6) flows in an upward fashion. This is in violation of a generally accepted rule that flow lines should normally progress either downward or to the right. However, it will be discovered that it is not always practical to rigidly follow this rule and, if the distance of the flow line is not too long or so involved as to be unclear as to what is desired, the variation may be acceptable. In fact, it may even be clearer than using connectors such as (9) and (18). Also, both the calculations in (5A) and (5B) could have been indicated in the processing symbol at (5A) and then the flow line would have been acceptable. The main objective to be achieved is clarity and avoiding possible misunderstanding as to what is desired.

Step (6) calculates the regular amount of pay (RAMT) based on 40 or less hours of work during the week. Step (7) combines the results of (6) and (5B) to give the gross pay (GRPAY) for the individual for the work week.

Step (8) is a calculation to determine if the value of the social security taxable amount to date is equal to the current taxable maximum (CM) provided by law. Any amount lacking is to be stored as a taxable amount (TA) which will be used in this and perhaps succeeding weeks in tax computations.

Step (9) illustrates a *connector symbol* and indicates that the output flow at point *A* will continue at the input flow of point *A* elsewhere on the flowchart, which in this case is step (10).

Step (10) is a decision which can only have two possible answers as the social security deductions can never exceed the current maximum deduction allowed. If the taxable amount (TA) is zero we are ready to branch to step (14) to write out the new payroll master as there is no social security deduction required. If TA is some amount then we move to step (11) to determine the actual amount of the tax for the week.

Step (11) tests to see how much of the gross pay will be subject to the social security tax. If the week's gross pay is equal to or less than the taxable amount, the entire gross pay will be subject to the tax in step (11A). However, if gross pay is more than the taxable amount, only the taxable amount will be subject to tax in step (12).

In step (13) the social security tax amount determined in either step (11A) or (12) will be added to the total social security deducted previously (SS) to bring SS up-to-date so it will be available for next week's payroll calculations.

In step (14) the employee number, the earnings rate per hour, the withholding tax factor, the other deductions, and the new balance of social security taxable amount are put on a new Payroll Master File. This new file will be used in step (3) when the payroll is processed for the next week.

Step (15) is a computation of the current week's deduction for the withholding tax. The withholding tax factor is multiplied times the week's gross pay amount to determine the withholding tax to be deducted (WTDED) this week.

Step (16) is the computation of the net pay amount for the employee and is the gross pay amount less the total of the social security, withholding tax, and other deductions.

Step (17) is the preparation of the payroll check which is represented pictorially by the *document symbol*. Information would have to be presented at this point to provide all the information to be used and its placement on the check and on a stub which would show the detail of hours worked, overtime pay, regular pay, and all the deductions and related data.

Step (18) is another connector symbol but here it performs a looping function—rather than a continuing function—as it refers the program back to step (1) so that the payroll information may be gathered and a check written for the next employee as shown on the next time card.

In Summary. As indicated earlier, the flowchart serves a very important function in documenting a procedural application. If the flowchart is only to present an overview or overall summary then a systems flowchart may serve the purpose very well. However, if the detail of the application is to be shown or the flowchart is to be used in computer program preparation, then a program flowchart and its related information must be furnished. Even when time has elapsed after the program has been written and used, the program flowchart will serve as valuable documentation for reference purposes in case the program needs to be altered or new personnel desire to follow what is happening in the processing of the program on the computer. (See References 1. 2, 3.)

CASE ILLUSTRATION

One large manufacturer of candies and cookies solved its problems of converting its recordkeeping system from punched cards to a computerized system in the following manner.

The company was managed by a board of managers made up of the heads of the four principal operating divisions: manufacturing, distribution, finance, and administration. These men were personally convinced that a computer was what the company needed and were ultimately responsible for installing what has proven to be a highly successful computerized system.

The organization structure was clearly defined, and all echelons of management had a clear understanding of their authority and responsibility. The board of managers asked each member of the management team to enumerate all the information he or she would like to have, assuming that it would be obtainable, in order that he or she might more adequately discharge his or her responsibilities. When all of the managers' requests for information were compiled, it quickly became obvious that if all this information were to be provided, the members of management would be doing nothing but reading reports. A compromise was therefore worked out to provide only the most essential data.

The proposed complete computerized data processing system was then written up in booklet form describing (1) the various inputs to the system, how they would be prepared, and what they would contain; (2) all of the procedures which would be followed in connection with the recording and the processing of the data; and (3) exact copies of the proposed output reports. Sufficient copies of these booklets were prepared so that all members of management could have them to study. The proposed system was then discussed, criticized, and modified, where necessary, but every member of management was given to feel that he or she had a part to play in the development of the system. This involved two years work prior to the actual installation of the computer.

From the point of view of the board of managers, the computer installation has been an unqualified success, and they feel that much of the success is due to the planning which went into the installation.

REFERENCES

1. BOHL, MARILYN. *Flowcharting Techniques.* Palo Alto, California: Science Research Associates, 1971.

2. GLEIM, GEORGE A. *Program Flowcharting.* New York: Holt, Rinehart, & Winston, Inc., 1970.

3. LENHER, JOHN K. *Flowcharting: An Introductory Text and Workbook.* Princeton, N.J.: Auerbach Publishers, 1972.

4. ORILIA, LAURENCE S.; STERN, NANCY; STERN, ROBERT A. *Business Data Processing Systems.* New York: John Wiley & Sons, 1972.

QUESTIONS

1. What purpose does a data processing system serve in an organization?

2. Is it necessary for a business organization to have a data processing system?

3. What usually precipitates the management of a business deciding that a review of the existing system is necessary?

4. When the decision is made to review the data processing system of a business, what aspect of the existing system should be examined first? Why?

5. Following on your answer to question 4, what portions of the system would you next study and in which order?

6. Is change usually the best answer when the decision has been made to study what is presently being done in a data processing system? Explain.

7. Why is flowcharting recommended as a good way to study a data processing problem?

8. Differentiate between systems flowcharts and program flowcharts.

9. What purpose is being served by endeavoring to have the symbols used in flowcharting standardized on an international basis?

10. In systems flowcharting how is a looping procedure indicated?

11. What purpose does a looping procedure accomplish?

12. If when drawing a flowchart a decision were necessary, how should you indicate that you wanted to determine whether one number was larger than another number?

13. When a decision arises in a procedure, is it possible to only chart decisions which involve two possible alternatives? Explain.

14. Why can it be said that flowcharting is a good means of documenting a program?

15. Explain five flowcharting symbols with which you are acquainted.

16. When talking or thinking of systems analysis, it is always stated that the analyst should first carefully study the business under consideration and its related problems. What has this got to do with designing or redesigning any part of the total system? Explain. (Use illustrations if you think they would be helpful.)

13

Software Development

UP TO THIS POINT, our discussion of computers has emphasized the development and capabilities of the equipment, or *hardware* as it is often termed.

Equally important is the development and availability of software—usually in the form of programs—to assist in directing the computer in its processing of data through the equipment.

The computer is capable of solving problems of tremendous complexity with unbelievable speed and extreme accuracy. One of its most significant features is in its ability to solve problems from start to finish without human intervention in the intermediate steps of computation.

At first, the program of instructions to the computer had to be written in great detail. However, as will be seen, the depth of detail required in the program of instructions has been considerably reduced through the development of software.

STORED-PROGRAM CONCEPT

Since a computer must be directed as to the procedures to be followed, a program is basic to its operation. The program provides a complete set of coded detailed steps and procedures directing the computer to perform a data processing task. It will be stored in memory and interpreted by the control unit of the machine, making it possible for the computer's performance to be self-controlled. Any such self-controlled performance includes a series of actions or movements, each depending on another and requiring no operator intervention in the completion of the series. The series can be very short or very long; it can be completely sequential or the next action to be taken can be chosen by the last action completed.

The operation of an automatic record player is a good example of a series of actions, each depending on the one immediately preceding it. When records are loaded on the spindle of a record player and the player is turned on, a record drops, the playing arm moves into position, and the record plays; upon completion, the playing arm returns to a neutral position and the next record in sequence drops into place; the playing arm returns to the starting position on the new record; this record plays, and the cycle continues, without need for intervention or assistance by anyone, until all of the records have been played. This series of actions is called a program, and it is stored in the record player (Figure 13–1).

Any person planning to code a program should have the following knowledge and background: (1) he or she should know precisely the information which is desired out of the system; (2) he or she should also be fully acquainted with all of the types of data which will be fed into the system; (3) he or she should know the characteristics of the files which will be used to store partially processed data; (4) he or she must understand the instructions which will be used to guide the computer in its operation; and (5) he or she must be aware of the characteristics of the equipment available to carry out the procedures.

In data processing systems, the program controls the entire flow of data in and out of various processing units. If, for instance, original data are punched into cards, the program controls the reading of these data and their transport to various processing areas for addition, subtraction, multiplication, division, modification, classification, recording, and any other kind of action to which data can be subjected.

In stored-program systems all of the instructions needed to complete a procedure are written in the form of program steps. These program steps are made available to the machine by various methods, the most common of which is punched cards. (However, most of the larger computer systems normally use magnetic tape.) The data processing system stores these program steps in some type of storage medium. (See Chapter 11.) Thus, when a procedure is to begin, the stored program is loaded into the system, and the entire procedure can be performed from beginning to end without further intervention. The program calls

FIGURE 13–1. Block Diagram of a Program

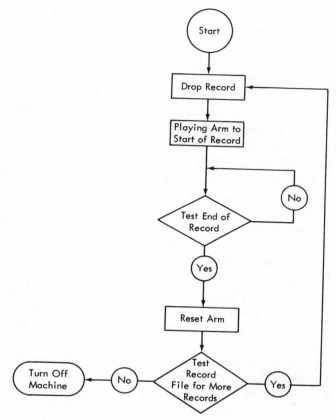

in the input data as needed, enabling the computer to perform in sequence the stages required in the processing of the data.

PROGRAMMING CLASSIFICATIONS

While the first computer programmers were, of necessity, jacks-of-all-trades, programming soon generated its own subspecialties. The first logical division of programming came with the distinction between applications programming and systems programming.

Applications Programming

The people who write applications programs are the ones who write the programs which cause the computers to accomplish certain data processing tasks, such as billing, payroll, and so on. They are usually individuals who have been trained or hired by a specific company and are highly knowledgeable of the problems they are programming.

Application programs are normally designed for a specific business firm and involve individual specific problems applicable to that firm's processing needs. This type of program provides the basic logic and instructions necessary to solve a given algorithm or problem.

Most application programs are unique to a given firm and are developed by the programmers of that firm. However, some types of firms—particularly those regulated by governmental agencies—have identical or similar applications. These and other general-purpose application programs may, at times, be acquired from computer-user groups or from the program libraries maintained by some of the computer manufacturers.

Closely associated with application programs are programs, which have become standardized over time, designed to take over or assist in the performance of routine but repetitive tasks often found in data processing operations. Programs of this type include *error routines, report generators,* and *utility programs.* Error routines provide a means of automatically initiating corrective action when errors occur. The presence of an error can be signaled on the console of the computer. Error routines are executed after programmed checks establish that an error exists. Programmed checks are often built into the computer or into the logic of the program itself. For example, one type of program check would be to run a sample program with similar programming and a known answer to see if it agrees with existing results.

A report generator is a program that can direct the production of output reports if the computer is provided with format and specification, input file detail, sorted input data, and input/output procedure rules.

Utility programs are standard routines used to assist in the operation of the computer, for example, a conversion routine, a sorting routine, a printout routine, and so forth.

Systems Programming

The systems programmers write the programs that run the computing equipment and generally are employed by the computer manufacturers. There are many computer routines which are common to many different data processing tasks, and it is these routines which are generally developed by these individuals. These programs are often referred to as program packages, and they can include such types as: control programs which operate the input and output equipment, testing programs which are designed to detect electrical and mechanical malfunctions, and utility programs which control output formats.

When a programmer who is writing an applications program comes to a point in the program where one of these program packages (macro instructions) would fit, he or she can utilize the program package which is obtainable from the computer manufacturer, rather than working out this part of the program independently. The programmer knows that this package has already been tested and proven. Through the use of such program packages, the writing of applications programs can be speeded up immeasurably, and the task of the applications programmer can be made a whole lot easier.

An important subdivision of systems programming is programming language development—producing the assemblers, compilers such as FORTRAN, COBOL, and other translation programs. With programming languages, applications programmers can instruct a computer in a language closer to English and normal mathematical notation rather than use the ones and zeros of machine language. Programming language development, then, is the creation of programs which permit the computer to translate a natural language statement into the numerical, machine language instructions, or object programs that actually operate the computer.

Machine Language Instructions.   When the first computer programs were written, they had to be written in a language acceptable to the computer. Since each make of computer had its own language, the programmer had to be trained in the techniques of coding for a particular computer system. This involved the writing of instructions in the form of long lists of numbers or number codes. Such a system, because of the detail and complexity involved, was prone to numerous errors. The possibility of transfer of knowledge between the coding required for two different computers was slight, and this created many difficult situations. For example, if a firm desired to change its computer, it also had to change all of its programs. Creating an equally difficult problem was the fact that the programs had to be prepared or coded in machine language. Obviously, coding in machine language made it necessary for the programmer either to memorize or to have readily available the many instruction codes which a particular computer used.

An even greater problem in machine language coding, however, was keeping track of the data and instruction locations as the instruction and data addresses were different for every instruction and for every program written. Thus, when the command to add was given in a machine language program, not only did the proper instruction code have to be indicated but also the specific memory address of the quantity to be added. Since all but the simplest programs contain several hundred coded instructions, and programs of thousands of instructions were not at all uncommon, keeping track of what was stored in various memory locations and determining which locations remain unused was quite an involved task. Furthermore, when changes had to be made or when errors were discovered in the program, all the address locations which followed usually had to be changed, necessitating an almost complete rewrite of that portion of the program.

Processor Programs.   Many of the difficulties and inconveniences of coding programs directly in machine coding can be simplified or eliminated through more advanced systems of program writing.

Experience has shown that computers can be programmed to recognize instructions expressed or written in other languages and to translate those instructions into their own language (processor programs).

For example, the first simplification of the programming process came with the use of letters and arabic numbers in place of basic number codes.

The programmer blocked out his or her problem and then used a series of symbols to represent each step in the process. Thus, for an instruction such as "load address," instead of writing a series of numbers for a code such as 01000001, the programmer needed only to remember "LA." A set of these symbols or *mnemonics,* when punched into cards and run through the computer, became the source program. The processor program, which was the translator program, was then used to translate the mnemonic instructions into a machine language to create the object program. In order for this object program to be used to produce the output results intended, it had to be read back into computer storage—along with the data to be processed—to produce the output desired in the form of tape or disk records, punched cards, or printed reports. (See Figure 13–2.)

FIGURE 13–2. Preparation of an Object Program

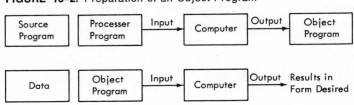

This technique simplified programming, but it still required one instruction for every step performed by the machine.

Not long after this advancement it became possible for the processor program itself to take on the difficult task of assigning storage addresses to data. This eliminated the need for the programmer to specify any addresses. He or she simply indicated how much storage would be required, and the processor took over the entire task of allocating storage to data and instructions.

INTERPRETER PROGRAMS.   Some early processor programs performed the function of translating source programs into machine language and also permitted the execution of the developed instructions at the same time. This type of processor program is termed an interpreter program. No object program is produced by the interpreter, so the data to be processed are fed in following the source program and are processed just as if an object program were provided. This characteristic has resulted in interpreters often being called "load and go" processors.

COMPILER PROGRAMS.   In programming, certain types of instructions are frequently repeated in the logic required in solving a given problem. Over and over, almost any program uses commands to read a card, update a disk file, move a record, perform some type of arithmetic calculation, and so on. In earlier processor programs, each time such an instruction appeared, the person coding the program had to write and rewrite the series of detailed instructions which told the machine exactly how to go about the particular task.

In the newer processor programs, which came to be known as *compilers,* much of the detailed series of machine commands for a given instruction in a source program could be generated by the computer through the utilization of *macroinstructions.* Macroinstructions are source language instructions that have the capability of generating more than one machine language instruction for a given source program instruction. In other words, through the use of macroinstructions, much of the repetitive work of programming could be eliminated by calling on a given "mini program" every time a particular instruction was given. These individual macroinstructions in the source program are processed by the compiler program, and the entire series of detailed machine language steps necessary to perform such a command as "read a tape" are produced in the object program. The use of compilers and macroinstructions has simplified the coding of programs and has led to the development of procedure-oriented languages in which the programmer can express his or her source program steps in terms of algebraic formulas or English language instructions which can then be compiled into machine language instructions.

Thus, the user of the computer language COBOL, which is a widely accepted language for handling business data processing problems (see Language Supplement B), must have a COBOL compiler for his or her computer in order to process programs written in COBOL and to translate them into machine language numeric codes which are understandable to the computer. Other compilers are required for a computer to accept any of the other computer languages commonly in use today.

Multiprogramming and Executive Programs

Chapter 6 described the evolution of computer hardware from its rudimentary beginnings in the early 1950s through four possible generations of development. During this period of time technological changes brought about infinitely greater operating reliability, speed of I/O devices, speed of access to all of the many forms of memory and storage, and storage of many times the amount of data in a much smaller area. All of this was accomplished with a reduction in the cost of the equipment per unit of data handled.

Memory devices were expanded both in size and capability and are now capable of holding many types of programs. Also, it is now possible to access the computer from many remote terminals at will. This last innovation gave rise to the multiplexor system which enabled inquiries to the computer, covering many different types of data processing operations, to be acted upon in the order of their arrival.

These new capabilities permitted the computer to do more than one programming application at a time, however, the computer's operation was now too fast for it to depend upon intervention to switch it from job to job. It was at this point that systems programmers created the concept of multiprogramming and a type of systems program known as an executive program evolved. Such a program was capable of controlling a system which only processed batch programs, a system dedicated to the control of telecommunication devices, or any combination of these two.

In addition to controlling the input from remote terminals, the responsibilities of the executive program were divided into the following classifications:

1. Scheduling the allocation of computing time to the tasks at hand.
2. Allocation of memory and storage involving the assignment and utilization of hardware.

3. Control of input and output for operating user programs.
4. Control over service operations.

All of these areas are closely interrelated and frequently depend on each other.

An example of how this might work would be as follows—when an inquiry is made from a remote terminal, the executive program must first determine the program which will be necessary to process the inquiry. It must then cause the necessary program to be brought into central core storage and assign space to it. At this point in time, another inquiry may be received from another terminal on an entirely different subject. This will necessitate the use of another program presently stored in off-line storage. So as not to keep the second inquiry waiting until the first one has been completely answered, the executive program will cause the computer to go back and forth between the two programs, processing a bit of each of the programs with each swing, but at such a speed that the persons making the inquiries will both feel that their inquiry is being immediately answered.

Multiprocessing. The words multiprogramming and multiprocessing are frequently used interchangeably and this is confusing because they are not the same. Multiprogramming is a technique for handling numerous routines or programs simultaneously by overlapping or interlacing their execution. Multiprocessing, on the other hand, has to do with the situation where there are several computers hooked together to handle a particular data processing task. For example, small computers might be collecting a particular type of data in outlying areas, summarizing it, and then communicating it to a central computer installation where the data would be compiled and utilized for the purpose intended. The act of doing this would be the multiprocessing of data.

DATA BASE

As the capacities of computers have increased and as the concepts of on-line real-time management information systems and time-sharing have emerged from the conceptual stages to the stage of reasonable working reality, the problem of organizing and maintaining data files for maximum utility has become significant. The question first raised was whether or not the data files, as they related to the operations of a company, might not contain data which was common to more than one operation. After study is was often found that this was true.

If one were to analyze the data processing systems in three separate but related departments one would probably find that a certain portion of the data found in one department would be common to data found and utilized in the other two departments. In the following illustration, the data in the shaded area would be the data that are common to more than one area.

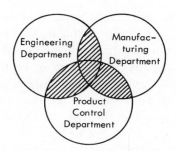

With this being true, why wouldn't it be possible to save storage space as well as access time by creating a common data base of the applicable data in the system? Doing this would (1) eliminate redundant data, (2) reduce program maintenance, (3) provide for consistency of data, and (4) help to insure the quality of the data. These ideas, when duly implemented gave rise to the term *data base.*

As an extension of this data base concept, planners brought to reality a complete management information system concept (working under a time-sharing or batch environment) with the equipment operating in an on-line real-time mode.

Under this system, which was called a file management system, a user first decided what data he or she had that was of value. The user then determined a hierarchy of values for all the data relative to the other data available and how all of the data related to this hierarchy. Other considerations included such key requirements as:

1. Which file access method is desirable?
2. The size of the file and its sub-files.
3. The design requirements of each item of the file with special emphasis on any unusual requirements.
4. A complete breakdown of the costs of initiating and maintaining the file and the media utilized.
5. The documentation of the steps involved in file maintenance processing.
6. How to protect the file data from unauthorized surveillance and usage.
7. How to physically protect the files from damage or destruction (intentional or unintentional).

As soon as an appropriate data base has been determined and stored, an appropriate system or method of communicating and selecting data from within the data base, so as to answer questions of a specific nature, had to be determined.

In an endeavor to facilitate the choosing of an appropriate method to select data from the data base, the United States government, in 1964, was instrumental in organizing the Codasyl Systems Committee. This committee was to participate with computer manufacturers and users in setting of standards (using the COBOL programming language) for the organization of the files and methods of access to the data base.

The thinking at this time centered around the conservation of data space and the rapidity by which data could be accessed in a particular installation.

It should be pointed out that, by having a common data base for much of the company data, the systems programs have to be far more sophisticated than those previously used. The reason for this is that the computer could now be asked a variety of questions, and the systems programs have to be adequate to allow the computer to make the proper solutions.

One of the data base recovery systems developed at that time was developed by IBM and was known as the Information Management System/360 (IMS). This system was installed at North American Rockwell in 1968 to meet the data base management requirements of the Apollo Program. An important feature of IMS was the Data Language–1 (DL–1) concept of controlling access to the files. This provided that a definition of the data would be stored in special libraries in a centralized control organization external to the using program. Tables were available which specified which programs were permitted access to each data base and whether only update and/or inquiry was permitted.

There have been many problems with the system. Most of these had been resolved by 1974. North American Rockwell felt that it is safe as well as practical to entrust its primary financial, product, personnel, and marketing data to on-line data bases. (See Reference 16.)

Another factor, working in a somewhat different direction, entered the picture about 1969. It was a trend among large computer users to move away from application-oriented data files to data bases which would serve many or all applications. They also wanted the data bases to be accessible to numerous programming languages.

In response to these demands a variety of File Management Systems have been placed on the market by computer manufacturers and software houses. Many of these systems remain, each of which is being used at a variety of locations. Among those being used are: Mark IV from Informatices, ASI–ST from Application Software, GIS-2 from IBM, and GIM from TRW. There is work yet to be done to have these systems working at the level of efficiency ultimately desired.

From what has been said one can see that there are a wide variety of efforts being carried out by quite a number of computer users to implement the data base concept. Some of the problems which potential data base users have found to be most difficult to cope with are as follows: (1) organizational—companies which are organized by division where the divisions have a high degree of autonomy, with little interdivisional commonality, do not appear to be prime candidates for a company-wide data base because they do not follow a common pattern for accomplishing their paper work; and (2) security—a big question which arises between divisions which are highly autonomous is which levels of management in the different divisions would be privileged to have certain data base information.

It is generally felt, however, that data processing is a corporate resource and that individual corporate units should not be allowed to go their own way. Funding for the necessary data base research should come from top corporate levels, but that applications of this research should be worked out jointly between the managements of the various divisions. (See References 2, 3, 4, 6, 7, 8, 9, 10, 11, 12, 13, 15.)

SOFTWARE DEVELOPMENT TRENDS

There have been a number of developments which have evolved fairly recently which have had and will—perhaps even more—in the future have an impact on software systems.

The use of data base systems has been growing rapidly in the last couple of years. Virtual memory or storage techniques have evolved which—to state it far too simply—permit on-line storage (usually disk) to serve as temporary "internal" memory which is called into real internal memory by segments before and as it is needed. There has been an ever-expanding usage of on-line real-time systems involving remote terminal and multicomputer systems with multiple users of programs and data files.

Each of these developments has had its own particular impact on software requirements. To explain these impacts simply is virtually impossible, but the net effect has been to massively expand the complexity of systems programming.

To date most of the specific needs have been met by a firm's programmers modifying existing manufacturers software to fit their own individual requirements. However, as complexity has grown there has been an ever-increasing time lag in meeting these needs and maintaining the programs. The problems and the resulting expense involved has become all but prohibitive. Seemingly, as one set of needs are met others present themselves and usually the entire programs have to be redesigned.

It seems that one possible economically feasible approach will be for this complex software to be written by the manufacturers or software firms (the announced DL–1 or Data Language–1 prepared by IBM is an example). These will apparently have to be subdivided into modular segments that can be added to or deleted from as needed. If modifications are required only given segments will have to be altered.

Regardless of how these complex software needs are met, there seems to be little question but what software will get even more complex and that there will be some major changes in the software approach in the not-too-distant future. (See Reference 14.)

Applications

The business world was among the first and has been the largest user of data banks. Credit companies, such as Credit Data Corporation of California, have started data banks involving the credit ratings of individuals. These ratings are usually sold to the subscribers of the credit bureau. The airline industry is another area of business that uses data banks. American Airlines, for instance, has one of the largest data banks and includes in one central location all the information they require including reservations and openings; connecting flights; names of passengers, flights they have traveled, time of day, telephone contacts, hotel and car reservations; maintenance schedules, meal planning and distribution; as well as historical record-keeping and other data. With this system, either teletype or on-line connections can make instant reservations on American flights.

Banks are another type of business making use of the data bank. Many banks are involved in some effort in this area. For example, the Federal Reserve Bank of Kansas City has a Management Information System system working reasonably well, and the Colorado Central Bank and Trust Company is working on a management information system using the TOTAL system. On the foreign scene, New Zealand now has a nation-wide data bank with the larger five banks in the country using nine computers to merge all their 1,129 trading bank offices and their agency customers into one file. This information is now available via an audio telephone link-up with the system.

Many large businesses with branch offices and factories in other parts of the country are using data banks to keep track of the companies' entire accounting and inventory systems on a day-to-day basis. This is done by each branch entering into the central computer through either terminal or on-line link-ups any changes in the inventory or other transactions and having the computer update the records. This updating may be done as the entry is transmitted if the system is a real-time one or, and more probably, the next morning if remote entry batch processing is utilized. Marketing has started utilizing the data bank concept in dealing with investments and in marketing products by storing the information by certain topical subjects. These may be used in making marketing projections based on the present and past facts stored in the computer.

Other areas including education, libraries, municipalities, medicine, law, and, of course, the various levels of government are all using data banks to some degree currently and are rapidly expanding their efforts in this direction.

Many of the above systems are not yet fully implemented, but they are slowly being brought to fruition. When and if these systems can be made workable, the industry will be much closer to having what can be truly called a management information system. (See Reference 1.)

PROGRAMMING LANGUAGES

FORTRAN—*Formula Translation*—is a language system written in the period 1954–56 by IBM personnel under the general direction of John W. Backus. It is a mathematical language and has its greatest use in scientific applications. Problems are coded for the computer in a style which closely resembles ordinary mathematical notation, and which requires virtually no knowledge of the computer on the part of the person doing the programming.

A typical FORTRAN statement might be as follows:

$$ROOT = (-B + SQRT [B**2 - 4.*A*C])/(2.*A)$$

to symbolize the mathematical formula:

$$\text{ROOT} = \frac{-B + \sqrt{B^2 - 4AC}}{2A}$$

With such a statement, the computer would search out the data enclosed in the innermost set of brackets and perform the calculations required, then progress to the outer set of parentheses, and finally divide by the sum of two multiplied by A. The double asterisk indicates exponentation; a single asterisk indicates multiplication; the minus sign, subtraction; the plus sign, addition; and the slash symbol, division.

FORTRAN has been adapted to both small- and large-scale computers and has been used extensively with IBM equipment. The ideas utilized in the design of FORTRAN have been adapted to other manufacturers' computers under many different program names. A detailed overview of the FORTRAN language elements and its program statements is provided in Language Supplement A along with an illustration of an application program.

BASIC is a language which has evolved out of the FORTRAN language. BASIC is essentially a subset of FORTRAN, which is particularly adaptable to time-sharing usage, that was originally developed for GE systems (now Honeywell). However, BASIC is now available for most of the computers of other manufacturers and is perhaps most widely used in conjunction with educational and other on-line systems involving terminal type I/O. Anyone familiar with the current versions of FORTRAN can easily adapt to a system utilizing BASIC.

The United States government is the largest single purchaser of computers for use in its many diversified applications. Purchases have been made from most, if not all, of the firms producing computers. It was this government ownership of many brands and types of computers that began to create major problems. If one agency outgrew a given computer, or if there was a need for one agency to share time on its computer with another agency, it was impossible to shift the programs created for one piece of equipment to another.

Finally, in 1958, the Department of Defense initiated the idea of having a joint committee formed which would be composed of representatives of the government, large private users, and the major computer manufacturers. These individuals were brought together to develop a language code which would enable one program to be translated into the machine languages required by other computers.

Due to the different coding techniques needed in mathematical and business coding it was decided that two standard program languages were needed rather than one. The outcome was the development of ALGOL and COBOL.

ALGOL, an *Al*gebraic-*O*riented *L*anguage, is an automatic coding language designed for wide usage in coding computational applications. It had been started in 1958 but was not extensively implemented until the early 1960s.

ALGOL's major usage to date has been with very large scientific-oriented computing systems. Consequently, the use of ALGOL has never been as extensive as originally thought probable. Also, as time passed, FORTRAN has evolved into a much more powerful and capable language than conceived in its early form. It has replaced much of the scientific language needs of the larger systems, as well as being very widely used on smaller systems.

COBOL, the *C*ommon *B*usiness *O*riented *L*anguage, like ALGOL, is not designed to be oriented to any particular computer in its utilization of a vocabulary of machine functions. When using COBOL, the coder is concerned with writing the functions he or she wants performed and not with exactly what machine instructions will ultimately be supplied by the COBOL compiler.

Each of the computer manufacturers who anticipates selling equipment to the government—and most of them do, of course—has written a COBOL compiler which translates the basic COBOL language into the machine language for their particular computer. In this way, a program written in COBOL could be compiled by an IBM System/360 Model 50 using its COBOL translator to produce a program for that computer. If a program was compiled by an NCR Century COBOL translator, a program would be produced for that NCR Century computer. Similarly, COBOL programs can be translated into machine language for any computer for which a COBOL translator has been written.

An overview of the basic components of the COBOL language along with illustrative applications may be found in Language Supplement B.

Programming Language–1 (PL–1) is a language originally developed by IBM to serve combination scientific and business needs by a merging of many of the capabilities of both ALGOL and COBOL. PL–1 has served some needs for such a language very well but has never really proven to be the "ultimate" language many thought it would be early in its development.

Basic Assembler languages are classified as being somewhat in between the compiler languages and machine languages. They have the capability of macroinstructions and are very fast running (in terms of machine time) languages and are mainly used on jobs that are highly repetitious in their usage. They are more difficult to learn and use because of the macroinstructions required and have very little to offer for applications that are to be run only a single time or even just a few times. (See Reference 14.)

OTHER TYPES OF COMPUTER SOFTWARE

In addition to the compilers and other processors already discussed, there are software techniques available from computer manufacturers and user groups which should be considered.

Debugging Aids

Certain debugging aids are essential in installing a computer. One of these debugging aids is a memory print (dump) program which will cause the contents of memory to be printed out in some form to permit it to be analyzed and edited by the programmer. Memory print programs can vary in their sophistication from a very simple program to one which will actually interpret the contents of each area of memory to determine whether the information in that area consists of data or machine instructions. In the case of instructions, the instructions can be edited from machine language into a mnemonic form, which is easier for the programmer to read. This is particularly important in computers where addresses or operations in the machine language would appear in binary or octal rather than decimal digits. In such cases, it is particularly important that the memory print program edit these binary or octal configurations into a number system form the programmer can easily read.

The tape print program is another important debugging aid. A tape print program in its simplest form reads the contents of a tape and prints it out. This enables the programmer to check the data written on the tape to see if the data are correct. The tape print program in a simple form would just print the data from the tape in a consecutive manner, item by item, for the entire length of the print line used by the particular computer in use. In more complex tape print programs, each tape record would be printed out on a separate line. Some tape print programs enable the programmer to type in the account number of the desired record. The program then searches the tape to find the indicated account number and prints the appropriate record for that account. These are some examples of the options that can be built into debugging aids to make them more effective. Programs such as the memory print and tape print programs are often called *utility routines.*

Operating Systems

An operating system is a group of programs designed to increase the efficiency and effectiveness of the computer in its day-to-day operations by reducing setup time through automatic program sequencing and selection. The program tape, which contains all of the installation's program, is the heart of the operating system. The program tape is created by converting the programs from punched cards to magnetic tape or by using magnetic tape as the output from the assembler or compiler.

One way in which an operating system might function would be the following: The first program on a program tape would be a program locator routine, which is followed successively by a production program, a locator, then another production program, and so on. This tape, when mounted on a tape unit, permits the operator to call in the first program from the tape (the locator) and specify the particular program he or she desires to run. The operating system automatically searches the program tape to find the program the operator has specified. The operating system would verify the tape labels for each input file and write tape labels on the output files. Control is then transferred to the production program, which performs its own processing. At the conclusion of the production program, the locator is read into memory to search the program tape for the next production program scheduled to be run. The automatic setup procedures are again performed without operator intervention or manipulation of card decks.

Another function of an operating system is to provide a method of dating reports, payrolls, and so on, and inserting variable constants (such as factors, rates, and dates) into the programs where they are needed. The dating systems provided by the manufacturers today vary from no dating system at all to rather complex dating systems which include calendars and tables of special dates used to vary processing requirements. Operating systems eliminate production program decks and their inherent disadvantages (such as getting cards out of sequence, dropping a deck, losing cards, and card reader jams, which may occur as frequently used program decks become worn). This eliminates the necessity of periodically reproducing the decks to keep them in good condition. Also, by automatically sequencing and selecting the production programs, these operating systems reduce operator intervention to a minimum. This tends to limit the opportunities for operator errors. Operating systems and instruction tapes are not new, as they were first developed for some of the earlier types of computers. It is just recently, however, that computer manufacturers have been including operating systems in their software packages.

Application Packages

Another type of software is the application program package. This is a program which has been written with a particular type of accounting or data processing problem in mind. For example,[1] in the International Computer Programs quarterly catalogue dated April 1973 there are many hundreds of application programs described which give their intended use, type of equipment on which they operate, and their cost. The types of application programs available are too numerous to enumerate and they have been written by industrial users as well as software houses. They include such subjects, however, as accounting, banking industry, manufacturing and inventory control, retail industry, and the utilities industry—each subject area providing many individual applications.

Some of these programs are quite specific in nature due to the fact that they have been written for a specific use. Others, on the other hand, are general because they have been written to try to appeal to a broad spectrum of users. Some of the software packages sold by computer manufacturers are in this category and are purposely broad in nature.

An example of this latter type of software package would be the program packages which are available to go with the IBM Systems/3. To tailor the software to the particular requirments of a user, the user is asked to fill out a questionnaire and a series of specification sheets so as to provide the information and/or method of presentation which is unique to a proposed application. The prospective user indicates how he or she wants this particular job done, identifies the calculations required, chooses how the application should be processed as well as the types of reports and layouts to be produced. These specifications are checked for completeness, and then the appropriate job segments are chosen from programs already written and on file. When necessary

---

[1] All other computer manufacturers and most software firms have similar listings of application programs.

they can be modified to satisfy the job specifications more precisely. With this approach the customer is producing documentation which explicitly defines the programming jobs to be done. This documentation defines the required programs in sufficient detail so that they can be coded by a newly trained but inexperienced programmer in the customer's employ. The programming language used in this case is RPG II (Report Program Generator). Such jobs as order writing, invoicing, inventory management, and sales analysis can be customized for use on the System/3 in this way.

The Burroughs Corporation has their 1700 series of computers designed with the same type of user and application in mind. In many ways this equipment and its accompanying software goes even further than RPG in providing the versatility the typical user needs. (See Reference 5.)

USER GROUPS

In August 1955, representatives of several airplane manufacturers met in Los Angeles to talk about their mutual computing problems. It was their feeling that with the difficulties involved in this area, they ought to get together and exchange programs and experience.

Out of that meeting came a remarkable idea for a new kind of organization: the computer user group. Since then, the growth of computer user groups has been phenomenal.

Following is a list of user groups who are currently within the Joint User Groups of the Association for Computing Machinery:

COMMON	Smaller IBM Computer Users
DECUS	Digital Equipment Computer Users Society
EDUCOM	EIN (Educational Information Network)
EMR Users	EMR Computer User Society
FOCUS	Control Data Users (3000 Series and below)
GUIDE	IBM Large-Scale Business Computer Users
NCR Users	Users of NCR Computers
PAL	RCA Users
SEL Users	Users of System Engineering Laboratory Computers
SERCUS	Users of Raytheon Computers
SWAP	Wang Laboratories Computer Users
USE	UNIVAC Scientific Exchange
UUA	UNIVAC Users Association
VIM	Control Data 6000 Computer Users
XDS	XDS Users

User group rules are simple. A computer installed or on order, attendance at one of the biannual meetings, a willingness to contribute worthwhile programs (conforming to certain standards of documentation), and discussion of information and ideas are all the credentials a prospective member needs. No dues are required, but a cooperative spirit and participation in project work are expected.

As a group member, the computer user can draw what is needed from a reservoir of superior computing thought distilled from a continual, critical interchange of ideas among the entire membership. More specifically, the user can expect to do considerably less programming and check-out on everything from utility routines to complete systems.

As computer users have become more sophisticated, they have paid more attention to specialized problem solving.

Application-oriented groups have been formed to help satisfy complex programming needs. These organizations include CEPA (Civil Engineering Program Applications); HEEP (Highway Engineers Exchange Programs); ACUTE (Accountants Computer Users for Technical Exchange) open to public accounting firms only; and ECHO (Electronic Computing—Hospital Oriented).

Out of the cooperative spirit of the users groups, IBM has established a program library in Hawthorne, New York. Members of the user groups are expected to contribute programs to this library on a nonproprietary basis. The programs, however, are available to all IBM users.

SOFTWARE PRICING POLICIES

As computers first evolved, software was included as a part of the price paid for the hardware in either an outright purchase or the rental of a given computer system.

By 1968, however, a great deal of pressure was brought on the larger manufacturers by court action and threats of action based on the monopolistic position of—particularly—the International Business Machines Corporation. Smaller firms had begun to develop, especially in the software area, and they wanted to break the traditional ties that existed between the user and the manufacturer of his or her computer so that they might sell the user their own products. In many instances, these software packages had been developed for particular models of equipment and were, at times, superior, in some ways, to those developed to generally work with families of models or equipment lines.

In 1969, IBM bowed to the pressure (a number of other major manufacturers followed) and "unbundled" by pricing hardware and software (and other services) separately. This change in sales tactics has not been in effect over a long enough period of time for its impact to be properly evaluated. However, there does seem to be some concensus of opinion that the user is having to pay more for the combination package than he or she previously did when it was all included under one price.

REFERENCES

1. ADL SYSTEMS, INC. "Good Management of Computer Operations." *Computers and Automation,* April 1973, p. 7.

2. BURCH, JOHN G.; STRATER, FELIX Q. *Information Systems: Theory-Practice.* Hamilton Publishing: Santa Barbara, Calif., 1974, Chapters 6 and 9.

3. COHEN, LEO, J. "Data Base Considerations and Implementation Techniques." *Data Management,* September 1972.

4. DODD, GEORGE G. "Elements of Data Management Systems." *Computer Surveys* 1 (June 1969) p. 117.

5. "Application Package Revisited." *EDP Analyzer,* July 1971.

6. "The Debate on Data Base Management." *EDP Analyzer,* March 1972.

7. "The Cautious Path to a Data Base." *EDP Analyzer,* June 1973.

8. GRAFTON, WILLIAM, P. "Data Base Recovery With IMS/360." *Data Base,* Spring 1972, p. 9.

9. HARRISON, C. W.; RADFORD, J. K. "Creating a Common Data Base." *Journal of Systems Management,* 23, June 1972, p. 8–15.

10. MCLAUGHLIN, RICHARD A. "Building a Data Base." *Datamation,* July 1972, p. 51.

11. PATTERSON, ALBERT C. "Data Base Hazards." *Datamation,* July 1972, p. 48.

12. PRICE, G. F. "The Ten Commandments of Data Base." *Data Management,* May 1972, p. 14–23.

13. SCHUBERT, RICHARD F. "Basic Concepts in Data Base Management Systems." *Datamation,* July 1972, p. 42.

14. SIMPSON, DUN. "Future Trends in High Level Language." *Data Processing,* March–April 1973, p. 89.

15. STEIG, DONALD B. "File Management Systems Revisited." *Datamation,* October 1972, p. 48.

16. VAN PADDENBURG, J. C. "Centralized Computing Services at North American Rockwell." *Datamation,* November 1972, p. 58.

QUESTIONS

1. Briefly describe the changes which have occurred in programming languages since the inception of the computer.

2. Clearly describe what applications programming and systems programming are and the distinction which should be made between them.

3. How should error routines and utility programs be classified? What is their function?

4. What are macroinstructions and what are their functions?

5. In what ways are compiler programs superior to machine language programs?

6. What type of programming did the multiplexor system facilitate? How?

7. What is the function of multiprogramming?

8. What is the role of an executive program in multiprogramming?

9. What had occurred in the hardware area which made the development of executive programming imperative?

10. Describe the development of the data base concept.

11. How has the data bank concept evolved from this?

12. What is the function of an operating system?

13. What is an application package? How might it be used?

14. What is the function and purpose of user groups?

15. Describe several of the recent developments which have taken place in the field of software design which are enabling computer users to more fully utilize the capabilities of the hardware which is presently available. Describe these developments in sufficient depth so that you can make it clear what they have really contributed.

14

Computer Systems Controls and Security

As business organizations become larger, management becomes less able to exercise personal control over the daily affairs of the business. Greatly increased physical size, geographical dispersion, and increasing numbers of employees make the job of overseeing and directing extremely complex. Management, to fulfill its responsibility, has to depend more and more upon systemization. This involves building a system to process the data, seeing that checks and controls are built into it, making sure that everyone understands the system, and then endeavoring, through both the internal and the external auditing functions, to see that the system is followed. This is done until the system is proven to be deficient or inadequate in some way, and then the system has to be altered to conform to changed conditions.

As clerical procedures have become more and more automated, fewer workers have generally been needed. It has become more difficult for one group to check upon the work of another. With the growth in size of the average business unit has come the mechanization, and later the computerization, of many of the clerical data processing activities. The net effect of all of this is that management has come to rely more on machines and less on people to see that procedures are being properly followed.

What assurance can management have that prescribed procedures are being followed and that the output of the machine is accurate? This problem is of particular relevance to the systems analyst who is called upon to remodel an existing data processing system or to design a completely new one. It is also important to the external auditor, the certified public accountant, who is called upon to certify as to the adequacy of the system of internal control which, in turn, will determine the extent of the audit checking which he or she must accomplish before he or she can certify as to the validity of the audited financial data.

It is, therefore, essential that anyone interested in the field of data processing realize how important controls are to the ultimate users of the data, whether they be management, creditors, stockholders, or the government. A thorough understanding of internal control is particularly important.

Many of the intermediate steps in traditional business information processing procedures (that is, maintenance of journals and ledgers) are either consolidated or nonexistent in an EDP system. This has resulted in the loss of an "audit trail," which has long been considered essential in tracing—backwards—from a record or statement to determine the individual originating documents and the basic transaction which led to the recorded end results. Chronological journals, classified postings to one or more classes of ledgers, listings, proofs, trial balances, and so on, could be produced in the computer system. However, this would be requiring paper work to be prepared just for testing or checking purposes. This would not only be expensive, but would also offset many of the advantages offered by an EDP system. Consequently, without visible evidence to support records, transactions, and other financial and nonfinancial data, the auditor must devise and adopt new procedures to verify the reliability of the information.

The audit of computerized accounting systems, as with manual and mechanical systems, must be planned to fit each individual situation. The planning and approach to such an audit engagement is, of course, left to the judgment of the auditor, but regardless of the approach used, the audit of any EDP system must be based on the sound verification of reliable source data. Equally important is the proving of the accuracy of the output of the system.

There are two distinctly different approaches to testing and verifying that the source data used in an EDP system are accurately developed and properly utilized in producing the end products of that system. One involves a direct verification of the output from the source data without really considering the method of source data conversion to its computer input form or the actual method of processing the data. This approach is usually referred to as the *around-the-machines* audit approach. The logic of this concept is that if input can be proven correct and was processed to produce the output, then it is assumed that the output must be equally correct. The manner in which the system operates in proceeding from the creation of the source data to the production of its output is of secondary importance.

Simplicity, logic, and familiarity are some of the advantages gained by the use of this approach. In addition, this method minimizes the need for specialized knowledge concerning EDP equipment, and there is little interference with processing operations during the conduct of the audit. There are, however, three main problems associated with the around-the-machines approach. First, the apparent or actual disappearance of the audit trail may make it difficult, if not impossible, to trace other than very large groups of data from its output form back to its source. Second, changes in operating instructions might make the sampled items used in the test applicable to only a limited number of transactions. And third, a large variety of transactions coupled with a large volume can make the testing of samples of data impractical from the standpoint of cost in comparison with the results obtained.

A second approach which does not require the tracing of input to output is referred to as the *through-the-machines* approach. This method involves a detailed examination of EDP operations and an evaluation of the accuracy and propriety of these procedures. The logic behind this method is that if correct source data are used and the processing procedures are accurate, then there is no need to trace input to output because the output of the system must be accurate. This approach is entirely dependent on the consistency of processing operations, which is generally quite satisfactory in most electronic business information systems.

The application of through-the-machines auditing requires a fairly comprehensive knowledge of machine operations and a good understanding of the techniques of systems design and of audit procedures which have been developed in conjunction with the growth of EDP.

Experience has shown that a combination of the applicable features of each method is perhaps the best approach to auditing an EDP system. The around-the-machines approach to auditing is familiar to all auditors, as it is the technique most often used in the audit of manual systems. The new control procedures used in the through-the-machines approach are not nearly so well known. Yet, a technical knowledge of the through-the-machines approach is extremely important in auditing EDP systems and should be familiar to all accountants, managers, and others concerned with the reliability to be placed on data produced in an electronic business information system.

There must be methods and procedures before there will be an EDP system to be audited, however. The systems analysis and design function must come first. Some person, or persons, must determine how data is to be processed and what procedures are going to be followed. What is decided in this case is of extreme importance to management because the ability of management to control effectively their individual areas of responsibility is diminished as the operations for which they are responsible increase in diversity and magnitude. Methods and procedures must be planned in such a way that the best known concepts of control can be incorporated into the system being designed.

INTERNAL CONTROL

The adequacy of the network of internal controls present in a system is generally recognized as the key element to be depended upon in determining the reliance to be placed upon the accuracy of the data processing system. Internal control has been defined as "the plan of organization and all of the coordinate methods and measures adopted within a business to safeguard its assets, check the accuracy and reliability of its accounting data, promote operational efficiency, and encourage adherence to prescribed managerial policies."[1] Because this is a very broad definition, a distinction needs to be made between types of control available and particularly between the administrative controls and internal accounting controls.

The Committee on Auditing Procedure of the American Institute of Certified Public Accountants made the distinction in this way:

a. Accounting controls comprise the plan of organization and all methods and procedures that are concerned mainly with, and relative directly to, safeguarding of assets and the reliability of the financial records. They generally include such controls as the systems of authorization and approval, separation of duties concerned with record keeping and accounting reports from those concerned with operations or asset custody, physical controls over assets, and internal auditing.

b. Administrative controls comprise the plan of organization and all methods and procedures that are concerned mainly with operational efficiency and adherence to managerial policies and usually relate only indirectly to the financial records. They generally include such controls as statistical analyses, time and motion studies, performance reports, employee training programs, and quality controls.[2]

---

[1] Auditing Standards Executive Committee, Codification of Auditing Standards and Procedures, *Statement on Auditing Standards No. 1,* Copyright 1973 by the American Institute of Certified Public Accountants, Inc., Section 320.

[2] Ibid., p. 28.

It should appear from this distinction that the systems analyst and designer, as well as the independent auditor, is primarily concerned with "accounting controls." Professors Bower and Schlosser point out that "the basic purposes of internal control are to bring reliability into the financial information system and to safeguard assets."[3]

There are certain characteristics or elements of a satisfactory system of internal control which must be recognized. They are as follows:

> A plan of organization which provides appropriate segregation of functional responsibilities,
>
> Personnel of a quality commensurate with responsibilities,
>
> A system of authorization and record procedures adequate to provide reasonable accounting control over assets, liabilities, revenues and expenses, and
>
> Sound practices to be followed in performance of duties and functions of each of the organization departments . . .[4]

The responsibility for their existence as well as their success rests solely with management.

AN ORGANIZATIONAL PLAN TO PERMIT
FUNCTIONAL RESPONSIBILITY SEGREGATION

Earlier chapters have stressed the importance of providing an overall plan of organization. Specific suggestions have included the development of an organization chart, the assignment of levels of responsibility with the authority to carry out each such assignment, an adequate chart of accounts, and a standardized account coding system. All of these fundamental approaches to an overall plan of organization lend themselves to providing a mechanism which permits the separation of the operating, custodial, and accounting functions among individuals and departments in order to serve as a check upon unauthorized activity.

An EDP system tends to eliminate much of the separation of duties and cross-checking formerly done. This is in part due to the decreasing number of workers involved. In assigning responsibilities for the control of EDP systems, many managements have sought to retain a basic division of duties by:

1. Making certain that the programming and systems development activity are kept organizationally separate from the operation of the equipment itself.

---

[3] James B. Bower and Robert E. Schlosser, "Internal Control—Its True Nature," *Accounting Review* 40 (April 1965) p. 339.

[4] Auditing Standards Executive Committee, *Statement on Auditing Standards No. 1*, pp. 28–29.

2. Holding the operating departments which supply the input data responsible for its authenticity, accuracy, and completeness.
3. Establishing the data processing center as a separate unit organizationally independent from the operating units, restricted from any direct control over the assets, and without authority to disburse funds, issue inventory, and so forth, in order to reduce pressures that may develop to process the data improperly either to manipulate the results or to cover fraudulent activity.
4. Requiring the recipient and user of the processed data to perform checking procedures to verify that the data which have been received are accurate. For example, comparing accumulated batch totals with the current output totals.

To emphasize the importance of control and the separation of functions, public accounting firms often use a checklist questionnaire to ascertain the existence of these controls in a client's EDP installation. (One section of such a questionnaire is shown in Figure 14–1).

PROVISION FOR PERSONNEL OF A QUALITY COMMENSURATE WITH RESPONSIBILITIES ASSIGNED

The qualifications of the personnel involved in an EDP system are considerably higher than is normally the case when clerical personnel are solely involved. On the whole, EDP personnel need to have a broader background with greater appreciation of what is taking place, both from an accounting point of view and from the point of view of the more technical aspects of computer operation.

The provision for personnel of a quality commensurate with their assigned responsibilities does not mean that only highly trained individuals with experience should be sought for the computer area. From an operating viewpoint, it would be wonderful to have only top-level personnel on the job; however, if individuals with this background were assigned to some of the strictly procedural or operational jobs to be performed on a steady basis they would soon be dissatisfied and either leave the firm for a more challenging position or build up a growing resentment to their assignment. In smaller organizations, which can afford to employ only a few computer personnel, employees must perform a wide variety of jobs. However, from an internal control viewpoint, it is best—wherever possible—to have employees working at positions which challenge them in the performance of their duties

FIGURE 14–1. Section of Internal Control Questionnaire

	Answer		Answer Based on		
Documentation of Systems and Programming	*Yes*	*No*	*In-quiry*	*Obser-vation*	*Test*
A. Does the current documentation for each computer program contain:					
1. A written description?	—	—	—	—	—
2. Flow charts and block diagrams?	—	—	—	—	—
3. Program listings?	—	—	—	—	—
4. Operator's manual?	—	—	—	—	—
5. Description of input and output elements?	—	—	—	—	—
6. Written procedures for testing new programs before use (test data)?	—	—	—	—	—
B. Does the operator's manual contain:					
1. Set-up instructions?	—	—	—	—	—
2. Description of input layouts?	—	—	—	—	—
3. Description of output layouts?	—	—	—	—	—
4. Operating messages (errors and halts and required action)?	—	—	—	—	—
5. Procedures for labeling and disposition of input?	—	—	—	—	—
6. Procedures for labeling and disposition of output?	—	—	—	—	—
C. Are there written procedures for program maintenance which provide for:					
1. A formal request for a program change?	—	—	—	—	—
2. Approval by a responsible individual for a change? If so, by whom?_____	—	—	—	—	—
3. A test of the change prior to acceptance?	—	—	—	—	—
D. Are duplicate copies of either the source decks, object decks, or program listings maintained away from the EDP premises as protection against loss?	—	—	—	—	—

rather than assigning them to positions with a classification level far below their training and experience background.

A SYSTEM OF AUTHORIZATIONS AND RECORD PROCEDURES TO PROVIDE ACCOUNTING CONTROL

The establishment of a system of authorizations is conceptually the same regardless of the type of system in use and, of course, refers to the requirement that written authority be obtained before performing some given duty. Common examples would include credit approval before completing a sale and payment approval before issuing a check to pay a vendor's invoice. In each instance, some form of check or investigation would be made before permission to take action would be granted. In the computer area, examples would include (1) a prepared and authorized list indicating individual jobs to be considered and the pattern to be followed in processing given procedural runs for a given day of the week, (2) authorization to alter the program steps in a given application program, and (3) permission to destroy the data (by recording new information) stored on a given reel of magnetic tape or disk file.

Providing a system of adequate record procedures tends to be involved in any data processing system, but thoughtful and careful consideration must be given to the documentation required in every computerized system.

Adequate program documentation, which is important for reviewing the proposed program, is close to essential for operating and modifying programs and reconstructing lost data. It is also necessary to enable other interested parties (management, auditors, system analysts, and outside agencies) to understand the operation of the system.

The basic test in judging the adequacy of documentation is to ask whether a typical programmer can follow the documentation provided in a given system and gain an understanding of the system without supplementary information and discussions. For a system of average complexity, this could require:

1. A general, written description of the overall system (including a statement of its objectives), a description of the basic flow of information through the system, and a broad description of the separate processing steps and interrelationships between computer runs.
2. A general system diagram to accompany and illustrate the description.
3. For each computer program, a description of the functions performed by the program and a general description of how the program accomplishes them, with particular attention to features of the program or logic that would otherwise tend to be obscure.
4. Block diagrams showing the sequence of operation performed by the programs, with one or two levels of detail, as required, for clarity. The most detailed level, however, should be less detailed than the source language listings.

5. Record descriptions showing the form and content of all inputs and outputs and memory locations.
6. Program listing in source language and in object code.
7. Program operating instructions for loading control cards, switch setting, halt procedures, sources of input, and disposition of output.[5]

Such a system and program documentation should convey a detailed understanding of what the system does and how it does it.

SOUND PRACTICES TO BE FOLLOWED IN DEPARTMENTAL DUTIES AND FUNCTIONS

"Sound practices," in the performance of duties and functions, refers to the ability to have control over both the accomplishment of the duties and the procedures involved in their performance.

Control Practices and Methods

Control practices in a manual system usually involve checks made in a variety of ways throughout the data processing activity. An automated or computerized system is no exception to this, although the checks and controls are of quite a different nature. There are controls that can be built into the data processing system itself (input-processing-output). Of equal importance are the controls which must be developed to protect the data and the equipment from accidental or intentional harm. There are also controls, whose usefulness must not be overlooked, which are built into the hardware by the equipment manufacturers.

All of these controls must be considered by the person designing a computerized data processing system. The controls utilized in a given system should be adequate to protect the owner of the system commensurate with the risk involved and the cost which he or she is willing to assume. The problem is not solely one of there being adequate ways to control the processing of data in a computerized system. Instead, it is a problem of anticipating and building into the system sufficient controls to be adequate to cope with the risks which will be encountered.

Controls are ineffectual by themselves, however. They must be incorporated into standard operating procedures to insure nonoccurrence

---

[5] International Business Machines Corporation, *Management Control of Electronic Data Processing,* F20–0006, 1965, p. 11.

of errors due to inadequate methods or failure to follow the established operating standards. Frequent reviews should be made of the operating systems to insure that the prescribed operating standards are being followed and are realistic in the light of existing circumstances. (See Reference 5.)

SYSTEM CONTROLS

Input Controls

The input of data into a computer system involves the most probable source of error in such a system. Obviously, machines will operate just as well with incorrect data as with correct data. A computer is accurate in its operation, but the results obtained can only be as accurate as the data fed into the system. Therefore, if an error is introduced anywhere between the origin of the transaction and its input into the computer, the error will be carried forward.

There are four distinct problem areas associated with error elimination in the input function. These may be classified as follows: (1) Those which assure that the data originated at the time of the transaction are adequately and correctly captured. This problem is usually a "people" problem. It involves several items associated with the design of a system which have been discussed earlier. These items include such areas as properly trained individuals, carefully designed forms, adequately documented procedural instruction, and so on. Though this type of problem is usually associated with people manually originating data, it may also include data which are badge or card fed, as in data collection systems, or data which are keyed into the system from remote terminal devices. Regardless of the entry method used in capturing the data, the important aspect must be that all the required data be entered and that they be correct. Standard procedures should be used and a periodic review made to insure that the procedures are being followed. (2) If the originated data are not captured in a machine-processable form (optically scannable, magnetic ink characters, punched card, magnetic tape, and so on), they must be converted to such a form. Unless this is a direct process (one not involving human action), great care must again be taken to assure that the originated data are properly—completely and accurately—transferred to the given processable code.

Once the data have been captured in machine-processable form, there are still two major hurdles to be passed in the input of these data into the processing system. The first of these (3) is to be sure that all the data so captured are fed into and properly processed by the information processing system.

The final major problem (4) is to be sure that the data provided are processed only a single time. Specific input controls (other than those associated with the organizational separation of functional responsibilities and the employment of personnel of a quality commensurate with their assigned responsibilities) may be classified as transcription controls, control totals, and labels.

Transcription Controls.   Transcription controls check the accuracy of the conversion of raw data into machine-acceptable language. If cards are keypunched from the source documents, independent verification of the accuracy of the data punched in the cards is necessary after they have been punched. While duplication of time and effort is necessary in this procedure, the verification of input data has, in many instances, proven to be an economical operation in the long run. If the data are produced in machine-processable form as a by-product of the transcription of the data on typewriters, adding machines, or cash registers (see Chapter 4), both the coded data and a copy readable by humans are also produced in the process. This permits the data to be checked visually and verified as to their accuracy either as, or after, they are prepared.

Control Totals.   Control totals also aid in establishing the accuracy of input data. Control totals are always taken on batches, or groups, of source documents. These are usually batches of preselected and sequenced logical transaction groups, as most EDP systems presently in use are serial-type processing systems. However, in a random access system, these batches may be composed of completely random and unrelated transactions, and the ability to process random data is one of the major advantages of such a system. Control totals for input data are usually obtained from adding machine tapes or from totals previously prepared by originating departments; they normally do not require any extensive additional work in their preparation. Careful planning and coordination in the use of control totals can help to provide a reasonably high degree of internal control with very little effort and consequently very little expense.

Batch totals are a form of control totals where input data are grouped into an economic processing unit. Totals of the batch may even be accumulated before source data are converted to input form. After data conversion is made to a machine-readable language, the batch totals previously taken may be compared to the totals on the input data. Thus, this is a good check to assure that all the source documents are being processed. As will be mentioned later under Output Controls, batch totals may also be used as a check on the processing unit through a comparison of output totals and the totals taken prior to the input of the data into the system.

An illustration of several programs where batch totals are used as control devices follows. This is a common routine where cards are used as input to a computer system. The flowchart, Figure 14–2, represents in diagrammatic form the way it is intended that the controls should work.

Step 1. The first step in the system would consist of the batch balancing and validation process. Transactions entering the system at this point could consist of batch control records containing figures to be utilized in balancing the batch, master file maintenance transactions to be applied to the good account master file and/or the general ledger file plus the accounting entries. In addition, if other computer systems existed within this organization, accounting entries might be generated out of the other computer systems, such as accounts payable, accounts receivable, payroll/personnel, inventory control, etc. These entries are depicted as being supplied into the general accounting system via magnetic files.

A good account master file is shown as input to the batch balance and validation program. This file could be a disk-oriented file containing all good account numbers and other codes utilized in the system. This good account file would be used by the program to validate codes contained in the input transactions.

The system could provide for processing and accumulating numerous batches of transactions prior to moving into Step 2 processing. This capability is indicated by showing the output from the validation program being a magnetic tape containing not only the current batch of transactions but all previous batches. If in the processing of Step 1, the current batch of transactions was not the last batch to be processed prior to month end, then the output file from the batch validate could become the input file for the next running of the validation program. The second and subsequent batches of transactions would then be added to the output file so that at month's end the batch file would contain all batches processed during the month.

Typically, the printed output coming out of Step 1 would be a proof list of the current batches processed, indicating all validation errors

FIGURE 14–2. A General Accounting System Illustration

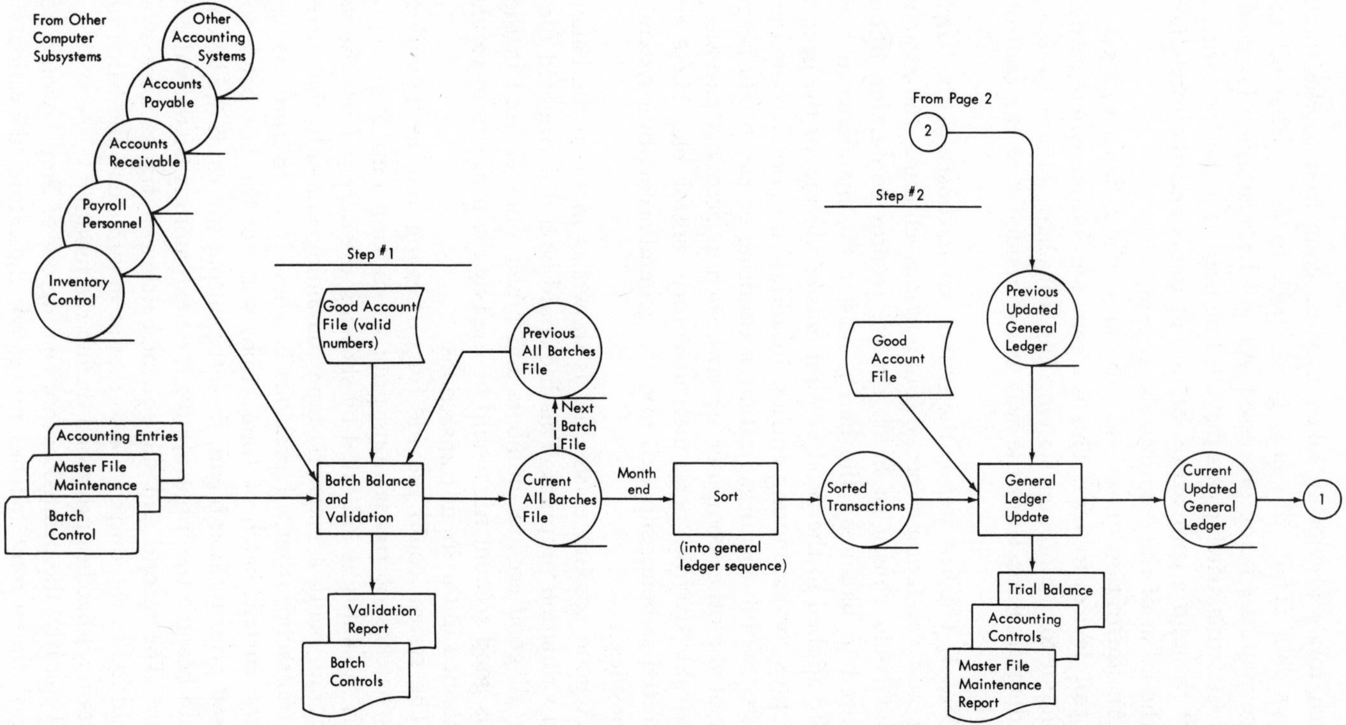

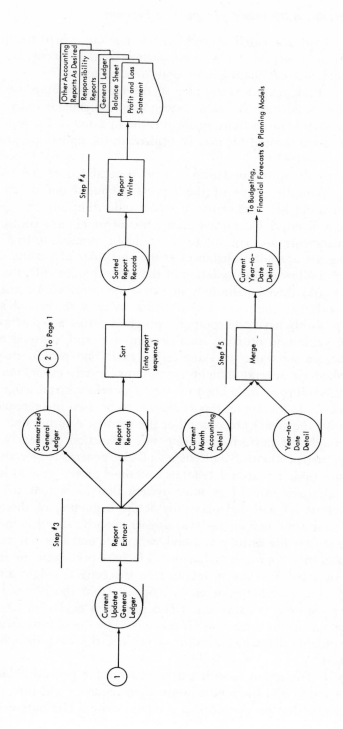

discovered, plus a batch control report showing where the program balanced the controls of the batch, such as zero balancing of journal entries and/or accumulating hash totals or total debits.

Step 2. Prior to processing Step 2, the tape containing the batches would be sorted into the same sequence as the general ledger master file. The sorted transactions would then be updated to the general ledger. The good account file may be utilized in the update program once more, if so desired.

As a result of the updating, a new general ledger file would be created. Typically, some of the reports produced out of an update program could be a maintenance report indicating any changes made to account descriptions or other master file information; a control report where balancing and control totals could be printed; a trial balance reflecting the accounting balances at the particular processing date.

Step 3. Following the updating of the general ledger file, the general ledger would then go through an extraction process. An installation having a larger computer and utilizing more sophisticated software would probably have one computer program called a report extractor. In an organization utilizing smaller computers and, consequently, less sophisticated software, the same report extraction process may be accomplished via several computer programs. In any event, the general procedure followed would be to extract from the general ledger master file a work file containing report records to be used in subsequent processing for the actual preparation of the reports. Another unit of work which might be performed during this extraction process would be to strip current month detail entries off the general ledger and at the same time update year-to-date totals contained on the general ledger.

An approach utilized in some system designs is that the general ledger starts off with balances only at the beginning of the year and grows in size throughout the year as each month's detail is maintained on the master file until year's end, when all detail is purged at one time. Another approach is the one which is portrayed on this chart where only balances are maintained on the general ledger and at the end of each month the detail is stripped from the file and merged into the year-to-date detail file. (This process is explained later.) Also coming out of this extraction process would be the summarized general ledger master file which would be utilized the next time Step 2 is processed.

Step 4. The report records extracted from the general ledger would first be sorted into the report preparation sequence and then processed by a generalized program called a report writer. The output from the report writer could include such things as profit and loss, balance sheet, general ledger, and possibly, responsibility accounting reports.

Step 5. The current month's detail extracted from the general ledger could be merged with previous year-to-date detail to build a new year-to-date file. In a more sophisticated system, the year-to-date detail file would then be utilized in budgeting the forecasting models or other planning-type computerized applications.

Hash totals are a form of batch total in which the totals of grouped data are not in dollar amounts. Hash totals, for example, are totals of data which would not normally be added, such as stock numbers, unit prices, and so forth. These totals are meaningless in themselves but are very useful for control purposes.

Record count controls can be found in many forms and vary considerably, depending upon the particular data processing system in use. Some of the more typical types of record count controls follow.

Record count control can be done by use of prenumbered documents in which appropriate accounting is made to see that each number is present or accounted for. When data are recorded in punched cards, a sample card count is a good control technique. The best technique would involve a card count that is independent of the computer operating group. This independent count may then be compared with the number of cards the operator processed to assure that all cards were subsequently processed. When paper or magnetic tape is being used, controls should also be established to assure that the number of records read on the tape agree with the number of source documents.

Record counts are usually carried at the end of the deck of cards being processed or the reel of tape, as the case may be, and compared each time the deck or reel is processed. As with batch and hash totals, record counts may also be used to check on the accuracy of the central processing unit. Although record counts may be a useful proof of processing, they will not indicate the occurrence of specific errors when the controls are out of balance. Duplicate records may be used in some cases to determine where the errors exist. In other situations, a rerun of the routine may help to eliminate the difficulty. This last is especially applicable in the processing of magnetic tape where machine errors may occasionally occur in reading the data from the tape.

External Labels. Aonther form of control over input is provided in the use of external labels which are visibly written on any type of data container. Such labels usually contain such information as serial number, length of tape, name, date of run, date of the last work processed, output tape (or other) address, the numbers of the runs it is to be used in conjunction with, and the tape (or other) address for each of these runs. This label should also contain the date on which it can be used again for new data. Thus external labels attempt to make certain that the operator will properly process the data file or program so that the data contained will not be destroyed until after their retention period has expired and the data contained are no longer of any value.

Processing Controls

It is difficult, if not impossible, to draw a fine line of distinction between different types of controls applicable to a computer installation (for example, between input controls and processing controls). What is important to recognize is what the different types of controls are, and their areas of applicability.

The Canadian Institute of Chartered Accountants says the following concerning processing control objectives:

> The four main control objectives which should be met by processing controls are the following:
>
> 1. To ensure the completeness of data processed by the computer.
> 2. To ensure the accuracy of data processed by the computer.
> 3. To ensure that all data processed by the computer is authorized.
> 4. To ensure the adequacy of management trails.[6]

Programmed Controls. Some of the more challenging and versatile controls available in a computer system are those which are written into the computer program by the programmers. Many such controls are available, all designed to test the validity of the data as well as the accuracy of the processing equipment. Some controls of this type are also provided in library routines available from the computer manufacturers.

The extent to which these programmed controls are utilized depends upon the ingenuity of the programming staff, the demands of the supervisory and maintenance personnel of the data processing center, the type and capabilities of the equipment, and the need for certain controls in a given processing run, weighed against the costs to be incurred because of the additional processing time required.

From the point of view of designing a system, it is a good idea to incorporate as many of the programmed controls as the designer

---

[6] Study Group on Computer Control and Audit Guidelines, *Computer Control Guidelines,* Canadian Institute of Chartered Accountants, 1970, p. 61.

of the system feels necessary into the program for the system and to insert them as close to the beginning of the system as possible. The sooner the user of a program can be assured as to the adequacy and completeness of his or her data the more accurately and smoothly the program ought to run. Consider the following examples.

Sequence checks may be incorporated into programs to ensure that the desired order of records is maintained. This not only applies to data comprising a group of similar transactions which have been sequenced for entry into the system, but to groups of data made up of presequenced sets of data groups where one or more items from each of the respective groups are required in the processing procedure. "By comparing sequential control numbers, such as voucher numbers, check numbers, stock numbers, and employee numbers from one record to the next, records which are out of sequence, gaps in the sequence, and duplicate numbers can be quickly and efficiently located and emitted for further attention."[7]

Internal labels are usually assigned to a group of data associated with given processing procedures or "runs." These are used extensively in magnetic tape records and are checked prior to processing in what is sometimes called identification comparison checks. These labels provide checks on the tape librarian and computer operator and on the equipment to assure that the proper tape and tape drive have been selected before the data are entered into the system.

A number of internal label routines are available for use today. The checking of an internal label is similar to checking the external label except that the actual check is usually performed through some combination of programming and checking by inquiry through the console typewriter. Information desired from internal labels is particularly concerned with data to determine if this is the proper tape to be used and if this is the only tape of its type necessary for this run or if a series of tapes is required.

Identification comparison is also used in avoiding the use of incorrect disk memory files. A comparison may be made of some common items appearing in the file and in the data to be processed. Such a comparison may be related to a memory address, stock number, or unit of issue.

Check points are sometimes used to facilitate the recording of data before the processing run is completed. This technique avoids the necessity of reprocessing an entire procedure should an error or machine

---

[7] U.S. Department of the Air Force, Auditor General, Comptroller, *Guide for Auditing Automatic Data Processing Systems* (Washington, D.C.: U.S. Government Printing Office, Nov. 1, 1961), pp. 6–8.

failure result before processing is completed. Check points also provide an intermediate starting point for any necessary rerun.

Balancing controls are very similar to those used in controlling manual processing procedures. Typical would be an accounts receivable posting procedure where, as the transactions are posted to the individual ledger accounts, beginning balances are added to transaction amounts to obtain a net balance of each account. The total of all the net balances of the individual accounts must then agree with the control balance in the "general" ledger account. Zero balancing may be used if the two totals are subtracted from each other to provide a zero answer if correct.

Crossfooting balance checks are used to determine if the sum of the horizontal totals of arrayed data agree with the sum of the vertical totals.

Limit checks, sometimes called tolerance checks, are programmed into the system to call attention to any data that exceeds or is less than certain predesignated limits. Typical limits would be a maximum dollar amount for payroll checks, a maximum number of inventory items to be issued at one time, percentage variations, minimum stock item levels, and maximum credit to be extended to a given individual. Any abnormal items would be printed out, noted on reports, or otherwise called to the attention of management for any action required.

Limit checks may also be provided to check the results of any arithmetic procedure and determine if the capacity of equipment accumulators or registers has been exceeded and if there is a danger of significant data being lost because of the overflow condition.

Some fields of data require the presence of blanks in their format. Where such fields are present, they must be checked in the processing procedure by blank transmission tests. Similarly, nonsignificant zeros should be removed before transactions are posted to data records, as these could replace significant data in the storage file.

Where a series of multiplications is to be performed, the final results may be checked through the use of proof figures. In such a procedure an arbitrary figure, larger than any of the data multipliers, may be selected as such a proof figure. Each multiplicand is multiplied twice, once by the data multiplier and then by the difference between the multiplier and the proof figure. The totals, of both multiplications, for the series of items are then compared with the product of the multiplication of the total obtained by the multiplication of all multiplicands and the proof figure.

Validity checks are comparisons of the account or file number recorded in the input data with lists of existing accounts or file numbers stored in internal memory to detect erroneous entries which might otherwise be made to existent accounts. For example, if a portion of a salesperson's payroll were coded for posting to a production expense account, it would be rejected as invalid, although the designated account exists.

Self-Checking Numbers. Incorrect identification numbers (accounts, files, products, employees, and so forth) can be detected with over 95 percent reliability by making certain mathematical calculations with the digits in the basic number and comparing a digit in the result with a check digit included as a suffix in the identification number. This technique is used most frequently when the code number is originally recorded by hand and subsequently keypunched. In such cases, the check is performed either by a device connected to the keypunch or by the computer in an input editing or checking run.[8]

There are many types of error routines. These serve to pinpoint error conditions, permit corrections to be made more easily, and give some assurance that correction has been taken before the data are reentered into the system.

Some error routines are termed diagnostic, as they are used to determine what caused the error condition found to exist. These are usually printed out to aid in their correction. If desired, the processing run may either be halted for correction or continued after a proper "note" of the error has been made by the computer. Other error routines are used after processing instructions, such as COMPARE, to analyze the results if an impossible or error condition is found in the comparison.

Failure to post to a disk memory file may be detected in an alteration test by comparing the contents of the file before and after each posting procedure to determine if the contents of the file have been altered.

If the total of a field of input or output has been prenumbered, the system can perform a check of totals by accumulating a corresponding total and comparing it with the predetermined total (See Reference 11.)

A good example of the location of this validation process can be found in Step 1 of the illustration on pages 328–29.

Output Controls

Control totals, previously mentioned under input controls, such as hash totals, dollar amounts, and record counts, are basic in the control

---

[8] International Business Machines Corporation, *Management Control,* p. 9.

of the output of data. As the batches of data are processed, the computer can be programmed to develop its own batch totals. These totals are then checked by an independent department—usually the internal auditors—to be sure that they agree with the previously prepared control totals. If these independently derived batch totals are in agreement, the data processed must be the data delivered to the EDP department for processing.

A periodic read-out or print-out of totals and account balances is sometimes used for an audit trail after a certain number of transactions are processed at specified time intervals. Magnetic disk, tape, and internal storage files may occasionally be "dumped" (printed-out) for similar usage. The extent to which such print-outs are performed is a decision which must be made by management after consideration is given to the usefulness and the cost of such a procedure. After such a print-out, an occasional hand check of data samples from source document through to a report, or from the report back to the source document, may be justified as a basis for a continuing assurance of the normal level of accuracy expected in output data produced by computer systems. The selection of the above data samples may be made through the utilization of some of the systematic sampling techniques available through the use of the computer.

Reports and analyses may occasionally be prepared for submission to the groups where transaction data originated for their approval. Typical of these groups would be credit departments, labor and personnel departments, and inventory control and purchasing departments.

Control by exception is another form of output control. If management can assume that the daily routine and nonexceptional items are satisfactory, then it may concentrate on the exceptional or special items in its decision-making function. These could involve a check of any error or unusual conditions found as a result of the programmed controls previously described. More probably, however, exception items of most concern to management would be those related to limit, tolerance, or reasonableness checks. Typical items might be sales which exceeded credit limits; proposed sales to customers who do not have approved credit; notice of a deviation from fixed sales prices previously established; differences discovered between priced items on purchase orders and prices on related invoices; notification of any unusual stock withdrawals, sales, or percentage changes; and exceeding of minimum, maximum, or other set limits. Control by exception is a widely used and most effective control technique.

The use of prenumbered standardized forms is another form of output control. Nonstandard or modified data forms will not be compatible with standard forms. If numerical accountability is required, then each form must be accounted for and the possibility of fictitious or fraudulent statements, invoices, or checks will all but be eliminated.

All of these controls can work well from a theoretical point of view. The most basic output check of all is to insure yourself that the user understands the data he or she is receiving and checks it to insure himself or herself of the reasonableness of the output. It is imperative that the ultimate user of the system understands how it works.

Built-In Controls

The use of parity bits is probably the most widely used control built in by manufacturers. The parity bit, described earlier in Chapter 7, is a binary digit (bit) which may be added in the parity bit channel when required to provide the proper number of bits to make the coded data either an all odd or all even number of bits. Whether this number is even or odd depends on the requirements of the system in use. These bits are counted every time the tape is processed to be sure that the correct number of bits are present. This is a very important control technique, as magnetic bits may be covered by particles of dust, not be readable because of tape flaws, or even become "lost" if a reel of tape is dropped.

Duplicate circuitry is occasionally provided for particularly critical circuits in some equipment to assure a high degree of machine accuracy. The space requirements and cost of this duplication prohibits its general use.

Used rather widely in early computers, but to a lesser extent today, is the utilization of double or reverse arithmetic. As implied, double arithmetic consists of performing the same operation twice and comparing results. An example would be in the multiplication of $A \times B$ to obtain C. B would then be multiplied by A, subtracting C to arrive at zero. These operations would be performed simultaneously, utilizing different circuits to obtain the results.

Echo checks are sometimes used at points in the procedure where data are transferred in the system. As this transfer is made, an echo is sent back to the original source of the data. If there is any variation between the transferred data and the original data, a machine failure is indicated.

In the discussion of magnetic recording devices in Chapter 11 it was mentioned that some equipment had combination read-write or dual reading heads provided. These dual heads serve as control devices in that data written may be read and checked for agreement with the original data, or the data may be read by two heads and checked for comparison.

Preventive maintenance, though not "built-in" as such, is one of the more important techniques used today in the avoidance of component and subsequent equipment failures. The components and circuitry of the computer of today are quite stable in their performance and are designed to operate over a reasonably wide range or level of operation with accurate results. Most component failures are preceded by a decline in efficiency and operation under reduced voltage conditions. If these components are tested periodically under such conditions, it is possible to determine their threshold, or lowest level, of proper operation. The items which are weakening and failing will normally be detected long before there is any loss of operating performance. The replacement of these failing components before they fail is certainly a positive approach in avoiding errors before they occur. (See References 15 and 17.)

ON-LINE SYSTEMS

In some cases, the computer may be operating on an "on-line" basis (also called a real-time environment) where system continuity becomes particularly critical. In such situations a second on-site system may be required to continue processing should the other system fail. The expense of providing this equipment would make this alternative reasonable in only the most critical situations. However, if more than one computer exists on-site, for other than back-up reasons, the necessary equipment for switching the network from one computer to another should be provided since the additional cost is relatively low. Should the system tolerate operation using a less efficient alternative for a period of time, the procedures to be followed should be clearly outlined.

In some cases data may be transmitted from remote locations by use of a network of terminals. To insure continuity of operations in such a data collection environment, recovery procedures should include some alternative means of data entry. Depending on the volume of data and speed of turn-around required, some on-site back-up equipment, such as keypunches, may be required to handle critical transactions. The recovery of data already entered on-line is usually accomplished through the use of a log tape or duplicate file copy of the data. The system and procedures should be designed to preclude the necessity for the terminal operators to reenter a significant amount of data due to a data loss in the system.

On-line updating of master files demands the most extensive fall-back, recovery, and restart procedures. The recovery and restart procedures for on-line updating must provide for continued operation in spite of the loss of the system or data at any time during the processing of an updating transaction. The procedures must further provide for rapidly returning the updated files to the status held at any point in time, normally to the last copy of the master files. It is usually also necessary to provide for the reapplication of transactions against the files. The primary tools used to effect recovery in this environment are logs of the transactions, modified data records, and copies of the data files taken at specified intervals. Usually, these applications are supported by batch operations on the files in off-line mode.

Where on-line files are updated in place, the previous status of an updated record is not automatically available unless special steps are taken to save it. Transactions generally arrive in random sequence and cannot be re-created unless steps are taken to log the transactions as they arrive. Periodic dumps of the files onto tape or other media, to-gether with a log of all transactions and modifications to the files, allow reconstruction of data in most cases. Back-up copies of these files should be verified for integrity, immediately after creation, by at-tempting to reload from the back-up tape to insure they are readable and in balance.

The computer should operate under a monitor which acts as an over-all guard to provide protection against accidental and deliberate at-tempts to misuse the computer. The monitor should be designed with adequate security measures to insure only authorized access to sensitive data and programs. Statistical data should be recorded, maintained, and periodically reviewed to insure that only authorized terminals have access to the master files. Sign-on/sign-off procedures are necessary to insure proper use of any terminal. Only authorized personnel should have access to these procedures and codes. (See Reference 6.)

COMPUTER SECURITY

The subject of the physical security of data processing facilities as well as the security of the data itself within any given installation or system should be a topic of considerable concern to people anywhere in the world where computers are used.

It has been observed in the United States and in Australia and New Zealand as well that the security of data and of the EDP facilities is recognized as a problem by management only in proportion to the risk which they feel they are running in data accumulation, transmission and processing, at their particular place of business.

An analogy to illustrate these two different points of view would be that in some of the large metropolitan cities of the world people are afraid to be on the streets at night, and as a result go to considerable expense to protect themselves in a variety of ways. On the other hand, there are other areas of the world where people feel perfectly safe to go anywhere at any time. In these areas, expenditures which would be made on personal safety would be minimal in comparison.

This analogy possibly describes the extremes of feeling that might be evidenced concerning data security. Most computer users will feel themselves to be somewhere in between. In these cases judgment will have to be made based upon the anticipated consequences of the loss, modification or disclosure of data, and/or damage to the equipment.

It is reasonable to say, however, that with government and business placing more and more reliance on computer-processed data and on the equipment which does the processing, greater and greater risks are being taken. More and more data, on an increasing variety of subjects, of great concern to many people, is being processed, transmitted, and stored in central locations with the equipment being controlled by a very small group of people. Prudent and conservative judgment on the part of top management should prevail as to the necessary security measures to be taken. The cost of the total avoidance of risk is prohibitive. The common sense approach is to use sound procedures so that risk may be reduced.

The security of equipment and data can be broken down into five main categories, namely: (1) facilities protection, (2) hardware back-up, (3) software protection and back-up, (4) insurance coverage review and evaluation, and (5) the utilization of the internal computer auditor function.

The department or agencies which should be most interested in equipment and data security, other than the owners and top management, are the internal and external auditors. The internal auditor is concerned with the conformity of the security to management policies, the soundness of the controls, and the quality of performance while the external auditor is concerned about the survival of the client as well as a quick reading of the client's controls.

Facilities Protection

There are two sources of peril to any computer facility: (1) physical perils, and (2) perils caused by people. Only the principal perils of each type will be illustrated. However, each peril should be considered in depth by every computer user.

Physical perils can be divided into those (1) which arise from fire, and (2) those which arise from all other forms of natural disaster, that is, flood, hurricane, and so forth.

Physical Perils—Fire. To give some idea of the variety and complexity of this area of problem, note the following:

1. Selection and implementation of adequate smoke and fire detection and quenching systems.
2. Construction of the computer area out of retardant flame materials.
3. Necessity for specific instructions to be drawn up and training given to all computer personnel relative to the procedures to be followed in the event of fire or fire alarms.
4. The placement of the fresh-air intakes for computer air-conditioning installations so as to be as free as possible from harmful pollutants (smoke, fumes) coming in from the outside.
5. Necessary liason with local fire departments in regard to their particular concerns or precautions in case of fire.
6. Precautionary measures to be planned for, within the computer area, should water be used to extinguish fire in the computer area.
7. Physical placement of the computer installation within the building complex so as to minimize the likelihood of loss to the computer in the event of fire.

Physical Perils—Natural Disaster. In areas which are susceptible to flood, computers should not be located in places where flood waters might reach them. If tornado or hurricanes are recognized possibilities within an area, computers should be located so that the risk of loss through either of these forms of natural disaster might be minimized.

Physical Perils—People. The fact that this subject is not highlighted in the organization of this section should not mislead the reader into thinking that the subject is of minor or lesser significance. It is placed in this position only because it appears logical. People have caused, either intentionally or unintentionally, a greater array of security problems for persons concerned with the security of computers and computer information than have all the other types of security problems put together.

Each of the problem areas which follow deserve study and planning in depth even though they are enumerated at this point. Many of the problem areas, it should be noted, tie directly back to the adequacy of the internal control procedures existent at a particular time and place:

1. Lack of control over persons who have access to the machines room and to the operation of the machines.
2. Inadequately defined areas of responsibility for the security of data, systems and programs.
3. Data processing personnel not adequately informed as to the importance and significance of their work as it ties into the continuity and prosperity of the firm.
4. Definite procedures for the handling of a disgruntled employee not established.
5. Physical placement of the data processing facility in as inconspicuous a place as possible relative to public access, and also removed as much as possible from any part of the business facility which might be peculiarly susceptible to any of the perils discussed in this section.
6. Inadequate assessment of the consequences of a power failure or voltage reduction to the EDP installation.
7. Inadequate protection of tape and disk libraries. Unrestricted access to programs and files of data is not advisable. Responsibility for the physical security of this data should be assured at all times.
8. Failure to use operational logs as security measures.

Hardware Back-Up

In theory it makes sense to provide for hardware back-up facilities. This would involve either of two alternatives: (1) provision by the user of duplicate computer facilities at a separate location, or (2) entry into a written agreement with another computer user in the area who has the same configuration of hardware.

Both of these alternatives have serious limitations, however. The first alternative involves an outlay of funds far in excess of what most managements are willing to afford. Only one firm observed followed this practice.

The second alternative, on the other hand, is equally difficult to carry out. To begin with, the ability of any company to find another local company within the vicinity which has the same equipment configuration is unlikely. Assuming such a firm was found, a written agreement should be entered into—clearly outlining the privileges, duties, and responsibilities of both parties. Experience demonstrates that this latter requirement is particularly difficult to achieve. Lastly, assuming that a company with a compatible computer configuration is nearby, and the management of the latter firm is willing to sign a contract permitting your company to use their computer facility for a given amount of time in the event of an emergency, there is still the problem of how all of this would be done should an emergency arise.

The chances of finding that the two computer systems are compatible is remote, and even more remote is the likelihood that any firm would be sufficiently concerned and foresighted to do what has been described.

Software Protection and Back-Up

Once programs have been developed, tested, and put in operation, they should be kept, along with the data files resulting from procedural operations, under the control of someone responsible for their safekeeping. This individual, or librarian, should be responsible for these files, usually in the form of reels of magnetic tape or disk packs. He or she should see that they are properly stored and cared for and that they are only issued to authorized personnel. A record, or log, should be kept of any withdrawals of these items indicating to whom they were issued, when they were issued, and when they were returned.

Another problem of control over the program and data files is closely associated with the familiar saying, "Don't put all your eggs in one basket." This suggests, in connection with data files, that perhaps a set of duplicate tapes should be stored in another geographical area to protect the data from a specific disaster which might occur in the computer area. If such a set of back-up tapes were available, loss of the original tapes would not paralyze the firm. Certainly, every precaution must be taken to make certain that at least key elements of the business accounts are safe.

On a smaller scale, protection of data tapes from the possibility of accidental loss in the form of a mutilated tape or a tape written over in error is usually provided in the retention of tapes prepared in the immediately previous procedures. The tapes retained are usually termed three-generation tapes and are often called "son," "father," and "grandfather" tapes. Some form of retention schedule must be adhered to.

The nature of the business often determines the number of copies of tape files or generations of files, which should be kept. For example, the Mountain Bell Co. is required by law to maintain 365 generations of tape in one particular instance. This is required by the U.S. Internal Revenue Service as a means of making it possible to use machine-generated information to document federal income tax returns.

Tape rings (Figure 14–3) are usually provided with reels of mag-

FIGURE 14–3. Tape File Protection Device

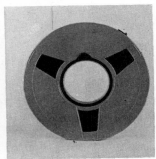

Courtesy of IBM

netic tape. These small plastic rings fit into the side of the reel holding the tape and must be inserted before data can be written on the tape. The presence of the ring does not hinder reading the tape. The ring is removed when the tape is just to be read to avoid any possibility of accidentally writing over data that are to be retained for future use. (See References 1, 2, 3, 4, 7, 8, 10, 12, 13, 14, 16 and 18.)

Insurance Coverage Review and Evaluation

Insurance may be purchased to cover almost any risk for a price. The ability of a company to insure itself against physical loss to its equipment and associated activities is available through at least one insurance company. The policy of this company is divided into six subsections. Each subsection has a different set of assumptions which governs the cost of the insurance and the conditions under which loss reimbursement occurs. The subsections are as follows:

1. Data Processing System Equipment
2. Data Processing Media
3. Extra Expenses

4. Valuable Papers and Records
5. Accounts Receivable
6. Business Interruption

The principle questions which need to be asked again, however, are: Is the insurance coverage adequate for conditions as they presently exist today? Is the company willing and able to pay these costs, or is the business over-insured in light of the risks which management views as existing at the present time?

Internal Computer Auditor

The concentration of information flow in a single computer complex has made it easier to commit computer fraud. Because of this problem a new functional area of expertise is emerging, the internal computer auditor.

The auditing of computers requires an in-depth technical knowledge and ability in three separate areas: accounting, auditing, and electronic data processing. In addition, the internal computer auditor must have thorough knowledge of the organization and functioning of the business enterprise as well as of industry practices. A person with these qualifications is difficult to find.

It is the feeling that such a person or department should be involved in the development of every computer system from the very beginning. This would involve monitoring the design work as well as approving the conversion and testing procedures, thereby making it possible for a post-audit to be made to see how successful the new system may be.

CASE ILLUSTRATION

A Small Inventory, Billing, and Accounts Receivable System[9]

This case illustration describes how a relatively small EDP user effectively organized the responsibilities and used programmed control and external control techniques to achieve a high degree of reliability in an EDP system for inventory, billing, and accounts receivable. It also

---

[9] Ibid., pp. 28–30.

illustrates some effective control techniques applied in connection with the use of disk memory units.

The EDP user is a wholesaler maintaining a warehouse which fulfills orders received either through salespersons or directly from customers. The EDP system maintains both the inventory records and the customer account balances on disk files which are updated as each transaction is processed. The details of the customer account balances are maintained in separate punched card files.

Division of Duties. The company's operations are divided into the following six groups, all of which report directly to a general manager: sales, warehouse operations, data processing, credit, cashier, and accounting. These organizational distinctions provide for a clear separation of duties between the sales personnel who contact the customers, the warehouse employees controlling the physical inventory, the data processing group which prepares the invoices and maintains the inventory and customer records, the credit manager who authorizes lines of credit and undertakes collection activity, and the cashier who handles the payments received from customers. In addition, the accounting department and its control records are segregated from the foregoing groups, and this department has no access to the company's assets or authority over its operation.

The common division of responsibilities between development of the EDP system and its operation was not carried out in this company because of its size. The systems development and programming was performed by the two employees who, together with three keypunch operators, currently operate the system. In the absence of this division of responsibilities, the general manager closely supervised the systems development and testing and continues to closely review its operations.

Source Data Control. The data processing cycle begins with the receipt of a customer order. Such orders are received by telephone calls either from sales personnel or directly from customers. The telephone operator prepares an order form which includes the customer's name, account number, and quantities ordered. In addition, the operator notes the number of different products ordered. No additional control procedures are exercised at this time as procedures have been incorporated in an editing run to ascertain the validity of the customer and reasonableness of the order. Since all sales are made at listed prices, there is no need to obtain approval for the prices of the items ordered.

Control of Input. The sales orders are forwarded by the telephone operator to the data processing unit, where the keypunch operators prepare punched cards recording customer's number, date, product code and quantity for each item ordered, and the total number of items ordered. Both the customer number and the item codes are self-checking numbers which are checked by the keypunch machine. Because of this control, plus the other control procedures in the editing performed by the computer, the company does not consider it necessary to verify the keypunching.

The customer orders are accumulated and three or four times a day are processed by the computer. In the first processing operation, the data from the cards are stored in work space on a disk file, and several editing routines are performed to detect errors in the input and to identify orders requiring the specific approval of an operating department:

1. The input is reviewed for completeness of data in all appropriate fields (for example, presence of a quantity when a product code appears).
2. The number of product items is counted by the computer and compared with the total-items-ordered field in the input to check against the omission of any items ordered.
3. The product code number in the input is traced to the inventory file to check its validity (both the inventory and customer account disk files are on-line during the editing run).
4. The customer account number in the input is traced to the customer account file to ensure its validity.
5. Approximate sales values are calculated when the inventory files are checked and are accumulated with the customer's account receivable balance to determine whether the customer's credit limit will be exceeded by the new order.
6. The customer's account file is searched for the presence of a "do not bill" code which indicates that for credit or other purposes, no further sales may be made to this customer without prior approval.
7. All quantities expressed in individual units are reviewed to ensure that they are less than a case quantity as a check on the order quantity recorded (if they exceed a case quantity, there is a probability that the quantity amount is incorrect).

In addition to the editing procedures at this time the computer establishes a hash total control over the customer numbers and counts the number of individual orders included in the batch.

Errors and other unusual items disclosed by the editing routines are printed on exception listings and forwarded to the appropriate operating department for its review or authorization. For example, orders from customers for which no master file has been established are reported to the sales department for their investigation and authorization of a new customer file. The sales department will also be advised of orders with improper product codes or other missing input data, and individual item quantities in excessive case units, for checking to the order form or clarifying with the customer. Orders which would exceed the authorized credit limits and orders received from customers subject to a "do not bill" code are reported to the credit department for disposition.

By these editing procedures and referral of errors and orders requiring specific authorization back to an operating department, the company has clearly asserted the responsibility of the source operating departments for the accuracy and authorization of the input data. The completeness of the input data is not assured by these procedures, but the company believes that, because its orders are for current delivery, the loss of an order would result in its not being shipped and would be promptly reported by a customer. Alternatively it would appear that the orders written by the telephone operators could be numbered and noted in a simple register which could be proved daily against the total orders processed or referred to the sales and credit departments. This could also control the orders being held by the latter two departments.

Billing and Recording Controls. The customer orders passing the editing test and stored in the work area of the disk file are processed in a second operation to prepare the sales invoice and update the customers' accounts and the inventory records. Invoices with preprinted numbers are used, and the number of the first invoice is inserted at the beginning of the processing in order that the customers' records will contain the invoice number for reference. During the processing customer account numbers are totaled and orders counted for comparison at the completion with the totals accumulated during the editing process to ensure against loss of data. The sales prices stored in the inventory master files are used to calculate the invoices. No checking of this calculation is performed by the computer. However, it is considered that the credit limit check, which is performed a second time when a customer account file is updated, serves as a limit control against any possibly large overbillings.

The customer account numbers and the product numbers are also used as the address of the file locations in the disk files. Such numbers are also stored in each file record. As a check that the proper file location has been addressed by the computer, the customer and product numbers in the input data are compared with the numbers stored in the master files before processing such files. The possibility of writing over and destroying an active account when opening a master file account for a new customer or product is controlled in two ways. A punched card file is maintained for all unused addresses of customer accounts and product files. When new accounts are to be opened, the addresses are selected from the card file and the address selected is withdrawn from the file. As a second check against writing over an active file, before a new address is used it is searched for the presence of a code symbol which should have been recorded when the address location was previously erased at the time of closing the prior account at that address.

Interesting control procedures are followed in posting inventory master files during the billing process: The balance at the beginning of the day is not altered for each transaction, but instead, each sale (or receipt) and the new balance resulting are posted in separate fields. This provides a restart point in the event of error or computer malfunction during the day's operation. It also permits the computer to check its own processing the following morning when each inventory file is checked to ensure that the prior balance, plus the receipts and less the sales, equals the recorded closing balance, and only then is the prior balance adjusted to the new balance. During this daily balancing routine, the inventory master files are reproduced on a separate disk file which is retained until the following day's master files are reproduced. The customer account master files are similarly copied each morning. The input for the transactions processed each day is filed together and, with the copied master files, provides a means of reconstructing current master files if such becomes necessary.

Sales are posted to the customer account master files during the billing run and are also accumulated in a separate record for the day. A daily report is prepared by the EDP system, showing the sales for the day and the invoice numbers used. A copy of this report and a punched card record for each customer invoice is forwarded to the accounting department, where a control total of the accounts receivable is maintained together with a punched card file of the details of each customer's balance.

Use and Review of Processed Data. Copies of all sales invoices are forwarded to the warehouse supervision to serve as shipping instructions. The preparation of the invoice in advance of the shipping is possible in this company as it very seldom encounters an out-of-stock condition. The warehouse supervision is also furnished by data processing with a unique aggregate shipping manifest. The manifest is prepared from the inventory master files and reports the total of each product item to be shipped each day. On the basis of this manifest the products are withdrawn from their storage locations and brought to the shipping department, where they are then broken down by invoice quantity. Separate performance of these two functions assures that the quantities being billed agree with the quantities by which the inventory records have been reduced. It also helps the warehouse management to separate the shipping function from the storage operations of the warehouse and thereby adds to the physical control it can exercise over its products which are very subject to pilferage.

Comprehensive sales reports are prepared daily by the EDP system. These reports to the sales department and general manager indicate sales by product, product group, sales personnel, district, and type of customer, and show both daily sales and cumulative sales for the month. These reports, designed principally for operating purposes, provide a sensitive analysis of the operations as recorded by the EDP system. Management believes that its daily review of these sales reports and the attention given to them in the sales department would disclose any significant error in the recorded data. It is also believed that the monthly commission statement prepared for each salesperson also would be a likely source of notice of any error not otherwise detected.

The accounting department also checks the reliability of the EDP system. It reviews the sales register and accounts for all of the pre-printed invoice forms used during a month. By comparing the total sales reported in the sales register for the month with similar totals on the various sales analyses, it checks that the data reviewed by management is the same as entered in the accounts. The total sales are posted to a manually maintained summary account used to control the total accounts receivable. The credits to this control account for cash received are derived from two sources: (1) the cashier, who reports directly to the accounting department the cash received and deposited, and (2) the EDP system, which reports the net cash received, the commission allowed, and the total credit to the customer accounts. The accounting department ensures that both of the cash amounts agree, reviews the reasonableness of the total discount allowed, and then posts the total cash credit to its accounts receivable control account.

At the end of each month, the punched card file containing the detail of the customers accounts receivable (which is culled daily for items paid) is processed with the customer accounts master files to prepare statements for the customers of their balances. In this processing the computer checks the balance it has recorded in each customer master file with the balance indicated by the punched cards. The grand total of all the customer statements is checked by the accounting department to its control total of accounts receivable.

Two external control methods are used by the company to ensure the reliability of inventory records maintained by the data processing system. First, each week the system produces a list of the balances on hand for each product. This listing is checked by warehouse personnel by physically counting the inventory present in the warehouse. The second control over the inventory records is exercised by the accounting department. Each month it reviews the sales and cost-of-sales report produced by the data processing system from the data recorded in the inventory master files. With the statistical data accumulated from the purchases and sales prices, the accounting department is able to closely forecast the gross profit relationship for each product group; it uses this information to check the cost-of-sale amounts received from the inventory.

REFERENCES

1. ALLEN, BRANDT. "Danger Ahead! Safeguard Your Computer." *Harvard Business Review,* November–December 1968, p. 97.

2. BERGART, JEFFREY G.; DENILOFF, MARVIN; HSIAO, DAVID K. "An Annotated and Cross-Referenced Bibliography on Computer Security and Access Control in Computer Systems." The Ohio State University, November 1972.

3. BROWNE, PETER S. "Computer Security—A Survey." *Data Base,* Fall 1972, p. 1.

4. CHASTAIN, DENNIS, R. "Security vs. Performance." *Datamation,* November 1973, p. 110.

5. CUNNINGHAM, JAN. "Establishing Internal Controls for a COM Operation." *Information and Records Management,* June 1973, p. 30.

6. EASTIN, CAROL P. "System and Software Controls for On-Line Systems." *Management Controls,* June 1972 p., 141.

7. "EDP Security: Is Your Guard Up?" *Price Waterhouse Review,* July 1971, p. 46.

8. International Business Machines Corporation. *Considerations of Data Security in a Computer Environment.* G520–2169–0 (Repr. 7/70).

9. "Magnetic Larceny." *Modern Data,* October 1973, p. 31.

10. McCalmont, Arnold M. "Communications Security for Voice—Techniques, Systems, and Operations." *Telecommunications,* April 1973, p. 35.

11. Mason, John O. Jr., Connelly, William E. "The Application and Reliability of the Self-Checking Digit Technique." *Management Adviser,* September–October 1971, p. 27.

12. Palme, Jacob. "Software Security." *Datamation,* January 1974, p. 51.

13. Rittersbock, George H. "Data Processing Security: A Selected Bibliography." *Management Adviser,* September–October 1973, p. 52.

14. Sobczak, Thomas V. "Protection for a Most Valuable Asset: Business Information." *The Data Communications User,* March 1974, p. 113.

15. Study Group on Computer Control and Audit Guidelines. *Computer Control Guidelines,* Canadian Institute of Chartered Accountants, 1970.

16. Tassel, D. Van. *Computer Security Management.* Englewood Cliffs, N.J.: Prentice-Hall, 1972.

17. Weiss, Harold. "The Danger of Total Corporate Amnesia." *Financial Executive,* June 1969, p. 69.

18. Weiss, Harold. "Computer Security: An Overview." *Datamation,* January 1974, p. 42.

QUESTIONS

1. How has the auditing of computerized systems created problems for the auditor which did not exist before? Explain.

2. In a general way describe the pattern of philosophical reasoning which has been developed to make the auditing of a computerized system a greater reality.

3. Differentiate and explain the differences which exist between the "around-the-machine" audit approach and "through-the-machine" approach.

4. Clearly distinguish between "accounting controls" and "administrative controls."

5. From an organizational point of view, what is the best way to set up the organization structure for a computing section?

6. What does the word documentation mean when applied to computer systems?

7. How is it possible to tell whether a particular system has been provided with adequate documentation?

8. When does a systems designer know that he or she has used enough controls?

9. Discuss in some detail the importance of two different types of input control. Would they be any more applicable in one situation than another?

10. Of what importance is the inclusion of programmed controls as close to the beginning of the program as possible?

11. Discuss in reasonable detail some programmed controls you feel might be particularly important to include in a program. Why would you emphasize these particular ones?

12. Describe an output control which you consider to be of special importance. How would you make it operative?

13. What is the purpose or function of the parity bit?

14. What does preventive maintenance have to do with computer controls? Explain.

15. Briefly describe the four main categories of computer security. Is one of these any more important than another?

16. What should be the role of the internal and external auditors when considering the problems of computer systems control and security?

17. Discuss five points of concern to a company installing a computer insofar as protecting the computer from fire.

18. Enumerate several of the better ways you feel there are to protect computer installations from "people."

19. What are the problems in providing for adequate hardware back-up?

20. Discuss a few of the more common ways to provide software protection.

21. Briefly describe two different types of controls which a systems designer should probably incorporate into the design of any computerized data processing system. Give several examples to illustrate each type of control and indicate what it is that each form of control is designed to provide to the data processing system.

15

An Integrated
Management Information
System for Planning
and Control

TEN YEARS AGO Norman E. Sklar defined an integrated data processing system as:

> a network of related subsystems developed according to an integrated scheme for performing the activities of a business. It is a means of uniting men, materials, and machines to accomplish the objectives of the business. It specifies the content and format, the preparation and integration of information for all functions within a business that will best satisfy the planning, organizing, directing, and controlling needs of the various levels of management.[1]

This concept unites data accumulation, communication, computation, processing, and control. The product of such a system is information in a form that can be used by all levels of management in the performance of their duties.

Today, when a complete management information system is spoken of, exactly the same ideas prevail except that the system is computerized and completely automatic. The system will be on-line to all levels of management and will be capable of supplying information in real-time in a wide variety of forms. Ideas such as this have always held a great appeal to computer enthusiasts. In many of their writings over the past ten years, they have held that when such a system could be

---

[1] Norman E. Sklar, "Integrated Information Systems," in *Business Systems* (Cleveland, Ohio: Systems and Procedures Association, 1963), 2, pp. 21–24.

made operational it would provide the "ultimate" for modern-day management. (See Reference 11.)

There have been companies which have attempted to achieve this type of system. A few years ago in one very large and well-known American corporation which manufactures data processing equipment the best minds available within the company were given an ample budget and charged with developing a truly integrated management information system for their company. To this date, they see the present system they have developed as satisfying only the needs of operational management.

One of the primary reasons for their system's failure to satisfy functional needs is because more of the problems of their top managements are of an unstructured nature. The decisions involved are not particularly objective or quantifiable.

They are finding that it will take tremendous more amounts of time and money to develop and implement a system which will also satisfy the needs of functional management. (See Reference 7.)

On the other hand, there are companies where the problems or decisions of management concerning resource allocation have been highly structured and thus more consistently understood. An example is the set of production decisions in an oil refinery (based upon product requirements, costs, schedules, and production capabilities) where the technique of linear programming has been successfully applied and widely accepted as a valid tool for this purpose.

It should be recognized that all so-called integrated management information systems (MIS) do not cover the same range of management activities. Most such systems include information which is primarily of concern only to operating management.

Typically, the operational aspects of business can be more readily quantified and measured than can the more subjective types of information which have bearing on the decisions which top management must make. Top management is concerned with the future and what it may hold for the business. The types of information which bear on this are not nearly as readily determined and quantified.

Another factor which has an impact on the ability of a company to develop an integrated MIS system is the manner in which it is organized. Through interviews with a large number of companies in the United States and Australia it was found that those companies which appeared to have had the greatest success to date with their integrated MIS systems were those which had the most clear-cut organization structure. Their lines of authority and responsibility were clearly understood and common systems and procedures had been utilized by all departments, divisions, and subsidiaries for considerable periods of time.

PLANNING FOR A MANAGEMENT INFORMATION SYSTEM

Before making any plans to integrate more fully an existing data processing system, those doing the planning should stand back and take note of the objectives of the business as well as the objectives which top management holds for the data processing system itself. Many of our largest corporations have not clearly set corporate objectives, and still fewer have long-range goals for their computerized information systems. It is only after such objectives and goals have been analyzed and considered that the planning for a successful MIS system can be started because, without them, data processing applications often do not ever get beyond those which were originally set when the initial conversion to computers occurred.

In large complex business organizations today there is need for continuous planning and control. Problems, conditions, and relationships are continually arising, reacting to, and interacting with one another. This is brought about by the changes which occur in the environment in which business operates today. A few years ago it was sufficient for most firms to plan and then control only on a periodic basis. Continuous planning and control is now necessary because general management must direct both the resource managements and the functional managements on a continuous basis. One group of managements cannot be allowed to dominate another group. Decisions must be reached bringing both groups into accord with each other. (See References 3 and 9.)

Figure 15–1, the organization chart of the data processing equipment manufacturer mentioned previously illustrates the above point. Reading the chart vertically, the process or functional managements include the functions of development, manufacturing, marketing, service, and finance, while the resource managements reading horizontally on the chart include cash, personnel, organization, and product information systems. It should be noted that these functions pervade and have an intimate connection with all of the activities of the various process or functional managements. For example, the importance of cash to the operation of all of the processes is apparent. No process can be carried on without adequate cash. The general manager has the task, therefore, of coordinating the sometimes conflicting aspirations of the

FIGURE 15–1. General Manager's Business Unit

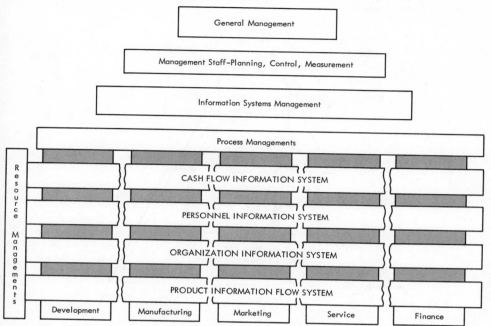

Source: S. D. Catalano and P. D. Walker, "Designing the General Manager's Information System," *International Business Machines*, July 1969, p. 14.

treasurer and those of the marketing or production manager so as to achieve the goals of the organization.

Figure 15–2 is a further breakdown and elaboration of Figure 15–1. If a company is to develop a true management information system, the top corporate planners must first determine corporate objectives, strategic plans, and so on. To do this, they must consider the effects of environmental factors. These include customers and how they react to the products and services received; government and the types of regulatory practices being considered regarding pricing, advertising, and so on; investors and their appraisal of management in terms of the growth and stability of the business; the public and its influence on corporations' growing social conscience; competition; and how technology may affect new products and merchandising tactics. All possible courses of action must be considered and carefully evaluated before a corporate goal or objective is set.

This goal, or goals, must then be translated into policies and plans which it is agreed can be implemented and which are understandable and acceptable to general management. The importance of the com-

FIGURE 15–2. Conceptual Diagram for Planning, Control, and Measurement Hierarchy

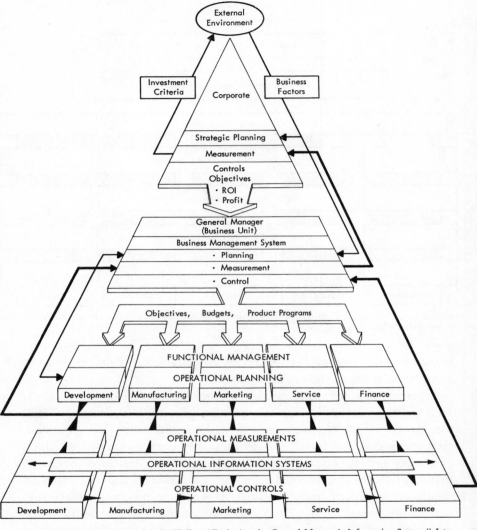

Source: S. D. Catalano and P. D. Walker, "Designing the General Manager's Information System," *International Business Machines*, July 1969, p. 15.

munication process cannot be minimized in any management situation, and it is no less true in this case. There must be a continuous interplay of plans and ideas among all levels of management at all times.

Broad plans and objectives are then reduced to the world of reality in the form of annual and monthly budgets, specific product programs, and so on. Such budgets spell out in detail the working relationship which must exist between the functional areas and the resource areas of the business in terms of resources—money as well as time. In short, who has to do *what,* and *when.*

This pattern of reasoning in turn implies that everyone in the organization is dedicated and cooperative toward the accomplishment of these corporate objectives or goals and that all the resources of the firm will be dedicated to their accomplishment. This also implies that the data gathering system will be designed to gather and summarize pertinent data to facilitate and insure the accomplishment of these corporate goals and objectives. (See Reference 6.)

TECHNOLOGICAL DEVELOPMENTS MAKING MIS POSSIBLE

Progress in Programming

The "art" or "science" of programming has made great strides during the last 20 years. This development can be easily noted in the discussion of software development in Chapter 13. Twenty years ago it was necessary to write a program in machine language in order to communicate with the computer. Today the person who has the problem can communicate with the computer in the language which she or he knows best, and the communication will be either expressed in mathematical terms or in English sentences and phrases.

Communicating with the computer must be made obviously easy to convince management of the virtue of using its capabilities.

Greatly Enlarged Memory Systems

A management information system implies that all the information necessary for management to carry out its functions, namely that of planning, organizing, and controlling, will be contained within the computer system. Many types of storage devices are available today which can store tens of millions of digits of data at a reasonable cost. These devices are discussed in Chapter 11.

Improved Means of Capturing Source Data

The MIS system almost automatically implies great quantities of inputs into the system. Without accurate and speedy means of accommodating these inputs, the MIS system, as such, would not be feasible.

Fortunately, optical scanners and magnetic ink character recognition, as examples, have been developed, and have been proven to be economic, to provide the inputs for this type of system at the speed which is necessary.

Improved Terminal Devices

It is now possible to make inquiry to the computer from remote locations at what would appear to be the same time, and to obtain nearly instantaneous responses. These reponses can be in the form of visual displays, or nearly instantaneous hard copy (microfilm). (See Reference 1.)

FACTORS HINDERING DEVELOPMENT

Walker and Catalano say:

> Very few firms have established objectives and strategies for their information systems. There is a lack of top management understanding of, or involvement in information systems efforts. Corporations have not mounted well-defined programs to set priorities for committing resources. Scarce resources (particularly human resources) continue to be used for low-value activities or insignificant evaluations. Today's measurement systems are based on a calendar year, but the general manager's system requires commitment to projects which may evolve over a decade. Many of today's operational managers, the ones handling day-to-day activities, tend to make decisions in the interest of a small portion of the firm, rather than in the best interest of the total organization. This type of manager is usually very aggressive in resisting change. Many of today's computer specialists are so involved with technical problems that they often lose sight of overall organizational objectives.[2]

INFORMATION NECESSARY TO FACILITATE PLANNING FOR AN MIS SYSTEM

Knowledge of the external environment in which the firm operates is of fundamental concern in planning for a management information system. This is true because the effects of outside forces on the future actions of the firm should not be overlooked. For example, the activity

[2] P. D. Walker and S. D. Catalano, "Next in MIS: 'Data Managed' System Design," *Computer Decisions,* November 1969, p. 30.

of competitors can have a direct bearing on future plans and decisions made by the management executives of the firm. Also, forecasts of economic activity—regional, national, and international—must be considered in the plans of executives because the activities of a large company planning a management information system are probably nation wide, if not world wide, in character and any change in the economic outlook would probably have direct repercussions on the company involved. The same would be equally true for the mood and activities of government as it would affect business. The decision of a government to tax business more or less heavily would undoubtedly shape both short- and long-range plans for many years to come. (See References 2, 5, and 13.)

The external environment, however, should not be the only concern of the planner. The resources internal to the firm are of equal importance. Planning cannot be adequately accomplished if the executives doing the planning are not thoroughly aware of the resources which are available to the firm. These resources would include all types of administrative and scientific talent within the firm, and cash, equipment, and raw materials, as well as an organization which has objectives toward which it is constantly striving.

The planners need also to be aware of any management policies which might act as a constraint upon future plans. Such a policy might be that the firm will not diversify its products.

One will quickly recognize that some of these areas of concern can be much more easily expressed in quantitative terms than others. In order for any of these concerns to be utilized as a parameter (a definable characteristic) in a computer model or an MIS program, it must be capable of being expressed quantitatively. This in turn means that all of these concerns, even though they are important, cannot be recognized or cognizance taken of them in a computerized MIS program with equal verifiability. (See Reference 10.)

A MANAGEMENT INFORMATION SYSTEM MUST ALSO BE A CONTROL SYSTEM

Information from an MIS system can be of the greatest value when it is compared with a previous plan which has been expressed in quantifiable terms. Assuming that responsibility has previously been delegated for the accomplishment of the plan, control takes place when these same individuals are called upon to account for deviations between the plan and actual results.

Hodge and Hodgson have described the characteristics of this type of system in the following ways:

1. A computer-based system.
2. A system that interfaces directly with management and provides management with the information required to operate the facility the manager controls.
3. A system that incorporates the manager's needs into the system in the form of budgets, targets, limits, goals, and so forth.
4. A system that the manager can communicate with to obtain information as required.
5. A system that as a minimum provides the current status of the facility the manager controls, in a realistic time frame.
6. A system that maintains the historical results of the facility.
7. A system that can project, even if in simple terms, the future behavior of the facility.
8. A system that operates in a decision-making environment and not merely in a reporting environment.[3]

The above description of a management information and control system sounds direct and reasonable. To plan and to integrate what has been described into one unified system is the ambition of the planners in many large and complex companies. The realization of it is, as yet, still far beyond the grasp of most. This is due to the complexity of the problems involved, the difficulty of quantifying them, and the difficulty of moulding the thinking of a large group of managers in any firm into a common objective and a common approach for solving problems. (See Reference 6.)

SPECIALIZED TYPES OF MANAGEMENT INFORMATION SYSTEMS

There have evolved, over the past few years, several limited specialized types of MIS. Some of these provide concepts which may eventually permit the implementation of MIS in the broad sense previously discussed. These types include the on-line real-time, and time-sharing systems. (See Reference 12.)

On-Line Real-Time Systems

The term "on-line real-time" is of comparatively recent origin in the computer field. It implies that everyone using the system has a point-of-origin device or terminal which provides a direct keyed entry to the system via teleprocessing. Each such device permits a two-direc-

---

[3] Barton Hodge and Robert N. Hodgson, *Management and the Computer in Information and Control Systems* (New York: McGraw-Hill Book Co., 1969), p. 93.

tional information flow such that the person using it receives responses to his or her request in sufficient time that the information received can be useful in making decisions. In many such systems there is direct visual output via cathode-ray tube devices or in typewritten message form.

In the earlier years of computer usage, data was processed in batches. Like data, as evidenced by business documents, was gathered together and made into a batch. The batch was converted into machine-processable form, and then processed by the computer. As soon as this batch of data was fully processed, another batch of a different type would be processed.

A real-time system is quite different in that in order for a response to be received in real-time, all transactions must be processed in random order. This involves the updating of the master file or description of the current situation with every transaction, regardless of the type of transaction or how frequently the transactions occur.

Response time is the time the system takes to react to a given input. If a message is keyed into a terminal by an operator and the reply from the computer is typed at the same terminal, "response time" may be defined as the time interval between the operator pressing the last key and the terminal typing the first letter of the reply. For different types of terminals, response time may be defined similarly. It is the interval between an event and the system's response to the event.[4]

The speed of the response time differs from system to system, depending upon the actual needs. The more rapid the response time, the more sophisticated must be the equipment and the programming, and all of this makes for greater cost. For example, the speed of response varies from the airline reservation systems which give a maximum response time of about three seconds to the system used for controlling production in a paper mill where a five-minute response time is adequate.

There have had to be a number of technological advances to make such a system workable:

1. The storage capacity of computers has been increased manyfold without a commensurate increase in cost.
2. The speed of access to stored data has also been increased manyfold without a corresponding increase in cost.
3. The operating speed of computers has increased from millionths to billionths of a second for one calculation with an actual decrease in cost of equipment.

---

[4] James Martin, *Telecommunication and the Computer* (Englewood Cliffs, N.J.: Prentice-Hall, 1967), p. 453.

4. Terminals have been developed to directly link the computer with a telecommunication network.
5. Completely new programming techniques have been developed to cope with the problems created by this type of data processing whereby it is possible for many remote terminals to make inquiries of the computer at the same time.

Remote terminal devices are usually attached to the central processing unit of the computer via input/output synchronizers, which are storage devices used to compensate for a difference in the rate of flow of information. The synchronizer may contain several core buffers or intermediate storage devices which form an interface between the input/output (I/O) devices and the computer. Input data is generally transferred to the buffer. When a buffer is full, the central processing unit will be interrupted. Information can be read from, or placed into, buffers by ordinary read-and-write commands.

In order to make all of this possible, executive programs, which were described in Chapter 13, are used.

A good example of an on-line real-time system which has been developed by Datafile Systems Corporation, Blue Bell, Pennsylvania follows:

> Datafile 500 provides invoicing and a broad range of accounts receivable, inventory, sales, and profit reports, the company says.
>
> Keyboard printer terminals are located at the user site and linked on-line to Datafile's two 3500 Burroughs computer systems in Blue Bell. The system has immediate random access to the customer file and the inventory file to allow updating for invoicing and inquiry purposes. Datafile says its system collects and monitors the usage for each item in inventory and can automatically adjust reorder points.
>
> Payments are entered into the system by referencing the customer, invoice, amount, and date. Datafile 500 then produces an aged (30–60–90) open item A/R trial balance and, optionally, delinquent lists by salesmen and aged open item statements. The system can point out vendor shipments which are critical or late.
>
> Reports are produced at the terminal sites either daily or monthly. Invoices are produced immediately after an order is entered.
>
> Costs for Datafile/500 system are based on the services used.[5]

Time-Sharing

One application of real-time systems is in the area of time sharing. The concept of time sharing is typified by having a large, general-pur-

---

[5] *Management Adviser,* March–April 1971, p. 11.

pose computer facility available to many users who are in themselves remote from each other. The service which the users receive is instantaneous (it seems to the user), although the users and the system are independent of each other. (See Reference 14.)

These benefits are made possible because of the system of executive programming (mentioned above and further discussed in Chapter 13). Through this system, the central processor devotes only a short period of time to each user's program before going on to the next, but the delay is not apparent to the user. Assuming 20 users of the system made inquiries, almost simultaneously, the computer would process a small segment of the program of each user going from one to the other in rapid succession. It can act with such speed that each user will commence receiving a response to his inquiry almost as soon as she or he completes the inquiry.

The individual user of the computer time-shared system has a console or teletypewriter in his or her office. The user is connected by telephone line to the central computer. When the user wants to use the system, he or she will dial the identification number or password and then type out the inquiry. The computer takes over at this point and prints out the result of the inquiry on the user's same teletypewriter.

It is possible through time sharing to achieve a continuous video presentation that keeps up with changing environmental factors. For example, engineering drawings can be examined and modified at will on this video display screen.

The computer time-sharing industry has experienced extremely rapid growth since its inception in the early 1960s. According to Robert F. Guise, Jr. of Com-Share, over $300 million was spent in 1970 by approximately 150 time-sharing users with just the firms belonging to the Association of Data Processing Service Organizations.[6] (See References 7 & 8.)

During 1969 Honeywell began offering time sharing along with batch data processing and contract software in regional computing centers established throughout the nation. Honeywell's time-sharing services are primarily tailored to the needs of scientists and engineers. The Control Data Corporation, UNIVAC, and General Electric (GE) are also expanding their services. GE is now one of the largest suppliers of time-sharing services. The GE system will be able to process local batch, remote batch, and time sharing concurrently. This means a user can handle all of his or her data processing with a single system, a capability that is unique at the moment. Remote batch processing is

---

[6] Robert F. Guise, Jr., "Statistics Time," *Modern Data,* October 1971, p. 36.

somewhat different from batch processing as described in Chapter 6. It has been described as follows:

> In a Remote Batch Entry mode of computer operation, the user's terminals are geographically dispersed and connected to the computer by telephone lines. Data to be processed are batched (collected over a period of time), and entered into the computer system through a terminal. The terminals can read punched cards, and generally have a line-printing capability of several hundred lines a minute. The terminal capability and, naturally, the class of jobs done are what distinguish RBE from the interactive time-sharing mode characterized by a teletypewriter terminal.
>
> Remote batch entry systems lend themselves best to the running of jobs with fairly heavy input/output. RBE use comparable to a batch service bureau operation with the notable exception of having the input/output facility on the user's premises, thus replacing the messenger with phone lines.[7]

Risks in Time-Sharing. Management must plan the type of safeguards the system must provide for its data. If the system is to be eventually a general one—that is, a total system—then it will ultimately be used by people at a variety of levels of responsibility in many different areas of the organization. As a result, it may be necessary to limit the access to certain information to specific individuals or groups.

For example, in one of the GE time-sharing installations, each typewriter terminal has a number assigned to it. This number is not changeable except through mechanical alteration at the terminal site. Data storage areas in the computer system are set aside for each user, and these areas are internally coded according to the individual user's identity code. An internal cross-reference table specifies which terminals are permitted access to which data storage areas.

Costs. One obvious advantage to the user of a time-sharing system is the avoidance of substantial outlays for site preparation and computer installation. Generally, the only equipment needed by a time-sharing customer is a single teletype terminal, which can easily be fitted into an area equivalent to that occupied by a normal-size office desk and chair.

Another advantage is that the user of a time-sharing system only pays for the actual amount of time that he or she uses the computer. The cost of participation in a computer time-sharing system is generally the sum of three items: rental of a teletypewriter, charges for actual computer time used, and charges for telephone calls covering the length of time the terminal is connected with the time-sharing system.

[7] *Coopers Lybrands Newsletter* 11, no. 10 (December 1969) p. 8.

However, if the potential user wants to store data files at the time-sharing center, he or she may find this to be quite expensive. Often company records contain many thousands of characters to be stored and the programs to manipulate the files may also need to be stored on-line. This storage may add considerably to time-sharing costs as a typical monthly charge is $1 for every 1,000 characters of data stored.

Computer Languages. Most time-sharing suppliers offer a choice of several algebraically oriented programming languages. The problems of many business people who might be potential users of time sharing are largely those of an accounting nature. To use the algebraically oriented languages for accounting reporting purposes often demands a higher level of skill and proficiency than the employees of a smaller business may have. This may make the use of time-sharing expensive and awkward. Also, in many cases the languages offered by time-sharing companies do not include COBOL which is the language most widely used in the majority of companies today and with which their employees are most familiar. This makes for an added difficulty in using time sharing.

Software. In order to make time sharing appealing to the smaller business user, packaged accounting programs have been developed to handle some of the most frequent types of applications which are desired. For example, IBM's CALL/360: BASIC is a package of accounting programs which have been written to fill many of the average data processing needs of a typical business user. The name of this package is somewhat misleading in that the programs available are not only written in the BASIC language, but also in FORTRAN and PL-1.

However, for the prospective smaller business user to utilize this package, he or she must have the capability to use one of these languages (BASIC, FORTRAN, or PL-1). If the user already has some of his or her computer work written in COBOL, as might frequently happen, that particular group of programs would have to be rewritten into either BASIC, FORTRAN, or PL-1 or the packaged programs rewritten in COBOL. Either of these revisions could easily involve a significant amount of time and money. (See Reference 4.)

Service Bureaus

A similar, but in some respects a different, alternative to time sharing is to utilize a service bureau. To do this, the same type of economic decisions would have to be reached based on a comparison of the costs and benefits to the prospective user. Factors to be considered would be: (1) the type or types of data processing operations to be performed (mathematical calculations vs. large masses of identical types of data); (2) the volume of data to be processed; (3) the accessability to the user of either time-sharing or service bureau facilities; (4) the speed at which the data needs to be processed; (5) the rate of flow of the data; (6) the compatibility of data communication media between the prospective user and the service bureau; (7) the security of the data; (8) the cost of meeting these requirements; and (9) the benefits to be derived from such a decision.

There are three basic types of service bureaus. Time sharing and service bureaus are not dissimilar operations because a time-sharing facility is one form of service bureau. It permits the user to have direct access to a large computer. Access is through a console located on the users premises and output is received through the same device. The main advantage to this arrangement is that a small user has access to a powerful computer. The principal disadvantage is the relatively slow speed of the remote input/output device, particularly if there is a large volume of data to be processed.

Another type of service bureau is a batch processing operation where the user gathers the documents, codes them, prepares a control tape and forwards it to a service bureau. The information on the tape is converted into machine-readable form, processed and summarized in report form, and returned to the user.

The third type is a remote batching operation which follows the same principles as time sharing except that the user has more powerful input/output devices enabling larger blocks of data to be processed at one time.

In Australia, a fourth type of service bureau has evolved. It is organized with the intention that it be utilized by the chartered accountant in conjunction with his or her work in summarizing and analyzing the financial statements of clients. It provides complete accounting systems with all of the necessary reports as outputs, for various types of smaller business enterprises. This, in turn, allows the accountant greater time for financial analysis work with the client.

In Retrospect—Problems of Accomplishment

Excellent examples can be found of on-line real-time systems which are operational and are performing functions at a cost and in a way that previously would never have been possible. These systems are, however, operating primarily within one functional area of the business. They do not often cross over functional lines. The reason for this being so is that each functional area of a typical company is so different in nature from each of the others that it has been most difficult to create one universal information system meeting the needs of all of the functional areas.

Professor John Dearden, in a recent article in the *Harvard Business Review,* at this point raises the following question: "Why not have a group of experts, one from each functional area, pool their knowledge to create an overall system?" He answers the question by saying, "because it would increase the problems of coordination of information. The information systems for such complex functions as marketing and production would be the responsibility of the staff group rather than the line executives who must actually manage marketing and production . . . if any of the MIS people are competent to tell the functional experts what to do, they should be in the functional area."[8]

Another type of problem which frequently arises, whether it be within a functional area or between functional areas, is the question which all systems designers must ask management, and that is, what information do you require in order to make adequate decisions? This assumes that such information is available.

> There is evidence that many managers cannot reduce the decision-making process to quantifiable expressions. This may not be an unwillingness on the part of the managers to cooperate, but rather a genuine inability to comply, since in order to identify the information that one needs, one must first have a model of how he makes decisions. Until a model of this process exists, one cannot specify the information required, and, too often, mathematical concepts cannot capture the expressions of human values which often dictate decisions.[9]

The adequacy of the existing accounting system is of crucial importance also. How clearly does it depict what is going on in the organization? Just because a company makes use of a computer does not mean that it has an adequate accounting system presently in existence. This can be attributed to a variety of things: (1) organizational authority and responsibility have not been clearly defined, (2) the chart of accounts does not measure costs in accordance with prescribed areas of responsibility, (3) costs have not been classified according to their fixed

---

[8] John Dearden, "MIS is a Mirage," *Harvard Business Review,* January–February 1972, p. 90.

[9] P. P. Schoderbeck and S. E. Schoderbeck, "Integrated Information Systems—Shadow or Substance?" *Management Adviser,* November–December 1971, p. 28.

and variable components, (4) the reporting system is meager and not well understood, and (5) the management of the firm has never felt that the accumulation and summarization of numeric data was particularly important.

To summarize to this point in time: (1) without question, tremendous strides have been made by some business firms in developing integrated management information systems, as defined in this chapter, (2) the cost in terms of time and manpower has been much greater than most planners believed possible, and (3) the problems of getting all segments of management to determine and be willing to follow a standardized approach to the solution of their problems has been more than firm managements have been willing to cope with.

Problems such as these have slowed down the rate of progress considerably in the accomplishment of integrated management information systems. In the future it is quite likely that top managements will insist more strenuously that further work of a more sophisticated nature in this area must be cost justified before it will be allowed to proceed. The cost of developing such a management information system is usually large and is becoming increasingly difficult to justify. This along with the time required and the effort which must be expended will probably tend to continue to delay extensive management information systems development—at least in the near future.

CASE ILLUSTRATION[10]

Consolidated Freightways can now locate in seconds any of the company's 8,200 line-haul tractors and trailers from coast to coast. The nation's largest motor common carrier can tell who's driving, where he's going, when he should get there, and how much freight is aboard. With this information, the company can route tractor-trailers across 43 states and 90,000 highway miles for maximum profit and service.

Helping to make this data available is a new IBM computer program called FIRST (Fast Information Retrieval for Surface Transportation). The program was developed by Consolidated Freightways, working with IBM under a Custom Contract Services agreement. IBM is offering FIRST to other motor freight carriers under a license agreement.

"This is a powerful tool for us," says Donald E. Moffitt, vice president, financial planning. "All but one percent of our shipments fall into the less-than-truckload category. The average customer order is

---

[10] "A First for Consolidated," *Data Processor,* March 1972, p. 24.

only 540 pounds with a revenue of less than $35, so we have to come up with more efficient techniques to remain profitable. At the same time, FIRST has already meant significantly improved service to our customers."

As trailers are loaded and dispatched from Consolidated Freightway's 152 terminals, information about each trailer and the shipments on board is keyed into IBM 2740 communications terminals. Arrivals and exchange of equipment with other carriers are reported in the same way. This data is flashed to CF's data processing center in Portland, Oregon, and added to the files of a System/360 Model 50.

Using the 2740s, employees at each of the company's motor freight terminals can obtain information from the data base about equipment en route to their locations. Meanwhile, at the Menlo Park, California, control office, data is immediately available about all operations throughout the system. For terminal managers, the report on shipments en route tells where and when the loads originated, when and in what order they should arrive, how much freight is aboard, the drivers' names and number of customer shipments. This data helps the managers plan their shipping dock crew and driver schedules.

Headquarters traffic specialists can identify tractors and trailers remaining in one place too long and see that they are put to work. They can also keep track of the use by CF of other carriers' equipment. Reports on the movement of empty trailers are another significant piece of information not previously available on a daily basis.

REFERENCES

1. ARNDAHL, LOWELL D. "Computers and Communications—New Trends and Applications." *Telecommunications,* January 1974, p. 32.

2. BENTON, WILLIAM K. *Use of the Computer in Planning.* Reading, Mass.: Addison-Wesley, 1971.

3. BRINK, VICTOR Z. *Computers and Management: The Executive Viewpoint,* Englewood Cliffs, N.J.: Prentice-Hall 1971.

4. DREIER, STEPHEN I. "Capital Expenditure Analysis with Timesharing." *Financial Executive,* July 1973, p. 46.

5. DRUGER, LEONARD N. "Computer Timesharing Aids in Forecasting." *Financial Executive,* August 1972, p. 20.

6. FOLSOM, DONALD J. "A Control Guide for Computer Systems." *Management Accounting,* August 1973, p. 49.

7. HAIDINGER, TIMOTHY P. "Computer Time-Sharing: A Primer for the Financial Executive." *Financial Executive,* February 1970, p. 26.

8.   HILLEGOS, JOHN R.   "Piecing Out the Timesharing Puzzle." *Computer Decisions,* February 1973, p. 24.

9.   HINDMAN, WILLIAM, R., and KETTEMAN, FLOYD F., JR.   "Integrated MIS: A Case Study." *Management Accounting,* August 1973, p. 21.

10. HOLMES, ROBERT W.   "Areas to Investigate for Better MIS." *Financial Executive,* July 1970, p. 24.

11. KANTER, JEROME.   *Management-Oriented Management Information Systems,* Englewood Cliffs, N.J.: Prentice-Hall, 1972.

12. SCHIFF, FREDERICK S.   "The Use of Time-sharing in the CPA Firm." *Journal of Accountancy,* January 1974, p. 62.

13. SCHODERBEK, PETER P., and SCHODERBEK, STEPHEN E.   "Integrated Information Systems—Shadow or Substance?" *Management Adviser,* November–December 1971, p. 27.

14. WOODFIN, PAUL B.   "Should Your Company's Taxmen Be Using Computer Time-sharing?" *Price Waterhouse Review,* Summer–Autumn 1972, p. 23.

QUESTIONS

1.   What is a Management Information System?

2.   Why is it that the greatest number of working applications of MIS are found in the operating divisions of companies?

3.   Are there certain types of companies where MIS seems to be more easily and readily possible? Explain.

4.   What seems to be inherent in large-scale business today which makes Management Information Systems indispensable?

5.   Technologically, are Management Information Systems feasible?

6.   What have been some of the reasons why there has not been more accomplished in this area?

7.   What do you understand when it is stated that a system or a machine is "on-line?"

8.   What is meant by "real-time?"

9.   As the owner of a small but profitable business, what types of accounting help in the way of prepared programs might you expect to find available to you at any well-known time-sharing computer company?

10. Summarize the benefits which one might expect to accrue to a business enterprise which installed a time-sharing terminal in its office?

11. Might this same business enterprise, mentioned in question 10, have any problems in trying to make use of its time sharing terminal? Explain.

16

Management Information Systems—Applied

EARLY DIGITAL COMPUTERS were bulky, heavy, generated an excessive amount of heat, and were relatively expensive per digit of data processed. Programming was a difficult and time-consuming task, and there was little assistance available from the manufacturers in the form of software. In short, the early users of digital computers were hardy souls who had to have a great need for the processing capability and comparatively greater speed the computer had to offer to cause them to venture into the maze of problems involved in converting their mechanical or punched card accounting systems to one of the early computerized systems.

The many initial problems surrounding the use of computers made a conversion to a computerized system a very expensive undertaking. In the beginning it was quite natural to consider a conversion, for example, because a clerical bottleneck existed or there was a need to provide better service to customers. The computer could also usually handle the clerical work more quickly with fewer personnel, and many of the earlier computerized systems were justified solely on the basis of cost saving in the performance of clerical tasks. Those firms, however, who have allowed their computers to remain in their office strictly as a bigger, better calculating machine have not realized the full potentialities of the equipment and, in most instances, have soon become disenchanted and dissatisfied with their installations.

The greatly increased I/O speeds, memory capacity, access time, and diminishing costs per unit of data processed, as well as the availability of greater software assistance, have made it possible for the computer to be used in a much wider variety of ways to perform a greater scope of services for management.

Information accumulated and summarized by computers is being used, for example, to measure performance, evaluate progress, assist in decision making (by simulating assumed conditions), forecast business conditions, set company objectives, set standards, and allocate resources.

Applications for digital computers have been found in almost every conceivable activity, for example, to maintain and continuously update all of the files and records in a large metropolitan school district; to help to increase the security and simplify time and attendance reporting at a large city hospital; to provide both current and accurate data about contract requirements and shop performance in a large aeronautical company; to speed up the operation of a county court system; to monitor the purity of the water provided to a city; to maintain continuous and updated records as to the care of the patients as well as to maintain a continuously updated record of the charges being incurred by the patients in a hospital. Innumerable other examples could be cited with equal validity.

Many of the earlier business users of computers have gone through an evolutionary process in the development of their computerized systems. The computer has made it possible for them to go from the relatively simple automation of clerical tasks to complex applications and improvements in existing procedures which assist management in top-level decision making and in controlling and coordinating widely scattered business units.

AUTOMATION OF CLERICAL TASKS

When business personnel started looking at computers as a means of assisting them in some of their data processing tasks, the tasks which they first considered were those which had large volume, where the clerical operations were largely repetitive, and where there were peaks in the periods during which the data had to be processed. The computer, with its speed, seemed to be ideally suited for this type of operation. Payroll and billing applications were usually among the first to be converted to computers. Sales analyses and the updating of inventory records followed as a logical outgrowth of the billing operation.

Applications such as these have generally been chosen first for computer application because (1) there was a felt need, (2) existing system could be relatively easily programmed and made operable on a computer, and (3) there was an obvious immediate and easily calculable cost saving.

Churchill, Kempster, and Uretsky, in a study sponsored by the National Association of Accountants, found in their observations of 12 firms that the ways in which computers were being utilized in business and industry had progressed a long way in the 15 years since computers were first adapted to business usage. Overall, in terms of numbers, users have increased from a few hundred or thousand during the early years to tens of thousands of users 15 years later.

In the study, they state:

> The computer has come of age in clerical operations. Almost all of the routine, structured operations are on the computer except for those where personnel considerations indicate a postponement or where low volume or present efficiencies preclude economic justification. This automation has changed the content of many basic jobs; altered and, in general, increased the skills required; and, in many areas, reduced the number of people employed in "paper processing" activities.
>
> While the initial applications involved separate systems, an increasing amount of integration is now taking place; applications are being combined and related tasks performed as one system, even where it cuts across functional lines. Some activities are automated, although not economically justified individually, because of their relationship to other computerized activities or because of the economies automation brings to the operation as a whole.[1]

Such statements are perfectly correct when based on studies of a limited number of firms. However, a word of caution should be mentioned in conjunction with this statement in applying it to computer installations in general and particularly in areas of the world which are not highly industrialized and mechanized. This usage is probably correctly stated in regards to the larger companies' installations in this country and even in industrial areas in Europe. However, in many small firm installations in the United States and especially in Australia and New Zealand the touted "integration" of applications and related tasks into single systems has not taken place to any large extent.

---

[1] Neil C. Churchill, John H. Kempster, and Myron Uretsky, *Computer-Based Information Systems for Management: A Survey* (New York: National Association of Accountants, March 1969), p. 140.

Computer applications are integrated, extended, and improved only as the management of the firm sees reasons for doing so. To do any of these things costs money, and if management is not interested in additional or improved applications for the computing facility, the likelihood is that nothing will be done.

In personal contacts with many chief accountants, controllers, and treasurers of firms with computer facilities in the United States, Australia, and New Zealand, one of the questions asked was, "How much encouragement or help do you receive from your top management to investigate further applications for your computer facility?" In many cases, unfortunately, the reply to this question was, "Little or none" and "any improvements that we make in our present system we have to propose ourselves. We have to try to find the time and money to obtain the programs in one way or another, and then endeavor to sell top management on utilizing what we have tried to develop." In most instances, all that the data processing people have to sell to management is ideas. Ideas are hard to sell as it is difficult to quantify many of the advantages that would accrue from such areas as improved customer relations, improved employee relations, newer types of reports, and more timely reporting. Any or all of these, if they were adopted by management, could have a strong impact on the competitive position of the company. Ideas must be sold, though, before funds are provided to implement them.

It is probably safe to predict that many firms today will have difficulty in progressing—at least for some time—beyond the current stage in their computer development of automating clerical tasks. When the initial conversion was made to computerized equipment, it was usually done because the company had certain clerical problems which needed to be done more rapidly. Objectives and plans were not usually made at that time for a complete revision of the data processing system in line with computer capabilities. Since that time, it has cost the company increasing amounts of money just to maintain the existing computing facility and to keep the existing programs up-to-date.

In addition, top managements have not been convinced that there is any real value to the firm in going beyond this stage. Top managements tend to learn from and to imitate each other, and when the general feeling prevailing in an area or in an industry is that computers are primarily useful for repetitive clerical tasks, that is probably the level of achievement most computer users will attain until economic conditions require it changed or general acceptance of newer methods develop. (See Reference 1.)

IMPROVEMENTS OVER PREVIOUS DATA PROCESSING SYSTEMS IN ASSISTING IN THE MANAGEMENT FUNCTION

On the other hand, it was pointed out earlier in this chapter that there has been a clearly perceptible evolution in the way computers are being utilized throughout American industry and commerce. This conclusion was reached in a survey of 12 large companies, located in the eastern part of the United States, made by Churchill, Kempster, and Uretsky.[2] They found that a new computer user usually first considers automating existing clerical routines. As soon as these operations are mastered, and the user begins to realize more fully the capabilities of the computer, he or she generally endeavors to improve upon his or her existing data processing system. For example, in using the computer the user is often impressed by the ease and speed with which data can be accumulated and summarized, as well as the many different ways whereby accounting functions can be integrated because of their use of identical data. With greater amounts of current information available it is possible for the planning function (standards, budgets, forecasts) to be carried out in a much more complete and adequate manner.

To further explain this point, a study made in 1972 by the Diebold Research Program indicated that of the 245 companies questioned, 31 percent of their computer effort was involved with finance and administration, compared with 44 percent as found in the Booz, Allen, and Hamilton Study in 1968.[3] The manufacturing activity followed this with 24 percent and marketing with 14 percent of the total computer effort.[4]

The point to be noted here is that although companies are using less time for financial and administrative work than they did four years ago, the total amount of time being spent on utilizing computers to facilitate the planning function of the firm is still so negligible it is hard to measure.

In far too many instances, top managements are not yet ready to put their faith in quantified predictions of the future to determine their courses of action. A primary reason for this feeling is that there are many variables in most businesses to be considered in making business

---

[2] Ibid.

[3] "As Companies Gain More Experience with Computers Emphasis Shifts Away from Financial Applications," *Management Services*, May–June 1968, p. 13.

[4] "Company Size Does Not Affect Allocation of Funds to EDP," *Management Adviser*, March–April 1972, p. 15.

decisions and the techniques for adequately determining, considering, and quantifying them, as well as the education to understand and believe in their validity, has not yet been attained.

Of course, one can find instances where this statement would have to be modified in one way or another. For example, the public utility industry has, for many years, known that their future plans for the demands made upon them, were largely tied to changes in population in the territory which they serve. Ways and means of statistically predicting population trends have been proven accurate over many years of use, and these methods are accepted and followed by the industry. The use of the computer to facilitate the planning function is an accepted tool in this application.

In most firms whose management has the training—and a belief in—the newer techniques and tools now available through the utilization of the computer in decision making, the previously referred to study sponsored by the National Association of Accountants found that:

> Decision-making capabilities on a basic, but increasingly sophisticated, level are being incorporated into computer applications. While exceptions are still treated by human decision makers, many previously considered "exceptions" are now handled automatically by computer programs. This moves the point of managerial decisions ahead in time, for now management must pass on decision rules rather than on decisions themselves. The need for planning is increasing while the time spent on expediting, routing control is reduced through the use of computer-based systems.[5]

One should also realize that all of the purposes (planning, control, administration) for which computerized information is being used are part of the management function. In other words, the computer has progressed from merely being a clerical tool to one which management looks upon as being capable of providing meaningful assistance in the management function.

The experience of a Caterpillar Tractor Company franchise dealership furnishes an interesting illustration of the use of a computer for control purposes. The dealer headquarters maintained 13 widely dispersed warehouses and commercial outlets for the parts inventory for their line of products. This necessitated the maintenance of approximately 40,000 different types of spare parts at each of the 13 warehouses. The management of this franchise was highly conscious of ser-

---

[5] Churchill, Kempster, and Uretsky, *Computer-Based Information Systems,* p. 141.

vice to their customers and as a result felt that it was imperative that an adequate stock of parts be maintained at each warehouse and commercial outlet.

Maintaining such a sizable parts inventory, as well as the storage, protection, and maintenance of this stock, necessitated a tremendous investment. It was a continuous problem, therefore, to attempt to provide the service which management felt was paramount, try to minimize the investment in inventory, and at the same time have the parts available at all of the warehouses when they would be asked for.

Initially, the company attempted to keep its inventory records with cardex cards and then switched to bookkeeping machines. From this they went to punched card equipment. In all three instances, however, they were highly dissatisfied with the inaccuracy of the information they received as well as with the slowness with which it was provided. They felt that the inaccuracy was due to the poor quality of clerical employees they were able to hire but that the equipment was responsible for the lack of speed. Both of these factors materially reduced the service the company could render to their customers.

As a means of solving the problem, top management installed an IBM System/360 Model 40 computer and completely standardized the clerical procedures surrounding the preparation of input data for the computer. All of the 13 warehouses were then connected by teletype, so that all of the input data could be fed continuously to the computer, which was centrally located.

By having accurate inventory information more quickly, they were able to reduce their investment in inventory by approximately 20 percent, in addition to being able to render much better service to their customers, which in turn enabled them to increase their sale of parts. They obtained a great deal of information about their sales which was not available on a timely basis before, as well as being able to determine the quantities to be ordered for replacements by means of an economic order quantity formula.

To this point, the computer is still being utilized primarily by operating management.

TOP-LEVEL ADMINISTRATION AND EDP

Different levels of management have quite differing responsibilities. Most of the hierarchies of management, below the top level, are primarily concerned with current operating problems. How to keep the various segments of the firm operating efficiently and to make sure that they conform to budget standards is a never ending source of concern to all operating management.

The prime responsibility of those in top management, on the other hand, is to be concerned with the future. They should be frequently asking themselves "what if" types of questions. What would be the position of the company if this or that happened in the future? Operations research techniques can often be of assistance with problems of this type. Operations research has been described as:

> An examination of the problems of an organization having as its aims the identification, definition, and interrelation of individual problems, the study of the underlying human and mechanical variants that delimit their solution, the selection of possible goals, the development of one or more practical solutions, the staff training required to give effect to them, and management reports capable of leading to decision and action; more narrowly, the application of management science to the solution of particular problems. Operations Research is ultimately concerned with the welfare of the organization as a whole; intermediate purposes include the best uses of men and machines, the stabilization of production, and the maximization of profit. Typical operation research studies proceed by means of models, especially mathematical models, which are suited to the use of such tools as linear programming; the skills of engineers, psychologists, mathematicians, economists, and accountants are often combined in such examinations.[6]

In considering the use of computers in management decision making, be assured that no complicated "human type" of decisions have yet been made by a computer as such. It is possible, however, for a computer to utilize programmed instructions, which must be written by humans, to make such decisions as to whether one amount is larger or smaller or equal to another amount, or, if certain conditions are present, to decide whether the conditions fulfill the answer to a "yes" or "no" question. These programmed instructions can be quite complicated in nature at times, and it is very important to realize that the use of the computer in solving this type of problem is limited only by the ingenuity of the programmer.

Only in the sense that the human decision process is based on the recall of information stored in the mind—and is influenced by the experiences the individual has had—can there be any parallels in the thinking processes of humans and machines. However, as computers grow in complexity and storage capacities to the point where they more

---

[6] Eric Kohler, *A Dictionary for Accountants,* 4th ed. (Englewood Cliffs, N.J.: Prentice-Hall, 1970), p. 333.

closely follow the patterns of the human mind, and as these computers reach maturity in terms of experiences—it is not too far in the realm of fantasy for them to more nearly equal their glamorous billing as "giant electronic brains."

To answer "what if" types of questions often involves the use of simulation techniques. Simulation is the designing of models of real-life situations in numeric form and then utilizing a computer to determine the outcome of a wide variety of assumed circumstance by varying different factors in the model. An interesting problem in simulation involving linear programming which came to the authors' attention is that of a large pulp and paper manufacturer. This problem involves the question of how much money should be spent on the propagation of a forest and at what point in time the timber should be harvested. The trees which the company is planting come to maturity within approximately 30 years. They can be harvested sooner or later than this as the occasion may dictate.

In the initial stages, one of the big costs is the planting of the forests. Following this, the trees must be pruned. The pruning of the lower branches is done to provide a greater amount of air circulation among the trees, which in turn provides for healthier trees. It also serves to reduce the danger of fire.

There is also the matter of "high thinning." This involves the trimming of the trees much further off the ground as the trees grow older, and this has to be done by hand with long ladders and saws. When there are millions of trees involved, this can involve a lot of human labor. The thinning of the trees when they come to a certain size is also a considerable cost item.

These are the major cost factors involved. The other side of the coin is, of course, the amount of lumber and, eventually, the amount of revenue which will be derived from the forest if it is harvested within a varying amount of time, probably a six- or eight-year period. One of the factors which can be varied is the second trimming. This is the "high trimming." However, if the trees are not high trimmed, there is going to be more trimming in terms of hand labor when the trees are felled.

The company has put in a great deal of time, money, and effort in developing models which are as nearly typical of the situation as possible so that top management can have better information on which to make future policy decisions when and as these mathematical models have some relevance to the decision being made.

The reader should note in the previous example that the management intended to use the results of the computer simulation as an adviser in the solution of the problems enumerated. As effective as the new mathematical techniques may be, they still do not necessarily give the answers to the problems which have been posed. They are not a substitute for management experience and judgment.

Capital investment decisions are another of the concerns of top management. Return-on-investment analysis is one means of assisting management to make these decisions. One large tire manufacturer has been using this procedure to determine the average net return on possible investment opportunities by using present value factors to discount each year's outflow or inflow of cash by trial and error until a discount factor is found which equalizes the inflow with the outflow. In 1967 the firm developed a computer program to do this. To use this program, it was necessary to define the study in terms of:

a.   Annual sales.
b.   Net current investment as a percentage of sales.
c.   Net fixed investment as a percentage of sales.
d.   After-tax profits as a percentage of sales.
e.   Investments.
f.   Type of depreciation (straight line, sum of the years' digits, or double declining) for each investment.
g.   Depreciation of life of each investment.
h.   When to start depreciation (the same year or the following year) for each investment.
i.   Before-tax income or savings.
j.   Before-tax one-time costs or expenses.

Each item of input data can be entered annually to show virtually any type of business operation desired. The program will handle up to nine separate investments in every year, each with a different depreciation schedule. Also, to simplify input data, annual sales can be entered before tax income or savings, and before tax expenses as a percentage increase or decrease from the previous year.

The data are fed into the computer on punched cards, all calculations are performed internally, and the computer prints out the complete return-on-investment study, showing for each year:

a.   Sales forecast.
b.   Annual sales increase.
c.   Current-investment increases or decreases.
d.   Fixed-investment increases or decreases.

e. Annual depreciation.
f. Net investment increases or decreases.
g. Annual after-tax profits or savings.
h. Annual after-tax expenses.
i. Annual net profit.
j. Annual net cash flow.
k. Annual discounted cash flow.
l. Annual return on investment (annual net profit divided by cumulate net investment).

The print-out also contains the residual value and the average discounted cash flow return on investment for the project.

One of the major benefits the company has realized by letting the computer do the calculations has not been the direct labor savings but the freedom it now has in looking at each investment in various parameters—playing "what if" games with the input data. The firm now looks at such things as, what if:

a. the initial investment is $X more than originally estimated?
b. sales follow a different pattern than projected?
c. profits are different than projected?

In this it can look at each investment in terms of:

a. the most likely view.
b. the most pessimistic view.
c. the most optimistic view.

By doing this, the management is better able to see the alternatives available, but they must make the final decision.

A large natural gas transmission company has simulated a long-range financial planning model for the firm. This financial model is a series of computer programs which provide the financial results of a long-range forecast of operations. Given beginning balances, estimates of revenues and expenses, and forecasts of anticipated capital expenditures, the system will perform all accounting and financial computations by year. Principal calculations made by the system are book and tax depreciation, book and tax depletion, income taxes, financing requirements, net income, and cash balances. The projected results are reported in financial statements which may be generated for periods up to 99 years. (See References 1, 3, 5, 6, 7, 8, 11.)

The Weyerhaeuser Company of Tacoma, Washington, one of the largest paper-making companies, has been an aggressive advocate of the use of the computer to facilitate the finding of optimal solutions to the decision-making problems of all levels of management. The company has been actively involved in endeavoring to accomplish this objective since 1962. Ten years later they came to the following conclusions:

> From the very beginning we were all aware of the need to have our line management involved in and committed to the use of these tools. We still feel that this is an area in which we must continue to work. Two of the principal ways we have sought to achieve this involvement are:
>
> 1. By firmly establishing that the business manager is the planner and that the planning staff supports him in his role.
> 2. By giving the business manager the responsibility to justify and to assure the effective implementation of computer systems. Similarly, he is responsible for the effective use of support staff for planning, control, and systems development.

BUSINESS PLANNING FOR SUPPORT FUNCTIONS

We have achieved a certain degree of maturity in planning our material flows and investments in plants and equipment. We are now learning to plan for professional support functions and their relationship to the ongoing businesses. This is particularly necessary for research, development and engineering, and business systems. The principle is that our plans for these functions must be related to our business plans in order to be effective.

TOUGH JUSTIFICATION OF EXISTING AND NEW SYSTEMS

In the early days we took a somewhat paternalistic view of systems and operations research projects because we wanted our management to gain a familiarity with these tools. We now feel that the continued existence of existing systems and the acquisition of new systems must face a tough justifications test just like any other investment. For existing systems we have asked our business management to look at what can be dropped to make room for new development. In the recent economic squeeze we tightened up on existing systems and on new development rather than simply freezing development. We think this type of orientation will continue.

PIONEERING IS A TRICKY BUSINESS

For projects in systems as well as research, development, and engineering, we are looking explicitly at whether or not we want to be a pioneer, a fast second, or a follower. We have learned that being a pioneer has a number of unexpected pitfalls that make it a risky proposition and generally requires much management attention. The principle we are following is to make very visible which strategy we are pursuing, what the potential benefits are, and what the risks are.

COORDINATION OF INFORMATION PROVIDING FUNCTIONS

The planning, control, and systems staffs in each of our businesses have been put under one organization tent. We felt that as these functions matured in their support of the businesses, there were increasing overlaps in the problems they were attacking. We feel that bringing them together as relatively mature functions will enhance each of their roles and will provide an organizational incentive for developing more compatible and useful information for management.

FUTURE

Some of the areas that we need to work on in the future are:

1. We need a vehicle that allows us to get at management information needs rather than individual manager's wants. We have spent a lot of time customizing complete systems to a particular manager's style and have found ourselves without a useful system when he moved on.

2. We feel we need some sort of framework for relating the key decisions and leverage points in our business to how we define organizational responsibilities and provide for information and analysis needs. We do not have the answers, but we have tried looking at parts of this question and found it difficult. For example, I tried to reorganize the fiber group using an identification of key decisions made in each of the businesses as a starting point for defining organizational responsibilities. It helped but it was certainly not a clean process. Perhaps we expect too much, but we will keep trying.

3. There is a considerable amount of external data about the economy, markets, and competition that we must relate to our business planning. We have not yet learned to really take advantage of this information.

4. Because we are in processing businesses, we are making good use of computers for process control. We expect that to continue and to see data from the process control applications more tied in with our management information systems.

5. We are now seeing a movement of people with management science and systems professional backgrounds into planning and into our line operations. These moves have been fairly successful and have allowed us to make effective use of the tools of these professionals. We would expect this movement of people to continue.

6. The question that really puts us to the test is: How much of a particular support function like computer systems can we afford as a company? In other words, how can top management evaluate the effective return on its investment in these areas?

We know that magic is not going to solve all our problems in these areas. It is going to take tough-minded management in the areas of planning, management science, and computer systems to get effective results for our business. We expect to get these results and to have them contribute handsomely to the growth of the Weyerhaeuser Company.[7]

This is typical of the type of hard-minded thinking that the managements of some of the companies which have been most favorably disposed toward the use of computers in the planning function have been doing, however.

Case Illustration A at the end of this chapter is an example of a very large computer installation, but even it is not necessarily used for forward planning purposes.

HOW TO OPERATE A COMPUTER INSTALLATION PROFITABLY

Importance of Cost Control

Many business computer systems have been installed in the past 10 or 12 years with little consideration being given to the fact as to whether their cost could be justified. Some systems were installed because they felt that it was the "thing to do." Other firms quickly found an initial need, which was quickly taken care of, but nothing more was done. Times were prosperous, and the computer budget was not a large part of the total company budget. As a result, no one paid too much attention to what the computer system was costing. Also, in many cases, the computers had not captured the interest of top and line management because most looked upon the computer as a technical tool.

With these factors at work, it was not difficult to see, when the economic recession began in 1969, that computer departments became a primary target for cost cutbacks. Normal criteria for judging cost effectiveness had not been applied, in many instances, to what computer departments were spending their time doing. As a result, the functions and activities of these departments came under close scrutiny from all sides. Out of all of this has emerged, however, a management methodology which makes the costs of this activity more controllable. The key to much of this is through the careful planning, development, and implementation of new EDP systems.

---

[7] M. D. Robison, "Weyerhaeuser Approach to MIS," (Unpublished speech to Pulp & Paper Group), pp. 73–74.

Planning Makes Cost Control Possible in EDP Systems Development

The key to the success of computer cost control is tied into obtaining the interest and complete cooperation of all management personnel. If they don't evidence interest and concern in the use of the computer, it won't take the other personnel long to find this out. As a result the system will not be nearly so effective as it otherwise could be. This is true because it is characteristic of human beings to resist change. Rank and file employees are expected to put the system into effect. If those in authority are not enthusiastic and interested in the proposed changes, the average employee finds little reason to become concerned personally; especially if the change involves his or her work.

Two authors, writing in the October 1971 issue of the *Financial Executive* concerning the ability of top management to cope with EDP project management put it this way: "Work is divided into three phases: planning, development, and implementation. Within this framework, specific activities are established, and reviews by management are scheduled at key points within this activity structure. Under this approach, systems development projects become both standardized and consistent."[8]

Within the planning phase of project management the first step is for top management to determine in what areas computer proposals are likely to be useful. This means analyzing the strategic objectives of the business. Risk analysis and production scheduling are typical areas where computer applications might be profitably utilized.

Once the objectives have been set, it is important for top management to have standards which proposed projects must meet before they are embarked upon. An anticipated rate of return on the .money to be expended could be one such standard. Payback period would be another.

As soon as the "go-ahead" has been given to a project, periodic reviews of progress should be made, so that each stage of the development of the system can be studied and ratified before the next phase takes place. In this way, top management has more complete involvement in what is being done at all times, and is in a position, where necessary, to curtail or modify the development of the system in the light of the then current economic picture by choosing between short-term and long-term payoffs.

Using such a project structure approach, the benefits to be achieved

[8] Donald R. Wood and Arnold E. Ditri, "Managing EDP Costs," *Financial Executive,* October 1971, p. 73.

from the system are assigned to the user departments, which are the only groups in a position to realize them. However, if this is the case, the user departments should also be involved in the setting of standards for judging performance. If they know and understand these standards, the greater the possibility that they will be met, and that the computer system will be profitable.

One Approach to Solving the Problem. As the complexity of the EDP environment has increased and the seemingly never ending additions and changes in systems, equipment, and software continues, there is tremendous pressure on management to plan and evaluate computer systems. One attempt to provide greater control has been in the development of a series of computer programs for simulating proposed and existing computer operations. This set of programs known as SCERT (Systems and Computer Evaluation Techniques) serves as a working tool which permits users to compare actual and predicted results and to even evaluate combinations of hardware and software to handle anticipated future workloads.

SCERT has five functional phases, which are employed for each EDP system hardware/software/combination that is simulated.

1. First SCERT builds a model of the specific EDP system and workload, basing it on a description of this system written in a systems-oriented definition language (that is, sort, merge, update, validate, table look up, and so forth). The system description is documented on special input forms, and also includes such pertinent environmental considerations as size of staff and their years of experience and salary levels, and the equipment on which their experience was acquired. From this information, SCERT generates a mathematical model of the EDP system and workload.

2. Then, separately, SCERT models any hardware and software configuration to be evaluated. In its constantly updated hardware and software factor library, SCERT maintains full performance files on every major computer and piece of peripheral gear on the market. The factor library contains over 2.5 million elements of information.

3. SCERT then merges the workload model and the hardware/software model in presimulation—a linear representation of what happens in the performance of each task requested of the functioning system.

4. Full simulation then takes place. Here the multiprocessing, multiprogramming, time-sharing, and real-time characteristics of the total system are also taken into account. In this phase, the entire system functions as it would in actual working environment with all the hardware and software in place and debugged.

5. The last phase of SCERT produces output management reports, giving detailed cost/performance data on the overall system and on every individual facet of it. The reports identify inadequacies and bottle-necks, thus guiding the user to change any element of his system and/or environment definition, and resimulate with SCERT, until an optimal system is found and confirmed.

Essentially, SCERT may be used in three major areas: hardware/software selection, systems design, and management planning.[9]

Cost Control within Existing Systems

Improved Scheduling of Work. There are two problems which may exist in improving the scheduling of work to be performed by the system. (1) A problem may exist in scheduling the flow of work through the people who must take the initial data and transform it into machine-processable form. (2) All of the computer equipment on hand may not be utilized as fully as it could be, due to the fact that its use had been poorly scheduled, or due to the fact that the configuration of the equipment is inadequate.

Looking at the first problem, it may be found that the overall efficiency of the keypunch operators is poor or that their cost is excessive One of the big eight public accounting firms has observed among some of its clients that between 20 to 30 percent of the keypunching costs may be saved by increasing the productivity of the keypunch operators. For example, (1) This may be done by setting standards of productivity for the operators. Or, (2) not requiring operators to verify 100 percent of all data entries because much of this can be done by computer editing. (3) The keypunch operator should not be forced to search for out of sequence data. The data should be prepared in proper sequence in the first place. (4) Many of the manufacturers of keyboard-to-tape and keyboard-to-disk-to-tape equipment are claiming that from 10 to 50 percent of data entry costs can be saved by using their type of data entry equipment.

Once the data reaches the machines' room, the problem may not yet be over. It is often found that machine operators have to search for job elements or documents when the work is scheduled to begin. Or, they may have an excessive amount of clerical work to do before they can begin a scheduled run. These occurrences can also cause costly delays.

When considering the second problem, that of central processing

[9] "How SCERT Works," *Coopers and Lybrand Newsletter,* April 1970, p. 15.

and peripheral device utilization, one national public accounting firm found that a careful analysis of equipment usage records could produce considerable cost saving. A typical example was as follows: "A warehousing organization installed a disk storage computer system with terminals attached for writing orders and billing. Because of the need to prepare orders at any time, the computer was reserved for this purpose only; other usage during the day was minimal. Analysis showed that the order writing and billing application, with some modifications, could be performed by paper-tape reading and punching devices with printing and calculating capability. Since this application had been the primary justification for the computer, management found that it could accomplish the same results at 20 percent of the present cost, using the alternate equipment."[10]

Another suggestion was that a periodic report should be made which accounted for the total hours of operation of each major device in the computing department showing productive as well as nonproductive time. An analysis of this report could show that a firm had not optimized its equipment configuration as well as it should or that data had not been processed in the time that had been forecast.

One possibility for improving the equipment configuration might be to attempt to smooth the work load, possibly by downgrading the response times furnished to some users.

If the data processing work had not been accomplished in the forecast time, an explanation should be obtained as to why it had not been accomplished, and steps should be taken to see that this did not happen again for the same reason.

Use of One Supplier for EDP Forms.   The money that is spent on forms by a typical EDP user is considerable. One suggestion which has been made to cut down on this sizable expenditure of money is to have bids solicited for an annual supply of forms as soon as the detailed specifications of the forms have been determined. The suppliers of these forms will generally give a discount when they are purchased on a volume basis.

Forms Salesmen Often Have Innovative Ideas.   Consult with them when determining the specifications for new forms. It is likely that they can make some cost-saving suggestions.

Use of Independent Suppliers for Peripheral Devices.   A number of new companies have been formed in recent years to manufacture and sell various types of peripheral devices which are interchangable

---

[10] "Techniques for Reducing EDP Operating Costs," *Coopers and Lybrand Newsletter,* January 1971, p. 11.

with similar equipment of major computer manufacturers. In some instances, the monthly rental on such equipment is less than if the equipment has been obtained from the computer manufacturer. In addition, this equipment may also provide improved performance due to its greater accuracy and reliability. (See References 2, 4, 9, 10.)

Bill Every Department for Data Processing Services. In companies which have large data processing organizations, it is often the practice for the data processing department to bill the user departments for services rendered. If each user department has to budget for data processing expense and justify it to their own management, they will probably think through their proposals much more carefully.

Build Flexibility into Present Programs. This may well make current programs less efficient, but it will enable them to be modified in the future as the needs increase at much less cost than trying to modify a program with little or no flexibility.

When information is processed manually, all kinds of exceptions and errors are processed and corrected unconsciously by the person doing the work. The payroll clerk will unconsciously detect the time card which claims 160 hours for one week, and correct it accordingly. No computer program is capable of handling this problem unless the problem has been anticipated in advance. Since all exceptions or problems cannot be anticipated in advance, it is for this reason that the plea is made for the writing of programs in flexible style.

Improve Quality of Programs Used in System. This argument could be made as directly in opposition to the point made above. The more efficient the programming language, library routines, utility programs, application programs, the greater the productivity which can be obtained from the existing hardware.

Improve Operator Training. Equipment capacity cannot be defined in a vacuum. Capacity is the result of the interaction of all aspects of the system. To increase capacity, for example, the quality of the operators may be improved through training so that they can take better advantage of the system.

CASE ILLUSTRATION A[11]

Fifteen to twenty billion dollars a week of interbank transfers are now being handled by a computerized communications network, CHIPS.

---

[11] "Major New York Banks Now Have Automated Transfer of Funds," *Management Adviser*, March–April 1971, p. 10.

Nine New York City banks are using CHIPS (Clearing House Interbank Payments System). The system is responsible for 3,000 separate transactions a day on behalf of foreign banks with a total of more than 4,000 accounts. According to John F. Lee, executive vice president of the New York Clearing House Association (NYCHA), CHIPS represents the first true employment of electronic money within the commercial banking system.

CHIPS has eliminated more than 15,000 checks each week that were necessary for interbank payments. The messengers who moved these checks along the streets of the financial district are also no longer needed.

The banks participating in CHIPS are The Bank of New York, The Chase Manhattan Bank (N.A.), First National City Bank, Chemical Bank, Morgan Guaranty Trust Company of New York, Manufacturers Hanover Trust Company, Irving Trust Company, Bankers Trust Company, and Marine Midland Bank–New York.

Each participating bank has two leased telephone lines connecting the terminal computers, 42 Burroughs TC 500s in the nine banks, to the central computer, a Burroughs B3500 installed in the Clearing House building. Each bank also has an additional dial line to be used in case the leased lines should be unavailable.

How It Works

The Clearing House central computer stores and forwards interbank payment messages as they are approved for release during the day by sending banks. The central computer at the end of the day correlates all the transactions, nets out the debits and credits, and prints detailed reports showing which banks owe money to other banks and which banks have money due them. The next business day a copy of summary information is delivered to the New York Federal Reserve Bank, where adjustments on the appropriate books of account are made.

"While we are dispensing with official checks, we are not dispensing with commercial payment instruments. Hard copy records created at both sending and receiving terminals, in conjunction with end-of-day computer reports, can be used to prove the accuracy of electronic transmission," NYCHA Vice President Lee said.

Lee looks forward to larger networks for payment exchanges and interconnected networks covering large geographic areas. "This will have to evolve, however, as costs, capacity, and needs are evaluated. The point is that we have developed the system, and we have the computer equipment and programs available to make expansion, in terms of single or multiple systems, entirely feasible," he said.

Another computerized service being offered bankers is for the management of collateral loans. Called Margin Monitor, it is offered on an on-line or off-line basis by the Bank Computer Network Corporation (BankCom), Chicago.

Margin Monitor provides description, daily pricing, and detailed analysis of a bank's security and chattel collateral for loans outstanding. For banks with lower loan value, mailed reports are substituted for direct computer connection.

BankCom assures that bank file integrity is maintained in the Margin Monitor system. A three-level security code system is used, and while low-level personnel can enter information, they cannot retrieve it.

Margin Monitor daily updates prices and dividends for 8,000 securities. BankCom claims that even the off-line version provides management with more timely and detailed collateral situation reports than are available by traditional in-house manual methods.

CASE ILLUSTRATION B

How Financial Planning and Control Are Facilitated by a Computer Corporate Model in a Meat Freezing Works

Many thousands of sheep, lambs, hogs, and cattle are slaughtered and frozen for export by the meat freezing companies of New Zealand every year. The problem of planning for this accurately is of great financial importance to these companies because neither the number of animals to be slaughtered nor the revenue to be derived from the sale of the meat can be readily determined in advance.

The Freezing Works slaughter and freeze sheep and cattle for farmers on two different bases: (1) the animals are bought outright from the farmer by the Freezing Works with all of the proceeds from the slaughtering operation belonging to the Freezing Works, and (2) the Freezing Works will slaughter cattle for a farmer with the farmer retaining title to the meat, which will be turned over to him as soon as it is ready. In order for the latter to be accomplished a standard costing system is used as a basis for charging the farmer to whom the meat belongs, for the cost of slaughtering it. By far the greatest amount of the work performed by the Freezing Works, however, falls under the first category.

The planning process begins each year when the corporate officer in charge of livestock purchasing is asked to prepare a budget one year in advance predicting the flow of animals through the Freezing Works. He will base his estimate on his intimate knowledge of the animals which are being raised in his buying area. The estimate must include not only total numbers of each type of animal for the year, but also the rate of their flow into the Freezing Works. It is necessary to have an even rate of flow of animals to keep a trained staff busy. Based on this estimate an annual budget broken into weeks is prepared utilizing a standard costing system.

When the Freezing Works buy the animals from the farmer, the animals are paid for on a "per animal" basis. In other words, each animal is graded and paid for based upon what the Freezing Works estimate that animal will produce in saleable meat and by-products.

When the Freezing Works has prepared its estimate of the weekly through-put of animals to be slaughtered, and has an up-to-date standard cost accounting system, it is then in a position to utilize a packaged simulation program which is available from the ICL Corporation. This program is designed so that the user may manipulate a large number of variables by altering various inputs into the program. It is well suited to this application since the physical characteristics of the animals may change from week to week as well as the type of animal to be slaughtered.

For example, to illustrate the changing of the variable data, on a given week the anticipated number and type of sheep and lambs to be slaughtered are entered into the "program model" as well as the estimated weight of these animals. When these two factors are known, the program is able to cause the computer to determine, on average, the weight of the meat that will be produced by these animals. Also, related to the weight of the carcass will be the weight of the recovery of offals, fat, bonemeal, dried blood, wool, and the type of skins suitable for export. As another product of this operation, the "program model" will calculate the direct cost of making the kill of a particular week, the transfer prices which will be charged for the kill as it is transferred from the killing area to the freezing area and it will also make allowances for including costs of any other direct expenses that may be incurred.

Figure 16–1 is an illustration of one of the outputs of this corporate modeling program. It illustrates the value of the various grades of animal as determined, the amounts allowed for the animals which were

FIGURE 16–1.

THE CANTERBURY FROZEN MEAT CO. LTD.

PARTICULARS OF STOCK RECEIVED AT
FAIRFIELD
(PHONE ASHBURTON 5018)

REFERENCE		
DATE	CLIENT No.	MOB No.
3 MAY 73	45659	9962

OFFICE COPY   W.R. BROWN,
3 R.D.,
CROMWELL.

L1

ACCOUNT: C.F.M.   DRAFTER: MR P.C. CLARKSON
TRANSPORT: UPPER CLUTHA TSPT   TYPE: WOOLLY LAMBS

DESCRIPTION	CARCASES	LBS	AVERAGE WEIGHT	PRICE	VALUE
FAQ-YL	70	1565	22.4	22.30	369.00
FAQ-YM	1	29	29.0	22.30	6.47
ALPHA	34	596	17.5	20.20	120.39
C.OVIS 10 HEAD					
TOTAL EXPORT	105	2190	20.9	21.73	475.86
REJECT REJ-2ND	2	45	22.5	8.80	3.96
REJ-3RD	3	54	18.0	2.00	1.08
CONDEMN	5	108	21.6		
TOTAL RECEIVED	115				480.90
SKINS	115	WOOL	1.65	3.70	625.50

REJECT DETAILS			
Lympho		Arth.	5
Bruise	7	Pleurisy	4
Spare		Overfat	
Serko.		Abscess	2
Periton.		Yellow	
Coarse		Callous	
Seedy		Emac.	
Mela.		Fever	
C. Ovis		Other C.	4

GROSS PROCEEDS

115	C/S	7.88	906.40

LESS
TRANSPORT   ROAD 50.0   57.50-
RAIL

PER HEAD $3.50
GAIN AGAINST SCHEDULE

NETT PROCEEDS	848.90

N.B. ALL STOCK AND PRODUCTS HANDLED SUBJECT TO THE COMPANY'S PUBLISHED CONDITIONS rejected primarily for health reasons, the health reasons, as well as the net proceeds due the farmer for his shipment.

REFERENCES

1. ADAMS, WAYNE. "New Role for Top Management in Computer Applications." *Financial Executive,* April 1972, p. 54.

2. BATTAGLIA, VINCENT J. "Cutting Computer Costs." *Financial Executive,* August 1972, p. 26.

3. BUCATINSKY, JULIO. "Ask Your Computer, 'What if'." *Financial Executive,* July 1973, p. 56.

4. "Get More Computer Efficiency." *EDP Analyzer* 9 (March 1971).

5. "Financial Modeling and 'What if' Budgeting." *Management Accounting,* May 1972, p. 25.

6. GUSTAFSON, GEORGE A. "Computers—Lease or Buy?" *Financial Executive,* July 1973, p. 56.

7. GORMAN, THOMAS J. "Corporate Financial Models in Planning and Control." *Price Waterhouse Review,* Summer 1970, p. 41.

8. KRUEGER, DONALD A., and KOHLMEIR, JOHN M. "Financial Modeling and 'What if' Budgeting." *Management Accounting,* May 1972, p. 25.

9. RAU, PAUL. "Evaluating the EDP Function." *Datamation* 18 (September 1972) p. 72.

10. SMITH, LEIGHTON F. *An Executive Briefing on the Control of Computers,* Data Processing Management Association, 1971.

11. WHISLER, THOMAS L. *Impact of Computers on Organizations.* New York: Praeger Publishers, 1969.

QUESTIONS

1. Discuss two reasons why you feel that computer installations as a whole have not accomplished more in the field of integrated data processing than they have on an average to date.

2. Why does it seem to be so difficult for a firm with a computer to expand and integrate its computing operations as time elapses?

3. Why does it seem to be especially difficult for more firms to have computer applications in the planning area?

4. Why is it easier for some industries to be able to use the abilities of the computer to facilitate their planning activity more readily than others?

5. Give three examples of how you feel that Operations Research techniques could be of the greatest assistance to top management in their discharge of the planning activity?

6. Why have so many computer users raised the question of the cost of computer usage in recent years?

7. How can computer users hope to obtain the greatest value in return for their investment? Discuss.

8. Discuss two methods of cost control in the computer facility which you feel could be most readily implemented. Explain why you feel as you do.

IV
Implementation of Information Systems

17

Justifying the Use of
Computerized Equipment

IN THE LAST DECADE the economic scene over the world has experienced more change than in all prior years combined. Economists, sociologists, and business leaders predict that there will be a continuation of this change at an accelerated pace in the immediate years ahead. Today's managers are faced with the serious prospect of competing within this environment of accelerated economic and social change. The successful managers will be ones who are able to anticipate, plan, and cause change rather than merely attempting to react to change caused by external factors.

The widespread and in some cases commonplace use of computer technology in the processing of data has developed during this same period of time. The ways of introducing the computer into a data processing operation have taken on a variety of forms as time has passed.

1. Outright purchase of the equipment, endeavoring to design and implement over a period of time a system, as fully integrated as possible, to utilize the capabilities of the equipment.
2. The equipment can be either leased or rented to accomplish the same end.
3. The management of a company or department may decide to computerize only certain critical data processing areas. Here also, the equipment they use may be purchased, leased, or rented.
4. There are many service bureaus and time-sharing facilities available to the users in various facilities throughout the world where the

advantage of computerized data processing can be obtained without the physical problems of having to acquire and operate the equipment.

The problems associated with the processing of data through a service bureau or a time-sharing facility are different from a company or department doing it for itself, and costs can vary widely. (See previous discussion in Chapter 15).

The justification of computer equipment, at least in some phases of the activity, is not as much a question today as it was 10 to 15 years ago. At that time computer applications were being justified for a variety of reasons: (1) on the basis that "it was the thing to do;" (2) "our chief competitor has one, therefore we must have one too;" (3) to alleviate immediate bottlenecks and provide capacity for expansion to different and additional applications in the future; and (4) on the basis of a cost-saving analysis. (See Reference 6.)

It can be legitimately questioned how many of the firms which changed from manual, mechanical, and punch card installations to computerized installations during that period of time seriously considered how their existing system might have been improved so as to alleviate the problem or problems which appeared to exist before they made the change. The computer had come of age and change was in the air.

This attitude has been unfortunate for some companies because, in the economic recession of 1969–70, many companies began to question themselves as to how best to cut costs.

The data processing departments came under closer scrutiny because their costs had risen rapidly, and it was difficult to justify these increasing costs in the light of diminishing profits.

Since 1971 the emphasis placed in justification of an initial computer installation or the enlargement of an existing installation has been on a cost-justification basis. This is not to say that planning for a greater capacity to meet future demand is not being considered, but rather that the immediate cost implications are having a greater impact than they have had previously.

It is safe to say, that when profits are readily made, the average business person is much less concerned with ways of becoming more efficient and more profitable. Cost justification becomes of greater importance when the profit outlook is not as good. (See References 1, 3 and 4.)

In many companies contemplating the acquisition of a computer it is possible that the data processing procedures will have to be centralized in place of the decentralized system currently employed. Such a change may result in the complete disruption of presently established lines of communications or work patterns which may have evolved over years of operations and are now firmly established in the firm's corporate structure. On the other hand, even though there may not be a relatively complete change in operations, there will probably be many major changes required in almost any firm involved in such a systems-change decision. New managerial policies will undoubtedly have to be implemented, and different methods of providing and capturing the originating data may have to be devised. Not only will there be probable changes in the data itself which may be required for newly proposed reports and analyses, but many of the conventional reports of the past, which have become a tradition in the minds of those relying on them, may be completely eliminated.

In some instances new and unfamiliar job titles will replace the old ones which disappear. Normally, however, most of the current job classifications will remain, even though many of these will be completely changed as to the routines and procedures to be followed. This will undoubtedly bring about many changes in personnel requirements. Existing employees may have to be shifted into other positions, the duties of which are new and different, and this will probably involve the development of training programs to aid these employees in learning their new jobs. Additional personnel may be required for some of the more technical and highly skilled positions which will be developing.

The work area required in the processing of data will also probably be changed or altered in terms of the actual amount as well as type of space required.

Thus, it must be realized that any organization considering the adoption of electronic data processing (EDP) must consider a multitude of problems which will be precipitated by a change to EDP. Such a decision is of significant importance, both to present and future operations, in the development of the firm. The monetary outlays required are certainly major, but they may be relatively insignificant in relation to the effects the change to EDP may have upon the organizational structure, the physical facilities, and perhaps most important of all, the personnel of the firm. (See References 5 and 9.)

APPROACH TO THE INVESTIGATION

There are a number of situations which may be encountered.

1. The problem of justifying a computer installation for a firm which has not had one previously.

2. Utilizing an off-premises computer for some part of the data processing operation where this has not been done previously.
3. Expanding the utilization of an existing computer facility.

All of these problems are similar in some respects and quite different in others. In any of these circumstances, it is well to make a cost-benefit analysis or cost-justification study in light of the proposed system. The planning, design, and control of effective, workable systems has proven to be the key stumbling block in many cases to having a profitable and effective operation.

Whatever is being attempted, a necessity of the greatest importance is to have the full interest, cooperation, and support of top management. Whenever any proposal is made to change the way that things are going to be done, people are involved. People (employees) do not take to change readily. Unless employees can see that the proposed change is fully supported at the top management level, problems are almost certain to occur. Many examples can be cited to illustrate this point.

As a means of meeting this problem, one lending institution's top management made frequent visits explaining to the employees in various branch offices the anticipated changes in procedures which were to be made, and in addition issued a series of clever brochures to all employees explaining the reasons for computerizing the clerical operations and the advantages which would accrue to the company and the employees alike when the proposed changes were carried out. The change over from mechanical to computerized operations was accomplished smoothly and easily.

System Objectives

Whenever computers are considered for use in carrying out data processing operations, management must endeavor to think through the long-range objectives they have for such a system. The reason for this is that if the computer is utilized with the view of only alleviating an immediate problem, the likelihood of it being utilized more fully or effectively is greatly diminished. The costs of hardware as well as program maintenance are rising all the time. There must be definite objectives with long-range plans, determined in advance and backed up by a commitment to attain them.

Typical objectives that may encourage a firm to automate its office may include one or more of the following items, which are only representative of the many conceivable reasons which may be proposed by any specific firm:

1. Attempt to reduce clerical costs through a reduction in the required clerical force. (Part of the gains here may be offset by a general upgrading of the positions retained.) If there is a reduction in clerical help, some savings in the office space requirements may result.

2. Eliminate conflicting and overlapping services by combining some of the many functions and activities now performed by separate departments and branches in the preparation and processing of data and in duplication in file maintenance.

3. Improve employee relations by providing them with additional information in such reporting areas as those of payroll, pensions, taxes, insurance, and so on.

4. Increase the productivity of clerical operations through greatly improved processing techniques which are not only faster but which also become more accurate with the elimination of human intervention in the processing and preparation of reports.

5. Obtain greater operating efficiency in data processing through increased speed, improved accuracy, and decreased equipment idleness due to infrequent "downtime" and reliability of the computer system.

6. Reduce expenses through faster billing procedures. This may be realized in the reduction of interest charges on borrowed capital previously necessary because of the longer carrying time on customer accounts.

7. Provide more flexibility for the expansion of the firm's data processing capabilities as growth occurs.

8. Improve customer relations and competitive position through accuracy and timeliness in reporting, billing, and in the notification of scheduling or shipping changes or delays.

9. Permit more timely decisions by management. This is made possible through the current reports and data provided by the speed of the computer and more complete reporting in the form of information which would not have been economically feasible or available using conventional methods.

10. Gain greater control of information and a consequent strengthening of the organizational structure through improved system and accounting controls which minimize human intervention by incorporating checks and balances which are automatically performed as the data is processed.

11. Permit the use of operations research and other management science techniques which could bring such typical future benefits as the reduction of inventory investments and other working capital requirements; reductions in production costs through more efficient scheduling, parts control, and costing techniques; and reductions in selling costs through improved market and sales analyses.

As a summary, the basic objectives of any EDP study must be to enable the firm to earn a larger net profit than is possible under its present system of operation. The larger net profit must accrue through improvement in many specific areas of operation such as: savings in clerical work, improved overall clerical performance and greater operating efficiency in the processing of data, speedier collections on accounts outstanding improved customer relations and services, and better and more timely reports for use in management decisions. (See References 8, 9, 10 and 11.)

Justification Study Group

It would be well for a firm confronted by any problems similar to those just enumerated to form a study group made up of members of the staff, or the management of the firm may take its problem to its public accounting firm for its expert advice. If the organization forms its own study group, the members should be familiar with company philosophies, systems, objectives, and existing accounting systems and procedures. If the public accounting firm makes the study, it will already have much of this information in its files from its audit examinations.

Authority Delegation

The authority delegated to the group should be clearly outlined. This is necessary because not only those conducting the study but those with whom they will have contact must fully understand the powers and responsibilities which have been assigned to the group. This is particularly essential where functional procedures tend to cut across departmental lines, as departmental jealousy or fear of loss of departmental controls may lead to noncooperation or even downright hostility to any proposed change.

It is not unusual for some segment of top management, as well as many of those in the various levels of middle management, to be outright dubious about the necessity of even considering an electronic computer. The assignment of authority from top management may have to be used at times to override, to hopefully overcome any resentment to the study being made or the interruption of work that will occur as the study progresses, and to lessen the general resistance that is always present in any change. Support of top management throughout the assignment is an absolute requirement for the success for any systems-change decision.

ANALYZING THE PRESENT SYSTEM

As soon as the justification study group has been organized, and the management has outlined to them the problems confronting the company, a survey of the existing system is the first task to be accomplished. The overall reason for studying the present system first is to learn what is going on as well as to ascertain whether the existing system may be at fault in some way, or whether computerizing a particular problem area or areas may be the best solution to the problem or problems.

In reviewing the present operations, care must be taken to obtain clear and concise information. The information should include the organizational structure and the chain of command within the firm. The review should spell out the procedures currently in use and indicate the function every person concerned with each given procedure performs. The existence, maintenance, and proper use of policy and procedural manuals, if any, should be documented.

Flowcharting should play an important role in the review of the organization's current operations. These flowcharts should include each department's procedures, and these should provide an overall chart which shows the main lines of movement of the data required. These charts should indicate the origination of data into the system, the files maintained, the sequence of operations, and the reports produced.

At this point, it might be a good idea for the committee or consultants to meet as a group to challenge the existing operations. Questions should be asked in respect to the purpose and results of each of the procedural operations. Some examples of typical questions include the following: Have conditions changed since the operation was established? Is the operation a result of habit? Is the operation created by an incomplete previous or subsequent operation? How necessary is the result obtained in each operation? Is there any possibility the end result could be changed and the procedure eliminated? Can the needed results be secured as a by-product of another operation or in some other manner?

Other information which may be required in such a review concerns equipment and office layout. Detailed diagrams could be made, disclosing the floor plan in relation to the flow of work. The present office layout should be challenged as to whether it serves a functional purpose in aiding the flow of work.

Existing equipment used in the current operations should receive much attention. Consideration should be given to its operating condition as well as to the possibility of its obsolescence in a systems change. The use of the equipment should also be investigated. Just how much is the equipment used? Are existing machines operating close to capacity? Is proper control exercised over equipment to prevent unauthorized functions from being performed?

Though personnel is discussed in more detail later, part of the review should include a listing of job classifications and the number of employees. Notes should be made on employee turnover, morale, training, supervision, and how each would be affected by a change to an EDP system.

In summary, the survey of existing procedures and operations should reveal relationships of personnel, equipment, documents, processing procedures, resulting records, and final reports.

Analysis of Forms and Reports

The forms and reports used in the current operations will be noted on the flowcharts previously prepared in the review of present operations. Detailed analysis of these should be made questioning each item as follows:

.01 Is the form being made out in proper place and by the proper person?

.02 Is all the information really needed? Is all the necessary information included?

.03 Do we get the correct number of copies? Are the proper persons receiving them? Is the line of transportation the best?

.04 Is the form designed for the best use, for both maker and reader?

.05 Could the form be eliminated through substitution as a by-product of another form?[1]

---

[1] U.S. Treasury Department, Internal Revenue Service, Data Processing Division, Systems and Procedures, *A Notebook for the Systems Man* (Washington, D.C.: U.S. Government Printing Office, February 1963), p. 13.

Additional questions should be those concerning the descriptive headings used, the sequence of the data, the reason for this sequence, how often the form is referred to in its normal usage, and what are its file retention requirements.

As the data on each of the different forms are assembled, the committee or consultant will have to study each form in its relation to the present system. The use of each of the present forms in both the current and the proposed EDP system should be questioned. The firm should not accept the data collected or the reporting forms used in their present operations as either ideal or even usable for the new system to be developed. Every effort should be expended at this stage in the study to provide more efficient forms for use in future operations—regardless of the equipment system to be implemented.

In addition to the attempt to develop more efficient forms, special attention should also be given to the possibility of a standardization of forms. This requires that care be taken to avoid duplication of data so that information provided on one form is not also being provided on other forms.

Forms which are improperly designed will lead to unnecessary and even duplicated effort. This will quickly be reflected in a loss of efficiency in their use.

The same review procedures should be applied to report forms which are prepared for management. It is important to remember, at this point, that the data included on the present reports—as well as the reports themselves—may have little relevance to the information management actually needs.

The information determined necessary should be presented in a format that is understandable and convenient to use and that requires very little effort in its interpretation. Timing is a very important consideration, which should not be overlooked when evaluating reports for management. Each report should be available by the time it is needed and when it will serve management best.

From the analysis of existing forms and reports, the committee should know the wants and needs of management. It should have, in part, revealed whether or not the currently used forms and reports are all necessary; it should have uncovered the possibility that additional reports or data forms might be necessary to facilitate managerial decisions.

The various input and output devices used by EDP systems, as well as the types of forms which various systems are able to utilize in the production of reports, should be carefully analyzed before considering new forms and reports. Different types of forms and reports recommended by equipment manufacturers should be carefully considered and studied to determine which will best provide for the requirements of the firm.

When the committee has completed the analysis of existing and possible new forms and reports, it should then reach a decision regarding the reports to be recommended to be produced, the data to be included, the format in which these data are to be presented, the number of copies required, and when the reports are to be produced. This information is vital in the design of any system. The volume of data to be presented and the pattern of the format to be used can not only have considerable effect on the output equipment requirements but also on the acceptability of the document produced by those who will be using it in their daily routine.

It must be constantly kept in mind that one of the major considerations in changing to an EDP system is that of improving the quality, quantity, and timing of needed reports. In some cases, reports of given types, particularly those involving extensive mathematical computation, cannot be produced manually due to the excessive costs involved and time required for their production. These may, however, be made available through a modern computer system at a cost which can be justified, and the reports can still be timely enough to aid management in its decision-making processes.

Work Volume Determination

A careful analysis should be made regarding the work volumes required in each individual department of the firm relative to every clerical procedure with which it is concerned. This information will be required in determining present cost of operations as well as in estimating costs of proposed systems to be considered.

Some of the procedures to be followed in determining departmental work volumes are:

1. Check the procedural flowcharts previously prepared for the work to be performed in each individual department.
2. Determine the data required by every function performed by the department in each procedure which flows through this area. This not only includes the data originating in the department, but the data, probably already in some type of report form, required from others.

3. Analyze the reports prepared by each department's personnel as to what data are included, for whom the report is prepared, the number of copies required, and the use to which the data will be put.
4. Build a file of each procedural flow and attach a copy of each related report prepared by the various departments.

After this information has been recorded for each individual department, it can be combined to determine the work volume of the entire company.

This work volume data should then be analyzed, both as a whole and by the individual department, to determine if the work volume findings will be adaptable to an EDP system. Where the work volume is small and the procedures required are varied, it is quite probable that EDP would neither be practical nor economical. However, when it is found there is a large amount of work involving duties of a similar nature in several areas, an EDP system should probably be considered.

Work volumes may also be used to determine procedural areas which may be consolidated or otherwise simplified to either improve the system in general or to cut the costs involved, or both.

Work simplification and standardization should be given special consideration. This may involve only the procedural aspect or it may also include form design or redesign. A typical procedural improvement might be in the preparation of a machine-processable document at the time of the recording of the original transaction. A form improvement might be to include additional data on a standard report preparation which would serve the needs now filled by two or more reports. This might be accomplished by using partial carbons for some copies of the report, which would omit some of the data included on other copies but not needed or desired by some users of the report. This might involve cost or profit data which some users should not have access to.

Depending on the depth of the completed work volume study, the findings in procedural areas which appear to be subject to systems improvement may have to be supplemented by additional depth of detail regarding the procedural flow of the data.

The quantitative data gathered on the number of various transactions which occur throughout the firm's operation should be analyzed in terms of the work loads which may result. If the daily level of these transactions is fairly constant, then summarization of the data will be relatively simple for determining work loads for the day, week, month, or year. However, when there are definite cyclical effects present in the business cycle of the firm, additional consideration will be required to prevent "bottlenecks" developing in the system in these periods of exceptional activity. This information is necessary in the determination of the operational time required in the schedules to be developed for processing the various procedures involved.

Other quantitative data to be gathered in work volume determination is that which concerns the files required for both the originating and reporting data. Here, not only the number and types of files and records required are important but also the information concerning what data are stored in these files and records and how the data are to be utilized. This knowledge is vital in determining the size and type of electronic memory storage required of an EDP system.

Cost of Present Operations

At first, many of the applicable costs related to as broad an area as the clerical systems and procedures of a given firm may appear to be rather nebulous and hard to determine. However, such an analysis is a vital and necessary requirement in a justification study, as it is impossible to ascertain if a change may be feasible until the present cost of these operations is known and is compared with the estimated costs of the new system.

Some of the major areas of costs to be considered include those of personnel, forms and supplies, equipment, and the physical space required to house the staff, files, and equipment. These costs may be determined, for some time period which allows a comparison of present and future costs, either by departmental or by functional analyses, whichever method is easier in the particular firm under consideration. How this is done may, in part, be set by the manner in which the system study is performed. If the entire system is to be replaced or revised, as it would be in a completely integrated system, then costs may be "lumped" together to a much greater extent than is possible in partial automation. In such a major revision, costs of individual procedures would no longer have the comparability possible where only selected procedures are to be automated and present procedural costs can be directly weighed against the new.

Personnel. Personnel costs, at first glance, may not appear to be too difficult to determine, as clerical personnel are usually separated both physically and functionally from production personnel. Where this is the case, these costs can be fairly easily determined unless the systems analysis was made by function. In this case, personnel costs would have to be allocated, on some predetermined basis, to each function performed by each individual. However, it will normally have been discovered in the systems study that, particularly in the origination of data, this clear-cut demarcation is not always present.

To mention an example of job classifications in which clerical functions may be present, in addition to the primary function, foremen may be used to prepare a roster of production workers present (or absent)—though in a firm of any size this will probably be part of the duties of timekeeping, which is a clerical function. The foremen, however, will probably either oversee or perform the duty of recording the time spent by each worker (and maybe each machine) on each job or contract—unless a data collection system is in use, and this probably would not be the case if office automation is not already a de facto condition.

Other mixed functions to be found in the plant, among many, would be:

1. In receiving and shipping, where records may be kept on incoming and outgoing items, on the related freight charges on these goods, and on the physical condition of the merchandise received.

2. In materials inventory control and maintenance where records may be kept of such things as goods on hand, the minimum and maximum stock levels of each item recommended, order quantities and normal suppliers of each type of good, and to whom and for what purpose items are to be released into the production stream.

3. In tool and miscellaneous supply storage, where the records needed would be somewhat similar to those above in material inventories, along with data on frequency of use and stock item condition in the case of such items as tools which are checked out, used, and returned.

4. In equipment maintenance shops where detailed records will be kept on downtime and on the labor supplies, and parts used in maintaining each piece of equipment. Many of these records, and their associated duties, may be replaced either totally or in part in the systems change, depending on the extent of the automation deemed feasible.

Forms and Supplies. The current cost of forms and supplies used in the present system is largely a matter of record. However, if it is anticipated that only part of the procedures are to be automated, the affected forms and supplies for these procedures will have to be separated costwise from those which will continue to be used.

When new forms are to be designed, there will be initial setup costs for their reproduction as well as the costs involved in the time spent on the actual design of these forms. This last cost may be more than anticipated, as form design is exacting work and requires consideration of all the related procedures and documents as well as the technical requirements of any new equipment under consideration.

Equipment. The cost of the equipment presently in use should also be easily determined by consulting the accounting records. Here, however, the net or book value of these items may have little relationship to either actual market value or their value in terms of the ability of the equipment to serve the firm over an extended time in the future. Depreciation previously recorded on this equipment may not have been properly determined in the first place, such as where an error was made in estimating the life of the equipment or where one of the accelerated methods of depreciation may have been utilized for tax purposes.

A new life estimate may have to be made if the equipment is to be considered for use in the future, or a salvage or disposal value may have to be determined if it will be replaced by other equipment in the newly proposed system.

Equipment costs to be considered are those on all the items of equipment used in the clerical operation. This will not only include the bookkeeping equipment itself, but the files, desks, chairs, cabinets, typewriters, calculators, and any other related equipment. Many of these items may not be required in the new system if there is a reduction in clerical personnel.

Physical Space. If a detailed cost system is in use, the cost of the physical space required in clerical procedures may already be allocated to the record-keeping function. If not, some method of allocating these costs should be determined, as some of these costs may be transferred to other functions if a new electronic computer is installed.

Operational Expenses. Operational and the many types of expense, such as light, heat, air conditioning, and personnel related costs, such as life insurance, hospitalization, and pensions, should all be determined and detailed, in as much depth as feasible, as many of these costs will be severely altered if the system is automated.

PERSONNEL REQUIREMENTS AND CONSIDERATIONS

It is important that the employees be advised as early as convenient in the planning stage of the fact that a possible systems change is under consideration. Experience has demonstrated, in studies made of the impact of automation on office personnel, that if management will impress upon the employees the need for a systems change and then keep them informed of progress as it is made, employee problems will normally be minimized. These studies also indicated that in instances where management deliberately avoided discussing the systems change with employees, knowledge of the study prevailed anyway, unfounded rumors quickly became rampant, and the feasibility study failed to proceed smoothly.

Resistance to change is inherent in most of us for the basic reason that we are sure of the familiar and fearful of what we do not understand. Fear and misunderstanding usually take over when management does not explain the benefits, in human terms, to be derived from new methods and equipment. This may result in the plans for the change being handicapped by the withholding or delay in providing needed information, and the possible results of the change may very probably become severely distorted by these efforts to resist change.

The more the employee knows about the changes to be implemented, the more he or she will become aware of the fact that business automation still requires people to get the work ready for the machines, requires people to tell the machine what to do, requires people to operate them, and also requires people to interpret the results obtained.

All workers associated in any way with clerical procedures must be made to feel that they are not on the outside, but that the success of the entire project depends on each playing some part in it. They should be encouraged to submit ideas and suggestions concerning the change-over. Careful consideration and acknowledgment should be given to any constructive ideas forthcoming.

Fear of loss of jobs and of the future are natural reactions to any mention of the word *automation.* There is plenty of justification for these fears as far as the production line, and its associated machinery, is concerned, and there is little question that these fears have received considerable publicity in connection with our continuing national unemployment problems. However, nearly every study made of business office automation, and there has been a large number of these studies, has concluded that very few personnel have been displaced as a result of it, that most of the positions affected have been upgraded, and that often after a short period of adjustment, the total staff is as large as it was before automation. *The Wall Street Journal,* in a recent report on a New York State study, again confirmed that computer-caused layoffs proved to be rare. The installation of computers at 277 firms employing 577,000 persons led to the firing of only 628 workers. Another

2,164 whose jobs were eliminated quit or retired. About 6,593 were retrained for new positions.[2]

The clerical positions which are normally affected by office automation are those which involve repetitious and routine procedures. There is generally a large turnover of the employees holding these positions because of the dullness and drudgery associated with these positions. Many of these people have relatively little training for more advanced work, and there is a tendency for them to shift positions relatively often in hopes of finding "greener pastures" and more challenging positions. Others who have training or special abilities tend to advance from these routine jobs as new positions present themselves. This turnover rate is the answer to the low displacement record in office automation. It is not unusual for the systems-change decision along with the period of preparing and waiting for the equipment to be delivered after the order is placed (usually 12 to 18 months) and the actual conversion to computer processing to require a time period of not less than one year and as long as three years for completion. This time lapse allows the firm to consolidate its work loads, hire temporary replacements where required, and use the attrition due to retirement to its advantage in the reduction of these routine-type positions.

A number of the individuals who have training or special aptitudes and abilities will be needed in the new operations. These people will have an exceptional opportunity to advance to more challenging positions in the firm. Training programs, furnished by both the firm itself and the computer manufacturer, will be available to them, and completely new vistas of job opportunity will open up for those capable and interested. These individuals will, almost without exception, be upgraded in both position and compensation.

Additional procedures involving techniques not previously available will be economically feasible with the new computer installation to guide management in the decision-making processes. These techniques may involve the addition of personnel to gather additional detailed information needed as well as technical personnel such as mathematicians, statisticians, engineers, and others.

Historically, the introduction of machines into industrial and office operations has, on the whole and in the long run, increased employment and raised the standard of living. The fact is that electronic data processing has and will replace some people, but there is little evidence to support any doubt of the increased productivity gains that will be available and the probable increase in total employment that will accrue as a result. Certainly, business office automation has resulted in a de-

---

[2] *The Wall Street Journal*, August 26, 1969.

crease in the drudgery present in the day-in—day-out functions required in work involving masses of figures and data and has freed many individuals to do analysis and more advanced work which will better serve the needs of management. It opens opportunities for more people to work at jobs involving the use of intelligence and judgment. In fact, all classes of jobs from office clerk to top-level management will be affected quantitatively and qualitatively as electronic computers are installed and properly utilized.

The fears and misconceptions the average worker has concerning electronic systems can only be overcome through education. Employees can be persuaded to accept office automation by making them feel more important as a result of using the new equipment and by encouraging them to make suggestions as to how the electronic data processing system can be adapted to the needs of the firm.

Retaining sound relationships with employees is possibly one of the hardest parts of the study, but in turn it is probably the most important aspect of all. Disorganization and dissatisfaction on the part of the employees will not only have its effect on the study itself but may be extended into continuing and long-run personnel problems.

The time spent in evaluating human relations problems, getting essential information to the employees, and keeping open channels of communication is a vital part of the program for the introduction of an electronic data processing system or any other major change in processing business information. (See References 2, 5, 7, 12 and 13.)

CONCLUSION

All of the information collected should be looked at by the committee in the light of whether or not the information needs of not only the present users but also the potential users of the system at all levels of the organization can and will be met.

The volume of information needed as well as the response time needed by the system users must be considered in the light of the projected growth of the organization as well as the light of the immediate needs of management.

The completion of the analytical process to this point will supply the study group with a thorough understanding of the present system, as well as the cost of operating it. This should serve as a basis for considering or rejecting the use of computers as a solution to the problems revealed in the present system.

Such a study could also serve as the basis for an alternative solution to the problem. Many firms have found that their chief problem was that the existing system was not working as it was originally intended, rather than that they needed to find another way of processing a particular type of data in order to achieve a desired result. Computerization is not always the best solution to an information or data processing problem. (See References 1, 10, 11 and 12.)

REFERENCES

1. ANDERS, DONALD H.   *Computers and Management.* New York: McGraw-Hill Book Co. 1970.

2. BATTAGLIA, VINCENT J.   "Cutting Computer Costs," *Financial Executive,* August 1972, p. 26.

3. BOARDMAN, LANDSDALE.   "Must We Repeat the Same Mistakes in Computer Installation?" *Financial Executive,* March 1969, pp. 61–66.

4. BRANDON, DICK H.   "Computer Acquisition Method Analysis." *Datamation,* September 1972, pp. 76–79.

5. BURNS, PATRICK D.   "Preparing for a Computer Installation." *Cost and Management,* April 1966.

6. DORN, PHILLIP H.   "So You've Got to Get a New One?" *Datamation,* September 1972, pp. 58–59.

7. GARRITY, JOHN T., and McNERNEY, JOHN P.   "EDP, How to Ride the Tiger." *Financial Executive,* September 1963, p. 19.

8. GARRITY, JOHN T.   "Management and the Computer—Who's in Charge." *Financial Executive,* June 1971, pp. 38–44.

9. *Planning for an IBM Data Processing System* F20-6088–1.   White Plains, N.Y. International Business Machines Corporation, General Information Manual, January 1961.

10. McMAINS, HARVEY J.   "Planning—The Role of Humans in Information Systems." *Data Processing Yearbook, 1965.* Edited by Edith Harwick Goodman. Detroit: American Data Processing Inc., 1964, pp. 158–68.

11. ORILIA, LAURENCE S.; STERN, NANCY; and STERN, ROBERT A.   *Business Data Processing Systems.* New York: John Wiley & Sons, 1972.

12. RAMSGARD, WILLIAM C.   "Evaluate Your Computer Installation." *Management Services,* January–February 1971, p. 37.

13. WASHINGTON, FREDERIC G.   "Should You Upgrade?" *Datamation,* September 1972, pp. 58–59.

QUESTIONS

1. How might the financial bases for justifying the acquisition of computerized data processing facilities for a governmental unit differ from those for a business enterprise? Explain.

2. Might any other bases of justification, other than financial, be different for governmental units and business enterprise? Explain.

3. Why does cost justification of computer acquisition and usage seem to be so much more significant today than it was 6 to 8 years ago?

4. Why do you suppose it might be less costly to have a centralized computer operation than it would be to have a decentralized noncomputer operation?

5. What might be the effects of such a change as mentioned in question 4 other than financial? Give thought to this in some depth.

6. Why is it imperative for any organization before installing a computer to have clearly conceived objectives in mind for the equipment to accomplish with a commitment for their accomplishment?

7. What is the first thing a justification study group should concern itself with when it is organized? What types of questions should it ask?

8. What should be the areas of concern to be studied?

9. What factors should be considered when the study group turns its attention to the cost of present operations?

10. Many firms that have grown rapidly during the last ten years are presently finding that their methods of keeping track of data have not improved and progressed at the same rate as the business growth. As a result, many of them have stated publicly that a computer appears to be the only answer to their needs. Several of these firms have come to you asking you to assist and guide them as to the path of action which they should follow. In outline form, please indicate to these firms the path of action which you would recommend that they follow.

18

Preparing for and Introducing Electronic Equipment

WITH THE COMPLETION of the justification study and its associated analysis of the business information system, a decision must be made regarding the feasibility of acquiring a new or different electronic data processing system.

If the decision is made to automate, thereby acquiring a new system, the firm must then approach the problems which will accompany such a conversion. These problems will, of course, vary to some degree with the business firm and the equipment system to be acquired. However, considerations involved in the selection of equipment, the acquisition and training of qualified personnel, the plans necessary in the conversion of present methods and procedures over to the new system, and the provision for the physical facilities needed by the computer and its associated peripheral equipment all have some common features regardless of the particular system to be installed.

SELECTING EDP EQUIPMENT

The selection of the perfect computer for a given information system is rarely, if ever, possible. If for no other reason, it may be because of rapid changes in the demands for data required in the system of any modern dynamic business firm.

There are, however, certain basic facts which must be considered in equipment selection. These include the characteristics of the computer and associated equipment; aids available through some of the computer manufacturers; and company policy, which is often expressed in terms of financial, personnel, or physical limitations.

Computer Characteristics

Only after all facets of the previously prepared systems study have been carefully examined and the needs of the new information system have been determined can a list of specifications for the equipment required be prepared. These system requirements will then have to be matched against the functions performed by the various available computer input, storage, and output devices and other special equipment such as that required in input preparation, filing, binding, mailing, and so on.

Alternative approaches to meeting the general specifications of the system must be considered, keeping in mind the importance of selecting the best equipment available—for the price. Such equipment must not only be able to do the current job but must be expansible to meet the future needs of the firm. This may not only be in terms of larger storage capacity and greater processing speed in accomplishing current requirements but may also include the computer system's incorporation into a full-fledged integrated data processing system involving communication and transmission systems and other on-line devices.

To obtain an initial idea of the types of equipment available which might perform the data processing work required, those in charge of planning the new system, along with officials of the firm, may follow several methods of procedure:

1. Invite representatives of the various computer manufacturers into the firm for initial discussions of the firm's needs.
2. Visit demonstration equipment showrooms of these manufacturers.
3. Visit computer installations of other business firms, particularly those with similar systems problems, and discuss with management how it solved these problems. Ask for advice—the people involved may have made some decisions regarding their own installation that they would not care to repeat if they were starting over again.
4. Consult trade organizations for general recommendations.
5. Attend seminars, institutes, and lectures on data processing.
6. Review the various forms of literature on the subject, such as texts and other books, trade magazines, and data processing periodicals in general.

A particularly effective method of determining equipment which may meet the specifications of a particular company is to request given computer manufacturers to submit bids or proposals on the basis of the specifications and procedural flowcharts submitted.

The list of specifications, based on the system requirements, should include, as a minimum, the following:

1. Data Origination
   a. How data originates
   b. How data is collected
2. Data Communication
   a. Data developed in the immediate system
   b. Local data transmission
   c. Distant data transmission
3. Input Data
   a. Format
   b. Coding
   c. Volume, including cyclical peaks
   d. Hourly rates of input
4. Storage Files
   a. Volume
   b. Method of maintaining and updating
   c. Code requirements
   d. Types of access (random or serial)
5. Data Handling
   a. Types of transactions
   b. Kinds of computations
   c. Types of decisions required
6. Output Reports
   a. Kind
   b. Distribution of data
   c. Volume of each type
   d. Formats
   e. Need for timeliness
7. Special Requirements
   a. Time cycle for unit processing (speed)
   b. Common-language compatibility
   c. Expansion possibilities
   d. Cost limitations
   e. Space limitation or requirements
   f. Maintenance requirements
   g. Date of delivery and installation
   h. Site preparation requirements

   i. Personnel training

   j. Manufacturer's assistance in programming, and so forth

   k. Other special requirements

The manufacturers, in turn, will respond to the bid invitation with specific proposals for implementing the system. Through this approach, management can gather the information needed and emphasis can then be placed on the relative efficiency and cost of the various makes of equipment. Today, the competence and continued support of the equipment manufacturer can be assumed, as the computer business is a highly competitive one and any major manufacturer will do its utmost to assist its customers.

Aids from Computer Manufacturer

Many benefits are to be expected from the rental or purchase of a computer from its manufacturer other than the functions performed by the equipment. These include maintenance of the equipment, training programs and educational facilities, programming assistance, and program libraries. These must all be considered and the expected benefits weighed before selecting a computer system.

Maintenance. Most computer manufacturers provide the maintenance required to keep the equipment in top operating condition under rental agreements. This must, however, be a separate consideration when outright purchase of the equipment is contemplated. Then it may, depending on many factors, be better for the firm to train its own staff of maintenance personnel rather than enter into a separate maintenance contract with the equipment manufacturer.

Under rental agreements or separate maintenance contracts, the availability of the manufacturer's servicing personnel must be a consideration in selecting equipment. It is a serious problem if the equipment becomes inoperable for even a short period of time, as the volume of work performed in such a system means that, with any delay at all, a backlog of data processing information will quickly develop.

In larger electronic computer systems the manufacturer may assign maintenance personnel to a specific system or to a few similar strategically located systems. In either instance the user of the equipment will be expected to provide the office and equipment space required for this personnel.

In smaller electronic computer systems the maintenance will probably be performed from a central office of the manufacturer. Here, the factors to be considered are the distance from this office and the general reputation of the manufacturer as determined from talks with other business firms who have installations serviced in this manner.

In conjunction with maintenance, the availability of other systems compatible with the one under consideration, through which the work could be performed on an emergency basis, should be investigated. Though the probability of a major system breakdown is remote today, it is always a possibility and could be a near disaster under some circumstances.

Training Schools. Previous to "unbundling" most computer manu-facturers provided training programs for their various customer's per-sonnel. Though this training was "advertised" as being without cost to the customer, this was not the complete picture. All personnel sent by the customer to this school were on the customer's payroll, and he or she also provided any transportation expense involved as well as housing, meals, and incidental expenses in some instances. Today, the extent of "free" training and the cost of nonfree training programs vary considerably from manufacturer to manufacturer and usually depend on the amount or degree of unbundling for the given manufacturer.

Typical areas of training include both seminars and classroom-type courses, such as those for a broad survey of office automation in general for executives, department heads, and even staff members as a group; training for operating personnel on both the computer system and the supporting peripheral equipment; detailed training in the technical per-formance of the equipment in developing programmers and systems analysts; and, where a firm purchases the equipment and desires to do its own maintenance, training of selected personnel in the technique and use of equipment necessary to do this type of work.

It is to be expected that a more extensive training program will be necessary as the size or type of system increases in complexity and capacity. However, the quality and depth of training programs may vary from manufacturer to manufacturer on a system of a given size, and the end result of quality personnel must be a factor to consider.

Programming Assistance. The amount of programming assistance to be expected can vary from a complete package of tested programs down to no assistance at all—again depending on the degree of unbundling.

At first mention, the completed package of tested programs sounds too good to be true. This may not be the case, however, as these will probably be very general programs for the given procedural application. This is understandable if one stops to think that these programs must be equally applicable for all other firms with similar procedural applications. Each firm has its own unique peculiarities, and if the program is broad enough to cover most of the possible differences, then it will generally be inefficient, in terms of processing time required, for any given firm. Such a program, however, may serve as a good starting point, and with the expenditure of a great deal of effort, selecting what is appropriate and then condensing it to fit a specific need, it may become a satisfactory program.

Some manufacturers will, if requested, furnish, on a full-time basis in the preparation stage, an experienced lead programmer or systems analyst to work with and guide a company's newly trained personnel in their work. This may be good under some circumstances, but care must be taken that this individual doesn't do the bulk of the work requiring real ingenuity in the techniques and decisions to be made. If this is the case, the company employees will not be developing as they should, and they will still be inexperienced programmers and systems people when the initial work is completed. Systems work and programming are never-ending jobs. As conditions and policies change, improvements can seemingly always be made. Company personnel will have this responsibility as soon as the system is in operation.

What is appropriate for one firm in programming assistance will not necessarily be so for another, so this must be a matter of executive judgment as to the capabilities of the personnel, the time to be allotted for the completion of the work, and the expense to be involved.

Program Libraries. Many of the computer manufacturers keep files of programs which have been developed for either specific problems or general applications. These may be in the form of a listing of detailed instructions, a deck of punched cards, or a reel of magnetic tape, to provide a given program. Normally, these are available without charge to customer users of a manufacturer's equipment.

Many of these represent specific "routine programs"—so called because they represent programmed procedures which will be utilized over and over. A typical example would be in the case of mathematical problems where the square root of a number or a given trigonometric function of a triangle may be needed. It would be ridiculous to write a new program to do either of these calculations every time such a procedure is called for.

Some of the library programs—often called "canned" programs—represent the development of extensive programs for specific applications. Generally these are applications with broad usage in a particular industry or type of business.

Program libraries are also available from various user groups. These may be groups of users who have similar problems or, more commonly, groups formed by users of specific models of a given manufacturer's computers. As the individual member of the group develops or improves upon programs which serve a common purpose for the group, these are put in the user-group file which is available to all members of the group.

Members of such user groups are usually charged a very nominal fee for membership, and each appoints one or more representatives to attend the various meetings held by the group. These groups may be limited in membership to local users or extended to a regional or even a national group organization.

PURCHASE VERSUS LEASE OR RENTAL CONSIDERATIONS

A decision to purchase must, of course, reflect the availability of capital funds—or the ability to secure borrowed funds at a satisfactory interest cost. There must also be serious thought given to the "opportunity cost" of alternative uses to which those funds might be applied if a decision to lease rather than purchase were made.

Usage requirements will have a bearing on the decision to purchase or lease, as overtime usage results in an additional rental charge—though at a reduced rate. Consequently, a two- or three-shift operation may be the factor that results in a buy decision.

Purchasing allows the substitution of fixed costs for the major variable costs of a computer system. Therefore, a firm must be conscious of the cost-volume-profit interrelations present. The break-even point (where the revenue from sales is just sufficient to meet the total, fixed and variable, expenses involved) will be raised with the purchase of a computer, so a serious consideration must be given to sales potential—just as it would in any other major asset investment.

Technical obsolescence is not always the problem that it appears to be. If the firm has planned properly and purchased a system which is adequate and provides for anticipated growth, there should be no consideration given to replacing it unless revolutionary changes threaten to give competition an insurmountable advantage in the market. Leasing or renting provides some protection against such a contingency, but any change will probably involve considerable expenditures and some certain resulting disorganization, which must be given proper weight in any decision to change systems. Also, the rental price itself must include some provision for the possibility of obsolescence, as the supplier must protect its own investment.

Amortization of the purchased investment through depreciation tends to counter the tax advantage of expensing rental payments. In fact, some of the accelerated depreciation methods permissible may even be an advantage in that the majority of the cost of the computer may be "charged off" in the early years of its use.

Another, but lesser, tax consideration is that purchase will result in additional property taxes. However, these taxes will also have been included in the determination of the rental fee.

If a change in computers is dictated after a few years use, it must be remembered that there is only a limited secondhand market for used computers. If disposal is made through a "trade-in" on a new system, this will probably "tie" the purchaser to the manufacturer who sold the previous equipment. This may prevent having the freedom desired in selecting the "best" equipment for the job. Developments, both in the purchasing firm and in the company manufacturing the equipment, may be such that a change in manufacturer is the only way to assure the achievement of the performance desired in a system. In the past, many computer firms have been absorbed by others through purchase or merger and their equipment modified or discontinued; others have stopped manufacturing computers completely, and some have not advanced technologically as fast as their competitors.

As previously mentioned, maintenance will normally be included in the rental fee quoted on the equipment, but it will be an additional expense if the computer is purchased.

Most leasing contracts allow part of the rental fee to be applied toward purchase of the computer. Such an alternative permits a "trial run" of the system before the firm must make a final decision to invest in computer hardware.

In most instances, leasing is more expensive than purchasing; however, leasing can certainly be justified if the usage is to be temporary, if only a few applications are to be employed, if the firm anticipates the introduction of improved models in the relatively near future, or, of course, if capital funds are not available for the investment required.

The decision to lease or purchase must be based on facts applicable to the particular firm, and management must consider all these facts, in terms of the impact the alternatives will have upon the firm, before finalizing its decision to purchase or lease the equipment. (See References 2, 4, 5 and 6.)

OTHER CONSIDERATIONS

Management should not build up high hopes of a new system substantially reducing the cost of the data processing operation. If it does, experience indicates that it will likely be disappointed.

The expected reduction in cost is often projected as a result of decreased labor costs through the reduction of the clerical staff. Quite often, this benefit fails to materalize. The savings from the reduction in the number of people employed is usually offset by the general upgrading of the positions retained.

To utilize the full capability of a computer system, the functions it performs must be extended beyond the conventional record system. This may involve additional managerial reports, such as detailed costing procedures would provide, or it may result in the use of some of the newer operations research or management science techniques. This utilization will, of course, increase costs but at the same time will provide better managerial control and greater anticipated returns from operations.

Another factor that tends to keep computer costs up is that it normally is not economically feasible to program a computer to handle all situations which may arise; therefore, it is necessary to retain a skeleton force to operate a manual system to handle exceptions and special cases. It is also important for some personnel to be around to know how it was intended to have the computer system operate. Computers have had malfunctions and breakdowns of various types.

Although the cost of operating the system may remain relatively constant or even increase, the increased managerial control that is possible through a soundly conceived system should ultimately make it a profitable investment. This may, however, be hard to prove in dollars and cents, as better control and an ability to make better decisions are hard to quantify.

Finally, automation should never be considered in the anticipation of short-run gains or for automation's sake itself. Instead, the cost of automation should be regarded in exactly the same light as any other major capital expenditure—a carefully planned investment which is expected to produce long-run benefits over the life of the asset being acquired.

PERSONNEL REQUIREMENTS

As previously discussed, personnel throughout the organization must be aware of the capabilities and limitations of an EDP system. Cooperation can only occur if the employees are favorably convinced from the beginning that the success of any system is dependent upon them individually and as a group.

Displacement Problems

To date, most of the companies involved in changes to computerized data processing systems have taken a "social trust" viewpoint toward their personnel and have generally been able to maintain sound employee relationships throughout the course of the changes. The vast majority of the studies made on employment displacement in changes to computer systems have shown very few people to have been displaced as a result of EDP. This problem, historically, hasn't begun to approach the magnitude that is generally assigned to it. Automation of the factory, however, has been another story and normally has involved sizable personnel displacement; but automation of the office seldom has.

Since the introduction of any EDP system requires an extended time period for it to be planned, installed, and put into operation, there is usually ample time to plan for the reorganization of the staff. Jobs of routine nature may be eliminated by normal attrition. These positions are usually staffed by young women among whom, traditionally, the turnover rate is very high. However, the total force may not be reduced because the computer system can perform so many additional activities which may require personnel in data gathering and analytical interpretation procedures.

Displacement in the managerial ranks can be a major cause of internal dissension. If a firm changes its traditions by hiring people trained outside of the firm and by altering the established avenues of promotion, the result could be failure of the EDP system. The company's normal procedures regarding security of employment and opportunities for promotion must remain intact if the installation is to be successful.

Personnel who have proven themselves satisfactory employees in the past should not be discharged but, if at all possible, should be retained for new responsibilities within the firm. Those who are not suited for or are not interested in the new, and often technical, positions should be provided jobs elsewhere in the organization. Whenever possible, these new positions should be commensurate in salary, prestige, and in all other respects to their current positions.

A technique which has sometimes been adopted regarding employees nearing retirement age, who might have a particularly hard time in adjusting to the changes necessary, is to accelerate their retirement.

This should be carefully planned, however, to permit a continuing use of the employees' experience and abilities on a part-time or consulting basis and to allow them to retain their ties with the firm so that they will feel they are still needed and are not being thrust "out in the cold."

Employee Acquisition

The firm must, of course, know which jobs are to be filled before any action can be taken. Job analyses, based on the functional descriptions developed in the feasibility study, should have resulted in definite job classifications and procedural descriptions of the positions which will be required. This permits the recruiter as well as the applicants to know exactly what is required and expected.

Past experience has shown that it is normally easier to train a person thoroughly versed in the firm's operations to do computer work than it is to train a computer specialist to have the required in-depth insight of the firm's policies and operations. However, once it is determined that qualified personnel are not available from the internal staff to fill the new positions, then management will have to turn to the labor market for personnel. Only people with a potential for growth should be hired so that normally expected promotions and advancement may be forthcoming as time passes.

Applicants must be tested for their ability to perform a given task and for their aptitude to learn the things required in the position. These tests may be designed by the firm, standardized tests may be purchased, or a professional testing service may be used. Tests, to be fair and accurate, must be professionally administered, scored, and interpreted.

Finally, after testing has been completed, interviews will also need to be conducted to delve into the applicants' personalities. Interviews are necessary since tests cannot adequately reveal indifference, ambition, or personal difficulties. The workers must be interested in the job. They should be able to pay attention to detail and have the ability to think logically and abstractly. Not only should a person have these analytical capabilities, but he or she should be aggressive in his or her actions while retaining the ability to get along with others.

The final selection of the technical personnel required can only be made after testing and interviewing the applicants.

Training

Although most of the training required is in the area of specific skills which are to be applied in the area of EDP, it must not be forgotten that EDP presents a new challenge for management also. Management personnel at virtually every level—even though they will have no direct connection with the program—must be orientated as to the potential and limits of an EDP system through educational programs. Again, full cooperation is necessary and a broad background is desirable so that the supervision and coordination of the data processing operation will be successful.

Systems analysts, programmers, and operators must also be trained. The systems analysts should have a broad general training so that they will understand the principles involved in programming the specific computer in operation. They should have a thorough familiarity with the way the business operates and must be aware of the existing internal control system. They must have formal training in EDP, but only the background of at least two years' experience can develop a top-notch analyst.

Programmers, console operators, and maintenance personnel are usually trained in their highly specialized skills in formal schools conducted by the manufacturer of the computer to be used. Again, however, proficiency can only come through experience.

A point that is sometimes overlooked is that even after the staff is complete and the systems change is in operation, there is a continuing need for a personnel development program in the firm. There is a strong demand for employees with computer-orientated training and experience, and the turnover of personnel in this area may be somewhat higher than might normally be expected. Regardless of this demand, however, there is always a need in every firm for better-trained personnel who can assume the positions which will become available through the firm's growth and normal attrition. (See References 1 and 3.)

DEVELOPING PROCEDURAL APPLICATIONS

The development of the various procedural applications to be processed on the new computer system is a joint responsibility of both the systems staff and line management. These procedural applications will be determined by (1) the output reports and their information which is desired from the system by the various levels of management; (2) the inputs into the system which must be planned in order to provide the data for the desired outputs; and (3) the basic files of data which must be maintained in order to provide summaries of data at periodic intervals.

Procedures to process the data will then be determined which utilize the particular type of equipment which has been selected. Flowcharting is an easily understood method of presenting procedures in a diagram form. From these flowcharts, programs must be written, debugged, tested, and converted into working realities.

Flowcharting

Systems and program flowcharting, as previously discussed, form the basis for the programmed instructions which must be prepared to guide the computer in its processing procedures. These flowcharts will probably have been developed in basic form as part of the systems survey, but once a given computer is decided upon, these will have to be re-analyzed in terms of the fundamental requirements of the system to be used. Every major type and model of computer system has its own special requirements. Some of these are the following: only certain types of input and output devices may be acceptable, both in terms of equipment and of data presentation; each processor has its own unique combinations of instructions, data, and internal codes as well as "decision-making" circuitry; and each system is a combination of various input, output, and internal and external storage devices. The net effect of these requirements will be reflected in the detailed steps necessary for a given computer system to complete a given processing procedure.

Programming

Programming is time consuming and an expensive job, so the initial preparation should begin as soon as an EDP system is decided upon. The programming effort should be closely supervised by someone who is thoroughly familiar with company operations and the objectives of management.

Previously prepared flow diagrams are studied by the programmers so that they will be familiar with exactly what the computer is expected to do. The basic idea of programming is to develop the most efficient way of transforming the source data into usable output. This is accomplished in EDP equipment by making use of four fundamental steps:

1. The transcription of the data into a medium acceptable by the machine through a set of coded instructions.
2. Programming (instructing) the machine in the necessary operations to be performed on the data to produce the desired results.
3. Reading (feeding) this data into the central processing unit through the various types of input devices available.
4. Writing out the processed data in the form desired.

There can be thousands of individual logical instructions involved in some of these steps.

In addition to writing his or her own programs, a programmer has several sources of information to turn to as he or she develops a program. Canned programs are also available through both the manufacturer and user groups, and consulting services may be provided by manufacturers, consulting firms, and service organizations.

Debugging the Program

Debugging is the process of detecting and correcting the errors which have been made in systems design, systems analyses, coding, and programming. This is the final check for the exceptional items for which there is no provision but which may appear from time to time.

The debugging process begins at the time the program is planned and continues as the program is written and finally implemented. In the beginning stages, programmers check on each other, but as the program enters the completion stage, tests are made with pilot runs to check the program's performance on the computer with actual data whose processing results are already known.

The two major types of errors found in computer programs are logical errors and clerical errors. Logical errors, usually extremely difficult to detect, are a result of a fundamental lack of understanding of what is desired in a given situation. Clerical errors, which might be something as simple as giving two files of data the same name, are discovered and corrected by testing techniques developed specifically for that purpose. If this program was written in COBOL, the compiler would have caused the machine to print out a diagnostic error which would be an attempt to describe the type of error which had been made, and its location would be identified.

Testing the Program

Testing is accomplished by applying specially designed hypothetical data, which requires only a small amount of machine time, to a program to see if the desired result is achieved. This procedure is relatively ineffective in eliminating logical errors. These may, in fact, not all be discovered until the program is actually put into use.

The two most common ways to locate errors in a program are by using *postmortems* and *traces*. A postmortem involves the selection of data after a mistake has caused the program to stop running and analyzing pertinent areas as to why the program halt occurred. This analysis could result in the use of the trace technique, which involves going through the logic of the program, instruction step by instruction step, to understand where and how the error developed.

CONVERTING

During the preparation for conversion, a systems manual should have been prepared prescribing the details of the early operation of the system. This may need to be revised as the system matures. The study and organization required in the preparation of such a manual will prevent many problems in the early stages of conversion and operation from occurring providing the manual is carefully followed.

The far-reaching changes introduced by an EDP system require a careful appraisal of the basic functions of the organization and of the manner in which the new procedures may assist in performing those functions. The personnel whose job it is to guide the conversion in the most efficient manner must have as their major concern the overall welfare of the firm. As management attempts to solve technical and administrative problems, it must, however, remain conscious of personnel problems and try to maintain equilibrium in the organization.

The final step in the integration of the computer into the system requires the conversion of files from written or punched card form to magnetic tape or some other medium which is acceptable as an input to the computer. Those responsible for this conversion may find that existing files are inaccurate, incomplete, and inconsistent, and that they even deviate from the correct format.

At the beginning of the period when the computer system is first used, the old noncomputer processing system should be operated concurrently—in parallel—for a period to assure the accuracy of the new system. Cross-checking will establish confidence in the adequacy of the new system. Discrepancies, whether due to inadequacy of the old system or oversights or mistakes in the new program, will be corrected without the loss of valuable data, operating efficiency, or continuity.

It is usually best to convert one or two procedures at a time so that disruption and confusion can be kept to a minimum. This allows the people involved to adjust to the changing conditions. If various departments or divisions have previously automated independently, overall efficiency and economy may suffer as personnel try to adapt to another computer system. They must not be allowed to feel resentful and fear a loss of status.

Management can expect an EDP system to offer solutions to many problems associated with:

1. An increasing volume of paper work.
2. A short supply of suitable office personnel.
3. The ever-increasing cost per unit of the performance of the information processing functions.
4. New requirements for managerial, accounting, statistical, and tax data.

To achieve these benefits, management must seek cooperation and understanding from all who are in contact with the EDP system. Management must remember that conversion, which is a trying experience for all concerned, may turn out to be a never-ending task as more uses are found for the computer and as new and better equipment becomes available.

HOW TO TRANSLATE SYSTEMS DESIGN TO EQUIPMENT REQUIREMENTS

What has been said under the topic of Developing Procedural Applications is broad in nature. There is no standardized way of designing a computerized system. This is the reason that the statements which have been made are stated as they are.

For a person interested in more of the specifics involved in turning the computerization of a plan into a working reality, the Case Illustration on page 440 is an outline used by one of the "Big 8" international public accounting firms illustrating how they recommend to their staff that this job be accomplished. The working papers which accompany the outline are predicated on the assumption that the outline is being used to analyze the feasibility of computerizing the payroll system of a client. It is the intention of the persons preparing this outline to seek bids from computer manufacturers on the requirements as outlined in the working papers.

Physical Facilities

The physical requirements of an electronic computer system can create many problems. If some effort is not made to determine these in advance and make preparations for them, serious problems will develop.

Floor Space and Design Requirements

While the actual computer installation may not take up any more floor space than present equipment, space may be a greater problem than was anticipated. You will have to have sufficient area for the dual operation of the new and at least part of the old equipment for a period of time. You may have to provide space for repairs and perhaps extensive modifications which will probably have to be made to meet the requirements of the computer system. Also, you will probably have to reorganize completely the data collection, handling, and storage areas for their most efficient use.

An existing floor with adequate structural qualities may be available, but it must also have adequate recessed channels to carry the power lines and other interconnecting cables for the equipment. These cables are fairly massive and require considerable space. They have critical lengths to be considered, as electrical power deteriorates as it travels through the wires. Also, some interconnected units of the equipment operate at speeds of millionths or, more recently, even billionths of a second, and the time it takes the signal to travel from one unit to another—even though it travels at approximately the speed of light—may be longer than can be tolerated. Normally then, these cables must be run in a direct path between these critical equipment units. Another problem is that the floor must be vibration-free for satisfactory performance of some of the units utilizing high-speed rotating mechanical devices.

If adequate cable channels are not available or if the floor structure is not satisfactory, then a false floor must be constructed. This permits more even loading of the existing structure, tends to cut down on vibration, and provides sufficient space underneath to permit the cables to be laid in the most efficient manner. This space may, where necessary, also be used for air-conditioning and/or heating ducts.

Other problems arising from the computer room itself include acoustical floor, walls, and ceiling to cut down on noise. The materials used for this purpose must also have qualities which make them as dust- and lint-free as possible. Special nonflaking floor wax and wall paint should be used, along with special cleaning procedures. Foreign particles can, if they reach some of the magnetic data-carrying medias or reading and writing heads, either cause data to be masked and not read or cause the foreign particles to be read as data. This, of course, cannot be tolerated.

Observation windows to the equipment should normally be planned for the use of employees and visitors so as not to disturb operations. Visiting executives, employees' families, and college students are all fascinated by the data processing center.

Preventive and corrective maintenance require that space be provided on all sides of the computer to facilitate the removal of panels and to swing out hinged sides or tops to permit access to the interior components. Large pieces of test and repair equipment on wheels or carts must have room to move between the equipment. Data will also move within the computer room on racks, stands, and hand trucks. To obtain efficiency, data must travel a direct and short route between points of use.

For effective supervision while operating the console, the operator must be able to see the indicator lights on all on-line input and output units and the front side of the magnetic tape units.

After the technical requirements for the computer room have been met, the remainder of the data processing center can be established. The storage vault should be near those who will use it. Spare maintenance parts can be located at a distance from the center, but maintenance technicians must be able to locate them conveniently. The floor space required by the input preparation room may make it necessary to locate it some distance from the computer. However, storage and data movement must be planned to avoid congestion in the computer room and surrounding areas.

Offices for the analysts and programmers are best located some distance away from the actual computer room to avoid the noise, distraction, and confusion that exists there.

Specific floor design and space requirements are influenced by the type and brand of equipment purchased and the size and scale of the operations planned.

Power Supply

The location of the computer will not generally affect the location of the power equipment. The major consideration when designing a power system is the continuous level of electrical power between a narrow range of tolerances. Electrically triggered circuits in a computer cannot adjust to much variance in the power level. There must be no interference from varying loads of power used by other equipment.

It may be wise to consider some means to provide for contingencies which lead to power interruptions. A substitute power device with an automatic cut-in may be an inexpensive investment in the long run if there is any previous history of power failures. First, it can be quite expensive to adjust, repair, and replace computer components after power failures or surges. Also, when your computer is down, or out of order, processing will either be at a standstill or, if another computer is available, data will have to be transported to the supporting computer system.

The actual cost of power is a minor consideration in a computer installation. The required voltage levels now range from 115 to 230 volts, but with the use of transistors and semi-conductors the need for high amperage capacities has been lowered.

Lighting

Management is faced with a difficult decision when choosing the proper level of illumination, because different chores, which may require different light levels, may be performed simultaneously. Any clerical work necessary to the operation requires a good level of illumination. Maintenance personnel need a high degree of flexibility as well as adequate illumination to enable them to distinguish colors and small component parts. On the other hand, operators can best observe indicator lights and read test equipment at a lower level of intensity. A partial solution to the problem is in the use of dimmer controls for the general lighting facilities and hoods or shields for consoles and test equipment.

Air Conditioning

The constant need for air conditioning often suggests the installation of a separate cooling system for the computer complex. However, the noise generated by air-conditioning equipment requires that it be placed at some distance from the computer facilities.

Even though the newer equipment does not generate vast quantities of heat, a fairly powerful air-conditioning system may still be required. Both machines and people are most efficient at constant temperature and humidity levels. A high percentage of humidity would damage such storage devices as paper tape, punched cards, and magnetic tape. Air must be circulated so as to be completely changed every few minutes. Air intakes and ducts, however, must be situated so that drafts and hot spots are not created. Dust must be filtered from the room, as it interfers with the efficient use of magnetic tape and disk units. The air conditioner also provides a slight increase in air pressure which inhibits the infiltration of foreign particles when doors are opened.

Planning is a very important requirement in the development of an effective air-conditioning system.

Other Areas of Environmental Control

The most effective use of a computer complex is derived from a controlled physical environment.

Usually, smoking will not be permitted in the computer room due to the ash problem and fire hazard. Carbon dioxide fire extinguishers may be the solution to the fire hazard. Sprinkler systems should not be used because of possible damage to the computer and the danger of electrical shock to the operators. Insurance contracts requiring a sprinkler system may complicate this problem.

Workers should be made fully aware of the high voltage utilized in the equipment and the possibility of shock or mechanical accidents.

Intercommunication systems should be employed and external telephones should be available for the use of personnel.

SYSTEM FOLLOW-UP

As with any extensive installation, the business information processing system must be observed, checked, and rechecked to determine if it is functioning in an efficient manner. As time passes, this check should be extended to include the possibility that changes should be made to incorporate any new managerial policies and functional or procedural requirements which have developed since the system was installed.

A checklist for both a checkup and reexamination of a system would include the following points.

1. Make a thorough checkup as soon as possible with these objectives:
    - .01 To see that all parts of the system have been installed and are working properly.
    - .02 To see that the procedures are being followed.
    - .03 To make modifications which may be required by operating experience.
    - .04 To measure the results achieved against the objectives and expectations originally predicted.

      a. See if the quality and quantity of work comes up to expectations.

      b. See if man-power savings are being realized or delayed.

2. Make regular postinstallation audits with these objectives.

  .01 To prevent inefficient or unnecessary steps creeping into the system.

  .02 To make sure that new personnel are fully indoctrinated before they begin to operate the system.

  .03 To see if the original objectives are being accomplished.

  .04 To see if the expected benefits continue to be realized.

  .05 To look for the possibility of further improvement through the introduction of new equipment or new techniques.

  .06 To look for opportunities to apply work simplification techniques.

      a. Assuming that the procedures are now accomplishing the desired results, look for possible ways to improve the methods of doing the work. This is the essence of a work simplification program—making improvements at the work stations.

      b. The actual work simplification should be done by the worker, by the supervisor, or by the worker and the supervisor working as a team.[1]

CASE ILLUSTRATION

I. How to Translate System Design to Equipment Requirements
  A. Preliminary steps
    1. Reporting requirements
      a. Inventory of reports
      b. Report information worksheet (Exhibit A)[2]
      c. Report samples
    2. Designing the processing flow
      a. Basic guidelines (Exhibit B)
      b. Systems flowcharts
    3. Defining the file requirements
      a. List of master files
      b. Information matrix
      c. Master file information worksheet (Exhibit C)

---

[1] U.S. Treasury Department, Internal Revenue Service, Data Processing Division, Systems and Procedures, *A Notebook for the Systems Man* (Washington, D.C.: U.S. Government Printing Office, February 1963), p. 27.

[2] Only a few selected exhibits are shown, beginning on page 445.

4. Determining the input requirements
   a. Input documents summary
   b. Input document information worksheet (Exhibit D)
   c. Samples of key source documents (Exhibit E)
B. Establishing parameters for equipment valuation
   1. Relationship to other preliminary Systems Design (PSD) steps
      a. Proper time frame
      b. System design must be complete
      c. Parameters established before selecting vendor
      d. Parameters established prior to economic evaluation
   2. Prerequisites for establishing the parameters
      a. Awareness of equipment market
      b. Knowledge of how hardware affects throughput
      c. Knowledge of how software affects processing time and CPU size
      d. Other factors to consider (future growth, and so forth)
   3. Selecting the configuration
      a. Decisions required
         (1) Number, size, and speed of CPU's
         (2) Number, type, and speed of peripheral devices
         (3) Channel and controller characteristics
         (4) Potential for multi-programming
         (5) Overall computer time requirements
      b. Major classes of configurations
         (1) Card
         (2) Tape
         (3) Direct access
         (4) Combination of tapes and direct access devices
         (5) Real-time systems
      c. Steps in determining the configuration
         (1) Use basic configuration as a starting point
             (a) Memory size   4K
             (b) I/O devices   5 (4 data + 1 op. system)
             (c) Channels   2
             (d) Printer   1
             (e) Card reader/punch   1
             (f) Console   1

       (2)   Refine the basic configuration
           (*a*)   Determine available time
       (3)   Separate the basic I/O operations
           (*a*)   Printer speed, and number of printers
           (*b*)   Number, type, and speed of card reader/ printers
           (*c*)   Requirement for special peripherals
       (4)   Determine file and CPU requirements
           (*a*)   Type of data files (card, tape, disk)
           (*b*)   Number of file devices
           (*c*)   Maximum memory requirements
           (*d*)   CPU model (size vs. speed tradeoff)
       (5)   Relate refined configuration to the processing
           (*a*)   Requirements of the proposed system
       (6)   Estimate the operating time to determine if the configuration is adequate
       (7)   Estimate the cost
       (8)   Repeat 2nd thru 5th steps until configuration provides a reasonable balance of cost, processing time, and expansion capability

   d. Other factors affecting selection of configuration
       (1)   Management preference
       (2)   Existing systems
       (3)   Multiple locations (centralized vs. decentralized proc.)
       (4)   Future growth

4. Estimating computer time
   a. Importance of timing
       (1)   Can be a costly mistake
       (2)   Estimate (within reasonable limits) should be done in PSD
       (3)   Estimated time is checked during detail system design
       (4)   Final time estimates compared to original estimates during system testing

   b. Program time computations
       (1)   Simultaneous operations
       (2)   Standard software time by program
       (3)   Process time by program (Exhibit F)
       (4)   Tape time (Exhibit G)
       (5)   Total time requirements

  c. System time computations
    (1) Individual program time is focal point
    (2) Program testing
    (3) Planned growth
    (4) Rerun time
    (5) Setup time
    (6) Contingency factor
    (7) Example
  d. Other techniques for estimating time
    (1) Guess
    (2) Rules of thumb
    (3) Benchmark programs
5. Defining criteria for selection
  a. Definition of criteria
    (1) Capacity (speed of equipment)
    (2) Operating cost (including alternative rental arrangements)
    (3) Availability of hardware
    (4) Availability of software
    (5) Expandability of equipment
    (6) Availability of special devices
    (7) Field testing
    (8) Cost of conversion
    (9) Contract terms
    (10) Support
    (11) Compatability with equipment bench replaced
  b. Determining relative importance of criteria
  c. Selecting the equipment
    (1) Summary of functional requirements (Exhibit H)
      (*a*) Preparing manufacturers specifications
        (*i*) Outline of spec book content
        (*ii*) Excerpt from spec book
      (*b*) Evaluating proposals
        (*i*) Summary of manufacturers proposals (Exhibit I)
        (*ii*) Computer evaluation summary (Exhibit J)
        (*iii*) Detail timing summary
      (*c*) Negotiating contract terms

                (*i*)   Economic analysis of contract con-
                       siderations (Exhibit K)
               (*ii*) Contract points
             (*iii*) Summary of contract points

II.   Cost Justification of a Computer System (economic evaluation)
     A.   Estimate proposed system costs
         1.   Personnel requirements
         2.   Equipment requirements
         3.   Other requirements
         4.   Summary of proposed system costs
     B.   Estimate operating savings
         1.   Personnel affected
         2.   Equipment released
         3.   Other savings
         4.   Summary of current operating costs
     C.   Summarize intangible considerations
     D.   Estimate installation costs (one-time costs)
         1.   Personnel requirements
         2.   Other one-time costs
     E.   Overall economic analysis

EXHIBIT A

Company Name *ABC Company*		*D-120* Index No.
REPORT INFORMATION WORKSHEET		*10* Item No.
Systems Development *Payroll and Personnel Records*		

Prepared by *Joe Campbell*	Reviewed by *O. Bailin*	Approved
Date *4-2-70*	Date *4-4-70*	Date

Report or Source Document Name:

Current Payroll Journal

Description: *The Payroll Journal provides a detail listing of all employees paid setting out hours worked, gross pay, deduction and net pay. Report totals provide basis for control totals and entries to the General Ledger*

Frequency: *Weekly / Semimonthly*

Estimated Volume: *650/150 pages*

Distribution:
Control clerk.
Payroll Department
Accounting Department

Key	Data Name	Comments
1	*Employee Name*	
2	*Department Number*	
3	*Section Number*	
4	*Employee Number*	
5	*Hourly Rate*	*½ monthly salary for semimonthly payroll*
6	*Hours Worked*	*Includes overtime*
7	*Regular Gross Pay*	*Gross pay for 40 hours work*
8	*Overtime Gross Pay*	*Gross pay for excess of hours worked over 40*
9	*Social Security Amt.*	
10	*Federal Withholding Amt.*	
11	*State Income Tax Amt.*	
12	*Life Ins. Deduction - fixed deduction per payroll*	

EXHIBIT B

ABC Company
Basic Guidelines
Payroll and Personnel Records

O. Berlin 4-18-70

D-200
Index No.

Guideline	Reasoning behind Guideline	System Effect
The system should provide both hourly and salaried employees.	Company does not want to design separate systems for each type of payroll.	Program identifying gross pay must utilize both hourly and salary calculations.
Both payrolls should be issued at the same time.	To minimize setup and processing time.	Design criteria must be established indicating when periodically switched over to the mode?
Master file should be located on magnetic tape.	We will provide uniformity within present techniques of other divisions of the parent company.	Processing techniques and backups should provide for a tape master file.
Payroll checks must be issued the Monday morning following the billing close.	Requirement of union contract.	Company employees responsible for check balancing and replacement of incorrect programs must be on premises on or case Saturday and/or Sunday. Otherwise, employees if one payroll will not be issued. Checks twice adequate payroll.

EXHIBIT C

Company Name __ABC Company__

D-330
Index No.

MASTER FILE INFORMATION WORKSHEET

10
Item No.

Systems Development __Payroll and Personnel Records__

Prepared by _Joe Campbell_	Reviewed by _R. Bailin_	Approved
Date _4-22-70_	Date _4-28-70_	Date

File Name: _Employee master file_

Purposes: _To maintain payroll and personnel data for all employees employed during the current fiscal year and medical and receivable data on employees under current employment_

Sequence: _Payroll code, Employee number, record code_

Media: _Tape_

Frequency of Access–
Reference: _Weekly / semimonthly_
Updating: "   "

Record Types

Key	Record Name	Comments	Estimated Volume
1	Employee Payroll record	Current payroll and personnel data	9,000
2	" Prev. Empl. History "	Previous company history with noncontiguous employment	250
	" Medical "	Major medical history record	100
	" Receivable "	Amts. due company for employee sales and advances	650
			10,000

Data Included

Key	Data Name	Number of Characters	Comments
1,2,3,4	Payroll code	1	
	Employee number	6	
	Record code	1	Identifies the specific type of record
1	Dept. + Section code	9	Dept. is 6 characters Section 3
	Social Security No.	9	
	Pay Rate - Hourly	4	Two decimal places
	" " - Semimonthly	6	
	Deduction code # 1	1	
	" " 2	1	
	" " 3	1	There is a provision for a maximum of 8 deductions.
	" " 4	1	
	" " 5	1	Those not used will be blanked.
	" " 6	1	
	" " 7	1	
	" " 8	1	

EXHIBIT D

Company Name ABC Company		D-420
		Index No.
INPUT DOCUMENT INFORMATION WORKSHEET		10
		Item No.
Systems Development Payroll and Personnel Records		

Prepared by Joe Campbell	Reviewed by R. Bailin	Approved
Date 4-23-70	Date 4-23-70	Date

Source Document Name:

Payroll deductions

Description:

a document for adding, changing, or deleting a specific deduction type and/or deduction amount.

Frequency: Daily	Estimated Volume: 25
Source:	

Personnel Department

Key	Data Name	Comments
1.	Employee Name	
2.	Pay Period Date	Pay period that transaction will become effective
3.	Employee Number	
4.	Transaction Type	add, change, or delete
5.	Social Sec. No.	
6.	Life Ins. Code	
7.	Life Ins. Amt.	
8.	Contribution Code	
9.	" Amt.	
10.	Saving Bd. Code	
11.	" " Amt.	
12.	Misc. Ded. Code	

EXHIBIT E

SOURCE DOCUMENT NAME *Payroll Deductions*

FREQUENCY *Daily*

SOURCE *Personnel Department*

D-430
INDEX NO.
10
ITEM NO.

J. Campbell
4-23-70

ABC COMPANY

PAYROLL DEDUCTIONS

Pay Period Ending Date

	Mo.	Day	Yr.
② 3	0 6	0 5	0

Employee Name *John T. Horton* ① Employee Number ③ 11 | 1 | 5 | 3 | 5 | 8 | 5 |

Type of Deduction Activity (Check only one):

Authorization   OR

Change   OR

Cancellation   OR

④ {
17 □ 108
17 ✓ 109
17 □ 107
}

Social Security Number (last four digits) ⑤ 20 | 5 | 3 | 2 | 2 |

---

1. AUTHORIZATION OR CHANGE

A. PERMANENT LIFE INSURANCE:

Identification Code ⑥   24 | 2 | 0 |

Deduction Amount ⑦   26 | | | | | ▲ |

C. CHARITABLE CONTRIBUTIONS:

Identification Code ⑧   24 | 3 | 0 |

Deduction Amount ⑨   26 | | | | | ▲ |

E. STATE, CITY INCOME TAXES

Identification ⑭   24 | 9 | 0 |

	1ST	2ND	3RD
State, City Code ⑮ 26			

Marital Status Code ⑯   35 □

Number of Exemptions ⑰   36 □ □

B. U.S. SAVINGS BONDS:

Identification Code ⑩   24 | 4 | 0 |

Deduction Amount ⑪ 26 | 0 | 0 | 2 | 0 | 0 |

D. MISCELLANEOUS DEDUCTIONS:

Identification Code ⑫   24 | |

Deduction Amount ⑬ 26 | | | | ▲ |

Approved By _____

EXHIBIT F

PROCESS TIME BY PROGRAM

Program Number	Number of Input Records	Type A Processing — Number of Records × Standard Time (minimum) — A	Type B Processing — Number of Records × Standard Time (minimum) — B	Type C Processing — Number of Records × Standard Time (minimum) — C	Total A + B + C (minimum) — D	Character Interrupt Time — Total Characters — E	Character Interrupt Time — Time per Character (us) — F	Character Interrupt Time — E × F (minimum) — G
10	66,000	2.67	_____		2.67	10,865,000	1	.18
20	44,000	1.78	_____		1.78	7,257,000	1	.12
50	110,000	3.96	_____		3.96	66,155,000	1	1.10
70	212,000	1.91	_____		1.91	33,726,000	1	.56
80	5,000	.92	2.53		3.45	23,965,700	1	.40

	Time (us)
Tape Time – 1 character	10
Interrupt Time – 1 character	1
Available for Processing	9

EXHIBIT G

TAPE TIME FOR EACH FILE BY PROGRAM

Tape I.D. Code	DATA RECORD — Number of Records — A	DATA RECORD — Numeric Characters — B	DATA RECORD — Alpha Characters — C	DATA RECORD — Total Tape Characters — D	Records per Block — E	Characters per Block D × E — F	BLOCK TIME — Character Time (MS) — G	BLOCK TIME — Gap Time (MS) — H	BLOCK TIME — Total G & H (MS) — I	TOTAL — Number of Tape Blocks A ÷ E — J	TOTAL — Tape Time (x) + 60000 (min) — K
10-1	66,000	60	40	82	8	656	6.56	10	16.56	8,250	2.27
20-1	44,000	60	40	82	8	656	6.56	10	16.56	5,500	1.52
30-1	66,000	60	40	82	8	656	6.56	10	16.56	8,250	2.27
30-2	44,000	60	40	82	10	820	8.20	10	18.20	5,500	1.67
30-3	100	50	35	73	20	1,460	14.60	10	24.60	5	.002
40-1	44,000	60	40	82	8	656	6.56	10	16.56	5,500	1.52
40-2	66,000	60	40	82	10	820	8.20	10	18.20	6,600	2.00
50-1	175,000	70	35	88	10	880	8.80	10	18.80	17,500	5.48
50-2	110,000	60	40	82	10	820	8.20	10	18.20	11,000	3.33
60-1	212,000	50	35	73	10	730	7.30	10	17.30	21,200	6.11
70-1	212,000	50	35	73	10	730	7.30	10	17.30	21,200	6.11
80-1	103,200	130	10	108	10	1,080	10.80	10	20.80	10,300	3.57
80-2	5,000	50	35	73	15	1,295	12.95	10	22.95	333	.13
80-3	100	100	0	75	20	1,500	15.00	10	25.00	5	.002
10-2	500	60	40	82	20	1,620	16.20	10	26.20	25	.011
10-3	500	60	40	82	20	1,620	16.20	10	26.20	25	.011
10-4	40,000	30	25	48	20	960	9.60	10	19.60	2,000	.65
10-5	500	90	40	108	20	2,160	21.60	10	31.60	25	.013
10-6	195,000	50	35	73	10	730	7.30	10	17.30	19,500	5.62
10-7	14,000	110	10	93	15	1,395	13.95	10	23.95	933	.37
10-8	100,000	70	55	108	10	1,080	10.80	10	20.80	10,000	3.47
10-9	50,000	50	35	73	15	1,295	12.95	10	22.95	3,333	1.28

EXHIBIT H

ABC Company

Summary of Functional Requirements
Payroll and Personnel Records

G-110

O. Berlin
4-27-70

Nature of Requirements	Statistical Data			Comments
	Stan./Point	Quantity	Cross Reference to W/P	
Basic Type of Computer Processing				Batch
Future System Equipment Requirements	To drive available/Model 8070		6-110	
Maximum Time Requirement for Payroll & Personnel Record System	Hours/Day Hours/Week Hours/Month	.5 4 30	6-110 -2	
Maximum Program Core Requirements	Memory in Bytes	45,000		
Acceptable Programming Language				Assembler, Cobol
Basic Backup Configuration				65K, 4 Tape, 3 Disk, Card Reader, Printer
Location of Backup Equipment				15-Mile Radius of Company Location
Optimum Equipment Delivery Date				9-15-71
Number of Physical Location for Input of System Data				
Method of Converting Source Data to Machine Readable Form				Keypunch
Peripherals: Tape Drives Disk Drives Card Reader Card Punch Printer				4 Drives; 30-40 KB; 9 Track; 800 BPI 3 Drive 1 Reader; 800-1000 Cards per Minute 1 Punch; 200-300 Cards per Minute 1 Printer; 1000-1200 Lines per Minute
Location of Operating System Residence				Disk
Executive Software Requirements				Program to Program Control, Dating, File Control, etc.; Journal and Aging of Files, Field Checking, etc.; Equipment Integration, Information, Multi-Programming, Upward Compatibility
Software Packages Required				Sort; Card to Disk, Disk to Card, Card to Tape, Tape to Card; Tape and Disk Comparators; Tape and Disk to Print; Test Data Generation; Memory Dump; Compiler; File Modification Software

EXHIBIT I

ABC Company

Summary of Manufacturers Proposals   O.8 ?? 5.18.70

Payroll and Personal Records

Cross Reference No.	Description of Considerations	Classification Rating	Importance Rating	Manufacturer #1	Manufacturer #2	Manufacturer #3	Manufacturer #4	Manufacturer #5	Manufacturer #6
I-2a	What is the preventive maintenance policy of the company for the equipment recommended?	S	12	Monthly or weekly as required	weekly-all equip	weekly-all equip	weekly-all equip	weekly-all equip	weekly all equip
I-2b	How many hours per week are required for preventative maintenance?	S	12	4	3	5	5	4	1
I-3	Will preventative maintenance be permitted outside the normal working shift?	S	12	Yes - at against notice	yes	no	yes - no extra charge	yes	no
I-4	How many maintenance personnel will be available? — on site	P	3	0	1	0	1	1	0
	— on call			1	1	3	2	2	2
I-5a	Where would the back-up equipment be located?	S	13	Chicago	Chicago	Chicago locally	locally Chicago	Chicago	St. Louis
I-5b	When would the back-up equipment be installed in relation to the Company's installation?	S	13	6 months later	same time	2 months earlier	already installed	already installed	same time
I-5c	What part of the day would the back-up equipment be available for the Company's use?	S	13	7pm-8am	5pm-8am	after 5pm	Anytime	8am-12am	4pm-11pm

EXHIBIT J

ABC Company
Computer Evaluation Summary
Payroll and Personnel Records
O. Berlin
6/1/70
G-400
1 of 3

Selection Criteria	Signature Pending	Difference Favors	Manufacturer #1	Manufacturer #2	Manufacturer #3
Primary					
Capacity	1				
Monthly System Time (minutes)		mfr. #1	1252	1298	12.75
Total Monthly Elapsed Time (hours)		mfr. #1	162	168	165
Operating Costs:	2				
Monthly Rental (one shift)		mfr. #2	$11,600	$9,950	$10,250
Monthly Rental with Overtime		mfr. #2	$13,165	$9,950	$11,670
Prompt Emergency Service:	3				
Number of Engineers on site		mfr. #2	0	1	0
Total Daily on-site Availability (hours)		mfr. #2	0	8	0
Equipment Availability:	4				
Schedule Delivery Date		1	September 15, 1971	September 15, 1971	September 15, 1971
Installation Assistance:	5				
Number of Analysts Full Time		1	3	3	3
Total Cost of Assistance		mfr. #2 & mfr. #3	$43,200	0	0
Secondary					
Software Availability:	6				
Program Maintenance Software Delivery Date		—	Available Now	Available Now	Available Now
Program Development Software Delivery Date		—	Available Now	Available Now	Available Now

EXHIBIT K

ABC Company
G-510
Economic Analysis of Contract Consideration O. Bestin 5-28-70
Payroll and Personnel Records

Effect of Contract Consideration by Manufacturer

Contract Consideration	Manufacturer #1			Manufacturer #2			Manufacturer #3		
	Index	Cost without Consideration	Cost Affecting Consideration	Index	Cost without Consideration	Cost Affecting Consideration	Index	Cost without Consideration	Cost Affecting Consideration
Preinstallation Items:									
Systems Analyst Assistance	G-510/1	43,200	43,200	G-510/2	43,200	—	G-510/3	43,200	—
115 Hours Computer Test Time (includes rental cost)	G-510/4	8,625	750	G-510/5	9,475	3,750	G-510/6	10,050	4,775
Programmer Training	G-510/7	720	720	G-510/8	720	—	G-510/9	720	—
Computer Site Layout Assistance	G-510/10	320	—	G-510/11	3	—	G-510/12	320	—
Testing of Existing Magnetic Tapes for sale with new equipment	G-510/13	240	—	G-510/14	240	240	G-510/15	300	300
Cost of Software Programs Specified in addition G-510/1	G-510/16	5,110	5,110	G-510/17	—	—	G-510/18	—	—
Programmer Assistance	G-510/19	2,640	2,640	G-510/20	2,640	—	G-510/21	2,640	—
Penalty for Attrition of Configuration prior to Delivery	G-510/22	11,000	—	G-510/23	9,500	—	G-510/24	10,000	—
		71,855	52,420		66,015	3,990		67,230	5,075
Continuing Items:									
60 Hours Overtime per month	G-510/25	1,565	1,565	G-510/26	—	—	G-510/27	1,420	1,420
Customer Engineer on-site full time During prime shift	G-510/28	750	—	G-510/29	685	—	G-510/30	705	—
Cost of 10 hours Computer time on backup equipment should client's machine go down	G-510/31	750	—	G-510/32	600	—	G-510/33	625	—
		3,065	1,565		1,285	—		2,700	1,420
		74,920	53,985		67,380	3,990		70,030	6,495

REFERENCES

1. "Computer Evaluation and Selection." *Journal of Data Management,* June 1968.

2. HEILBORN, GEORGE H. "EDP Equipment: Purchase, Trade-In or Sell?—An Analysis." *Data Processing Magazine,* August 1965, pp. 44–46.

3. HILLEGAS, JOHN R. "Systematic Techniques for Computer Evaluation and Selection." *Management Services,* July–August 1969, p. 35.

4. RAVER, ROLAND. "Computer Leasing Provides Future Flexibility." *Financial Executive,* May 1967, p. 18.

5. SABEL, THOMAS A. "Purchasing a Computer." *Management Accounting,* October 1972, p. 43.

6. WOLF, EDWIN D. *Rental versus Purchase of Data Processing Equipment.* Adapted from an article by Edwin D. Wolf in the February 1962 issue of *Management Controls.* Reprinted in *Management Services Handbook,* edited by Henry De Vos, chap. 5, pp. 296–302. New York: American Institute of Certified Public Accountants, 1964.

QUESTIONS

1. Enumerate and discuss in reasonable detail five possible constraints which might easily apply in any business intending to install a computer.

2. Keeping in mind your answer to question 1, describe the planning which is necessary in order to make a proposed computer installation operate effectively. What things must be made compatible with other things?

3. Briefly describe three of the aids which are often provided by a computer manufacturer to a first time user of their equipment.

4. Do you feel that the relative importance of each of these aids, one to the other, may be different today, to an average computer user, than they would have been 15 years ago? Explain why.

5. Under what circumstances can you imagine that a firm might decide to buy a computer rather than to lease or to rent it?

6. What types of personnel problems can arise within a firm when the announcement is made that the company is going to place certain of its clerical activities on a computer which it is acquiring?

7. What type of training is generally recommended for those people hired to work in the data processing area?

8. What steps should be taken before application programs are written? Why?

9. What sorts of things are involved in the debugging operation?

10. What is meant when it is said that the old and new system should be run in parallel for a short while? Why is this done?

11. Study the case illustration. Describe your reaction to this outline. If your CPA had completed this study for your company, how would you react to it?

12. Briefly describe the things which must be planned for in order to provide adequate housing for a new computing facility.

13. What is the purpose of having a periodic system follow-up?

Topics for Research

1. What is the market today for used computers with their accompanying peripheral devices?

2. What effect did the modular concept, introduced by IBM with their System/360 series, have on the computer hardware market, and might this have had any effect on the lease, rent, or purchase decision in more recent years?

3. In your opinion, can computers be cost justified? Explain.

4. How have some of the personnel problems referred to in question 6 been alleviated, if not solved, by firms which have gone through this experience?

V
Computer Programming

A

FORTRAN IV
Programming Language

THE MOST COMMONLY used computer language for the manipulation
of numerical data in solving arithmetical problems is the FORTRAN
(*Formula Translation*) language. A number of variations of
FORTRAN have been developed, with FORTRAN IV currently being
the most widely used. Each variation has had its own particular features—in its time—but FORTRAN IV is more advanced in its capabilities and permits the use of additional techniques which simplify certain
complex mathematical problems. This last advantage of FORTRAN
IV is not generally a necessity in the solution of simple business-type
problems.

Though the use of FORTRAN is quite prevalent in major computer
systems, each such system must be investigated to determine the particular version that is acceptable to it. In addition, a given version may
have been, or will have to be, modified (sometimes extensively) for
its adaptation to a given computer.

Our approach in this supplement is to provide a limited programming
capability that will permit the student to acquire a working knowledge
of FORTRAN IV as it is applied in relatively simple business types
of problems. To become proficient in the preparation of programs and
to fully utilize the power of this version of FORTRAN, the student
need only to refer to one of the many excellent books available on
this language for the few additional statements that are particularly
applicable to more involved problem-solving techniques.

The contents of this supplement will acquaint the student with the characteristics of programming in general, the terminology associated with FORTRAN IV, and a basic programming capability along with an understanding of the duties and problems of programmers. Specifically, a student completing this material will be able to communicate with programmers, have some empathy in connection with the art of programming, and be able to follow the logical steps of business applications programmed in the FORTRAN language.

FORTRAN IV

As in the case of all symbolic computer languages, FORTRAN IV requires the use of a compiler program which is part of the software provided through either the manufacturer of the computer in use or a software development firm. This compiler permits the computer to accept a program written in the FORTRAN language as input and to produce as output a program written in the computer's own machine language. The compiler as well as the object program it produces will be different for each make and, usually, for each model of computer. In organizations with sophisticated programming talent available, the compiler may be modified to extend its capabilities or to just do a specific job more easily. In fact, most of the different versions of FORTRAN have had as a basis of their development either the design and incorporation of improvements made on the language by programmers working on government projects or for business firms.

The FORTRAN compiler program is fed into the computer and is followed by a source program—which is the set of instructions necessary to solve a given application problem—written in a symbolic format. (This symbolic format or language will be explained in the following material.) The result, in the form of computer output produced by the reading and processing of the compiler and source decks, is a third program, known as an object program. It is this compiled object program, which is processed in turn with data (pertinent information related to the given problem in the form of constants), that executes or produces the solution to the problem in the form of the answer(s) specified by the original symbolic language program.

In some installations the student may never have access to the compiler program as it may be stored previously on magnetic disk, magnetic tape, or in the internal memory of the computer. In such instances, the student will have to prepare specific control cards to call in the FORTRAN compiler from storage and to indicate when the particular compilation is completed as well as providing the source program and its associated problem data. The information for the control cards required for your system will have to be furnished either by your computer center or instructor before your coded problems will be acceptable to the system.

In addition to these specific system control cards (or a compiler program deck), your source program and data information will have to be punched into cards for entry into the system. The data cards will, as you will learn as you study format statements, have to conform to the specific pattern you specify in these statements. The source program cards, however, have to conform to rigid rules which must be precisely followed if your program is to "run" satisfactorily.

FIGURE LS A–1. FORTRAN Program Card

The FORTRAN program card (Figure LS A–1) utilizes the standard 80-column card; however, only columns 1 through 72 may contain source program information. The remaining columns, 73 through 80, may be used for notation or comments by the student, but they will not enter into the execution of the program itself.

Each card in the program is to represent a single statement, with columns 1 through 5 providing an entry for a particular statement number (where one is desired or required). Normally the program advances from statement to statement (card by card), and except for instances where one program statement refers to another, there is no need for statement numbers unless they are desired for card arrangement purposes.

In addition to the statement number usage, column 1 is used for the entry of the letter C where a *comment statement* (for information only) is desired. Following the C in column 1, the comment statement may utilize any or all of the remaining columns of the card. Comment cards may be placed as desired throughout the program and will be printed out in the program listing but will not enter into the execution of the program in processing data.

Columns 7 through 72 are utilized for the actual program statements. In instances where program statements are too lengthy to fit into these columns, they may be continued in a second (or more) card(s) by inserting any valid FORTRAN character (other than a blank or zero) in column 6 of the second and other additional cards. Normally, some successive series of numbers or letters are used to assist in the orderly arrangement of the cards.

A typical program would be as shown in Figure LS A–2, with each

FIGURE LS A–2. Payroll Calculation Program

```
Card                    Card Column Numbers
No.              IIIIIIIIII2222222222333333333344444        777777778
        1234567890123456789012345678901234567890I2345        234567890

 I      C  PAY AMØUNT = HØURS * RATE
 2            READ (1,1) HØURS, RATE                          READDATA
 3         1 FØRMAT (F5.2, F4.2)
 4            PAYAMT = HØURS * RATE                           CØMPUTE
 5        10 FØRMAT (F15.2, F15.2, F20.2)
 6            WRITE (3,10) HØURS, RATE, PAYAMT
 7            STØP
 8            END
```

line of the program being punched into a single card. Briefly, these cards are designed to serve as follows. Card 1 is a comment card whose only function is to describe the program which is to be performed. Card 2 instructs a card reader (number 1) to read data HØURS and RATE from format statement number 1. The information in columns 73 through 80 in both cards 2 and 4 is ignored by the computer in the compilation of the object deck and serves only as information to anyone looking at the program cards or the program listing.

Card 3 is statement number 1 and indicates HØURS will be found in card columns 1 through 5 and have two decimal places and that RATE will be in columns 6 through 9 (the next four columns) and also contain two decimal places. Card 4 is the first and only arithmetic statement in this program and states that the answer PAYAMT is the sum of HØURS multiplied by RATE. Card 5 is format statement 10 and indicates the placement of data. The first data are to be placed in positions 1 through 15 with two decimals (position 1 is, however, a nonprinting position as will be explained later). The second data are to be placed in positions 16 through 30 and the third in positions 31 through 50 with both sets of data to contain two decimal place positions. It should be noted that the data to be placed in these three write positions are not large enough to require this size format. Thus, the unused left-most positions will be left blank and serve as spacing between the three sets of numbers. Spacing may also be provided by specific format specifications to be presented later.

Card 6 is a write statement instructing a printer (number 3) to print data for HØURS, RATE, and PAYAMT according to the format specified in statement 10 (card 5). Cards 7 and 8 are required at the end of each program to specify that this completes the cards contained in a particular program.

Data card or cards would follow the program deck of cards, with the data punched into fields in the cards to meet the specifications indicated by the read format statement. Generally speaking, data may be any valid FORTRAN character except the 0–2–8 punch for b (blank). However, the set of characters on a given printer may be limited and, if so, the use of any "not available" characters must be avoided.

FORTRAN Character Set

The basic FORTRAN character set (Figure LS A–3) is composed of the following alphanumeric characters.

1. The numeric characters are the digits 0 1 2 3 4 5 6 7 8 and 9.
2. The alphabetic characters are the capital letters A B C D E F G H I J K L M N O P Q R S T U V W X Y and Z. The dollar symbol $ is also classified as an alphabetic character.
3. The delimiting characters are the . (which serves as a decimal point representation) , ( ) and a small b (a 0–2–8 punch which represents a blank or empty character space and differs from a nonpunch which represents a spacing blank) along with the five algebraic symbols + — * / and =. Card column 73 also serves as a delimiter.

One of the rules required in writing FORTRAN statements is that one or more of these delimiters must be used to terminate every word, name, and number used.

In handwritten programs, there is occasionally an interpretation

FIGURE LS A–3. FORTRAN Character Set

problem—for the person performing the card punching—in distinguishing between some letters and similarly formed numbers. The techniques used to avoid these problems vary from installation to installation, but the most commonly found technique is to use a capital I for the letter and a 1 for the number one; a capital Ø with a slash through it for the letter O and an open 0 for the zero; and a capital Z with a dash through it for the letter Z and a 2 for the number two. These conventions will be used in the illustrations that follow in this supplement.

ELEMENTS OF FORTRAN IV

There are several kinds or classes of elements applicable to FORTRAN IV. These elements may be found as types of numbers, variable names, arithmetic expressions, words, and statements. Each set of these elements has its own specific set of rules that must be observed if meaningful results are to be forthcoming from the program's operation.

Numbers

There are three major modes or forms of numbers used in the FORTRAN IV language. These are composed of two basic types of numbers which are classified as counting, integer, or fixed-point numbers and as measuring, real, or floating-point numbers which may be expressed in either single-precision or double-precision as the mode of operation in a given FORTRAN statement.

Integer Mode. The integer mode indicates that the numbers used will always be whole numbers (integers) and *must not be* written with a decimal point or embedded commas. The size maximum and minimum range for integer numbers is $+2147483647$ to -2147483648 (10 digits). The I specification (described later under statements) is used for both input and output formats in integer mode.

Valid Integer Numbers	Invalid Integer Numbers	
0000	0.0	(decimal point)
6	12,467	(embedded comma)
–786	3465294682	(too large)
1764986274	–4321968475	(too small)

Real Mode (Single-Precision Numbers). The real mode indicates that the numbers used may be either whole numbers or decimal fractions and *must be* written with a decimal point. Single-precision real mode numbers may be up to seven significant digits in length. If the value is written without an exponent, the F specification is used in formats.

If the value is written to be followed by the exponent E, it must be followed, in turn, by a single or unsigned one- or two-digit integer constant. The maximum range of this exponent, however, is from approximately 10^{-75} to 10^{75} (actually 16^{-63} through 16^{63}). Single-precision real values written with an exponent utilize the E specification in formats.

Valid S. P. Real Numbers		Invalid S. P. Real Numbers	
+.0		0	(no decimal point)
898.9898		–1,357.2	(embedded comma)
–9.898989		3457.6491	(over seven digits)
45.7E+0	$[45.7 \times 10^0 = 45.7]$	123.E	(no integer after E)
4.5E–2	$[4.5 \times 10^{-2} = .045]$	19.E–87	(value exceeds 16^{-63})
4.5E2	$[4.5 \times 10^2 = 450.]$	492.E.8	(decimal in exponent)
472.E–03	$[472. \times 10^{-3} = .472]$	3714.1E+678	(three-digit integer)

Double-Precision Real Mode. The double-precision mode permits a real number to have its maximum range extended to provide up to 16 digits. Numbers with 1 to 7 digits must be followed by a D exponent, however, those entered with 8 to 16 digits will be automatically handled as valid double precision as the D exponent is optional with this number of digits. The magnitude of the range of double precision numbers is still 16^{-63} through 16^{63} as was in the case of single precision real numbers.

Valid Double Precision Real Numbers

4562396472.698476	[4562396472.698476]
4562396472.698476D–7	[456.2396472698476]
–563.87693D4	[–5638769.3]
47.93D+2	[4793.]
4.79D–3	[.00479]

Invalid Double Precision Real Numbers

574.9D	(no exponent value)
78.5E3	(needs D exponent)
4,567.2D2	(embedded comma)
468.42D91	(value exceeds 16^{63})
9.8D1.2	(decimal in exponent)

In FORTRAN IV, some models of equipment (IBM System/370 for example) permit a mixing of the modes of operation explained above. This is not recommended, however, even on these models, as an assigned hierarchical pattern of operations may alter the results desired under certain sequences of assignments. A good habit to acquire is to always use the same mode in a given arithmetic statement. The hierarchy assigned to the modes is:

1. If all operands are integers the results will be expressed as an integer.
2. If at least one of the operands is a single precision real number and the balance are integers or an integer, the results will be expressed as a single precision real value.
3. If one or more of the operands is (are) a double-precision real number(s)—regardless of the mode(s) of the other operands—the resulting value will be expressed as a double-precision real number.

Another word of caution is to avoid the division of one integer number by another, as the answer will also be an integer and any remainder will be truncated cut off and lost (not rounded). Thus, 15 ÷ 4 will provide a resulting answer of 3 and not 4 or 3.75.

Constants. Numbers which are used in computations that do not change from one execution of the program to another are called *constants*. The form of these constants is always numerical, but they may be either whole or fractional numbers. Examples of both integer and real number constants are:

Integer Number Constants	*Real Number Constants*	
12	12.	
–1	–1.	
2012	20.12	
–256	6.95E+5	[6.95 × 10^5]
674	6.9E–5	[6.9 × 10^{-5}]

Variable Names

Symbolic labels assigned by the programmer to identify quantities or assume a value within the program (other than statement words described below) are termed *variables* or *names*. These must always be defined in the program before the variable name is used in calculating arithmetic statements or control statements (described later). This definition may be by the assignment of a value to the variable in a read statement or by setting the variable equal to some other known variables or values in an arithmetic statement. Such a name may be a single alphabetic character or contain up to six alphabetic or a combination of six alphabetic and numeric characters as long as the first character is alphabetic. No special characters are permitted.

In the integer mode, an expression which is to represent an item which is variable in the proposed program *must always* begin with either I, J, K, L, M, or N. In the real mode of operation (both single and double precision), the expression representing a variable name *must always* begin with the letters A through H or O through Z. Examples of integer and real number variables are:

Integer Variables	*Real Variables*
K9	HØUR
MANNØ	RATE
I	TIME
JØB	SALARY
NUMBER	B4

An exception to this rule is possible when an explicit FORTRAN statement defines a given variable as being an INTEGER, REAL, or DOUBLE PRECISION number. Examples would be:

```
INTEGER HØUR, RATE, TIME
REAL JØB
DØUBLE PRECISIØN MAN, JØB
```

Variables may also be subscripted in the common notation form A_i to provide a subindex to a series of variables named A. In FORTRAN language, this simple form of single subscripting is expressed as $A(I)$. For example, if an array is a list of numbers 3, 5, 9, 7, 6 and the name assigned to this array is LIST, then the third item of the array would be LIST(3), which would have a value of 9.

Variable names may also assume a subscripted form when they are used in the representation of arrays of either 1, 2, or 3 dimensions. If a two-dimensional matrix of values, or a table named MTBL, was in the form:

	Col. 1	Col. 2	Col. 3
Row 1	3	5	9
Row 2	7	6	4
Row 3	10	2	7

then the item in row 2, column 1 would be MTBL(2,1) and its value would be 7. Similarly, a given position in a three-dimensional array N might be subscripted N (1,3,1) and represent some given value assigned to this position of the array.

Arithmetic or Operational Expressions

Any valid series of constants, variables, and mathematical functions which are connected by arithmetic or operational symbols form an expression. Arithmetic expressions involve the use of FORTRAN arithmetic symbols which are:

$$+ \quad \text{addition}$$
$$- \quad \text{subtraction}$$
$$* \quad \text{multiplication } (\times)$$
$$/ \quad \text{division } (\div)$$
$$** \quad \text{exponentiation } (x^y)$$

The use of these symbols individually is in the traditional arithmetic sense (same as noted in parenthesis), and typical examples include:

$$X+Y \qquad A/B+C$$
$$A-B \qquad X**Y$$
$$K*J \qquad C*B**A/D$$

There is, however, a specific hierarchial relationship assigned to these symbols in the pattern of the processing to take place, when several of these symbols are used in a given algebraic formula, that must be remembered.

The first operation performed in the compilation of an algebraic formula in the FORTRAN language is to analyze the statement for parentheses. Then the processing sequence is performed as follows:

1. Operations inside parentheses.
2. Exponentiation (as it occurs right to left).
3. Multiplication and division (as it occurs left to right).
4. Addition and subtraction (as it occurs left to right).

The use of parentheses is most important in writing FORTRAN programs. Without the parentheses the statement

$$A/B+C$$

would result in A being divided by B and then the results added to C. This may not be what is desired at all, and the parentheses provide the technique that will permit A to be divided by the sum of $B + C$ as in

$$A/(B+C)$$

An extended example of how the computer would process a complex mathematical statement would be as follows:

$$A=B-(C+D)**E*F+G/(H+I)+J$$

The first step, as noted above, would be to analyze the statement for parentheses; then $(C+D)$ would be processed to produce a sum X (called X, and so forth, for convenience in explanation) and $(H+I)$ to produce a second sum Y, X would be exponentiated to the power E and the product would be multiplied by F to produce Z. G would be divided by Y to produce W. Now that all operations excepting addition and subtraction are performed, they will be processed in the order in which they occur, and Z would be subtracted from B, with the remainder added to W and J in turn. The net result of this calculation would then replace the value previously assigned to A.

Words

Labels which distinguish one kind of statement from another are called *words*. A list of the key words in FORTRAN IV, which have a specific purpose and usage, is shown in Figure LS A–4. These key words are all command statements. Many of these which are particularly applicable to business programming will be explained later, in detail, under FORTRAN statements. The student should become familiar with all of these words, however, to avoid using them as variable names in FORTRAN statements.

FIGURE LS A–4. Key Words in Basic FORTRAN IV

ABS	END	IFIX
	ENDFILE	INTEGER
BACKSPACE	EQUIVALENCE	ISIGN
	EXIT	
CALL	EXTERNAL	PAUSE
CØMMØN		
CØNTINUE	FIND	READ
	FLØAT	REAL
DABS	FØRMAT	RETURN
DBLE	FUNCTIØN	REWIND
DEFINE		
DIM	GØ	SIGN
DIMENSIØN	GØ TØ	SNGL
DFLØAT		STØP
DØ	IABS	SUBRØUTINE
DØUBLE PRECISIØN	IDIM	
DSIGN	IF	WRITE

Statements

Along with the arithmetic expressions, statements form the basis of a FORTRAN program. Each statement performs a single aspect of the given problem and serves to direct the manipulation of data by various equipment to produce the desired result(s) of the application program. These statements are classified in several different ways in various FORTRAN texts and manuals; however, our grouping will be arithmetic, input/output, format specification, control, and dimension statements.

Arithmetic Statements. This type of statement involves the use of the arithmetic symbol = as in

$$A = B + C$$

In all FORTRAN statements involving the use of the equal sign, the symbol is used in the sense of "being replaced by" rather than "being equivalent to." In the statement $A = B + C$ it indicates that what was previously stored in A is now replaced by what is stored in both locations B and C after they have been added together. B and C memory locations will remain intact after this statement is processed, but A has been replaced by the total, $B + C$.

Input/Output Statements. As might easily be surmised, statements which instruct the equipment in where to get data for the given application and what to do with the data after they have been manipulated in accordance with the instructions provided by the program are termed input and output statements.

There is quite a variety of I/O statements available in the many versions of FORTRAN, depending on the input equipment available and the form in which the data must be provided to be acceptable to each type of equipment. Punched card readers would require data to be punched in card code form; paper tape readers would only read certain paper tape codes (5, 6, 7 or 8 channel); magnetic tape units would only accept a specific size of magnetic tape (7, 8, 9, or 10 track) and given tape codes (binary, binary coded decimal, EBCDIC, or ASCII), and so forth. Output equipment will also vary with the given installation and might include line printers, punched cards or tape, magnetic disk, drums, tapes, and so forth.

In FORTRAN IV we are only concerned with READ and WRITE as input and output statements. Provision is made in the form of these statements to make them adaptable to reading from and writing onto, respectively, many different types of equipment. The data equipment designations used in illustrations to follow will be a 1 for the card reader, 2 for a card punch, and 3 for an on-line printer. These designations can vary from installation to installation depending on the particular equipment configuration available. If these designations are not applicable to your installation, you will be advised as to the numbers to be used by your instructor.

A typical example of the READ statement is shown as related to card columns as follows:

```
Card Col.  123456789------------------------>
           17 READ (1,10) HØURS, RATE
```

The first five-card columns are reserved for the statement number—if any—and in this illustration, statement 17. The READ statement starts in column 7 and progresses to the right. Enclosed in parentheses and separated by a comma are two integers. The first integer designates the particular reading unit—in this case a card reader—which is to read the data. The second integer refers to a format statement (described later) number 10, which explains the positioning of the data to be read from the data card. The variable names, HØURS and RATE, are the labels assigned to the fields reserved for the data to be read.

Thus, statement 17 is a read statement indicating that the amounts for hours and rate are to be read from a card in a card reader according to a specified format number 10.

It should be noted here and henceforth that any blanks (spaces) embedded within FORTRAN IV statements will be ignored by the processor as if they were not present. In writing these statements, it is good practice not to compress the items too closely, because people as well as machines may have to read the statements and spaces do help provide reading clarity.

Also, in all explanations and illustrations which follow, it will be assumed that card columns 1 through 5 will be reserved for statement numbers (except for comment cards previously explained) and column 6 will be reserved for use as a continuation card designation. Thus, all statements will start in card column 7.

A typical WRITE statement

$$244 \text{ WRITE } (3,12) \text{ HØURS, RATE, AMT}$$

would indicate that statement 244 is a write statement instructing a printer to write out (print) the amounts for hours, rate, and amt (amount) according to the arrangement dictated by the format specification found in statement number 12.

In the output of data on a printer, the first printing position of the format statement is reserved for a carriage control character. Consequently, data may not be printed out on printing position one regardless of whether a carriage control indicator has been provided in the statement or not. The first position must either be skipped (by techniques to be described) or the first printing field must be made larger than the data to be printed. As an example, at least five printing positions would have to be provided for a four-position data field.

Format and Specification Statements. The data to be read into the computer from its input form must have some orderly arrangement. In the case of punched cards, these data would have been assigned to predetermined columnar fields in the input. To be sure that the particular data needed in the given application are read from the card, there is a format statement that specifies how data are to be read.

Inasmuch as in some instances all the data in a card are needed, while in others only certain data are needed (and the balance not used), and that the data characters themselves may be in differing forms such as numbers, letters, and so forth, different types of format specifications are provided to permit the flexibility required.

Format statements by themselves do not cause anything to "happen" in the FORTRAN language in the compilation of instructions in the object program and thus are termed nonexecutable. It is when they are used in conjunction with executable statements that they serve to specify "how" the data are to be transmitted, either to or from the computer. It is in this "how" function that they prescribe the pattern (format) of the data to be read, printed, or punched when used with the executable statements READ or WRITE. The function of the format statement will be made clear as the various forms of such statements are described.

I SPECIFICATION.   The *I specification* is used to read data in integer form and later output data in this same form. Typical FORTRAN statements such as

READ (1,6) L, M, N
6 FØRMAT (I3, I10, I6)

would read data into memory, as from card columns 1 through 19 of a given card containing data, such as 321—456734896748315 as 321, —456734896, and 748315.

When this same data is output under the I specification as in

WRITE (3,7) L, M, N
7 FØRMAT (I10, I14, I10)

the resulting print out would be

bbbbbbb321bbbb-456734896bbbb748315

Spacing in this illustration was obtained by making the print fields larger than the data fields. However, if exact data field sizes are desired then spacing, as above, can also be obtained by the X specification explained below.

F SPECIFICATION.   The *F specification* indicates that the data to be selected is a real number which contains a decimal point. Statements such as

READ (1,30) A, S, W
30 FØRMAT (F8.2, F5.1, F5.0)

would indicate that the data are to be found in the card (Figure LS A–5) in three successive fields. The first field of eight-card columns would contain numerical data or blanks with two decimal places (such as 00462.12 and bb001.20). The second field of five-card columns would contain numerical data or blanks with a single decimal place (b23.4 and 024.0). The third set of data would follow in card columns 14 through 18 and would contain numerical data or blanks in five columns with no decimal place (03574 and 67890). It also should be noted that if the data examples above had not been punched with the decimal point, the computer would still have read the data as if the decimal was present. Frequently, on input, an expressed decimal point will override the specification.

FIGURE LS A–5. FORTRAN Data Cards

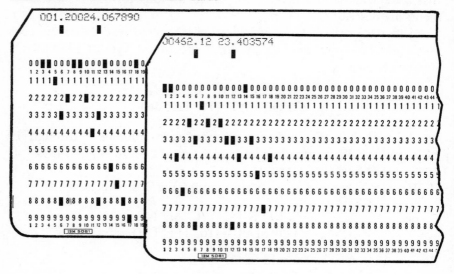

In the output of data using the *F* specification the statements

WRITE (3,12) HØURS, RATE, AMT
12 FØRMAT (F10.1, F8.2, F10.2)

would be printed out for given values of the variables as

bbbbbb40.0bbbb2.75bbbb110.00

If hours were always expressed as whole hours only this data could be expressed as an integer and statement 12 could be a mixture of I and F specifications as

WRITE (3,12) NHØURS, RATE, AMT
12 FØRMAT (I10, F8.2, F10.2)

and would be printed out as

bbbbbbbb40bbbb2.75bbbb110.00

X SPECIFICATION. The *X specification* is used when specific columns of the input card are to be ignored rather than accepting all the consecutive data from card column 1 to some other card column. For instance, data in a card such as 13.4465329674.8 may all be valid data. However, a given application may only be concerned with the first four and last five columns, and it is the X specification which permits the data in columns 5 through 10 to be ignored in a given reading of this card. The format statements to permit this selective reading of data would be

FØRMAT (F4.1, 6X, F5.1)

and the data read would be 13.4 and 674.8 with the six columns of data in between ignored.

The output of the data previously illustrated under the I specification could also utilize the X specification to provide the spacing desired on an output report.

WRITE (3,7) L, M, N
7 FØRMAT (7X, I3, 4X, I10, 4X, I6)

would produce a report as follows

|bbbbbbb321bbbb-456734896bbbb748315

which is identical to that produced by the previously used

7 FØRMAT (I10, I14, I10)

T SPECIFICATION. Another format code used to permit skipping over data to be read as input or to skip spaces in printing data out, is the T (tab or transfer) *specification*. Using the X specification illustration, above, in which a four-column field containing 13.4 is found in columns 1 through 4 and a five-column field containing 674.8 is found in columns 11 through 15, the T specification would be used to ignore columns 5 through 10.

FØRMAT (F4.1, T11, F5.1)

Note that T11 tabs (much as the tabulator bar on the typewriter does) directly to the next column to be read—from 4 to 11—while the X specification illustration skipped 5 through 10. The results are the same, but the technique is different as in T you merely indicate, by number, the first column of a field to be read, while in X you had to compute the spaces to be skipped.

In the output of data, the T specification is equally simple to use as you specify, by number, the first position of each field to be printed as in

WRITE (3,15) JAM, BØX, KAT
15 FØRMAT (T2, I5, T10, F5.2, T20, I7)

where the printed output of the values of the variables JAM, BØX, and KAT are 45678, 35.79, and 1872634 respectively, would be

| Print | 1 | 2 |
| Position | 0 | 0 |

```
b45678bbb35.79bbbbb1872634
```

E AND D SPECIFICATIONS.   The *E specification* is designed to handle single-precision real numbers in utilizing the E exponent, and the *D specification* is designed to handle double-precision real numbers utilizing the D exponent. These exponents are usually used in the input and output of large numbers (usually in scientific and mathematical applications). The scientific notation 3×10^4 (= 30,000) is written in FORTRAN as 3.0E04 or 3.0D04 with the E and D literally meaning "times 10 to the —— power" (in this case the 4th power).

Recall that earlier in this chapter, it was pointed out that real mode numbers not exceeding values ranging from 16^{-63} to 16^{63} could be expressed as exponents. If these numbers were seven digits or less, they could be expressed as either single- or double-precision numbers. However, real numbers of 8 to 16 digits in length could only be expressed as double-precision numbers.

The E (single-precision) and D (double-precision) specifications are provided so that data expressed with an exponent may be read or output in the FORTRAN language. With the exception of the number of digits allowable, however, the rules for the E and D specifications are the same.

Typical card input under the E and D specifications might be provided by

$$\text{READ (1,3) C, T}$$
$$\text{3 FØRMAT (E9.2, D12.3)}$$

which would read data into memory from a card. The letters E and D in the statement refer to the format in E and D notation form. The numbers 9 and 12 refer to the number of card columns to be read for each input data (this length must provide for the sign for a positive or negative number—if such a sign is present, the number or value, a decimal point when present, the E or D notation symbol, the sign of the exponent, and the exponent itself). The decimals .2 and .3 in the statement refer to the number of decimals to be read in the input number. Note that a decimal punched in the data to be read will override this statement decimal indicator.

The values for C and T would be found in a data card starting in column 1, with typical data being —4.56E-0713456.296D08 where the values for C and T would be −4.56E-07 and 13456.296D+08 respectively.

In output form the E and D specifications convert internal numerical data from single- and double-, respectively, precision real form to single- and double-, respectively, precision real form with an exponent. Typical output of stored data would include:

Stored Value	Format Specification	Printed Output
762.9	E12.5	b0.76290Eb03
762.9	D10.1	bbb0.7Db03
−762.9	E11.4	−0.7629Eb03
−3.7	D9.2	−0.37Db01
6.54	E11.4	b0.6540Eb01
.0123	D10.3	b0.123D-01
−.00123	E10.3	−0.123E-02
4567.89	D14.7	b0.4567890Db04
−4567.89	E13.6	−0.456789Eb04
98765.4321	D16.9	b0.987654321Db05

H SPECIFICATION. All of the specifications presented up to this point have been related to skipping data or spaces and to reading or printing numerical data. The *H* (named for Dr. Herman Hollerith) *specification* permits the reading of alphabetic and special characters, as well as numbers, from a program card and printing them out on a report or other form. Though the H specification is not recommended for use on the System/360—as another specification (the literal) is more efficient—this may be the only specification available to do its job on some computer systems.

A program to illustrate the use of the H specification in the preparation of a typical report with headings would be

```
      WRITE (3,6)
    6 FØRMAT (T30, 13HTRIALbBALANCE)
      WRITE (3,7)
    7 FØRMAT (T20,8HACCT.NØ.,T36,8HDR.bAMT.,T45,
      18HCR.bAMT.)          [a continuation card]
    8 READ (1,9) ACCT, DEBIT, CREDIT
    9 FØRMAT (I5, F8.2, F8.2)
      WRITE (3,10) ACCT, DEBIT, CREDIT
   10 FØRMAT (T22, I5, T35, F8.2, T44, F8.2)
      GØ TØ 8
      STØP
      END
```

After the headings are printed out according to format statements 6 and 7, statement 8 would read the data for ACCT, DEBIT, and CREDIT according to format statement 9 from the first 21 columns of each data card fed into the procedure.

The output of the report (for two given data cards) would be:

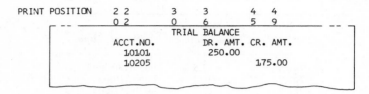

```
PRINT POSITION    2 2        3    3        4    4
                  0 2        0    6        5    9
                         TRIAL BALANCE
               ACCT.NO.           DR. AMT. CR. AMT.
               10101              250.00
               10205                       175.00
```

The GØ TØ 8 statement is a command statement to be explained later, but it instructs the program to return to statement 8 for additional data cards until all have been read. The final two cards instruct the computer the program is completed.

LITERAL SPECIFICATION.   The transfer of literal data, unlike the H specification, can be used both in the reading and printing of data. In reading data from a data card, as in

READ (1,5)
5 FØRMAT (T10, 'AAAAAAAA')

the eight As serve as a dummy name, and other characters—even in combination with blanks—would serve equally as well to read columns 10 through 17 of a data card. The same dummy name in format statement would, however, have to be used in printing this data out as in

WRITE (3,5)

where the data read in columns 10 through 17 would be printed out according to statement 5 in print positions 10 through 17.

The major usage of the literal specification is in reading data from a program (not data) card and printing it out as a report or other heading, and this specification has replaced the H specification in this usage in many computer systems.

Using the two format statements 6 and 7 illustrated under the H specification

6 FØRMAT (T30,13HTRIALbBALANCE)
7 FØRMAT (T20,8HACCT.NØ.,T36,8HDR.bAMT.,T45, 18HCR.bAMT.)

we can compare them with the literal specification which would be

6 FØRMAT (T30,'TRIALbBALANCE')
7 FØRMAT (T20,'ACCT.NØ.',T36,'DR.bAMT.bCR.bAMT.')

The output would be exactly the same for these two sets of format statements but not having to count the letters used makes the literal easier to use and avoids some possibility of error.

/ SPECIFICATION. If, in a report (such as the one illustrating the H specification) it is desired that additional line spacing be provided or if line spacing is desired between the items listed in a given write statement, the / (vertical spacing) *specification* may be used as in

WRITE (3,5) I, J, K
5 FØRMAT (///I4, ////I3, //I6, //)

in producing a report

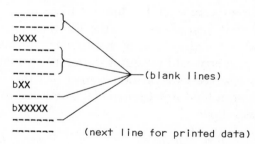

Print Positions 123456789

(blank lines)

(next line for printed data)

The three slash marks at the beginning of the format statement would cause the platen to rotate three positions or lines to provide two blank lines (note, the number of blank lines is one less than the number of slash marks) before printing the value of I. The four slash marks before I3 would cause three lines to be skipped between the values printed for I and J. The two slash marks before I6 would cause one blank line (double spacing) between the values for J and K. The remaining two slash marks would provide one blank line between the value of K and any data following to be printed out. Note that commas do not follow the slash marks.

If the statement is a punching statement

WRITE (2,6) I, J, K
6 FØRMAT (///I4, //I5, I4/)
[Cards affected 123 4 45 6   667]

the first three cards will be ejected without data. I (a four-digit integer) will be punched in columns 1 through 4 of card 4. The next two slashes will eject cards 4 and 5 and the five-digit integer for J and the four-digit integer for K will be punched into columns 1 through 9 of card 6. The last slash will eject card 6, and the final parenthesis will eject card 7.

The / specification may also be used to select specific cards of a data deck for input into the program for data. Statements

```
      READ (1,7) I,  J, K
    7 FØRMAT (///I4, //I3,  I6,/)
[Cards affected    123 4  45 6    6 6]
```

would read the following cards of a data deck. The first three slash marks would eject the first three data cards. Card 4 would be read for I. Cards 4 and 5 will be ejected by the two slash marks. Data for J and K will be read from columns 1 through 9 in card 6 and card 6 will be ejected.

CARRIAGE CONTROL SPACING.   Skipping lines by use of the / specification serves very well for limited form movement, but the use of multiple slash marks—even in the illustrations above—becomes awkward and, at times, confusing. Remember, previously it was mentioned that the printer would not print in the first print position, as this position was reserved as a carriage control whether or not such a control was present in the format statement. These controls are four in number and are as follows

First Instruction in the Statement	*Paper Advances (before printing)*
'b' (blank)	one line
'0'	two lines
'1'	to 1st line next page
'+'	no advance

Thus, following a WRITE statement, the format statement

16 FØRMAT (' ',I6)

would cause the paper-feed control to advance one line and print up to a five-digit integer (remember no printing in column 1). Technically the format statement

17 FØRMAT (I6)

would perform the same function if the first position of the six-digit integer is a blank. However, if it is a 0 or 1, the paper would advance two lines or to the next page, respectively, and in no instance would the first position of the six-digit integer be printed out. Care must be taken to avoid unwanted paper movement and the loss of printed information.

FORMAT PARENTHESES.   As has been illustrated, starting and closing parentheses are required to delineate the beginning and ending of each format statement. Additional pairs of parentheses may be utilized within the format statement to permit repetition of individual or groups of specifications.

WRITE (3,3) L, M
3 FØRMAT (T2, 2(I6))

would tab to the second print position and then print out two sets (the number depending on the integer before the second set of parentheses) of up to six integers. This avoids having to rewrite and repunch a second or more I6 format.

This technique may also be utilized within a group of format specifications as in

WRITE (3,4) X, J, L, M, N, A, B, C, D
4 FØRMAT (T2, F7.1, 4(I4), F3.2, 3(F6.3))

or in any other combination desired as long as the parentheses are in pairs.

It should also be mentioned that if a series of values called for by the write (or read) statement is larger in number than the format specification calls for, the format statement will be repeated until all demands of the write statement are met. In

WRITE (3,5) A,B,C,D
5 FØRMAT (3X, F4.2)

the output would be

| bbbX.XXbbbX.XXbbbX.XXbbbX.XX |

If this provision is used, care must be taken that the digit size and format specification(s) are sufficient to meet the requirements of the values for the variables.

OTHER SPECIFICATIONS.   Several other format specifications, including A, L, O, and P, are available in more sophisticated and advanced FORTRAN language developments. Each of these specifications has its own unique advantages. Some increase the capability of the language, while others increase the power by making it easier to perform more complex techniques. It is suggested if additional information is desired on these that an in-depth FORTRAN text or manual be consulted.

Control Statements. Most FORTRAN statements are performed sequentially in the order they are found in the program. However, in many programs it is necessary to alter this sequence to achieve the desired results. Statements which have this ability to alter the execution sequence of a program are termed control statements.

UNCONDITIONAL GO TO STATEMENT. When it is necessary to shift from the normal sequential execution of the program and it is desired to shift to a specific statement number in the program, the unconditional GO TO statement is used as in

$$\cdot \ \cdot \ \cdot$$
$$\cdot \ \cdot \ \cdot$$
$$X = 2$$
$$Y = 4$$
$$G\varnothing \ T\varnothing \ 5$$
$$10 \ X = 3.*Y$$
$$5 \ Y = 4.*X$$
$$\cdot \ \cdot \ \cdot$$
$$\cdot \ \cdot \ \cdot$$

where the GØ TØ 5 statement will shift the program to statement 5, which says Y should be replaced by 4 times X $(4 \times 2 = 8)$. Statement 10 would not be executed at this point in the program. However, it may be a point of entry from some other statement in the program.

COMPUTED GO TO STATEMENT. When it is desired to shift to another point in the program but you don't want to go to a specific statement number, as it depends on the value of some variable as to the exact point to switch to, another form of the GO TO statement is available. This is termed the computed GO TO, as the statement to be switched to depends on the "computed" value of the variable.

In this form of statement

$$G\varnothing \ T\varnothing \ (5, \ 10, \ 2), \ K$$

would indicate that if the value of K was 1, the next statement executed would be 5; if K was 2, the next statement would be 10; and if K was 3, statement 2 would be executed next.

IF STATEMENT. At times it is necessary to change the processing sequence of the program when certain conditions exist. In such an instance, it is necessary to test for the condition(s) which may exist. Thus, the IF statement makes a decision-making type of control available, as in a test to determine if the gross pay of an employee to date has exceeded the $13,200 level, at which point the employer stops deducting for the social security tax.

$$IF \ (GR\emptyset SS - 13,200) \ \ 10, \ 20, \ 30$$

If the gross pay minus $13,200 is negative (less than zero), statement 10 would be the next statement executed, and social security taxes would be calculated on the current pay amount. If the answer is exactly zero, then statement 20 would be executed next, and only the amount of current pay necessary to bring the gross up to $13,200 would be used in the social security tax calculation. If the answer to GROSS − $13,200 was positive, then statement 30 would be executed next, and no deduction would be made for the social security tax.

Another form of the IF statement is available, called the *logical IF statement,* which permits the use of logical expressions in a conditional statement to permit branching to another segment of the program. It is not too applicable to simple business programs and will not be discussed in detail in this text.

DO STATEMENT. One of the most powerful statements available in the FORTRAN language is the DO statement. In many programs it is necessary that a series of instructions be repeated for a given number of times with some subscripted variable (as in A_2) being modified each time the instruction is performed. A form of repeating instructions is possible using the IF statement in conjunction with other statements as in

```
      . . .
      . . .
      . . .
   10 J = 0
   20 J = J + 1
   25 ACR (J) = ACR (J) − PMT (J)
   30 IF (200 − J) 40, 40, 20
   40 . . .
      . . .
      . . .
```

in which a list of 200 accounts receivables is updated by deducting payments made on account. In the looping procedure to be followed, it is desired that each account (1 through 200) be updated for any payments to that account. J is first assigned account number 1 in statement 20, and statement 25 proceeds to update account 1. Statement

30 says 200 — J is greater than zero, so return to 20 where J becomes 2, and this account is updated. This looping continues until 200 — J = 0, at which time the program moves on to statement 40.

The looping procedure above required a minimum of three statements (10, 20, and 30) using the IF statement. This same procedure can be performed in a single statement using a DO statement as in

. . .

. . .

. . .

30 DØ 40 J = 1, 200
40 ACR (J) = ACR (J) — PMT (J)
50 . . .

. . .

. . .

in which case statement 40 would be performed for all accounts numbered 1 through 200, after which statement 50 would be performed.

If the increment steps in the numbers above had been desired to be 2, statement 30 would have been written

30 DØ 40 J = 1,200, 2

which would have updated only accounts 1, 3, 5, and so forth. Some of the specific rules governing the use of DO statements are as follows:

1. In some instances multiple looping is desired, and DO statements may be placed within other DO statements. However, each inner DO loop must be within the range of the outer loop.

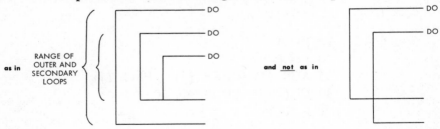

2. Transfers to statements out of the range of a DO loop are permitted, but it is never possible to return to the loop from outside that specified range.
3. When a DO statement is completed and passes control in a normal manner to the next statement, the index, the variable—J in the above illustration—may not necessarily continue to contain the last value assigned to it, and to reuse J it must be reassigned a value.

If transfer is out of the range, the value then assigned to J remains. The value of J also remains in the case of an inner loop procedure which is still within the range of a larger loop.

4. No statement within a loop may redefine the value assigned to the index of that loop. In the illustration the J of DØ 40 J = 1,200 may not be changed until after the loop is completed and the instructions which follow move beyond its range: statement 40.

5. The last statement in the range of a DO statement must be an executable statement. Statements such as DIMENSIØN and FØR-MAT and other information statements could not be used as a last statement.

CONTINUE STATEMENT.   The *CONTINUE statement* is not a control statement and causes no action when the object program is executed. It is included at this point, however, as it ratifies one of the rules of the DO statement that the last statement in the range of a DO must not be one that causes a transfer of control. A return to the DO is not possible, except to start at the beginning, when such a transfer is made. The CONTINUE statement may also be used to provide a transfer statement for an IF statement following the completion of a DO loop or following a FORMAT statement. An example of a CONTINUE statement would be

```
        . . .
        . . .
        . . .
30 DØ 60 J = 1, 200
40 ACR(J) = ACR(J) − PMT(J)
50 IF (ACR(J)) 80,70,60
60 WRITE (3,61) ACR(J)
61 FØRMAT (T20,F10.2)
70 CØNTINUE
80 GØ TØ 100
90 . . .
        . . .
        . . .
```

PAUSE STATEMENT.   When it is desired to temporarily halt the computer during an object program execution the statement

PAUSE

is used. After the reason for the halt has been corrected, the depression of the START key on the computer will cause the program to pick back up at the point it left off.

STOP STATEMENT. When it is desired that the program come to a final halt in its execution, a

STØP

statement is used. After a STOP is used, that run of the program is complete, and any continuation of the program is not possible.

END STATEMENT. The END statement is one of the previously discussed nonexecutable statements. However, it provides a signal to the FORTRAN processor that all the statements for a given program have been translated. Such a statement *is required* to be the last card of a FORTRAN program deck.

Dimension Statements. Just as in the case of FORMAT statements, the DIMENSION statement is a nonexecutable type of statement. The function performed by the DIMENSION statement is to provide the FORTRAN processor program with the information to permit it to allocate locations or positions in the computer's memory for data to be stored.

If only a single subscripted variable is to be stored in memory then a statement

DIMENSIØN RATE (3)

would serve to set aside three positions in memory for a variable named RATE, which might provide the rate per hour data to be used in computing payroll.

In the case of a two-dimensional array or table to store data, the statement

DIMENSIØN TABLE (5,6)

would provide memory storage for five rows of data six-columns wide. An example might be a table listing the number of stores in a region or state.

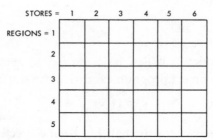

Similarly, variables which have triple subscripts, as in the case of three-dimensional arrays of data, would be described by a statement such as

$$\text{DIMENSIØN ØPR } (3,4,5).$$

Thus "operations" for a given firm might be a group of stores located in several states which in turn were classified into regions each encompassing several states.

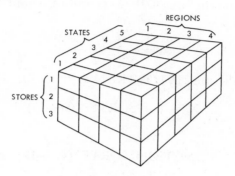

Subprograms

In instances where it is necessary to perform a given set of calculations a number of times in a program or to perform some standard calculations involving arithmetic functions, FORTRAN permits the use of two subprogram techniques.

The Function. First a given set of mathematical functions is available as an integral part of the FORTRAN compiler. These vary somewhat with the compiler but usually include the following:

Type of Function	*FORTRAN Name*
Natural logarithm	LØGF
Trigonometric sine	SINF
Trigonometric cosine	CØSF
Exponential	EXPF
Square root	SQRTF
Arctangent	ATANF
Absolute value	ABSF

Note that function names are always six or less alphabetical or numerical characters in length (no special characters), always start with a letter which must be an X if the value of the function is an integer.

(These restrictions apply specifically to FORTRAN II.) In many instances, programmers with ingenuity have developed additional functions which would follow the basic idea and patterns of those "built-in" functions listed above.

The function subprogram is used when a particular mathematical function cannot be defined as a single arithmetic statement. When such a calculation is performed, only a single value is provided to the main program.

An example of the use of these functions would be in solving an equation such as

$$X = Y + \sqrt{C + D}$$

which would be written in FORTRAN as

$$X = Y + SQRTF \ (C + D)$$

with

$$FUNCTIØN \ SQRTF \ (C + D)$$

being used to perform the calculation after both C and D had been defined.

The Subroutine.   Subroutine subprograms are usually used where one or more programs are part of a single, more comprehensive program or where more than one value has to be provided to the main program. These programs would usually be prewritten and found in a program library and would be predefined as to limits, variables, and so forth, applicable to each subroutine program, or they can be (and commonly are) written by the individual programmer.

To cause an exit from the main program to the given subroutine, the FORTRAN statement CALL would be used as in

$$CALL \ MEAN$$

which would cause the program to switch to the subroutine program named MEAN. This program would then be executed until it reached a statement at the end of the subroutine where the FORTRAN statement

$$RETURN$$

would then cause the main program to be continued at the point where it had transferred to the subroutine MEAN.

Various levels of subroutines may CALL in other subroutines which, in turn, may CALL in other subroutines before returning to the main program.

CASE ILLUSTRATION

FORTRAN Program to Prepare a Daily Cash Report[1]

The following data relate to the daily transactions of the Medina Federal Savings and Loan Association:

RMORT = Receipts on mortgage loans.
RSAV = Receipts on savings accounts.
COUT = Cash paid out.
CHAND = Cash on hand at end of day.
CHECK = Checks on hand at end of day.
FUND = A permanent cash fund amount which is required to begin each day's operation. If this amount is not in the fund, a check must be drawn and cashed to provide this amount.
RECON = A reconciliation to check for cash overage or shortage for the day.
RTOT = Total of fund and receipts.
OTOT = Total of on hand and cash paid out.
REIMB = Reimbursement of fund from cashing check.
DEPOS = Deposit.

Required. FORTRAN program to provide: (1) a reconciliation to determine cash overage or shortage; (2) a breakdown of the amount of cash and checks on hand at the end of the day; (3) a calculation to show any amount needed to reimburse the fund if fund is lower than requirements; and (4) the total amount of cash and checks available for deposit.

Flowchart. The logical flowchart of a procedure which will process the data given in this problem to produce the output required is illustrated in Figure LS A–6.

Description of the Program. The FORTRAN program (Figure LS A–7) to perform the logic of Figure LS A–6 is described as follows:

Line 1. A comment card for the name of the procedure.
Line 2. A comment card showing the person preparing the program.
Line 3. A comment card indicating the language used.

---

[1] Adapted from *A FORTRAN Primer with Business Administration Exercises* C20–1605 (White Plains, N.Y.: International Business Machines Corporation: 1964), pp. 40, 41, 110.

FIGURE LS A–6. Flowchart for Daily Cash Report

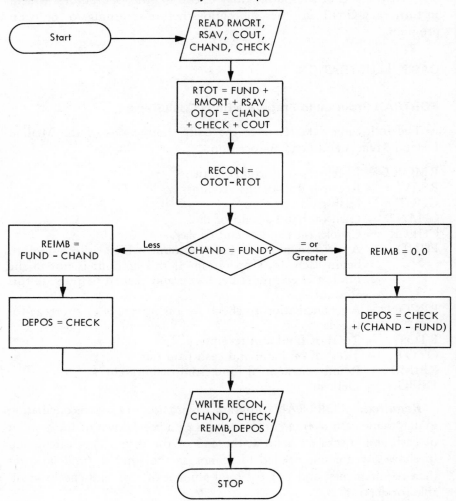

Line 4. Statement numbered 10 indicates that the format of the input card is 5 floating-point numbers, each of which takes up 8 columns on the card. Each of these numbers consists of 5 digits to the left of the decimal point, the decimal point, and 2 digits to the right of the decimal point (5 dollar and 2 cents positions maximum). The first number will be in card columns 1 through 8, the second in columns 9 through 16, and so on through column 40.

FIGURE LS A–7. FORTRAN Program

Line*

```
 1 C    DAILY CASH REPORT
 2 C    C TOM JONES EDP-245-01
 3 C    FORTRAN IV
 4   10 FORMAT(5F8.2)
 5      FUND = 40000.00
 6      READ(1,10)RMORT,RSAV,COUT,CHAND,CHECK
 7      RTOT = FUND + RMORT + RSAV
 8      OTOT = CHAND + CHECK + COUT
 9      RECON = OTOT - RTOT
10      IF(CHAND - FUND) 11,12,12
11   11 REIMB = FUND - CHAND
12      DEPOS = CHECK
13      GO TO 13
14   12 REIMB = 0.0
15      DEPOS = CHECK + (CHAND - FUND)
16   13 WRITE(3,14)RECON
17   14 FORMAT(F10.2,26H  OVERAGE(+) OR SHORTAGE(-))
18      WRITE(3,15),CHAND,CHECK
19   15 FORMAT(F10.2,13H  CASH ON HAND,F10.2,15H  CHECKS ON HAND)
20      WRITE(3,16),REIMB,DEPOS
21   16 FORMAT(F10.2,19H  TO REIMBURSE FUND,F10.2,12H  FOR DEPOSIT)
22      STOP
23      END
```

* The line numbers do not appear in the program or on the cards but are used here for ease of reference in the accompanying description.

Line 5. FUND is defined as $40,000.

Line 6. A READ statement indicating that cards will be provided in the FORMAT of statement 10 (line 4) with data for receipts on mortgage loans, receipts on savings accounts, cash paid out, and cash and checks on hand at the end of the day.

Line 7. RTOT is defined as the sum of the fund, the receipts on mortgage loans, and the receipts on savings accounts.

Line 8. OTOT is the sum of cash and checks on hand and cash paid out.

Line 9. RECON is defined as OTOT (Line 8) less RTOT (Line 7).

Line 10. An IF statement which says that if the cash on hand at the end of the day minus the $40,000 required in the FUND is: (1) less than zero—a negative amount—then the next statement is line 11 or (2) exactly zero or (3) greater than zero then the next statement is line 12.

Line 11. If line 10 was negative, this statement (11) calculates the amount required to reimburse the FUND.

Line 12. The amount to be deposited can only be the checks received if the FUND needs reimbursement in line 11.

Line 13. This is a GO TO statement which says the next program step is to be found in statement 13 which is found later in the program.

Line 14. Statement 12 was to be the next step if the FUND did not need reimbursement, so REIMB is set to 0.0.

Line 15. The amount to be deposited, if the FUND is satisfactory, is the sum of the checks on hand and the cash on hand above the FUND amount.

Line 16. Statement 13 is a WRITE command to print the amount of cash overage or shortage determined by the reconciliation. The format of the printed data is to follow that required by statement 14.

Line 17. Statement 14 indicates the format of some operation (WRITE in line 16) to be a floating-point amount of 10 columns with 2 decimal places followed by 26 positions of alphameric data containing OVERAGE(+) or SHORTAGE(−).

Line 18. A WRITE command which says use format statement 15 to print cash and checks on hand at the end of the day.

Line 19. The format specified by this statement 15 is to be a floating-point number of 10 columns, 2 of which are decimal places, 13 positions of alphameric data containing the words CASH ON HAND, another 10-column (2 decimal places) floating-point number, and 15 positions of alphameric data containing the words CHECKS ON HAND.

Line 20. Another WRITE command which will utilize statement 16 for a format to print data regarding amounts to reimburse the fund and to be deposited in the bank.

Line 21. This format statement is a 10-column floating-point number (2 decimal places) followed by 19 positions of alphameric data, TO REIMBURSE FUND, and a second 10-column floating-point number (2 decimal places) followed by 12 positions of alphameric data, FOR DEPOSIT.

Line 22. STOP indicates a permanent halt.

Line 23. END indicates to the FORTRAN processor that this completes the translation to machine language of the FORTRAN statements in this program.

Typical Output. A set of data which would represent typical output (based on specific given data) of the FORTRAN program illustrated is shown in Figure LS A–8.

FIGURE LS A–8. Daily Cash Report

COMPUTER OUTPUT

```
        -50.00 OVERAGE (+) OR SHORTAGE (-)
     35000.00 CASH ON HAND,   23000.00 CHECKS ON HAND
      5000.00 TO REIMBURSE FUND,   23000.00 FOR DEPOSIT
 STOP
```

QUESTIONS

1. Explain the function performed by a FORTRAN compiler. What are the steps that take place in the compilation and processing procedure for a given problem?

2. Briefly describe the composition of the basic FORTRAN IV alphabet.

3. What are the three major kinds of numbers used in the FORTRAN language? Describe or define these.

4. Name and describe the major elements of the FORTRAN language.

5. List examples of five of each of the following:
    a. Integer constants.
    b. Integer variables.
    c. Single-precision numbers.
    d. Real variables.
    e. Double-precision numbers.

6. Describe what is meant by arrays of 1, 2, or 3 dimensions.

7. What is an arithmetic statement? Describe its use.

8. List the arithmetic or operational expressions used in FORTRAN. Describe their function.

9. Describe the hierarchical assignment of processing steps involving an arithmetic expression containing several or all of the operational expressions.

10. Name and briefly describe the five groups of statements as they are classified in this text.

11. Name and describe the two types of subprograms.

B

COBOL
Programming Language

THERE ARE, of course, a number of different manufacturers of computers, and each manufacturer produces different sizes and models of equipment with differing characteristics and capabilities. This, in turn, has meant that different programming languages were usually more appropriate for certain models or groupings of equipment. The United States government has always been the largest user of computers and computer technology. Inasmuch as the government has always used a wide variety of the computers produced, it quickly became a problem that as departments or agencies outgrew a system the hardware was shifted to another agency needing it. With different models and makes of computers involved, this could require that all the programs of the agency receiving the new computer would have to be rewritten into a different programming language and this always involved a large expenditure of time and scarce funds.

The need to develop a programming language which would be equally applicable to all types of digital computers produced, became essential to the government as time went on. A language which could process vast amounts of data and prepare formatted, commercially oriented reports became a necessity.

This resulted in a proposal by the Department of Defense in 1958 that a committee of manufacturer and user representatives be organized to see what could be done to develop a language which would be compatible with the various makes of equipment. It was as a result of the efforts of this group that the COBOL[1] programming language was

---

[1] COBOL is an acronym for *Common Business Oriented Language*.

devised. Compilers were written for most of the major makes of hardware to translate the COBOL program to a machine language usable by each machine. In this way a COBOL program could be compiled on—for instance—either a IBM System/360 or a Honeywell 200 with only minor variations being required. This capability gave the user of any given computer system much greater flexibility in his or her operations than ever before.

COBOL has some distinct advantages over some other languages which should also be brought out. (1) All instructions are coded using English words and phrases which provide much greater or, at least, more easily understood documentation of the program for an auditor or another programmer other than the writer. (2) COBOL logic can be readily understood by those not familiar with the coded language. (3) The diagnostics generated by a COBOL compiler provides greater ease in debugging programs. (4) Having separate Data and Procedure divisions in the program makes it much easier to modify programs. Otherwise, a modification of a program could necessitate a complete revision of the program.

COBOL

Like the English language, COBOL is built up from its smallest possible units, a set of characters (letters, numbers, punctuation marks, and so on). These characters are used to form meaningful words by following certain rules, just as in English one finds different types of words, such as nouns, verbs, conjunctions, and so on. These types of words are combined, following the rules of grammar, to form expressions, statements, sentences, and paragraphs. Also, as in the English language, the different types of words in the COBOL language are combined, using COBOL's rules of grammar, into statements and sentences.

All computers are constructed so that certain sets of characters are meaningful to their operation. A set of such characters is referred to as a "computer character set." Because of the physical characteristics of each type of computer, the character sets for different types of computers may not be identical. Of course, all programs written in COBOL for a given computer must contain only characters from that machine's character set.

Names

Any language must contain words which stand as symbols for things. In English they are known as "names" or "nouns." COBOL also employs names which the coder uses to refer to things he or she is handling in his or her program. In ordinary language one does not usually have to distinguish consciously between the name of an object and the object itself, but this is very important in COBOL. A programmer must always keep in mind that when he or she gives an item of data a name and then refers to that item by writing the equivalent of its name in the program, he or she is referring to the data, not to the name. Thus, a name can be said to represent the value of the associated data item.

The portion of this supplement which follows will introduce the reader to COBOL. There are many more intricacies to writing a successful COBOL program than are explained here. The object here is only to give the reader a feeling for what the COBOL programming language is about.

There are four general categories of names in COBOL. They are data-names, procedure-names, condition-names, and special-names.

Data-Names.   Data-names are given to the data used in a program. As the reader will see, data-names usually will represent a number of values during the course of a program. For example, if a program is written to compute the payroll for a business firm, the coder might name one item of data MAN-NUMBER. Then, as the payroll is processed, the data-name MAN-NUMBER refers to the man number of the person whose pay is currently being computed.

Procedure-Names.   Procedure-names are assigned to individual portions of a program so that one procedure statement can refer to another by its individual procedure-name.

Condition-Names.   A condition-name is a name which is assigned to denote one of a number of values which may be assumed by an item of data. For example, suppose a dealer in tires identified each of his or her tire sizes in inventory by number. The number of tires on hand for any item of inventory will vary. Therefore, the tire size 850 × 14 will constitute a condition-name whose value will change from time to time.

Special-Names.   Special-names may be used to specify mnemonic names for hardware devices or to give names to console switches.

Rules for Forming Names

In COBOL, names may be formed by combining any of the following characters: the letters A through Z, the numerals 0 through 9, and the interior hyphen. In addition the following rules must be followed:

1. Names must not contain blanks.
2. They may contain from 1 to 30 characters.
3. They may neither begin nor end with a hyphen. However, hyphens may be used freely elsewhere in the name.
4. Data-names, condition-names, and special-names must contain at least one alphabetic character. Procedure-names may consist exclusively of numerals if the coder so desires.

Constants. The occasion often arises for data to have a fixed value never to be modified in a given program. Such a fixed value which never changes during the execution of a program is called a *constant* or *literal*. For example, suppose a program were written to handle the sales of a wholesale house. Assume that for certain types of items, a 10 percent tax must always be added. Since this value of 10 percent never varies, it would be convenient to be able to write it directly at the time the program is written, rather than having to enter it as data every time a sale of this type of item is made.

Program Divisions

A COBOL program is made up of four divisions, the Identification Division, the Environment Division, the Data Division, and the Procedure Division.

Identification Division. This division is used to identify or label the program and to provide any other such pertinent information required. This division may run from one to seven paragraphs long. Each paragraph can be identified in the following manner:

Program-ID—Program-name.
Author—Author-name.
Installation—Any sentence or group of sentences.
Data-written—Any sentence or group of sentences.
Data-compiled—Any sentence or group of sentences.
Security—Any sentence or group of sentences.
Remarks—Any sentence or group of sentences.

Only the Program-ID paragraph is required, and it must appear in the first paragraph of the program. The use of the other identification paragraphs is optional. The program-name should be used in referring to the source program, the object program, and all associated documentation.

Environment Division. This division is organized into two main sections—the CONFIGURATION SECTION and the INPUT-OUTPUT SECTION. The names of each of these main sections are fixed and must always be given at the beginning of their respective sections. The names of the paragraphs following each section are also fixed, and their names must also be given at the beginning of any paragraph used.

The portion of the structure of the ENVIRONMENT DIVISION which is required is shown below. Note the periods at the end of the division statements, the section statements, and the paragraph headings. It is important that these always be there.

```
ENVIRONMENT DIVISION.
    CONFIGURATION SECTION.
        SOURCE-COMPUTER. Computer name.
        OBJECT-COMPUTER. Computer name.
    INPUT-OUTPUT SECTION.
        FILE-CONTROL. SELECT_____ ASSIGN_____
```

The ENVIRONMENT DIVISION describes the equipment which will be used when the program is run. The computer upon which the program was written is described as the SOURCE-COMPUTER in the CONFIGURATION SECTION while the computer which will execute the object program (compiled program) is known as the OBJECT-COMPUTER in the same section.

The required portion of the INPUT-OUTPUT SECTION consists of the FILE-CONTROL paragraph which identifies and describes the files—usually at the least an input file and an output file. Most procedures call for reading data from one of several files, processing them, and writing them in one or more new files. For example:

```
FILE-CONTROL.
SELECT READUM ASSIGN TO CARD READER.
SELECT WRITUM ASSIGN TO LINE PRINTER.
```

The words SELECT and ASSIGN are required words in the format. The names READUM and WRITUM are names invented by the coder and given to the input and output files.

The ENVIRONMENT DIVISION is the portion of a COBOL program that would necessarily be changed when moving the program from one computer to another.

Data Division. The purpose of the DATA DIVISION is to describe the characteristics of the information to be processed by the object program. For example:

1. The input file(s), data records, and data items must be each assigned a specific name and then described.
2. The output file(s), data records, and data items must each be assigned a specific name and then described.
3. Any other data items stored must also be assigned a specific name and described.

The DATA DIVISION may be composed of three sections. These are:

         FILE SECTION.
         WORKING-STORAGE SECTION.
         CONSTANT SECTION.

If either of the last two sections are not required in the particular program being written, they may be omitted. The only required section is the FILE SECTION.

FILE SECTION. Files of data are always involved when dealing with business problems. In the illustration previously used of the FILE-CONTROL section, READUM constituted one file while WRITUM constituted the other. All files must have names. Any names are suitable as long as they conform to the COBOL rules for writing names.

Descriptions of the files to be used will follow the FILE SECTION heading and will be indented on the program worksheet and will be preceded by FD (File Description). The File Description will include a name for the file, such as described above; a description of the size of each individual record in the file; that is, if a standard punched card was being used it would be RECORD CONTAINS 80 CHARACTERS. If the file record is punched card or paper tape, the statement would read LABEL RECORDS ARE OMITTED. If the file record was on magnetic tape, the statement would read LABEL RECORDS ARE STANDARD. This is done because it is desirable for control purposes to place a label or name at the beginning of each program recorded on magnetic tape.

On a program work sheet, the description of the READUM FILE would be as follows:

         FD READUM
             DATA RECORD IS CARD-IN
             RECORD CONTAINS 80 CHARACTERS
             LABEL RECORDS ARE OMITTED.

The nature of the data on each record, described as CARD-IN in the previous example, must be carefully described. The computer needs to know the name of the items; whether the item will consist of numbers, letters, or a combination of numbers and letters; and the number of characters represented by the item.

Since a description of the CARD-IN record would be a subsection of the description of the READUM   FILE, the identification of the CARD-IN file is preceded by 01, while its description is preceded by 02.

```
01    CARD-IN.
      02   THIS-WEEKS-PAY PICTURE 9999.
      02   FILLER PICTURE X.
      02   WITHHOLDING PICTURE 999.
      02   FILLER PICTURE (72).
```

Note the position of the periods, once again, at the end of each sequence of information in regards to a specific item. They are essential to communicate with the computer.

A picture clause specifies a detailed description of an elementary item. The information following the word PICTURE is more fully described in the discussion of picture clauses. The word PICTURE is required in the format. The word FILLER is used to identify an un-used field or item, (in COBOL terminology) which is part of a larger group but which will not be necessary to be moved. The item will never be used individually, and therefore it does not need a distinctive name.

The following characters are typical of those which may appear in a picture clause:

Character   Meaning and Use

9   A 9 indicates that the character position will always contain a numeric character.

V   A V indicates the position of an assumed decimal point. Since a numeric item cannot contain any character other than numerals and an operational sign, the actual decimal point cannot appear. Therefore, an assumed decimal point is used to provide the processor with the information concerning the alignment of items involved in computation.

S   The character S is equivalent in meaning and use to the sign clause, it indicates the presence of an operational sign.

If used, it must always be written as the left-most character of the picture.

A   The character A, when used in a picture, indicates that the character position will always contain either a letter or a space.

X   The character X, when appearing in a picture, indicates that the character position may contain any character in the computer's character set.

Z   The character Z specifies zero suppression of the indicated characters. Zero suppression is the process of replacing unwanted zeros, to the left of significant digits, by blanks so they will not be printed.

$ The single dollar sign, like the S character above, is placed in the left-most position of a picture, and specifies that a dollar sign character is to be placed in that position in the data. The use of several $ signs at the left of a picture provides a floating $ symbol which will appear to the left of the first significant digit.

This character represents an actual decimal point. When used to describe a character position:
1. The data being edited is aligned by decimal point.
2. An actual decimal point will appear in the indicated character position.

Following is an example of how different pictures might look utilizing the symbols just given:

If Picture Is:	And the Characters in the Item Are:	Then the Item Will Be Used in Procedures As:	And Its Class Will Be:
99999	12345	12345	NUMERIC
999V99	12345	123.45	NUMERIC
S999V99	–12345	–123.45	NUMERIC
XXXXX	123AB	123AB	ALPHANUMERIC
AAAAA	ABCDE	ABCDE	ALPHABETIC
999X99	123.45	123.45	ALPHANUMERIC
999XX	123AB	123AB	ALPHANUMERIC

WORKING-STORAGE SECTION. The WORKING-STORAGE SECTION is used to describe areas of storage where intermediate results and other items are stored temporarily. If it is desired to have the computer print out information from what has been in storage, the format for the print-out must be indicated in this section in the same way the CARD-IN record was described. The same is true when it is necessary to update files. They must be brought into WORKING-STORAGE. The records which are to be retained in storage must also be described in the same way. Each record description entry begins with the level number of 01, except for those items which are "orphans"—that is not part of any group or not directly related data items in a group. Those items are given a level of 77 and must precede any 01 level items.

In order to update a file, the data must be brought into WORKING-STORAGE. Whenever information is moved from one location in memory to another, something is done with the information so that when it arrives in the new memory location it looks different from the way it looked before. This is editing. Pictures which cause editing can be used in record descriptions, for output files, and working-storage files.

CONSTANT SECTION.   This section is used to describe constants which will be used in the PROCEDURE DIVISION. It always begins with a CONSTANT SECTION heading.

In a payroll situation, the CONSTANT SECTION would probably contain the following tax withholding information because the associated constant rates would apply to all employees.

77   SOC-SEC-PERCENT PICTURE V9999, VALUE IS .0585.
77   STATE-UNEMP-PERCENT PICTURE V999, VALUE IS .027.

Procedure Division.   The first three sections of a COBOL program, the equipment, or the data, which are going to be used in a DIVISION, and the DATA DIVISION—are all describing the program, the equipment, or the data, which are going to be used in a particular program. It is not until one gets to the PROCEDURE DIVISION that one actually develops procedures. The output of this division is what creates a program which will direct the activities of a computer.

In this division the programmer specifies what he or she wants to do with the data described in the DATA DIVISION. His or her ideas are expressed in terms of meaningful English words, sentences, and paragraphs. Every COBOL sentence must end with a period. The programmer will naturally require the use of some action verbs. COBOL verbs form the basis for the writing of the PROCEDURE DIVISION of a source program. These verbs fall into two main categories—program verbs and processor verbs. The former denotes the data processing steps the object program is to perform, while the latter directs the processor.

The COBOL verbs are listed below:

	Program Verbs	Processor Verbs
Input-Output	OPEN READ WRITE CLOSE ACCEPT DISPLAY	ENTER EXIT NOTE
Data Manipulation	MOVE EXAMINE	
Arithmetic	ADD SUBTRACT MULTIPLY DIVIDE COMPUTE	
Decision-Making	IF	
Sequence Control	GO TO ALTER PERFORM STOP	

INPUT-OUTPUT VERBS. The verb OPEN is used to initiate the processing of one or more input and/or output files. At least one of the two optional clauses (input or output) must be written. An open statement can name just one file or it can name all of the files to be processed by the program. In other words, the coder can open all the files at one time, if desired, or he or she can open one or more at a time according to the requirements of the program. In any case, an open statement must be executed for a given file before a *read* or *write* statement pertaining to that file can be executed. Some examples of the use of the OPEN verb are:

OPEN INPUT BACK-ORDERS.
OPEN OUTPUT STATISTICS.

The function of the READ verb is to get the next record from an input file and make it available for processing.

The WRITE verb is used to release a record for its insertion into an output file. Examples follow:

WRITE INVOICE.
WRITE MASTER-OUT FROM WORK-AREA.
WRITE VOLUME FROM TABLE.

DATA MANIPULATION VERBS.   The movement of data from one place to another within the computer and the inspection of data are implicit in the functioning of several of the COBOL verbs. The two main data manipulation verbs are MOVE and EXAMINE. The MOVE verb has as its primary function the transmission of data from one area to another as in MOVE DATE-IN to DATE-OUT. EXAMINE involves the inspection of data within the computer, with or without movement.

However, other verbs may perform the manipulation function incidental to their main purpose. For example, execution of the COMPUTE verb can involve editing of, as well as movement of, the result.

ARITHMETIC VERBS.   COBOL also provides a verb corresponding to each of the four basic arithmetic operations: ADD, SUBTRACT, MULTIPLY and DIVIDE. A fifth arithmetic verb, COMPUTE, is sometimes provided to permit the programmer to include arithmetic expressions in his or her source program.

Recommended procedure for using add, subtract, multiply and divide. ADD literal TO literal; example: ADD 15 to 20 GIVING M. ADD regular hours TO overtime hours GIVING total weekly hours. SUBTRACT literal FROM literal GIVING B. MULTIPLY literal BY literal GIVING C rounded. DIVIDE literal INTO literal GIVING D rounded.

A *literal* is an actual value which you want to use in your program. It may either be numeric, alphabetic, or alphanumeric. Illustrations of a literal might be add *15* to *20,* with 15 and 20 being the literals. Or, add *0* to *carriage control.*

Arithmetic operations may also be performed by the use of +, −, *, and, /, for addition, subtraction, multiplication, and division respectively.

DECISION-MAKING VERBS.   When a decision is to be made in a program the word IF is used, followed by words containing a test with an indication of what is to be done based on the results of the test. Such a grouping of words is called a "conditional statement." Such a statement has four parts. First comes the word IF followed by a test which gives either "true" or "false." The next parts tell you what to do if the statement is "true" while the last one tells you what to do if it is "false."

> IF BALANCE ON HAND IS LESS THAN 100 GO TO
> REORDER ROUTINE.
> IF BALANCE ON HAND IS MORE THAN 100 GO TO
> NEXT STEP.

SEQUENCE CONTROL VERBS. These verbs are designed to specify the sequence in which the various source program procedures are to be executed. They are: GO TO, ALTER, PERFORM, and STOP. Unless one of these verbs or a decision-making verb is encountered, the statements, sentences, and paragraphs of the PROCEDURE DIVISION of a source program are executed one after another in the order of their appearance. The verbs GO TO and PERFORM are used to interrupt the normal execution sequence and to transfer control to some other point in the program. The other two verbs are supplementary—ALTER provides a means of modifying GO TO statements and STOP is used to halt execution of the program.

PROCESSOR VERBS. Processor verbs are those verbs which only serve to direct the processor in its work. The verb ENTER makes it possible to utilize existing routines already written. These are macro instructions and may or may not be written in another language. To return to the COBOL program the same verb would be used in ENTER COBOL. The verb EXIT is required following a PERFORM which has conditional action in its statement and NOTE is used, as it connotes, to make a note or record for information only.

The independence of the procedure and data divisions leads to a major advantage of COBOL. With rather minor changes a COBOL source program can be compiled for running on any computer for which a COBOL processor exists. The data division does depend somewhat on the object machine to take account of such machine characteristics as variable versus fixed word-length format, the handling of signs, and tape formats. It usually turns out, however, that changing the data division is far less work than rewriting the whole program, and the relative machine independence is in fact achieved.

In order to end the PROCEDURE DIVISION properly, the files which were opened at the beginning of the division must be closed.

> CLOSE READUM.
> CLOSE WRITUM.

Finally, the run must be stopped.

STOP RUN.

Control Cards

In order for a program to be run on a computer, and continuing our assumption that cards are being used as the basis of input to the computer, certain cards known as control cards must be included in specific places within the deck of cards submitted to the computer. Different sets of control card instructions are, however, used with different computer systems and equipment configurations.

As an example, the following would illustrate the required *control cards* and their arrangement in a given program deck to be used in conjunction with the program cards and data cards, for a particular CDC 6400 System installation.

Card 1—Job Card—This card identifies the user of the program, an estimate of the time it will take to run the program, and the amount of core storage the program will occupy in the computer.

Card 2—The person or department which is to be charged for running the program is indicated in coded form.

Card 3—Contains coded information calling a particular compiler from storage into main core memory.

Card 4—Multipunched 7, 8, and 9 (all punched in Column 1). This card serves to separate the instructions from the main body of the program.

The set of COBOL program cards:

Card 5—Multipunched 7, 8, and 9 (all punched in Column 1). This card separates the program deck from the data deck.

The data deck:

Card 6—Multipunched 6, 7, 8, and 9 (all punched in Column 1). This card indicates the end of the program.

COBOL PROGRAMMING ILLUSTRATED

In order for COBOL to be compatible with all makes and models of computers, it is necessary that separate compiler programs be written for each make and model of machine. The significance of these compiler programs was explained in Chapter 13. It should be remembered, however, that every computer has its own unique physical characteristics. The function of these compiler programs is to take a common programming language and cause it to be translated by a particular machine in such a way that the output of this machine will be consistent with the output of all other makes and models of computers.

The writing of a program in COBOL is not as simple as the above statement might make it appear, because all COBOL compilers are not written under the assumption that all COBOL programs are going to be written in the same way. Even in a given organization, there is rarely any attempt made to completely standardize programming techniques. First, the creative ability of programmers would possibly be hampered if strict standards were imposed and second, there is seemingly always a better—faster or more efficient—way of designing a program.

In short, *there is no absolutely correct way to write a program in COBOL.* In a general way, however, one can say that the programs are written in the same way, but when it comes to specifics—these are going to be determined by the way in which the compiler is written.

Payroll Program

This first example of a COBOL program is a complete but simple program which will be illustrative of most of the many points made in the first part of this chapter.

The Problem. Phillip Thompson, certified public accountant, has three employees. The weekly payroll is $850. Assumptions: (1) the employer is responsible for remitting 11.7 percent quarterly to the federal government for federal insurance contributions, 5.85 percent being deducted from employees' salaries and 5.85 percent representing the employer's contribution; (2) the employer is responsible for remitting a total of 2.7 percent quarterly to the state for unemployment and disability insurance, and .5 percent to the federal government; and (3) income tax withholdings amount to $210.

Required. Prepare a program to compute the amount of money Thompson must pay his employees this week.

It should be noted that the program is written on work sheet paper expressly designed for the purpose. (See Figure LS B–1.)

A series of numbers is used to identify each of the steps on the program sheet. The first three numbers of the series, at the top of the first page, indicate the page number, and the second set of three

FIGURE LS B-1. Program Work Sheet

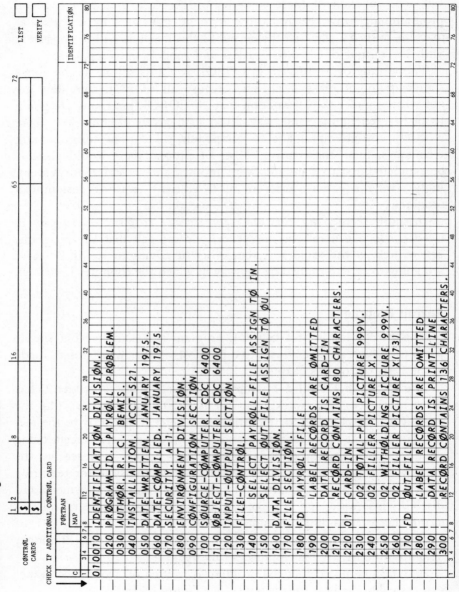

```
010010 IDENTIFICATION DIVISION.
   020 PROGRAM-ID. PAYROLL PROBLEM.
   030 AUTHOR. R. C. BEMIS.
   040 INSTALLATION. ACCT-521.
   050 DATE-WRITTEN. JANUARY 1975.
   060 DATE-COMPILED. JANUARY 1975.
   070 SECURITY. A-1.
   080 ENVIRONMENT DIVISION.
   090 CONFIGURATION SECTION.
   100 SOURCE-COMPUTER. CDC 6400
   110 OBJECT-COMPUTER. CDC 6400
   120 INPUT-OUTPUT SECTION.
   130 FILE-CONTROL.
   140 SELECT PAYROLL-FILE ASSIGN TO IN.
   150 SELECT OUT-FILE ASSIGN TO OU.
   160 DATA DIVISION.
   170 FILE SECTION.
   180 FD PAYROLL-FILE
   190 LABEL RECORDS ARE OMITTED
   200 DATA RECORD IS CARD-IN
   210 RECORD CONTAINS 80 CHARACTERS.
   220 01 CARD-IN.
   230 02 TOTAL-PAY PICTURE 999V.
   240 02 FILLER PICTURE X.
   250 02 WITHHOLDING PICTURE 999V.
   260 02 FILLER PICTURE X(73).
   270 FD OUT-FILE
   280 LABEL RECORDS ARE OMITTED
   290 DATA RECORD IS PRINT-LINE
   300 RECORD CONTAINS 136 CHARACTERS.
```

FIGURE LS B-1. *(continued)*

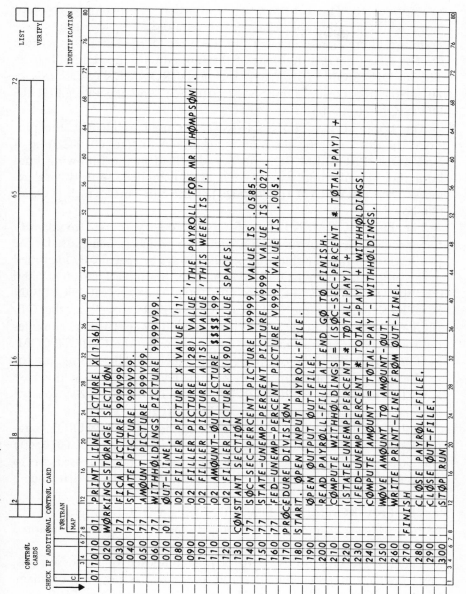

FORTRAN
MAP

```
010   01  PRINT-LINE PICTURE X(136).
020       WORKING-STORAGE SECTION.
030   77  FICA PICTURE 999V99.
040   77  STATE PICTURE 999V99.
050   77  AMOUNT PICTURE 999V99.
060   77  WITHHOLDINGS PICTURE 9999V99.
070   01  OUT-LINE.
080       02 FILLER PICTURE X VALUE '1'.
090       02 FILLER PICTURE A(28) VALUE 'THE PAYROLL FOR MR THOMPSON'.
100       02 FILLER PICTURE A(15) VALUE 'THIS WEEK IS'.
110       02 AMOUNT-OUT PICTURE $$$$.99.
120       02 FILLER PICTURE X(90) VALUE SPACES.
130       CONSTANT SECTION.
140   77  SOC-SEC-PERCENT PICTURE V9999 VALUE IS .0585.
150   77  STATE-UNEMP-PERCENT PICTURE V999, VALUE IS .027.
160   77  FED-UNEMP-PERCENT PICTURE V999, VALUE IS .005.
170       PROCEDURE DIVISION.
180       START. OPEN INPUT PAYROLL-FILE.
190       OPEN OUTPUT OUT-FILE.
200       READ PAYROLL-FILE AT END GO TO FINISH.
210       COMPUTE WITHHOLDINGS = (SOC-SEC-PERCENT * TOTAL-PAY) +
220       (STATE-UNEMP-PERCENT * TOTAL-PAY) +
230       (FED-UNEMP-PERCENT * TOTAL-PAY) + WITHHOLDINGS.
240       COMPUTE AMOUNT = TOTAL-PAY - WITHHOLDINGS.
250       MOVE AMOUNT TO AMOUNT-OUT.
260       WRITE PRINT-LINE FROM OUT-LINE.
270       FINISH.
280       CLOSE PAYROLL-FILE.
290       CLOSE OUT-FILE.
300       STOP RUN.
```

IDENTIFICATION

numbers indicates the line number on that page. Thus the first 010010 represents page 10, line 10. As you will note, the line numbers progress in stages of 10. This is to permit the insertion of other program steps when additions and other changes are required. When writing a program, to differentiate the zero from the letter O, the letter O is written Ø. The four principal divisions of the program are the IDENTIFICATION DIVISION (010010), the ENVIRONMENT DIVISION (010080), the DATA DIVISION (010160), and the PROCEDURE DIVISION (011170).

The IDENTIFICATION DIVISION is used to identify the program. In this case, the program is identified in line (010020) as a PAYROLL PROBLEM. It is further identified in the following lines by author, installation, date written, date compiled, security, and remarks. The PROGRAM-ID (010020) is the only entry which is essential, however.

The ENVIRONMENT DIVISION (010080) is used to identify the specific characteristics of the computer which is being used. The two sections in this division which must always be specifically identified in the program are the CONFIGURATION SECTION (010090) and the INPUT-OUTPUT SECTION (010120). The CONFIGURATION SECTION identifies the SOURCE-COMPUTER as well as the OBJECT-COMPUTER. The SOURCE-COMPUTER (010100), compiles the source program into machine language, while the OBJECT-COMPUTER (010110) is the computer upon which the object program (or machine-language program), will be run. Each computer in this case is a CDC 6400. The INPUT-OUTPUT SECTION (010120) consists of a single paragraph, the FILE CONTROL (010130).

In this problem the two files described in the FILE-CONTROL paragraph are the PAYROLL-FILE and the OUT-FILE, lines (010140) and (010150). They describe where the data to be processed are to come from, and the file where the data are to be placed after being processed.

The ENVIRONMENT DIVISION of a COBOL program is the portion which will normally be changed when the program is adapted from one computer to another.

The DATA DIVISION (010160) is composed of three sections, any of which may be omitted if the program has no need of them. The three sections consist entirely of entries and are the FILE SECTION (010170), the WORKING-STORAGE SECTION (011020), and the CONSTANT SECTION (011130).

The FILE SECTION describes the files which are mentioned in the

FILE-CONTROL section. A file description entry is always preceded by FD. This can be noted on lines (010180) and (010270). It is essential to identify each input and output record or file by a specific name, that is, PAYROLL-FILE (010180) and OUT-FILE (010270), and indicate the number of characters which represent it. Each item of information within a file, that is, CARD-IN (010220), must also be given a name and the number of digits which it will take to represent it. In this case, a description of the PAYROLL-FILE is contained on cards, and they are named CARD-IN. The arrangement of the data on the cards is described on lines (010230) to (010260). Total pay is indicated in the first three columns on the card, there is a space, and then the amounts withheld are contained in the next three columns. The rest of the card is blank.

Where either the input or the output files are not on magnetic tape the statement LABEL RECORDS ARE OMITTED, line (010190), is included.

The WORKING-STORAGE SECTION (011020) is used to describe areas of storage where intermediate results are temporarily stored. In this example, lines (011030 to 011060) describe the number of digits contained in the FICA payments, and the number of digits in the contributions payable to the state, as well as the digits in the net amount of the payroll and the digits in the total amount of income tax withholdings. If there is to be a print-out from WORKING-STORAGE, it must be remembered that in this particular illustration the print-out will be 136 characters wide. The width of the print-out carriage differs according to the make and model of machine.

The CONSTANT SECTION (011130) describes constants which will be used in the PROCEDURE DIVISION. In this case, the FICA contributions as well as the employer's contributions for Unemployment Insurance would be regarded as constants. The rate of tax in both instances would remain the same.

The PROCEDURE DIVISION (011170) develops the coded procedural steps in the program. It specifies what is necessary to be done with the data in the DATA DIVISION. Note the important position of the action verbs in each of the statements. They are START, OPEN, READ, COMPUTE, MOVE, WRITE, CLOSE, and STOP. The statements in this division are expressed in readily understandable terms. The PAYROLL-FILE and the OUT-FILE, both of which were previously described in the FILE SECTION, are opened. The data from the PAYROLL-FILE is read into storage. Necessary calculations are made. The net payroll is then moved to a location in storage called

AMOUNT-OUT. The next instruction is for the computer to print out the amount found in AMOUNT-OUT, following which the two files which have been in use are closed, and the run is STOPPED.

Program to Write Accounts Payable Journal

In this program you are to calculate and write an Accounts Payable Journal. The format of input cards is as follows:

1. Month Card
999	Columns 1–3
MONTH	Columns 4–15
Not used	Columns 16–80
2. Data Cards

Item	Columns
Date (MM/DD/YY)	1–8
Name of Firm Owed	9–39
Purchases	40–46*
Freight	47–51*
Not used	52–80

   * Note: These fields are dollar amounts and therefore have two (2) decimal places denoting cents.

The required printed output should show:

1. Date of purchase
2. Firm items purchased from
3. Purchase price
4. Freight charges (if any exist)
5. Accounts payable (calculated by adding purchase and freight)

As well as the above you should show the total figures for all of the above dollar amount items.

It was mentioned earlier in the text the importance of flowcharting a problem before endeavoring to code it (see Figure LS B–2). You should note that embodied in the flowchart is an assumption as to what the Accounts Payable Journal is to look like.

In reality, the coder must know all of the dimensions of the Accounts Payable Journal before the program can be written. Figure LS B–3 illustrates this point. As soon as this is done, hopefully, the program can be written (Figure LS B–4).

FIGURE LS B–2. Flowchart Preparatory to Writing Coded COBOL Program

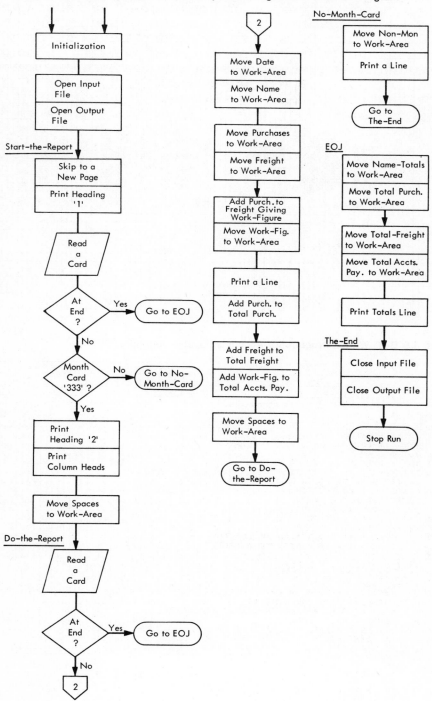

FIGURE LS B–3. Printer Spacing Chart

```
                         SUGAR CANE RACING ENTERPRISES
                         ACCØUNTS PAYABLE FØR NØVEMBER

      DATE      FIRM ØWED                           PURCHASES      FREIGHT     ACCTS. PAYABLE

      1/04/75   HAYS CLUTCHES AND FLYWHEELS         $ 2,837.50   $    89.23   $ 2,926.73
      1/04/75   ED PINK RACING ENGINES             $ 9,485.32   $   275.85   $ 9,761.17
      1/15/75   MØNDELLØ HEADS & HEADERS           $ 1,562.21   $    66.30   $ 1,628.51
      1/16/75   KEITH BLACK RACING EQUIPMENT       $ 2,625.30   $   125.50   $ 2,750.80
      1/17/75   CHET HERBERT,INC.                  $   191.60   $    21.34   $   212.94
      1/22/75   MW ENTERPRISES                     $   225.23   $     0.00   $   225.23
      1/25/75   F & M AUTOMØTIVE                    $   943.20   $     0.00   $   943.20
      1/28/75   SPICKLER AUTØMØTIVE                 $   842.75   $     0.00   $   842.75

                ** TØTALS **                       $18,713.11   $   578.22   $19,291.33
```

FIGURE LS B–4. Written Program for Accounts Payable Journal

COBOL Coding Form

SYSTEM		PUNCHING INSTRUCTIONS	PAGE 1 OF 6
PROGRAM		GRAPHIC	CARD FORM #
PROGRAMMER	DATE	PUNCH	

```
SEQUENCE  C
(Page)(Serial) O A  B          COBOL STATEMENT                          IDENTIFICATION
              N
000001   IDENTIFICATIØN DIVISIØN.
     5   PRØGRAM-ID.  ACCØUNTS-PAYABLE-JØURNAL.
    10   AUTHØR.  WM M GILLHAM.
    15   INSTALLATIØN.  UN ØF CØLØRADØ.
    20   DATE-WRITTEN.  1/11/75.
    25   ENVIRØNMENT DIVISIØN.
    30   CØNFIGURATIØN SECTIØN.
    35   SØURCE-CØMPUTER.  6400.
    40   ØBJECT-CØMPUTER.  6400.
    45   INPUT-ØUTPUT SECTIØN.
    50   FILE-CØNTRØL.
    55      SELECT READUM ASSIGN TØ INPUT.
    60      SELECT WRITUM ASSIGN TØ ØUTPUT.
    65
   100   DATA DIVISIØN.
   110   FILE SECTIØN.
   120   FD  READUM
   130       RECØRD CØNTAINS 80 CHARACTERS
   140       LABEL RECØRDS ARE ØMITTED
   150       DATA RECØRDS ARE MØNTH-CARD,  DATA-CARDS.
   160   01  MØNTH-CARD.
   170       05  TEST-FIELD        PICTURE 999.
   180       05  PRINT-MØNTH       PICTURE X(12).
   190       05  FILLER            PICTURE X(65).
```

FIGURE LS B–4. (*continued*)

COBOL Coding Form

SYSTEM			PUNCHING INSTRUCTIONS		PAGE 2 OF 6
PROGRAM			GRAPHIC		*
PROGRAMMER		DATE	PUNCH	CARD FORM #	

SEQUENCE (Page) (Serial)	CONT	A	B	COBOL STATEMENT	IDENTIFICATION
200	01		DATA-CARDS.		
210		05	DATE-IN	PICTURE X(8).	
220		05	NAME-IN	PICTURE X(31).	
230		05	PURCH-IN	PICTURE 9(5)V99.	
240		05	FRGT-IN	PICTURE 999V99.	
000250		05	FILLER	PICTURE X(29).	
000260	FD	WRITUM			
270		RECORD CONTAINS 136 CHARACTERS			
280		LABEL RECORDS ARE OMITTED			
290		DATA RECORD IS ACCTS-PAY-JRNL.			
300	01	ACCTS-PAY-JRNL	PICTURE X(136).		
400		WORKING-STORAGE SECTION.			
410	77	HEAD-1	PICTURE X(135) VALUE IS '		
420-		'	SUGAR CANE RACING ENTERPRI		
430-		'SES'.			
440	77	HEAD-2	PICTURE X(70) VALUE IS '		
450		'	ACCOUNTS PAYABLE FOR'.		
460	77	LINE-ACCTS-PAY	PICTURE 9(5)V99 VALUE IS ZERO.		
470	77	TOTAL-PURCHASES	PICTURE 9(5)V99 VALUE IS ZERO.		
480	77	TOTAL-FREIGHT	PICTURE 9(4)V99 VALUE IS ZERO.		
490	77	TOTAL-ACCTS-PAY	PICTURE 9(5)V99 VALUE IS ZERO.		
500					
510	77	COLUMN-HEADS	PICTURE X(135) VALUE IS '		
520		' DATE	FIRM OWED	PURCHA	

COBOL Coding Form

SYSTEM			PUNCHING INSTRUCTIONS		PAGE 3 OF 6
PROGRAM			GRAPHIC		*
PROGRAMMER		DATE	PUNCH	CARD FORM #	

SEQUENCE (Page) (Serial)	CONT	A	B	COBOL STATEMENT	IDENTIFICATION
530-			'SES FREIGHT	ACCTS. PAYABLE'.	
540	77	NAME-TOTALS	PICTURE IS X(31) VALUE IS '** TOTALS **'.		
550	77	WORK-FIGURE	PICTURE 9(5)V99 VALUE IS ZERO.		
000560	77	NON-MON	PICTURE X(135) VALUE IS		
			VALUE IS ZERO.		
000700	01	WORK-AREA-OUT.			
710		05	CARRIGE-CONTROL	PICTURE 9.	
720		05	FILLER	PICTURE X(24).	
730		05	DATE-OUT	PICTURE X(8).	
740		05	FILLER	PICTURE XXX.	
750		05	NAME-OUT	PICTURE X(31).	
760		05	FILLER	PICTURE XXX.	
770		05	PURCH-OUT	PICTURE $ZZ,ZZ9.99.	
780		05	FILLER	PICTURE XXX.	
790		05	FREIGHT-OUT	PICTURE $Z,ZZ9.99.	
800		05	FILLER	PICTURE X(7).	
810		05	ACCTS-PAYABLE	PICTURE $ZZ,ZZ9.99.	
820		05	FILLER	PICTURE X(27).	
830	01	BEGIN-HEAD-1 REDEFINES WORK-AREA-OUT.			
840		05	CARIG-CON	PICTURE 9.	
850		05	THE-HEADINGS	PICTURE X(135).	
860	01	BEGIN-HEAD-2 REDEFINES WORK-AREA-OUT.			
870		05	CAR-CONT	PICTURE 9.	
880		05	THE-HEAD-TWO	PICTURE X(70).	

FIGURE LS B–4. (*continued*)

COBOL Coding Form

SYSTEM		PUNCHING INSTRUCTIONS		PAGE 4 OF 6
PROGRAM		GRAPHIC	CARD FORM #	
PROGRAMMER	DATE	PUNCH		

SEQUENCE (Page) (Serial)	CONT	A	B COBOL STATEMENT	IDENTIFICATION
890		05 FILLER	PICTURE X.	
900		05 MØNTH-ØUT	PICTURE X(12).	
000910		05 FILLER	PICTURE X(44).	
002000		PRØCEDURE DIVISIØN.		
2010		BEGIN.		
20		ØPEN INPUT READUM.		
30		ØPEN ØUTPUT WRITUM.		
40		START-THE-REPØRT.		
50		MØVE 1 TØ CARIG-CØN.		
60		WRITE ACCTS-PAY-JRNL FRØM BEGIN-HEAD-1.		
70		MØVE ZERØ TØ CARIG-CØN.		
80		MØVE SPACES TØ THE-HEADINGS.		
90		MØVE HEAD-1 TØ THE-HEADINGS.		
002100		WRITE ACCTS-PAY-JRNL FRØM BEGIN-HEAD-1.		
10		READ READUM AT END GØ TØ EØJ.		
20		IF TEST-FIELD UNEQUAL TØ 999 GØ TØ NØ-MØNTH-CARD.		
30		MØVE SPACES TØ BEGIN-HEAD-2.		
40		MØVE ZERØ TØ CAR-CØNT.		
50		MØVE HEAD-2 TØ THE-HEAD-TWØ.		
60		MØVE PRNT-MØNTH TØ MØNTH ØUT.		
70		WRITE ACCTS-PAY-JRNL FRØM BEGIN-HEAD-2.		
80		MØVE SPACES TØ BEGIN-HEAD-1.		
90		MØVE ZERØ TØ CARIG-CØN.		
002200		MØVE CØLUMN-HEADS TØ THE-HEADINGS		

COBOL Coding Form

SYSTEM		PUNCHING INSTRUCTIONS		PAGE 5 OF 6
PROGRAM		GRAPHIC	CARD FORM #	
PROGRAMMER	DATE	PUNCH		

SEQUENCE (Page) (Serial)	CONT	A	B COBOL STATEMENT	IDENTIFICATION
10		WRITE ACCTS-PAY-JRNL FRØM BEGIN-HEAD-1.		
20		MØVE SPACES TØ WØRK-AREA-ØUT.		
30		DØ-THE-REPØRT.		
40		READ READUM AT END GØ TØ EØJ.		
50		MØVE DATE-IN TØ DATE-ØUT.		
60		MØVE NAME-IN TØ NAME-ØUT.		
70				
80		MØVE PURCH-IN TØ PURCH-ØUT.		
002290		MØVE FRGT-IN TØ FREIGHT-ØUT.		
002300		ADD PURCH-IN TØ FRGT-IN,		
10		GIVING WØRK-FIGURE.		
20		MØVE WØRK-FIGURE TØ ACCTS-PAYABLE.		
30		WRITE ACCTS-PAY-JRNL FRØM WØRK-AREA-ØUT.		
40		ADD PURCH-IN TØ TØTAL-PURCHASES.		
50		ADD FRGT-IN TØ TØTAL-FREIGHT.		
60		ADD WØRK-FIGURE TØ TØTAL-ACCTS-PAY.		
70		MØVE SPACES TØ WØRK-AREA-ØUT.		
80		GØ TØ DØ-THE-REPØRT.		
90		NØ MØNTH-CARD.		
002400		MØVE NØN-MØN TØ THE-HEADINGS.		
10		WRITE ACCTS-PAY-JRNL FRØM BEGIN-HEAD-1.		
20				
30		GØ TØ THE-END.		
40		EØJ.		

FIGURE LS B–4. (concluded)

COBOL Coding Form

SYSTEM		PUNCHING INSTRUCTIONS		PAGE 6 OF 6
PROGRAM		GRAPHIC		
PROGRAMMER	DATE	PUNCH		CARD FORM #

SEQUENCE		COBOL STATEMENT	IDENTIFICATION
50		MØVE NAME-TØTALS TØ NAME-ØUT.	
60		MØVE TØTAL-PURCHASES TØ PURCH-ØUT.	
70		MØVE TØTAL-FREIGHT TØ FREIGHT-ØUT.	
80		MØVE TØTAL-ACCTS-PAY TØ ACCTS-PAYABLE.	
90		WRITE ACCTS-PAY-JRNL FRØM WØRK-AREA-ØUT.	
002500	THE-END.		
10		CLØSE READUM.	
20		CLØSE WRITUM.	
002530		STØP RUN.	

REFERENCES

EDITORS AND STAFF. "COBOL Support Packages—Programming and Productivity Aids." *Data Processing Digest,* July, August, September, October, November 1971, and January, February, March 1972.

QUESTIONS

1. Discuss two advantages which COBOL has over other programming languages.

2. Are there any features to these advantages which would make COBOL particularly useful in a business data processing application?

3. What are the rules for forming a "name" in COBOL?

4. Name the divisions of a COBOL program.

5. What types of information are contained in each of the divisions of a COBOL program?

6. What purpose do the periods have in a COBOL program?

7. Specifically, what is involved in the description of a file in the DATA DIVISION? Why is it necessary to go into such detail?

8. Describe the significance of using the character Z in a picture clause?

9. What purpose does the WORKING-STORAGE SECTION serve?

10. Identify three functions which are performed by program verbs. What is the purpose of each function?

11. Under what circumstances would one use IF verb?

12. What statement must be expected for a given file before a READ or a WRITE statement can be executed?

13. What is the function of the READ verb?

14. Describe a literal. Give an example of one.

15. What must always be included at the end of a PROCEDURE DIVISION?

VI
Appendixes

A

Historical Background of Computing Devices

The recording of business transactions is almost as old as history itself.

Early in the development of man—who alone of all the creatures on earth has been credited with a combination of attributes that permit him to think, reason, apply logic, be inventive, and communicate through words with others of his kind—it became necessary for him to develop some technique which would permit the counting and recording of the transactions of the day.

EARLY MAN AND HIS RECORDS

During the Old Stone Age or Paleolithic period, man's principal concern was survival. This was the earliest and longest period since *Homo sapiens* emerged from his still more primitive ancestors. He was a nomadic hunter and food gatherer, lived in caves or rock shelters, and had only a few rudimentary stone tools. He knew about fire.

In the New Stone Age or Neolithic period, "industrial" development began with the emergence of pottery making, weaving, and carpentry.

As industry and agriculture developed, a need to count also developed. The earliest attempts at counting had been through the use of the first—and basic—"digital" computer—the fingers or toes. The digits, or fingers, were used to count by indicating one finger, two fingers, three, four, or by closing them all into a clenched fist, "many." The use of "many" was not too satisfactory, however, and after some time people switched from fingers (or toes) to pebbles which could be arranged in stacks to keep a record of totals.

These stacks of pebbles also created problems. They could be easily knocked about or "borrowed," and the record they provided would be destroyed. This led to the use, over time of course, of such techniques as marks in wet clay which could be baked or dried to preserve the information, the use of knots tied in fibers, which were the string of the day, and notches cut into sticks.

As limited specialization in production items developed over time, it also brought about the need to develop some common form of value. Often, this was either an item which was in great demand and could be converted to some real (actual) use in addition to serving as a medium of exchange or it was a relatively scarce item—which provided stability to the overall availability of such items. It is the latter type of exchange medium that has become money as we know it today.

EARLY DEVELOPMENTS BY CIVILIZED MAN

The ancient Egyptians discovered and perfected the use of papyrus (the source of our word for paper) to record their business and historical transactions. Their written language was in hieroglyphics, a form of picture writing. In Mesopotamia, Babylonia, Assyria, and Persia, cuneiform writing evolved which consisted of wedge strokes made with a stylus in soft clay or other material. Both of these forms of writing were slow and cumbersome, but they served to write the orders and historical records of the day and to provide records of the tax payments, deeds, leases, and purchase and sale of livestock, and to prepare storage receipts from granaries.

The Phoenicians inhabited the coast of the eastern Mediterranean and by 1250 B.C. were well established as sea traders and merchants. They extended their operations to all the seaports of the then known world. Extensive records were necessary to keep track of their business ventures, and to aid them in this, they developed the forerunner of today's alphabet. (See Figure A–1.) This 21-character alphabet was later extended by the Greeks to the 26 characters found in our modern alphabet.

In approximately 500 A.D., the Hindus began to develop a usable set of numbers. Previous to this, the form of the numbers used was such that it was impossible to perform any of the arithmetic functions so widely used today. This new set of numbers started by using an equivalent of the digits 1 through 9 with a small dot following the

FIGURE A-1. Evolution of the Alphabet

Courtesy of NCR

number to start a second series of numbers (1. for our 10, 2. for our 20, 1.. for our 100 and so forth). This was not too usable, as the dot could be overlooked, and a small circle was later substituted. In time the small circle became the same size as the other numbers and a full-fledged digit along with the others.

The development of the Hindu set of numbers, from which later evolved the Arabic, Spanish, and finally the Italian, number system (see Figure A-2), was a great improvement over the Roman numbers (try adding CVII to LXIV). For the first time, people had a set of numbers that could be manipulated to provide addition, subtraction, multiplication, and division as we know it today.

FIGURE A-2. Evolution of Numbers

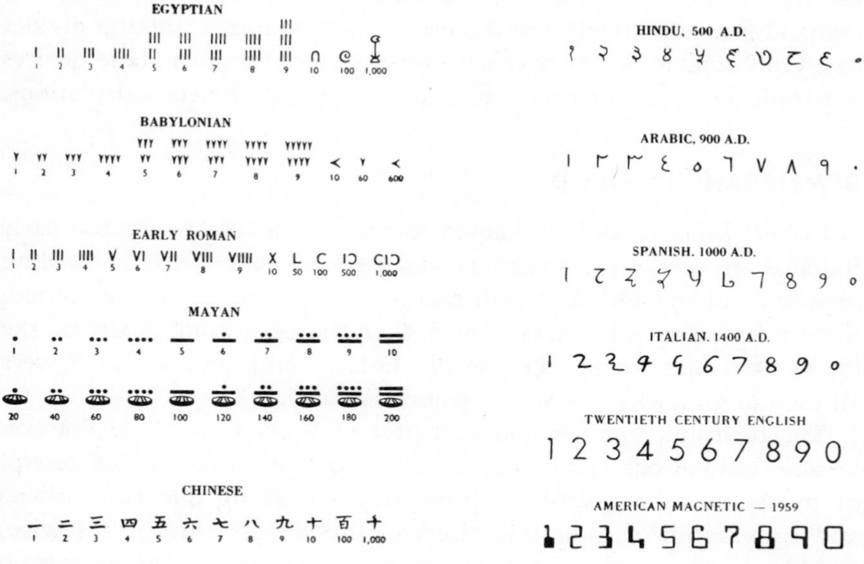

Courtesy of NCR

There appears to be considerable question as to the development of the first real computational machine or device. Various historians have dated the first use of the Chinese suan pan, or *abacus,* from as early as 1000 B.C. to as late as 200 B.C. (See Figure A–3.) Modifica-

FIGURE A–3. Abacus

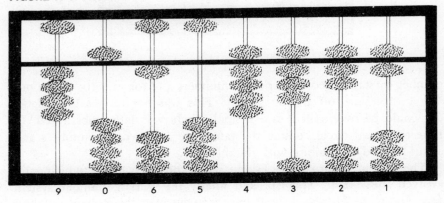

tions or variations of the abacus have been produced in many countries and are known as the *s'choty* in Russia, the *coulba* in Turkey, the *choreb* in Armenia, and the *soroban* in Japan. These variations include the use of one button above and four below the divider bar instead of two and five respectively and the use of nine buttons without a divider bar. Considerable dexterity can be developed by users of these devices to permit the performance of surprisingly rapid arithmetic calculations.

RENAISSANCE PERIOD

Record keeping as it is known today was developed by the early Italians—especially the Venetians and Genoese, who were the leading merchants of the 14th and 15th centuries. In this same general period, these people formed *bancos,* which were the early counterpart of the banks of today. Credit, the use of checks, notes, and so forth were all used in somewhat the same manner as today.

The twofold, dual, or double aspect of every business transaction became recognized. (As examples, every sale meant either the receipt of money or a "receivable" representing something due from others and a giving up of some trade item or the performance of a service; and the purchase of an item meant its receipt as well as its cost in terms of either the payment of money or the incurrence of a debt.) The recording and manipulation of the data resulting from business transactions utilizing this dual effect on the records became known as double-entry bookkeeping.

DEVELOPMENT OF CALCULATORS

Outside the development of the abacus, there was little, if any, attempt to develop mechanical devices to perform the laborious tasks of arithmetic computation until 1617. About this time John Napier, a Scottish mathematician, who earlier in 1614 had devised logarithm tables utilizing the base *e*, developed—just before he died—a device often called Napier's Bones, to perform multiplication problems.

FIGURE A-4. Napier's Bones

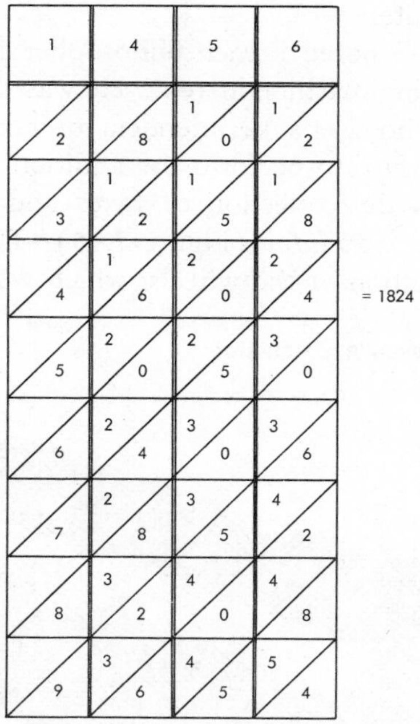

This device consisted of a set of *strips of bone,* each inscribed (Figure A-4) with one of a series of numbers representing progressive sums of that number added to itself eight times. In a given problem such as 4 × 456, one merely arranged the bone strips as shown in the illustration and listed from right to left the sums of the diagonals found in the "4" row. Thus the units position would be 4, the tens position would be $2 + 0 = 2$, the hundreds position $2 + 6 = 8$, and the thousands position a 1, for an answer of 1,824.

If the problem was 10×456 (to which the answer 4,560 is obvious) one could use 5×456 two times and add the answers together $(2,280 + 2,280 = 4,560)$, or use $(3 \times 456) + (3 \times 456) + (4 \times 456) = 1,368 + 1,368 + 1,824 = 4,560$, or any other combination of multipliers to equal the multiplier 10 in our problem.

Using the logarithm tables developed by Napier, William Oughtred, a British mathematician, inscribed *slides of wood* or ivory with relative points—based on the values of the logarithms. The first such device was circular in nature and was developed about 1622. In 1633, he produced a rectilinear device and the slide rule, as it is known today, came into existence. This development is now credited with being the forerunner of the analog computer, which is one of the two distinct families of computers.

Blaise Pascal—a noted French philosopher and scientist—developed the first true adding machine in 1642. He was then 19 and was working for his father, who was superintendent of taxes. He quickly saw the need for some device to perform the addition and subtraction calculations required in the collection of taxes and developed a *numerical wheel and rachet calculator* (Figure A–5). This calculator registered values by the rotation of the wheels, which were in the form of cylin-

FIGURE A–5. Pascal's Calculator

Courtesy of IBM

ders, by steps from 1 through 9, with a lever to perform the "carry" from one wheel to the next when the capacity of the first was exceeded.

About 1666, Sir Samuel Morland of England developed a more compact calculator which could multiply (by using cumulative addition) as well as add and subtract. This was a *stylus-operated* machine which is still advertised under various names today as a low-priced pocket calculator.

In 1694, Gottfried Wilhelm von Leibnitz, German philosopher and mathematician, completed a "stepped reckoner" which he had started in 1671. This machine had the capacity to perform all four basic arithmetical functions (addition, subtraction, multiplication, and division) as well as extract square roots. All these functions, however, were either performed by using simple addition, multiple addition, or reverse addition (subtraction) techniques.

In 1820, Charles Xavier Thomas of Colmar, France, developed a type of mechanical calculator. The major improvement over other models introduced up to this time was in the addition of a crank which would feed data into the machine. This machine, called an "arithmometer," was—in 1878—the first such equipment to be manufactured in a firm established just for this purpose. The founder of this firm was Arthur Burkhardt, a German. Some models of this calculator found their way to the United States and had a strong effect in stimulating developments in this country.

D. D. Parmalee obtained a U.S. patent in 1850 for the first *key-driven adding machine*. This equipment was very limited in its operation as only a single column of data could be added at a time.

Hill, who is sometimes described as being "the father of desk calculators in the United States," developed the first *key-driven four-process* calculating device in 1857.

In the 1870s, two parallel inventions were forthcoming. Frank Stephen Baldwin of the United States in 1872 (patented in 1875) and Willgodt Theophil Adhner of Europe in 1878 developed equipment which improved upon the design of the Leibnitz stepped-cylinder calculator. In each of the pieces of equipment, they used a thin but solid device, rather than a cylinder, to serve as the wheel to be rotated. This was accomplished by adding teeth to the edge of the wheel (much like those of a typical gear). Each tooth was assigned a given value from 1 through 9. This permitted the machine to be much more compact in size, and the idea has been carried forward in the design of most mechanical calculators to the present time. Baldwin's equipment is illustrated in Figure A–6.

FIGURE A–6. Baldwin's Calculator

Courtesy of Monroe

One of the first attempts to combine an *adding and printing device* together to produce a listing of the data was developed by E. D. Barbour in 1873. This was a very rudimentary form of listing machine and was not successful in its application.

In 1884, William Seward Burroughs developed a powerful adding-listing machine. This equipment (Figure A–7) was crank operated and had a *90-key keyboard* to handle a column of figures up to nine decimal digits. It was patented in 1888, and a manufacturing firm was set up to produce it in 1891.

Though not directly related to the calculators but somewhat associated in principle was the cash register (Figure A–8) which was invented in 1879 by James Ritty of Dayton, Ohio. This device was developed commercially in 1884 by the National Cash Register Company which is today one of the leading producers of cash registers, calculators, bookkeeping machines, and computers.

Around 1900, Hubert Hopkins of the United States developed the first practical billing machine utilizing a direct multiplication technique. In 1901 he also built the first adding machine to use *10 keys* instead of the "full-keyboard" set of keys.

Jay R. Monroe and previously mentioned Baldwin worked together to develop the first successful commercial *keyboard rotary calculator* in 1911 and established the Monroe Calculating Machine Company

FIGURE A–7. Burroughs Adding-Listing Machine

Courtesy of Burroughs Corp.

FIGURE A–8. The First and the Newest NCR Cash Register

Courtesy of NCR

in 1912. This firm still exists and is active in the calculator field today under the name of Monroe, a Division of Litton Industries.

Any number of specific brand-name calculators were put on the market from 1900 to 1930. Most of these, however, had characteristics similar to those already described and were essentially improvements in engineering design, appearance, speed, and ease of operation. Many of these were operated by electric motors, but all were mechanical in design.

Several models of punched card calculators were introduced in the late 1930s and 1940s. These will be noted and described in the following historical data on punched card equipment. Most of these were electromechanical in design, but a few others were truly electronic calculators. In the middle and late 1950s, the electronic calculators—which were quite expensive—were generally replaced by smaller electronic computers which, for the same expenditure of funds, could perform many other functions besides that of calculation.

Small desk-sized electronic calculators have been introduced in the immediate past few years by most of the equipment firms. These utilize microminiature integrated circuits to perform the calculations desired in microsecond (millionths of a second) speeds. These miniaturized components replace most of the mechanical parts previously required, and the equipment operates noiselessly. The information produced is displayed electronically and read visually on a small screen above the keyboard (Figure A–9).

FIGURE A–9. Electronic Calculator

Courtesy of Victor Comptometer Corp.

PUNCHED CARD EQUIPMENT

In the period 1725–45, Basile Bouchon, M. Falcon, and Jacques de Vaucanson, all Frenchmen, experimented with and developed textile-weaving equipment which utilized *punched holes* in either paper strips or cardboard to control the weaving of cloth. These were all very rudimentary in design, but they served to stimulate thinking along this line and helped lead to future developments.

Joseph Marie Jacquard, another French inventor, experimented for many years with the use of punched cards to control weaving looms. In 1780, he produced equipment which used an endless belt of punched cards to automatically control the weaving of intricate designs in the production of figured patterns. The development of this equipment and other inventions resulted in his receiving a Gold Medal in 1804 from the Inspectors of Paris.

Though there was a great deal of opposition from the workers to this "automation," his equipment was widely accepted and was used throughout the continent and in England. By 1812, 11,000 of these looms were in use in France alone. Modern models of Jacquard Looms are manufactured and used today in the production of cloth.

There is a story that the Dutch workers were so afraid of "automation"—just as their counterparts are today—that they developed a technique of "accidentally" dropping their wooden shoes (sabots) into the looms to delay production. This is said to be the origination of the word *sabotage* as it is used today.

Data Processing Equipment

In 1872, Charles Seaton, chief clerk of the U.S. Census Bureau, invented a mechanical tabulator which was capable of simultaneously registering both horizontal and vertical sums. This equipment could rapidly process, in sequence, large amounts of data and was used by the bureau in statistical analysis.

Even with the development of this mechanical tabulator, it still required seven and one-half years to compile all the statistical data then deemed necessary for the 1880 census. With the rapid growth in population, it was evident that, unless some new method of calculation was provided, a second census would be taken before they would be able to compile the information on the 1890 census.

Dr. Herman Hollerith, a noted statistician, had been experimenting with new techniques to compile statistical data, among which the use of punched cards was one method to show some promise. The U.S. Census Bureau heard of his experiments and engaged Hollerith as a special agent to aid it in solving its statistical data computation problems. At first, Hollerith punched data into a roll of paper using a ticket punch to punch the necessary holes. The use of paper did not prove satisfactory, so he substituted a 3- × 5-inch card divided into squares approximately ¼ inch in size. These squares were punched with the data, where applicable, from a given census form, thus developing what came to be known as a "unit record" of information. The punching was still performed by hand, using the ticket punch for some time, but eventually a device was developed in which a card was inserted and a key on a keyboard depressed to punch the hole (Figure A–10).

FIGURE A–10. Early Keypunch

Courtesy of IBM

The hole (or holes) in the card was read at first by inserting a different colored card behind it—to make the punched holes more visible to the eye—and it was manually read. Later, the cards were inserted individually into a holder which had small electrically wired cups of mercury below each hole position in the card. A pin-press was lowered that had spring-loaded pins for each hole position, and where holes existed, electrical contact was made and recorded on counters. This contact also opened a hinged box lid, and the card was removed by hand and filed in the compartment by given characteristics found in the card data. Thus, the punch, a manual feed reader, and a sorting box made up the original punched card installation in the Census Bureau. (See Figure A–11.)

An important concept was originated in the design of the punched card that was really not completely grasped until the advent of compu-

FIGURE A–11. Early Punched Card Equipment

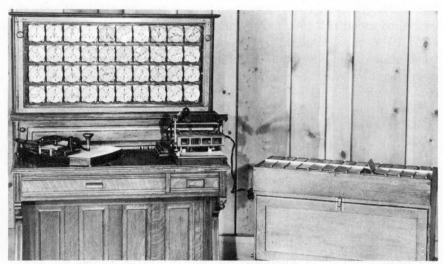

Courtesy of IBM

ters. This is the concept of "state" in which, in a given position in the card, there was either data (the punched hole) or no data (no punched hole) which easily adapted the punched card to the binary (two-position) number system (to be explained later). Also, for the first time, the hole in the card represented *data*—where previously the hole had merely indicated a control device (in the weaving loom)—which was electrically translatable into meaningful information.

This technique of manually punching the data into the card and individually reading each card was slow (50 to 80 cards per minute), but even with a one-fourth increase in population and an expanded statistical compilation, the 1890 census was completed in about two and one-half years time.

To promote the commercial potential of his inventions, Hollerith organized the Tabulating Machine Company in 1896. Several municipalities began using his equipment and this spurred him on to new developments. About 1900 a numerical key punch was developed, and before his retirement in 1914, he produced other equipment, which included an automatic electric-sorting machine which operated at an approximate speed of 300 cards per minute, a lever-set gang punch, and a semiautomatic accumulation tabulator.

In 1903, after some initial commercial success in marketing his equipment, Hollerith and S. N. D. North, director of the Census Bureau, had a disagreement over patents and finances, and Hollerith left the bureau to spend full time in the commercial field.

In 1911, the Tabulating Machine Company was merged with the International Time-Recording Company and the Dayton Scale Company to form the Computing-Tabulating-Recording Company. This company changed its name in 1924 to the International Business Machines Corporation, which is so well known today that it is most commonly referred to as IBM.

Shortly after Hollerith left the Census Bureau, Congress voted the bureau funds to establish an equipment development laboratory. James Powers was then hired by the Bureau in 1905 to develop a new and different set of punched card equipment. As a statistical development engineer, Powers soon proved himself to be well qualified for the position. By the time the 1910 census was ready to be compiled, he had developed a set of improved equipment, all mechanical in design, to punch, sort, and automatically file punched cards. About 300 pieces of equipment were produced in the laboratory for the 1910 census.

Just as Hollerith had in the past, Powers decided that his equipment had commercial possibilities, and he left the Census Bureau in 1911 to establish his own firm. The Powers Accounting Machine Company was organized in the state of Maine in the same year he left the bureau. This firm was merged with Remington Rand Corporation in 1927 and later became a part of the Sperry Rand Corporation.

A companion company of the Powers Accounting Machine Company, the Accounting and Tabulating Machine Company was organized to distribute Powers' equipment overseas through sales agencies.

After World War I, the British agency separated from the parent firm and continued to operate as an independent agency until 1929, when it combined with the French agency, Sociéte Anonyme des Machines à Statistics (Samas), to establish Powers-Samas Accounting Machines, Ltd., which, in turn, merged with the British Tabulating Machine Company in 1958 to establish International Computers and Tabulators, Ltd., now the largest computer firm in England.

Many functionally different machines and improvements were made in the next 30 years to provide a complete line of punched card systems equipment by both successor firms in the United States. Many of these were mentioned earlier in the book and they include card punches, verifiers, sorters, collators, reproducers, accounting machines, calculators, summary punches, statistical machines, and test-scoring machines, to name only the major units produced.

QUESTIONS

1. Why should people have some interest and concern in historical computing devices when we are living in the 20th century?

2. For what purposes were data manipulated and recorded in early Egypt and throughout the Middle East? Explain.

3. Would there be any correlation with your answer to question 2 and what you would find in our present-day environment? Explain.

4. What brought about the development of numbering systems, such as the Roman system? Explain.

5. Briefly, how does the abacus operate?

6. What was the economic environment in Venice and Genoa in 1494 when double-entry bookkeeping was first conceived.

7. Do you feel that your answer to question 6 could in any way explain why the double-entry system was conceived? Explain.

8. Briefly describe three of the early mechanical devices which were developed to perform arithmetic calculations.

9. Why do you suppose there were an increasing number of these inventions throughout the 17th and 18th centuries? What spurred the inventors?

10. Briefly describe some of the ways whereby punched holes in paper or cardboard were used to control machines.

11. Describe the background leading to the development of punched card equipment in the United States.

12. How has the design of punched card equipment changed and improved throughout the years?

B

Glossary of Terms[*]

Access time. The time interval between the instant at which data are called for from a storage device and the instant delivery begins.

Accounting machine. An equipment which reads information from a medium such as cards, paper tape, or magnetic tape and produces lists, tables, and/or totals on separate or continuous paper forms. Often called tabulating equipment or a tabulator.

ALGOL. A contraction of **Alogrithmic Language** or **Alg**orithmic **O**riented **L**anguage.

Algorithmic language. A standardized arithmetic language obtained as a result of international cooperation. Basically, a numerical language for computers, but also a means of communicating numerical procedures to individuals.

Alphameric. A contraction of either alphanumeric or alphabeticnumeric.

Alphanumeric. A contraction of alphabetic-numeric. To include the letters of the alphabet, numbers, and, at times, special characters such as: .,&, #, and so forth.

Application. The system or problem to which a computer is applied.

Application programmer. A programmer who writes programs for the needs of a specific application.

Arithmetic unit. The portion of the hardware of a computer in which arithmetic and logical operations are performed. The arithmetic unit generally consists of an accumulator, some special registers for the

---

[*] This glossary, except for some additions by the authors, is taken from "Automatic Data Processing Glossary," Executive Office of the President, Bureau of the Budget (Washington, D.C.: U.S. Government Printing Office, December 1962). Department of the Navy. ADP Glossary NAVSO P–3097. Supt. of Documents, U.S. Government Printing Office, December 1970.

storage of operands and results, supplemented by shifting and sequencing circuitry for implementing multiplication, division, and other desired operations.

Around-the-machines audit. A method of auditing involving the verification of the output from the source data without considering the method of source data conversion.

ASCII. American Standard Code for Information Interchange.

Audit trail. A method of providing a path or track which may be followed in tracing output data back through the processing steps used in converting input data to its final output form.

Automation. (1) The implementation of processes by automatic means; (2) the theory, art, or technique of making a process more automatic; (3) the investigation, design, development, and application of methods of rendering processes automatic, self-moving, or self-controlling.

Batch process. Is processing, without unscheduled interruption, of a group of items prepared or required for one or more related operations.

Batch total. The total or sum of specific data contained in a group or batch of documents containing similar characteristics. Used as control information to assure that all data of the batch have been properly processed.

Baud. (1) A unit of speed equal to the number of code elements per second. Sometimes used interchangeably with "bits per second."

(2) A digital data communications term designating the smallest unit of transmission signaling speed.

Baudot code. A five-channel paper tape code first used in telegraph communication. Developed by Jean Maurice Emile Baudot in 1870 while with the French Ministry of Posts and Telegraph.

Binary. A characteristic or condition in which there are but two possible alternatives.

Binary coded decimal. *See* Code, binary coded decimal.

Binary coded decimal number. A number, usually consisting of successive groups of figures, in which each group of four figures is a binary number that represents, but does not necessarily equal arithmetically, a particular figure in an associated decimal number, for example, the decimal number 262 would be expressed as the binary coded decimal number 0010 0110 0010.

Binary digit. A numeral in the binary scale of notation. This digit may be zero (0), or one (1). It may be equivalent to an on or off condition, a yes or a no. *See* Bit.

Binary notation. A number system written to the base two notation.

Bit. (1) An abbreviation of binary digit. (2) A single character in a binary number. (3) A single pulse in a group of pulses. (4) A unit of information capacity of a storage device. The capacity in bits is the logarithm to the base two of the number of possible states of the device.

Block diagram. (1) A graphical representation of the hardware in a computer system. The primary purpose of a block diagram is to indicate the paths along which the information and/or control flows between the various parts of a computer system. It should not be confused with the term *flowchart*. (2) A coarser and less symbolic representation than a flowchart.

Bookkeeping machine. A combination adding machine and typewriter which has been developed to do bookkeeping work.

Branch. A set of instructions that are executed between two successive decision instructions.

Broad band channel. Data transmission facilities capable of handling frequencies greater than those required for high-grade voice communications.

Budget. A formalized program or plan of action relating to the operation and control of a business firm.

Buffer. (1) An internal portion of a data processing system serving as intermediary storage between two storage or data handling systems with different access times or formats; usually to connect an input or output device with the main or internal high-speed storage. (2) A logical OR circuit. (3) An isolating component designed to eliminate the reaction of a driven circuit on the circuits driving it, for example, a buffer amplified. (4) A diode.

Bus. A pathway for the transmission of data, usually in the form of electrical impulses.

Byte. A sequence of adjacent binary digits operated upon as a unit and usually shorter than a computer word.

Calculator. (1) A device that performs primarily arithmetic operations based upon data and instructions inserted manually or contained on punched cards. It is sometimes used interchangeably with *computer*. (2) A computer.

Card column. A single line of punched positions parallel to the short edge of a $3\frac{1}{4} \times 7\frac{3}{8}$ inch punched card.

Card feed. A mechanism which moves cards serially into a machine.

Card punch. A machine which punches cards in designated locations to store data which can be conveyed to other machines or devices by reading or sensing the holes. Synonymous with card punch unit.

Card, punched. A heavy stiff paper of constant size and shape, suitable for punching in a pattern that has meaning, and for being handled mechanically. The punched holes are sensed electrically by wire brushes, mechanically by metal fingers, or photoelectrically by photocells.

Card reader. (1) A mechanism that sense information punched into cards. (2) An input device consisting of a mechanical punched card reader and related electronic circuitry, which transcribes data from punched cards to working storage or magnetic tape. Synonymous with card reader unit.

Cathode-ray tube (CRT). (1) An electronic vacuum tube containing a screen on which information may be stored by means of a multigrid modulated beam of electrons from the thermionic emitter storage effected by means of charged or uncharged spots. (2) A storage tube. (3) An oscilloscope tube. (4) A picture tube.

Cathode-ray tube display. A device that presents data in visual form by means of controlled electronic beams.

Central processing unit (CPU). (1) The central processor of the computer system. It contains the main storage, arithmetic unit, and special register groups. (2) All that portion of a computer exclusive of the input, output, peripheral, and in some instances, storage units.

Channel. (1) A path along which information, particularly a series of digits or characters, may flow. (2) One or more parallel tracks treated as a unit. (3) A path for electrical communication. (4) A band of frequencies used for communication.

Character. One symbol of a set of elementary symbols such as those corresponding to the keys on a typewriter. The symbols usually include the decimal digits 0 through 9, the letters A through Z, punctuation marks, operation symbols, and any other single symbols which a computer may read, store, or write.

Character recognition equipment. Equipment designed to be able to recognize automatically either magnetic ink characters, printed characters, printed codes, pencil characters, or perforated tags.

Character set. An agreed-upon set of representations, called characters, from which selections are made to denote and distinguish data. Each character differs from all others, and the total number of characters in a given set is fixed.

Check, automatic. A provision constructed in hardware for verifying the accuracy of information transmitted, manipulated, or stored by any unit or device in a computer.

Check bit. A binary check digit; often a parity bit.

Check, built-in. *See* Check, automatic.

Check, echo. A check of accuracy of transmission in which the information which was transmitted to an output device is returned to the information source and compared with the original information to insure accuracy of output.

Check, limit. Checks which can be written into a program to call attention to any data exceeding or less than certain predesignated limits.

Check, parity. A summation check in which the binary digits, in a character or word, are added and the sum checked against a single, previously computed parity digit, that is, a check which tests whether the number of ones in a word is odd or even.

Check points. These are predetermined points in a program where specific checks or tests are performed.

Check, sequence. A data processing operation designed to check the sequence of the items in a file assumed to be already in sequence.

Check, validity. A check based upon known limits or upon given information or computer results; for example, a calendar month will not be numbered greater than 12, a week does not have more than 168 hours.

CIM. Computer Input Microfilm.

Circuit. (1) A system of conductors and related electrical elements through which electrical current flows. (2) A communication link between two or more points comprising associated "go" and "return" channels.

Classifying. The identification of each item and the systematic placement of like items together according to their common features.

Closed loop. A loop from which there is no exit other than by intervention from outside the program.

COBOL. See Common Business Oriented Language.

CODASYL. Conference On Data Systems Language.

Code, alphabetic. A system of alphabetic abbreviations used in preparing information for input into a machine; for example, Boston and New York may in alphabetical coding be reported as BS and NY. Contrasted with Code, numeric.

Code, artificial. A code which does not follow some natural order in classifying data.

Code, Baudot. *See* Baudot code.

Code, binary. A code utilizing the characteristics of the binary number system in which there are but two possible alternatives or conditions or states.

Code, binary coded decimal. Describes a decimal notation in which the individual decimal digits are represented by a pattern of ones and zeros.

Code, block. A code which reserves a block or group of numbers for the classification of a specific block of items.

Code, channel. A code which utilizes paths along which information, particularly a series of digits or characters, may flow. Punched paper tape and magnetic tape codes are examples.

Code, computer. (1) A system of combinations of binary digits used by a given computer. (2) A repertoire of instructions.

Code, EBCDIC. An acronym for Extended Binary Coded Decimal Interchange Code.

Code, group classification. A code which uses one or more of its numbers to classify items into major and minor groupings.

Code, hexadecimal. A code based on the hexadecimal system of numbers which has 16 possible conditions or states.

Code, Hollerith. A widely used system of encoding alphanumeric information onto cards; hence, Hollerith cards is synonymous with *punched* cards. Such cards were first used in 1890 for the U.S. Census and were named after their originator.

Code, instruction. The list of symbols, names, and definitions of the instructions which are intelligible to a given computer or computing system.

Code, machine language. Same as Code, computer.

Code, MICR (Magnetic Ink Character Recognition). A specially designed group of ten arabic numbers and four special symbols printed in magnetic ink in designated field location along the bottom edge of a check or other document.

Code, mnemonic. A code in which the items are abbreviated and expressed mnemonically to facilitate remembering the item represented.

Code, natural. A code which follows some natural order of the data to be coded. Typical would be the arrangement of the accounts in a balance sheet.

Code, numeric. A system of numerical abbreviations used in the preparation of information for input into a machine; that is, all information is reduced to numerical quantities. Contrasted with Code, alphabetic.

Code, paper tape. A 5-, 6-, 7-, or 8-channel code used in conjunction with paper tape data processing.

Code, punched card. *See* Code, Hollerith.

Coder. A person mainly involved in writing but not designing computer programs.

Coding. The ordered list in computer code of the successive computer instructions representing successive computer operations for solving a specific problem.

Collate. To merge two or more ordered sets of data, or cards, in order to produce one or more ordered sets which still reflect the original ordering relations. The collation process is the merging of two sequences of cards each ordered on some mutual key, into a single sequence ordered on the mutual key.

Collator. A device used to collate or merge sets or decks of cards or other units into a sequence.

Column. A vertical arrangement of characters or other expressions.

COM. Computer Output Microfilm.

Command. A control signal. Loosely an instruction in machine language.

Common Business Oriented Language. A specific language by which business data processing procedures may be precisely described in a standard form. The language is intended not only as a means for directly presenting any business program to any suitable computer, for which a compiler exists, but also as a means of communicating such procedures among individuals. Synonymous with COBOL.

Communicating. As used in data processing, the act of assemblying and transmitting data through a data processing system so that the data may be acted upon, along with the distribution of the results of processing, usually consisting of reports to the users of the data.

Communication. The attainment of mutual understanding between the sender and the receiver. The act of transmitting and of receiving are pertinent to, but independent of "communication," just as are the equipment, and the storage or display media, such as remote interrogators, sensory devices, transmission channels, documents, records, reports, each of which is a tool for, but only the means to "communication."

Communication devices. Various types of units which permit the input and/or output of data transmitted to or between computer systems.

Communication link. The physical means of connecting one location to another for the purpose of transmitting and receiving data.

Communications channels. Transmission circuitry required in transferring data from point to point in connection with computer systems.

Comparison. The process of checking two or more items for identity, similarity, equality, relative magnitude, or order in sequence.

Compatibility, equipment. The characteristic of computers by which one computer may accept and process data prepared by another computer without conversion or code modification.

Compile. To prepare a machine language program from a computer program written in another programming language by making use of the overall logic structure of the program, or generating more than one machine instruction for each symbolic statement, or both, as well as performing the function of an assembler.

Compiler. A more powerful processor which can create a number of machine instructions from a single command.

Computer, analog. A computer which represents variables by physical analogies, such as: pressure, temperature, and so forth.

Computer, business. A type of digital computer designed to have the characteristics peculiar to the needs of business data processing.

Computer, desk-size. A small and compact computer. Usually a limited-capability machine and often closely associated with some advanced bookkeeping machines.

Computer, digital. A computer which processes information represented by combinations of discrete or discontinuous data as compared with analog computer for continuous data.

Computer, general-purpose. A computer designed to solve a large variety of problems; for example, a stored program computer which may be adapted to any of a very large class of applications.

Computer program. A series of instructions or statements, in a form acceptable to a computer, prepared in order to achieve a certain result.

Computer, scientific. A type of digital computer designed to have the characteristics desired in mathematical- and engineering-type computing.

Computer, solid-state. A computer built primarily from solid-state electronic circuit elements.

Computer, special-purpose. A computer designed to solve a specific class or narrow range of problems.

Computer, stored program. A computer capable of performing sequences of internally stored instructions and usually capable of modifying those instructions as directed by the instructions.

Computer utility. A service which provides computational ability. A time-shared computer system. Similar in concept to an electric utility.

Computer word. A sequence of bits or characters treated as a unit and capable of being stored in one computer location. Synonymous with machine word.

Configuration. A group of machines which are interconnected and are programmed to operate as a system.

Connector. On a flowchart, the means of representing the convergence of more than one flow line into one, or the divergence of one flow line into more than one. A means of representing on a flowchart a break in a line of flow.

Console. A portion of the computer which may be used to control the machine manually; correct errors; determine the status of machine circuits, registers, and counters; determine the contents of storage; and manually revise the contents of storage.

Control panel. An interconnection device, usually removable, which employs removable wires to control the operation of computing equipment.

Control total. A sum of numbers in a specified record field of a batch of records, determined repetitiously during the processing operation so that any discrepancy from the control indicates an error.

Control unit. The portion of a computer which directs the coded instructions and initiates the proper commands to the computer circuits preparatory to execution.

Controls, built-in. Techniques which are part of the design of the equipment to protect the processing of data and related data files.

Controls, input. Data control features or techniques applied to the input of data into a computer system.

Controls, output. Data control features or techniques applied to the output of data from a computer system.

Controls, processing. Various safeguards and techniques incorporated into computer programs or data files used in the processing of data.

Controls, security. Safeguard techniques utilized in protecting computer programs, data files, and equipment.

Controls, systems. Various controls or safeguarding techniques applicable to any part of the computer system.

Converter. A device which converts the representation of information, or which permits the changing of the method for data processing from one form to another, for example, a unit which accepts information from punched cards and records the information on magnetic tape, and possibly including editing facilities.

Copy. To reproduce data in a new location or other destination, leaving the source data unchanged, although the physical form of the result may differ from that of the source. For example, to copy a deck of cards into a magnetic tape.

Copy, hard. A printed copy of machine output, for example, printed reports, listings, documents, and summaries.

Core storage. A form of high-speed storage of data using magnetic cores.

CPU. Central Processing Unit.

CRT display. Cathode-ray tube display.

Data. A representation of facts, concepts, or instructions in a formalized manner suitable for communication, interpretation or processing by human or automatic means.

Data bank. A comprehensive collection of libraries of data. For example, one line of an invoice may form an item, a complete invoice may form a record, a complete set of such records may form a file, the collection of inventory control files may form a library, and the libraries used by an organization are known as its data bank.

Data base. The basic file(s) of the data required by a firm or organization. The data in this file(s) are changed as a result of the transactions associated with the firm's operation.

Data collection system. A system which records, in machine-readable form, the data pertinent to a transaction at the time and place the transaction occurs.

Data origination. The act of creating a record in a machine-sensible form, directly or as a by-product of a human-readable document.

Data-phone. A generic term to describe a family of devices available to facilitate data communication.

Data processing. (1) The preparation of source media which contain data or basic elements of information and the handling of such data according to precise rules of procedure to accomplish such operations as classifying, sorting, calculating, summarizing, and recording. (2) The production of records and reports.

Data processor. A device capable of performing data processing, including desk calculators, punch card machines and computers. Synonymous with processor.

Data punch. A portable, manual card-punching device which can punch six columns of numerical data into a standard punched card and simultaneously print the numerical figures with a single machine stroke.

Data transmission equipment. Equipment designed to transmit either card code or channel code over long distances by means of the telephone lines or by radio.

Debugging. The process of determining the correctness of a computer routine, locating any errors in it, and correcting them. This also involves the detection and correction of malfunctions in the computer itself.

Decision. A determination of future action.

Deck. A collection of cards, commonly a complete set of cards which have been punched for a definite service or purpose.

Density. The number of bits per inch of data which can be stored on magnetic tape or drum track.

Diagnostic. Pertaining to the detection and isolation of a malfunction or mistake.

Digital computer. A computer in which discrete representation of data is mainly used.

Direct access storage device. A device which permits direct addressing of data locations.

Disk pack. A portable set of magnetic disks which may be removed from the disk drive unit, allowing another set of disks to be placed on the unit.

Disk storage. The storage of data on the surface of magnetic disks.

Display tube. A tube, usually a cathode-ray tube, used to display data.

Documentation. The group of techniques necessary for the orderly presentation, organization, and communication of recorded specialized knowledge, in order to maintain a complete record of reasons for changes in variables. Documentation is necessary not so much to give maximum utility as to give an unquestionable historical reference record.

Downtime. The period during which a computer is malfunctioning or not operating correctly due to mechanical or electronic failure, as opposed to available time, idle time, or standby time, during which the computer is functional.

Dump. To copy the contents of all or part of what is in storage.

Duplex. In communication, pertaining to a simultaneous two-way independent transmission in both directions. Contrast with half duplex. Synonymous with full duplex.

Duplex channel. A channel providing simultaneous transmission in both directions.

Duplication. The copying of data from card to card (column by column) as performed on the card punch.

Edit. To rearrange data or information. Editing may involve the deletion of unwanted data, the selection of pertinent data, the application of format techniques, the insertion of symbols such as page numbers and typewriter characters, the application of standard processes such as zero suppression, and the testing of data for reasonableness and proper range. Editing may sometimes be distinguished between input edit (rearrangement of source data) and output edit (preparation of table formats).

EDP. **E**lectronic **D**ata **P**rocessing.

Emulate. To imitate one system with another such that the imitating system accepts the same data, executes the same programs, and achieves the same results as the imitating system.

Encode. (1) To apply a code, frequently one consisting of binary numbers, to represent individual characters or groups of characters in a message. (2) To substitute letters, numbers, or characters, usually to intentionally hide the meaning of the message except to certain individuals who know the enciphering scheme.

Equipment, off-line. Equipment or devices not in direct communication with the central processing unit of the computer.

Equipment, on-line. Equipment or devices which are under the control of, or in direct communication with, the central processing unit of the computer.

Equipment, peripheral. Devices which are necessary to a computer system. These may either be off-line or on-line devices.

Error. The general term referring to any deviation of a computed or a measured quantity from the theoretically correct or true value.

Error routine. A prepared diagnostic program which searches for predetermined types of errors and advises, by computer output, of any errors and the types of errors found.

Executive program. *See* Supervisory program.

Facsimile. A system for the transmission of images. The image is scanned at the transmitter, reconstructed at the receiving station, and duplicated on some form of paper.

Feasibility study. A study of applicability or desirability of any management or procedural system from the standpoint of advantages versus disadvantages for any given case.

Feed. (1) To supply the material to be operated upon to a machine. (2) A device capable of feeding, as in (1).

Field. In a record, a specified area used for a particular category of data.

File. A collection of related records treated as a unit or file.

File maintenance. The periodic modification of a file to incorporate changes which occurred during a given period.

Flowchart. A graphic representation of the major steps of work to be processed. The illustrative symbols may represent documents, machines, or actions taking place during the process. The area of concentration is on where or who does what rather than how it is to be done.

Flowchart, program. *See* Program flowchart.

Flowchart, system. A flowchart which shows the sequence of major operations which normally summarizes a complete operation.

FORTRAN. Formula Translating System. A programming language designed for problems which can be expressed in algebraic notation, allowing for exponentiation and up to three subscripts.

Gap. (1) An interval of space or time used as an automatic sentinel to indicate the end of a word, record, or file of data on a tape. (2) The absence of information for a specific length of time or space on a recording medium, as contrasted with marks and sentinels which are the presence of specific information to achieve a similar purpose. (3) The space between the reading or recording head and the recording medium, such as tape, drum, or disk.

Generator. A program which will adapt or modify a general-purpose program to fit a specific need.

GIGO. A contraction of "Garbage In, Garbage Out" which refers to the uselessness of invalid input data.

Graphic display terminals. Data terminals at remote locations at which data can be displayed graphically.

Half duplex. In communications, pertaining to an alternate, one way at a time, independent transmission. Contrast with duplex.

Half-duplex channel. A channel capable of transmitting and receiving signals, but in only one direction at a time.

Hardware. The physical equipment or devices forming a computer and peripheral equipment. Contrasted with Software.

Hash total. A sum of numbers in a specified field of a record or of a batch of records used for checking purposes. No attention is paid to the significance of the total. Examples of such numbers are customer numbers or part numbers.

Head. A device that reads, writes, or erases data on a storage medium.

Hexadecimal. *See* Code, hexadecimal.

IDP. *See* Integrated Data Processing.

Initialize. (1) To set various counters, switches, and addresses to zero or other starting values, at the beginning of, or at the prescribed points in, a computer routine; (2) used as an aid to recovery and restart during a long run.

Input-output. A general term of the equipment used to communicate with a computer and the data involved in the communication. Synonymous with I/O.

Inquiry station. A point of entry or access to the computer system.

Integrated data processing. (1) A system that treats as a whole, all data processing requirements to accomplish a sequence of data processing steps, or a number of related data processing sequences, and which strives to reduce or eliminate duplicating data entry or processing steps. (2) The processing of data by such a system. Synonymous with IDP. (3) The concept also applies to departments which should be unified on a departmental level to facilitate the automatic processing of data. The concept unites data accumulation, communication, computation, processing, and control.

Interface. A boundary which is common between automatic data processing systems or parts of a single system. In communication and data collection systems, this may involve such items as code, format, speed, or other required changes.

Internal control. The plan of organization and all of the coordinate methods and measures adopted within a business to safeguard its assets, check the accuracy and reliability of its accounting data, promote operational efficiency, and encourage adherence to prescribed managerial policies.

Internal label. *See* Label, internal.

Internal memory device. Storage devices that are an integral physical part of the automatic computer or central processing unit.

Interpret. (1) To print (in non-machine language) on a punched card the information punched in that card. (2) To translate non-machine language into machine language instructions.

Interpreter. (1) A computer program that translates and executes each source language statement before translating and executing the next one. (2) A device that prints on a punched card the data already punched in the card.

Interpreter program. A processor which translates a program into machine language and executes the instructions at the same time.

Key. (1) A group of characters which identifies or is part of a record or item; thus any entry in a record or item can be used as a key for collating or sorting purposes. (2) A marked lever manually operated for copying a character, for example, a typewriter, paper tape perforator, card punch, manual keyboard, digitizer, or manual word generator. (3) A lever or switch on a computer console for the purpose of manually altering computer action.

Key punch. (1) A special device to record information in cards or tape by punching holes in the cards or tape to represent letters, digits, and special characters (2) To operate a device for punching holes in cards or tape.

Keyed data terminals. Data terminals at remote locations in which data can be fed into the system through the manual keying of a keyboard.

Keysort cards. A manual device used to speed up the sorting function. Cards are notched in the margin and are sorted away from un-notched cards by means of a sorting needle.

Key-verify. To use the punched card machine known as a verifier, which has a keyboard, to make sure that the information supposed to be punched in a punched card has actually been properly punched. The machine signals when the punched hole and the depressed key disagree.

Label. One or more characters used to identify a statement or an item of data in a computer program.

Label, internal. When the label is recorded internally on the record or file, it is termed an internal label (contra to a label recorded externally).

Language. A system for representing and communicating information or data between people and machines. Such a system consists of a carefully defined set of characters and rules for combining them into larger units, such as words of expressions, and rules for word arrangement or usage to achieve specific meanings.

Language, common machine. A machine-sensible information representation which is common to a related group of data processing machines.

Language, object. A language which is the output of an automatic coding routine. Usually object language and machine language are the same; however, a series of steps in an automatic coding system may involve the object language of one step to serve as a source language for the next step and so forth.

Language, source. The original form in which a program is prepared prior to processing by the machine.

Library. (1) A collection of information available to a computer, usually on magnetic tapes. (2) A file of magnetic tapes.

Library routine. A proven routine that is maintained in a program library.

Line printer. A device capable of printing one line of characters across a page, that is, 100 or more characters simultaneously as continuous paper advances line by line in one direction past type bars or a type cylinder that contains all characters in all positions. Also type mounted on revolving chains.

Linear programming. In operations research, a procedure for locating the maximum of minimum of a linear function of variables that are subject to linear constraints.

Load. (1) To put data into a register or storage. (2) To put a magnetic tape onto a tape drive, or to put cards into a card reader.

Location. Any place in which data may be stored.

Log. A chronological record of everything pertinent to a machine run, including: identification of the machine run, record of alteration switch settings, identification of input and output tapes, copy of manual key-ins, identification of all stops, and a record of action taken on all stops.

Logic. (1) The science dealing with the criteria or formal principles of reasoning and thought. (2) The systematic scheme which defines the interactions of signals in the design of an automatic data processing system. (3) The basic principles and application of truth tables and interconnection between logical elements required for arithmetic computation in an automatic data processing system.

Logic, symbolic. (1) The study of formal logic and mathematics by means of a special written language which seeks to avoid the ambiguity and inadequacy of ordinary language. (2) The mathematical concepts, techniques, and languages as used in (1), whatever their particular application or context.

Loop. The repeated execution of a series of instructions for a fixed number of times.

Machine language. A language that is used directly by a machine.

Machine sensible. Pertaining to information in a form which can be read by a specific machine.

Macro instruction. A symbolic instruction in a source language that produces a number of machine language instructions. It is available for use by the programmer through an automatic programming system.

Magnetic card. A card with a magnetic surface on which data can be stored by selective magnetization of portions of the flat surface.

Magnetic core. A configuration of magnetic material that is, or is intended to be, placed in a spatial relationship to current-carrying conductors and whose magnetic properties are essential to its use.

Magnetic disk. A storage device on which information is recorded on the magnetizable surface of a rotating disk.

Magnetic drum. A light circular cylinder with a magnetic surface on which data can be stored by selective magnetization of portions of the curved surface.

Magnetic film. A layer of magnetic material, usually less than one-micron thick, used for logic or storage elements.

Magnetic Ink Character Recognition. *See* Code, MICR.

Magnetic ledger cards. A ledger sheet or card which has stripes (either on the front or back) of magnetic receptive material in which magnetic type coded data can be stored and read by machine.

Magnetic stripe. A stripe(s) or strip(s) of material coated with magnetic or other material on which information can be recorded and read in the form of magnetically polarized spots.

Magnetic tape. A storage device in which data are stored in the form of magnetic spots on metal or coated plastic tape. Binary data are stored as small magnetized spots arranged in column form across the width of the tape. A read-write head is usually associated with each row of magnetized spots so that one column can be read or written at a time as the tape traverses the head.

Magnetic thin film. A form of computer memory which varies in composition with the manufacturer but is in essence a thin-film base material which has been coated with a uniform deposit of magnetic storage materials.

Management information system. (1) Management performed with the aid of automatic data processing. (2) A data processing system designed to provide management and supervisory personnel with the information needed to manage and supervise a particular agency or function.

Manual of Procedures. Such a manual defines and sets forth company policies and procedures. It is more often found in larger businesses than smaller ones due to the fact that most smaller businesses do not feel the necessity to commit such things to writing.

Mark sensing. A technique for detecting special pencil marks entered in special places on a punched card and automatically translating the marks into punched holes.

Match. A data processing operation similar to a merge, except that instead of producing a sequence of items made up from the input, sequences are matched against each other on the basis of some key.

Mathematical model. The general characterization of a process, object, or concept, in terms of mathematics, which enables the relatively simple manipulation of variables to be accomplished in order to determine how the process, object, or concept would behave in different situations.

Matrix. An array of quantities in

a prescribed form; in mathematics, usually capable of being subject to a mathematical operation by means of an operator or another matrix according to prescribed rules.

Merge. To combine items into one sequenced file from two or more similarly sequenced files without changing the order of the items.

Microfische. A sheet of film, usually 4×6 inches in size, containing either negative or positive images, or frames, of printed material reduced from 12 to 38 times by photographic reduction.

Microfilm. A film often in the form of a strip 16 millimeters or 35 millimeters wide bearing a photographic record on a reduced scale of printed or other graphic matter.

Microsecond. One millionth of a second, 10^{-6} seconds, abbreviated *microsec.*

Millisecond. One thousandth of a second, 10^{-3} seconds, abbreviated *msec.* or *ms.*

Minicomputer. Generally, it is a small, general-purpose digital computer with a central processor and core memory (approximately 4,096 words), weighing about 85 pounds.

Mode. (1) A computer system of data representation, for example, the binary mode. (2) A selected mode of computer operation.

Monte Carlo method. A trial-and-error method solution of a problem. Often used when a great number of variables are present, with interrelationships so extremely complex as to forestall straightforward analytical handling.

Multiple. To interleave or simultaneously transmit two or more messages on a single channel.

Multiprocessing. Pertaining to the simultaneous execution of two or more computer programs or sequence of instructions by a computer or computer network.

Multiprogramming. Pertaining to the concurrent execution of two or more programs by a computer.

Nanosecond. A billionth of a second.

Narrow band channel. A channel which permits transmission of frequencies within the normal telegraph band of frequencies. Lower than the voice band channel.

Object language. The language to which a statement is translated.

Object program. A fully compiled or assembled program that is ready to be loaded into the computer.

Off-line. Descriptive of a system and of the peripheral equipment or devices in a system in which the operation of peripheral equipment is not under the control of the central processing unit.

On-line. Descriptive of a system and of the peripheral equipment or devices in a system in which the operation of such equipment is under control of the central processing unit, and in which information reflecting current activity is introduced into the data processing system as soon as it occurs—thus, directly in line with the main flow of transaction processing.

Operating system. Software which controls the execution of computer programs and which may provide scheduling, debugging, input/output control, accounting, compilation, storage assignment, data management, and related services.

Operations research. The use of analytical methods adopted from mathematics for solving operational problems. The objective is to provide management with a more logical basis for making sound predictions and decisions. Among the common scientific techniques used in operations research are the following: linear programming, probability theory, information theory, game theory, Monte Carlo method, and queuing theory. Synonymous with OR.

Operator, machine. The person who manipulates the computer controls, places information media into the input devices, removes the output, and performs other related functions.

Optical character recognition (OCR). The technique of using electronic devices and light in order to detect, recognize, and translate into machine language characters which have been printed or written on paper documents in a human-readable form.

Optical scanner. A device that scans optically and usually generates an analog or digital signal.

Optical scanning. The process which uses a machine to "read" human-recognizable language and decodes it into a machine language.

Optimize. To rearrange the instructions or data in storage so that a minimum number of time-consuming jumps or transfers is required in the running of a program.

Output. (1) The information transferred from the internal storage of a computer to secondary or external storage, or to any device outside of the computer. (2) The routines which direct (1). (3) The device or collective set of devices necessary for (1). (4) To transfer from internal storage onto external media.

Output device. The part of a machine which translates the electrical impulses representing data processed by the machine into permanent results such as printed forms, punched cards, and magnetic writing on tape.

Pack. (1) To compress data in a storage medium by making use of bit or byte locations that would otherwise go unused. (2) A shortened term for disk pack.

Paper tape. A strip of paper capable of storing or recording information. Storage may be in the form of punched holes, carbonization or chemical change of impregnated material, or by imprinting. Some paper tapes, such as punched paper tapes, are capable of being read by the input device of a computer or a transmitting device by sensing the pattern of holes which represent coded information.

Parity bit. A check bit appended to an array of binary digits to make the sum of all the binary digits, including the check bit, alway odd or always even.

Picosecond. One thousandth of a nanosecond, or 10^{-12} seconds; abbreviated *psec.*

Picture clause. Used in a COBOL program to indicate the size of an item, its class, the presence or absence of an operational sign and/or an assumed decimal point.

Plotter. A visual display or board in which a dependent variable is graphed by an automatically controlled pen or pencil as a function of one or more variables.

Polling signal. A centrally controlled, flexible, and systematic technique used to permit stations on a multipoint circuit to transmit without competing for the line.

Port-A-Punch. A portable keypunching device developed by the IBM Corporation whereby punched cards can be punched with a hand stylus.

Preventive maintenance. Maintenance specifically intended to prevent faults from occurring during subsequent operation.

Printers. Equipment which provides a printed output, usually in the form of reports or analyses.

Processing batch. Data which are similar are gathered into groups or batches and then entered into the processing procedure.

Processor. (1) A generic term which includes assembly, compiling, and generation. (2) A shorter term for automatic data processor or arithmetic unit. (3) A computer program which translates the symbolic (mnemonic) instruction codes into machine language instructions.

Program. (1) The complete plan for the solution of a problem, more specifically, the complete sequence of machine instructions and routines necessary to solve a problem. (2) To plan the proce-

dures for solving a problem. This may involve among other things the analysis of the problem; preparation of a flow diagram; preparing details, testing, and developing subroutines; allocation of storage locations; specification of input and output formats; and the incorporation of a computer run into a complete data processing system.

Program, coded. A program which has been expressed in the code or language of a specific machine or programming system.

Program control. A sequence of instructions which prescribes the series of steps to be taken by a system, a computer, or any other device.

Program flowchart. Designed to portray the various arithmetic and logical operations which must be accomplished to solve the complete problem.

Program library. A collection of available computer programs and routines.

Programmer. A person mainly involved in designing, writing, and testing of a program.

Programs, application. Computer programs designed to process specific procedural applications.

Programs, compiler. *See* Compiler.

Programs, executive. Extremely sophisticated computer programs used to control the operation of the equipment in scheduling tasks, allocating memory, utilizing various hardware units (including input/output), and control over service operations.

Programs, interpreter. A processor which translates a program into machine language and executes the instructions at the same time. No object program is created.

Programs, object. *See* Language, object.

Programs, processor. *See* Processor.

Programs, source. *See* Language, source.

Programs, systems. Computer programs designed to direct the operation of the equipment. Usually produced by the computer manufacturer.

Punch. (1) To shear a hole by forcing a solid or hollow, sharp-edged tool through a material into a die. (2) The hole resulting from (1).

Punched card. A card punched with a pattern of holes to represent data.

Punching positions. The specific areas, that is, row-column intersects, on a punched card where holes may be punched.

Queuing theory. A form of probability theory useful in studying delays or lineups at servicing points.

Random access. The ability to seek and retrieve data in a random manner from the files or memory of a computer system.

Random access processing. Access in a storage device under conditions such that the next address from which information is to be obtained is chosen in random order.

Read-in. To sense information contained in some source and transmit this information to a position in internal storage.

Read-out. To sense information contained in some internal storage and transmit this information to a storage external to the computer.

Read-punch unit. An input/output unit of a computing system which punches computed results into cards, reads input information into the system, and segregates output cards. The read-punch unit generally consists of a card feed, a read station, a punch station, possibly another read station, and one or more output card stackers.

Read-write head. A small electromagnet used for reading, recording, or erasing polarized spots, which represent information, on magnetic tape, disk, or drum.

Real-time. Connotes quick access to storage with an instantaneous response if desired.

Real-time processing. The processing of information or data in a sufficiently rapid manner so that the results of the processing are available in time to influence the process being monitored or controlled. Synonymous with Real-time system.

Record. A collection of related items of data, treated as a unit, for example, the line of an invoice may form a record, a complete set of such records may form a file.

Record length. The number of characters necessary to contain all the information in a record.

Recording. The act of capturing the pertinent data, at the source in reasonably permanent form, related to a business transaction.

Remote batch entry. Entering batches of data from remote terminals into a time-sharing system through a communication link.

Reporting. The technique of preparing various reports and analyses as an outcome of processing data.

Reproducing. The transfer of data from one card to another. This is performed in a single operation but partial or reordered information may be transferred.

Routine. An ordered set of instructions that may have some general or frequent use.

Row binary. A method of representing binary numbers on a card where successive bits are represented by the presence or absence of punches in a successive position in a row as opposed to a series of columns. Row binary is especially convenient in 40-bit-word, or less, computers, wherein the card frequently is used to store 12 binary words on each half of the card.

Scanner. An instrument which automatically samples or interrogates the state of various processes, files, conditions, or physical states and initiates action in accordance with the information obtained.

Scientific computer. A computer which has a large memory and is capable of handling extremely high-speed computations and many varieties of floating-point arithmetic commands.

Select. (1) To take the alternative *A* if the report on a condition is of one state, and alternative *B* if the report on the condition is of another state. (2) To choose a needed subroutine from a file of subroutines. (3) To choose specifically coded cards from a deck of cards.

Sequential processing. The procedure of processing data records in the same order that they occur.

Serial processing. The handling of one item after the other in a single facility, such as transfer or store in a digit-by-digit time sequence, or to process a sequence of instructions one at a time, that is, sequentially.

Simplex channel. A channel which permits transmission in one direction only.

Simulation. (1) The representation of physical systems and phenomena by computers, models, or other equipment. (2) In computer programming, the technique of setting up a routine for one computer to make it operate as nearly as possible like some other computer.

Software. The totality of programs and routines used to extend the capabilities of computers, such as compilers, assemblers, narrators, routines, and subroutines. Contrasted with Hardware.

Solid logic technology (SLT). Miniaturized modules used in computers which result in faster circuitry because of reduced distance for current to travel.

Solid state. The electronic components that convey or control electrons within solid materials; for example, transistors, germanium diodes, and magnetic cores. Thus, vacuum and gas tubes are not included.

Sonic delay line. A delay line using a medium providing acoustic delay, such as mercury or quartz delay lines.

Sort. To arrange items of information according to rules dependent upon a key or field contained in the items or records; for example, to digital sort is to sort first the keys on the least significant digit, and to re-sort on each higher order digit until the items are sorted on the most significant digit.

Sort, block. A sort of one or more of the most significant characters of a key to serve as a means of making workable-sized groups from a large volume of records to be sorted.

Sort, merge. To produce a single sequence of items, ordered according to some rule, from two or more previously unordered sequences, without changing the items in size, structure, or total number; although more than one pass may be required for a complete sort, items are selected during each pass on the basis of the entire key.

Sorter. A machine which puts items of information into a particular order.

Sorting. The arranging of items of information according to rules dependent upon a key or field contained in the items or records.

Sorting, alphabetic. To arrange a group of alphabetic data into an alphabetic sequence.

Sorting, block. A sort of one or more of the most significant characters of a key to serve as a means of making workable-sized groups from a large volume of records to be sorted.

Sorting, numerical. To arrange a group of numbers according to a numerical sequence.

Source language. *See* Language, source.

Stacker, card. (1) A receptacle that accumulates cards after they have passed through a machine. (2) A hopper.

Statistical data. Numerical facts which arise in the conduct of economic as well as physical activities.

Storage. (1) The term preferred to memory. (2) Pertaining to a device in which data can be stored and from which it can be obtained at a later time. The means of storing data may be chemical, electrical, or mechanical. (3) A device consisting of electronic, electrostatic, electrical, hardware, or other elements into which data may be entered, and from which data may be obtained as desired. (4) The erasable storage in any given computer. Synonymous with memory.

Storage, direct access. Those devices which serve as an extension of the internal memory of the central processing unit.

Storage, internal memory. Those devices which are used in conjunction with the central processing unit of the computer.

Storage, magnetic core. *See* Magnetic core.

Storage, magnetic drum. The storage of data on the surface of magnetic drums. *See* Magnetic drum.

Storage, magnetic tape. *See* Magnetic tape.

Storage capacity. The number of elementary pieces of data that can be contained in a storage device. Frequently defined in terms of characters in a particular code or words of a fixed size that can be so contained.

Storage dump. A listing of the contents of a storage device, or selected parts of it. Synonymous with memory dump, core dump, and memory print-out.

Store. (1) To transfer an element of information to a device from which the unaltered information can be obtained at a later time. (2) To retain data in a device from which the data can be obtained at a later time.

Stored program. A complete set of detailed steps and procedures stored within the computer directing it to perform a particular data processing task.

Storing. To put aside or accumulate in a safe place in some previously determined order so the information will be available when needed.

Summarizing. The accumulation of totals or amounts from data which have been classified and sorted into like groups.

Summary punch. A card punch operating in conjunction with another machine, commonly a tabulator, to punch into cards data which have been summarized or calculated by the other machine.

Supervisory program. A program designed to organize and regulate the flow of work in an automatic data processing system.

Symbol. A substitute or representation of characteristics, relationships, or transformations of ideas or things.

System. An assembly of procedures, processes, methods, routines, or techniques united by some form of regulated interaction to form an organized whole.

System analysis. The examination of an activity, procedure, method, technique, or business to determine what is required and how the requirements may best be accomplished.

System flowchart. A flowchart which shows the sequence of major operations which normally summarizes a complete operation.

System, information. The network of all communication methods within an organization. Information may be derived from many sources other than a data processing unit, such as by telephone, by contact with other people, or by studying an operation.

Systems programmer. A programmer who writes the programs which control the basic functioning of the computer.

Tabulating equipment. The machines and equipment using punched cards. The group of equipment is called tabulating equipment because the main function of installations of punched card machines for some 20 years before the first automatic digital computer was to produce tabulations of information resulting from sorting, listing, selecting, and totaling data on punched cards.

Tabulator. *See* Accounting machine.

Tape. A strip of material, which

may be punched, coated, or impregnated with magnetic or optically sensitive substances, and used for data input, storage, or output. The data are stored serially in several channels across the tape transverse to the reading or writing motion.

Test data. A set of data developed specifically, to test the adequacy of a computer run or system. The data may be actual data that have been taken from previous operations, or artificial data created for this purpose.

Through-the-machines audit. Does not require the tracing of input to output. The method involves a detailed examination of EDP operations with an evaluation of their accuracy and propriety.

Time-sharing. A method of operation in which a computer facility is shared by several users for different purposes at the same time.

Transcribe. To copy, with or without translating, from one storage medium to another.

Transistor. An electronic device utilizing semiconductor properties to control the flow of currents.

Unbundling. The separate pricing of software products and services from equipment charges.

Unit. A portion or subassembly of a computer which constitutes the means of accomplishing some inclusive operation or function.

Unit record. A separate record that is similar in form and content to other records, for example, a summary of a particular employee's earnings to date.

Update. (1) To put into a master file changes required by current information or transactions. (2) To modify an instruction so that the address numbers it contains are increased by a stated amount each time the instruction is performed.

Validity. The correctness; especially the degree of the closeness by which iterated results approach the correct result.

Validity check. *See* Check, validity.

Variable-length record files. Record files which will accommodate records of variable lengths.

Verify. To check a transcribing operation by a compare operation. It usually applies to transcriptions which can be read mechanically or electrically.

Voice band channel. A channel which permits the transmission of frequencies within the voice band. A channel suitable for the transmission of speech, digital, or analog data.

Word. An ordered set of characters which occupies one storage location and is treated by the computer circuits as a unit and transferred as such. Ordinarily a word is treated by the control unit as an instruction, and by the arithmetic unit as a quantity. Word lengths may be fixed or variable, depending on the particular computer.

Word length. The number of characters in a machine word. In a given computer, the number may be constant or variable.

Word length, fixed. Having the property that a machine word always contains the same number of characters or digits.

Word length, variable. Having the property that a machine word may have a variable number of characters. It may be applied either to a single entry whose information content may be changed from time to time or to a group of functionally similar entries whose corresponding components are of different lengths.

Zero. A numeral normally denoting lack of magnitude. In many computers there are distinct representations for plus and minus zero.

Zone. (1) A portion of internal storage allocated for a particular function or purpose. (2) The three top positions of 12, 11, and 0 on certain punched cards. In these positions, a second punch can be inserted so that with punches in the remaining positions 1 to 9, alphabetic characters may be represented.

Zone bit. (1) One of the two leftmost bits in a commonly used system in which six bits are used for each character. (2) Any bit in a group of bit positions that is used to indicate a specific class of items; for example, numbers, letters, special signs, and commands.

Index

Index